1776

*Also by David McCullough
in Large Print:*

John Adams

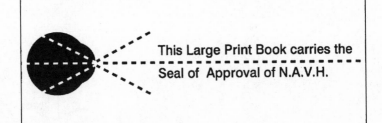

1776

David McCullough

Thorndike Press • Waterville, Maine

Published in 2005 by arrangement with
Simon & Schuster, Inc.

Thorndike Press® Large Print Nonfiction.

The tree indicium is a trademark of Thorndike Press.

The text of this Large Print edition is unabridged.
Other aspects of the book may vary from the original edition.

Set in 16 pt. Plantin by Minnie B. Raven.

Printed in the United States on permanent paper.

Library of Congress Cataloging-in-Publication Data

McCullough, David G.
    1776 / by David McCullough.
        p. cm. — (Thorndike Press large print nonfiction)
    Originally published: New York : Simon & Schuster,
c2005.
    Includes bibliographical references.
    ISBN 0-7862-7623-1 (lg. print : hc : alk. paper)
    1. United States — History — Revolution, 1775–1783.
2. Large type books.   I. Title: Seventeen seventy-six.
II. Title.   III. Thorndike Press large print nonfiction series.
E208.M396 2005b
973.3—dc22   2005004869

For
Rosalee Barnes McCullough

As the Founder/CEO of NAVH, the only national health agency solely devoted to those who, although not totally blind, have an eye disease which could lead to serious visual impairment, I am pleased to recognize Thorndike Press* as one of the leading publishers in the large print field.

Founded in 1954 in San Francisco to prepare large print textbooks for partially seeing children, NAVH became the pioneer and standard setting agency in the preparation of large type.

Today, those publishers who meet our standards carry the prestigious "Seal of Approval" indicating high quality large print. We are delighted that Thorndike Press is one of the publishers whose titles meet these standards. We are also pleased to recognize the significant contribution Thorndike Press is making in this important and growing field.

Lorraine H. Marchi, L.H.D.
Founder/CEO
NAVH

* Thorndike Press encompasses the following imprints: Thorndike, Wheeler, Walker and Large Print Press.

Contents

Perseverance and spirit
have done wonders in all ages.

— General George Washington

Part I

The Siege

The reflection upon my situation and that of this army produces many an uneasy hour when all around me are wrapped in sleep. Few people know the predicament we are in.
— General George Washington
January 14, 1776

Chapter One

SOVEREIGN DUTY

God save Great George our King,
Long live our noble King,
God save the King!
Send him victorious,
Happy and glorious,
Long to reign o'er us;
God save the King!

On the afternoon of Thursday, October 26, 1775, His Royal Majesty George III, King of England, rode in royal splendor from St. James's Palace to the Palace of Westminster, there to address the opening of Parliament on the increasingly distressing issue of war in America.

The day was cool, but clear skies and sunshine, a rarity in London, brightened everything, and the royal cavalcade, spruced and polished, shone to perfection. In an age that had given England such rousing patriotic songs as "God Save the King" and "Rule Britannia," in a nation that adored ritual and gorgeous pageantry, it was a scene hardly to be improved upon.

An estimated 60,000 people had turned out. They lined the whole route through St. James's Park. At Westminster people were packed solid, many having stood since morning, hoping for a glimpse of the King or some of the notables of Parliament. So great was the crush that latecomers had difficulty seeing much of anything.

One of the many Americans then in London, a Massachusetts Loyalist named Samuel Curwen, found the "mob" outside the door to the House of Lords too much to bear and returned to his lodgings. It was his second failed attempt to see the King. The time before, His Majesty had been passing by in a sedan chair near St. James's, but reading a newspaper so close to his face that only one hand was showing, "the whitest hand my eyes ever beheld with a very large rose diamond ring," Loyalist Curwen recorded.

The King's procession departed St. James's at two o'clock, proceeding at walking speed. By tradition, two Horse Grenadiers with swords drawn rode in the lead to clear the way, followed by gleaming coaches filled with nobility, then a clattering of Horse Guards, the Yeomen of the Guard in red and gold livery, and a rank of footmen, also in red and gold. Finally came the King in his colossal golden chariot pulled by eight magnificent cream-colored horses (Hanoverian Creams), a single postilion riding the left lead horse, and six footmen at the side.

No mortal on earth rode in such style as their King, the English knew. Twenty-four feet in length and thirteen feet high, the royal coach weighed nearly four tons, enough to make the ground tremble when under way. George III had had it built years before, insisting that it be "superb." Three gilded cherubs on top — symbols of England, Scotland, and Ireland — held high a gilded crown, while over the heavy spoked wheels, front and back, loomed four gilded sea gods, formidable reminders that Britannia ruled the waves. Allegorical scenes on the door panels celebrated the nation's heritage, and windows were of sufficient size to provide a full view of the crowned sovereign within.

It was as though the very grandeur, wealth, and weight of the British Empire were rolling past — an empire that by now included Canada, that reached from the seaboard of Massachusetts and Virginia to the Mississippi and beyond, from the Caribbean to the shores of Bengal. London, its population at nearly a million souls, was the largest city in Europe and widely considered the capital of the world.

George III had been twenty-two when, in 1760, he succeeded to the throne, and to a remarkable degree he remained a man of simple tastes and few pretensions. He liked plain food and drank but little, and wine only. Defying fashion, he refused to wear a wig. That the palace at St. James's had become a bit dowdy bothered him not at all. He rather liked it that way. Socially awkward at Court occasions — many found him disappointingly dull — he preferred puttering about his farms at Windsor dressed in farmer's clothes. And in notable contrast to much of fashionable society and the Court, where mistresses and infidelities were not only an accepted part of life, but often flaunted, the King remained steadfastly faithful to his very plain Queen, the German princess Charlotte Sophia of Mecklenburg-Strelitz, with whom by now he had produced ten children. (Ultimately there would be fifteen.) Gossips claimed Farmer George's chief pleasures were a leg of mutton and his plain little wife.

But this was hardly fair. Nor was he the unattractive, dim-witted man critics claimed then and afterward. Tall and rather handsome, with clear blue eyes and a generally cheerful expression, George III had a genuine love of music and played both the violin and piano. (His favorite composer was Handel, but he adored also the music of Bach and in 1764 had taken tremendous delight in hearing the boy Mozart perform on the organ.) He loved architecture and did quite beautiful architectural drawings of his own. With a good eye for art, he had begun early to assemble his own collection, which by now included works by the contemporary Italian painter Canaletto, as well as watercolors and drawings by such old masters as Poussin and Raphael. He avidly collected books, to the point where he had assembled one of the finest libraries in the world. He adored clocks, ship models, took great interest in things practical, took great interest in astronomy, and founded the Royal Academy of Arts.

He also had a gift for putting people at their ease. Samuel Johnson, the era's reigning arbiter of all things of the mind, and no easy judge of men, responded warmly to the "unaffected good nature" of

George III. They had met and conversed for the first time when Johnson visited the King's library, after which Johnson remarked to the librarian, "Sir, they may talk of the King as they will, but he is the finest gentleman I have ever seen."

Stories that he had been slow to learn, that by age eleven he still could not read, were unfounded. The strange behavior — the so-called "madness" of King George III — for which he would be long remembered, did not come until much later, more than twenty years later, and rather than mental illness, it appears to have been porphyria, a hereditary disease not diagnosed until the twentieth century.

Still youthful at thirty-seven, and still hardworking after fifteen years on the throne, he could be notably willful and often shortsighted, but he was sincerely patriotic and everlastingly duty-bound. "George, be a *King*," his mother had told him. As the crisis in America grew worse, and the opposition in Parliament more strident, he saw clearly that he must play the part of the patriot-king.

He had never been a soldier. He had never been to America, any more than he had set foot in Scotland or Ireland. But with absolute certainty he knew what must be done. He would trust to Providence and his high sense of duty. America must be made to obey.

"I have no doubt but the nation at large sees the conduct in America in its true light," he had written to his Prime Minister, Lord North, "and I am certain any other conduct but compelling obedience would be ruinous and . . . therefore no consideration could bring me to swerve from the present path which I think myself in duty-bound to follow."

In the House of Lords in March of 1775, when challenged on the chances of Britain ever winning a war in America, Lord Sandwich, First Lord of the Admiralty, had looked incredulous. "Suppose the colonies do abound in men, what does that signify?" he asked. "They are raw, undisciplined, cowardly men." And Lord Sandwich was by no means alone in that opinion. General James Grant, a member of the House of Commons, had boasted that with 5,000 British regulars he could march from one end of the American continent to the other, a claim that was widely quoted.

But in striking contrast, several of the most powerful speakers in Parliament, like the flamboyant Lord Mayor of London, John Wilkes, and the leading Whig intellectual, Edmund Burke, had voiced ardent support for and admiration of the Americans. On March 22, in the House of Commons, Burke had delivered in his heavy Irish brogue one of the longest, most brilliant speeches of his career, calling for conciliation with America.

Yet for all that, no one in either house, Tory or Whig, denied the supremacy of Parliament in determining what was best for America. Even Edmund Burke in his celebrated speech had referred repeatedly to "our" colonies.

Convinced that his army at Boston was insufficient, the King had dispatched reinforcements and three of his best major generals: William Howe, John Burgoyne, and Henry Clinton. Howe, a member of Parliament and a Whig, had earlier told his Nottingham constituents that if it came to war in America and he were offered a command, he would decline. But now duty called. "I was ordered, and could not refuse, without incurring the odious name of backwardness, to serve my country in distress," he explained. Howe, who had served in America during the Seven Years' War — or the French and Indian War, as it was known in America — was convinced the "insurgents" were few in number in comparison to those loyal to the Crown.

War had come on April 19, with the first blood shed at Lexington and Concord near Boston, then savagely on June 17 at Breed's Hill and Bunker Hill. (The June engagement was commonly known as the Battle of Bunker Hill on both sides of the Atlantic.) British troops remained under siege at Boston and were running short of food and supplies. On July 3, General George Washington of Virginia had taken command of the American "rabble."

With 3,000 miles of ocean separating Britain from her American colonies, accounts of such events took a month or more to reach London. By the time the first news of Lexington and Concord arrived, it was the end of May and Parliament had begun its long summer holiday, its members departing London for their country estates.

When the outcome at Bunker Hill became known in the last week of July, it only hardened the King's resolve. "We must persist," he told Lord North. "I know I am doing my duty and therefore can never wish to retract."

The ever-obliging North suggested that in view of the situation in America, it might no longer be regarded as a rebellion, but as a "foreign war," and thus "every expedient" might be employed.

At a hurried meeting at 10 Downing Street, on July 26, the Cabinet decided to send 2,000 reinforcements to Boston without delay and to have an army of no fewer than 20,000 regulars in America by the following spring.

Bunker Hill was proclaimed a British victory, which technically it was. But in plain truth His Majesty's forces, led by General Howe, had suffered more than 1,000 casualties in an appalling slaughter before gaining the high ground. As was observed acidly in both London and Boston, a few more such victories would surely spell ruin for the victors.

At summer's end a British ship out of Boston docked at Plymouth bearing 170 sick and wounded officers and soldiers, most of whom had fought at Bunker Hill and "all in great distress," as described in a vivid published account:

A few of the men came on shore, when never hardly were seen such objects: some without legs, and others without arms; and their clothes hanging on them like a loose morning gown, so much were they fallen away by sickness and want of nourishment. There were, moreover, near sixty women and children on board, the widows and children of men who were slain. Some of these too exhibited a most shocking spectacle; and even the vessel itself, though very large, was almost intolerable, from the stench arising from the sick and wounded.

The miseries of the troops still besieged at Boston, and of those Americans loyal to the King who, fearing for their lives, had abandoned everything to find refuge in the town, were also described in letters published in the London papers or in correspondence to friends and relatives in London. In the *General Evening Post*, one soldier portrayed the scene in Boston as nothing but "melancholy, disease, and death." Another, whose letter appeared in the *Morning Chronicle and Advertiser*, described being "almost lost for want of fresh provisions. . . . We are entirely blocked up . . . like birds in a cage."

John Singleton Copley, the American portrait painter who had left Boston to live in London the year before, read in a letter from his half brother, Henry Pelham:

It is inconceivable the distress and ruin this unnatural dispute has caused to this town and its inhabitants. Almost every shop and store is shut. No business of any kind is going on. . . . I am with the multitude rendered very unhappy, the little I collected entirely lost. The clothes upon my back and a few dollars in my pocket are now the only property which I have.

Despite the war, or more likely because of it, the King remained popular in the country at large and could count on a loyal following in Parliament. Political philosophy, patriotism, and a sense of duty comparable to the King's own figured strongly in both houses. So, too, did the immense patronage and public money that were his alone to dispense. And if that were not sufficient, there was the outright bribery that had become standard in a blatantly mercenary system not of his making, but that he readily employed to get his way.

Indeed, bribery, favoritism, and corruption in a great variety of forms were rampant not only in politics, but at all levels of society. The clergy and such celebrated observers of the era as Jonathan Swift and Tobias Smollett had long since made it a favorite subject. London, said Smollett, was "the devil's drawing-room." Samuel Curwen, the Salem Loyalist, saw dissipation and "vicious indulgence" everywhere he looked, "from the lowest haunts to the most elegant and expensive rendezvous of the noble and polished world." Feeling a touch of homesickness, Curwen thanked God this was still not so back in New England.

To much of the press and the opposition in Parliament, the American war and its handling could not have been more misguided. The *Evening Post*, the most partisan in its denunciations, called the war "unnatural, unconstitutional, unnecessary, unjust, dangerous, hazardous, and unprofitable." The *St. James's Chronicle* wrote contemptuously of "a foolish, obstinate, and unrelenting King." *The Crisis*, a vehement new paper, attacked "all the gaudy trappings of royalty" and the villainy of the King.

"What, in God's name, are ye all about in England? Have you forgot us?" asked a British officer in a letter from Boston published in London's *Morning Chronicle*. He wished that all the "violent people" who favored more vigorous measures in America could be sent over to see for themselves. Their vigor would be quickly cooled. "God send us peace and a good fireside in Old England."

The King, meanwhile, had recalled General Thomas Gage, his commander-in-chief at Boston, and in his place put the stouthearted William Howe. When, in September, an emissary from the Continental Congress at Philadelphia, Richard Penn, arrived in London with an "Olive Branch Petition" in hand, expressing loyalty to the Crown and requesting, in effect, that the King find a way to reconciliation, George III refused to have anything to do with it.

Behind the scenes, Lord North had quietly begun negotiations with several German princes of Hesse and Brunswick to hire mercenary troops. And in a confidential note dated October 15, the King reassured the Prime Minister that every means of "distressing America" would meet his approval.

By the crisp, sunny afternoon of October 26, as George III proceeded on his way to the opening of Parliament, his popularity had never seemed higher. Opposition to the war, as everyone knew, was stronger and more vociferous in London than anywhere in the country, yet here were crowds greater than any since his ascension to the throne. Further, they appeared in the best of spirits, as even the *London Public Advertiser* took note. Their "looks spoke peace and good humor"; there was "but little hissing"; the King could feel secure "in the affection of his people."

A boom of cannon saluted His Majesty's arrival at Westminster, and with the traditional welcoming formalities performed, the King assumed his place on the throne at the head of the House of Lords, flanked by the peers in their crimson robes. The members of the House of Commons, for whom no seats were provided, remained standing at the rear.

The magnitude of the moment was lost on no one. As expected, the King's address would be one of the most important ever delivered by an English monarch.

He had a good voice that carried well. "The present situation of America, and my constant desire to have your advice, concurrence, and assistance on every important occasion, have determined me to call you thus early together." America was in open revolt, he declared, and he denounced as traitors those who, by "gross misrepresentation," labored to inflame his people in America. Theirs was a "desperate conspiracy." All the time they had been professing loyalty to the parent state, "and the strongest protestations of loyalty to me," they were preparing for rebellion.

They have raised troops, and are collecting a naval force. They have seized the public revenue, and assumed to themselves legislative, executive, and judicial powers, which they already exercise in the most arbitrary manner. . . . And although many of these unhappy people may still retain their loyalty . . . the torrent of violence has been strong enough to compel their acquiescence till a sufficient force shall appear to support them.

Like the Parliament, he had acted thus far in a spirit of moderation, he said, and he was "anxious to prevent, if it had been possible, the effusion of the blood of my subjects, and the calamities which are inseparable from a state of war." He hoped his people in America would see the light, and recognize "that to be a subject of Great Britain, with all its consequences, is to be the freest member of any civil society in the known world."

Then came a new charge, based on opinions received from his commander at Boston. There must be no more misconceptions about the true intent of those deceiving the unhappy people of America. "The rebellious war . . . is manifestly carried on for the purpose of establishing an independent empire."

I need not dwell upon the fatal effects of the success of such a plan. The object is too important, the spirit of the British nation too high, the resources with which God hath blessed her too numerous, to give up so many colonies which she has planted with great industry, nursed with great tenderness, encouraged with many commercial advantages, and protected and defended at much expense of blood and treasure.

Since, clearly, it was the better part of wisdom "to put a speedy end" to such disorders, he was increasing both his naval and land forces. Further, he was pleased to inform the Parliament, he had received "friendly offers of foreign assistance."

"When the unhappy and deluded multitude, against whom this force will be directed, shall become sensible of their error, I shall be ready to receive the misled with tenderness and mercy," he pledged, and as evidence of his good intentions, he would give authority to "certain persons" to grant pardons "upon the spot" in America, though beyond this he said no more.

In sum, he, George III, Sovereign of the Empire, had declared America in rebellion. He had confirmed that he was committing land and sea forces — as well as unnamed foreign mercenaries — sufficient to put an end to that rebellion, and he had denounced the leaders of the uprising for having American independence as their true objective, something those leaders themselves had not as yet openly declared.

"Among the many unavoidable ill consequences of this rebellion," he said at the last, "none affects me more sensibly than the extraordinary burden which it must create to my faithful subjects."

His Majesty's appearance before Parliament had lasted just twenty minutes, after which, as reported, he returned to St. James's Palace "as peaceably as he went."

The members of the House of Commons filed out directly to their own chamber, and debate on the King's address commenced "brisk and warm" in both houses, the opposition marshaling the case for conciliation with extraordinary force.

In the House of Lords, expressions of support were spirited though comparatively brief. The King was praised for his resolution to uphold the interests and honor of the kingdom, praised for his decisiveness. "We will support your majesty with our lives and fortunes," vowed Viscount Townsend.

Those in opposition had more to say, and spoke at times with pronounced emotion. The measures recommended from the throne, warned the Marquis of Rockingham, were "big with the most portentous and ruinous consequences." The hiring of foreign troops was an "alarming and dangerous expedient." Even more deplorable was the prospect of "shedding British blood by British hands." Any notion of conquering America was "wild and extravagant," said the Earl of Coventry. The administration was "no longer to be trusted," said Lord Lyttleton bitterly.

"How comes it that the colonies are charged with planning independency?" the Earl of Shelburne demanded to know. "Who is it that presumes to put an assertion (what shall I call it, my Lords?) contrary to fact, contrary to evidence? . . . Is it their intention, by thus perpetually sounding independence in the ears of the Americans, to lead them to it?"

As the afternoon light began to fade and the chamber grew dim, the candles of the chandeliers were lit.

The one surprise, as the debate continued, was a vehement speech by the Duke of Grafton, Augustus Henry Fitzroy, former Prime Minister, who had not previously opposed the administration. Until now, he said, he had concurred in the belief that the more forceful the government in dealing with the Americans, the more likely matters could be "amicably adjusted." But he had been misled, deceived. Admitting to his ignorance of the real state of things in America — and inferring that this was no uncommon handicap in Parliament — he boldly proposed the repeal of every act concerning America since the incendiary Stamp Act of 1765.

This, I will venture to assert, will answer every end; and nothing less will accomplish any effectual purpose, without scenes of ruin and destruction, which I cannot think on without the utmost grief and horror.

The Earl of Dartmouth, Secretary of

State for the Colonies, was astonished. How could any noble lord possibly condemn the policies of the administration, or withdraw support, without at least giving them a fair trial?

It was in the Commons that the longer, more turbulent conflict ensued. Of the twenty or so who rose to speak, few held back. Attacks on the King, Lord North, the Foreign Ministry in general, and on one another at times brought the heat of debate to the boiling point. There were insults exchanged that would long fester, bombast and hyperbole in abundance, and moments when eloquence was brought to bear with a dramatic effect remarkable even in the Commons.

It was Parliament as theater, and gripping, even if the outcome, like much of theater, was understood all along. For importantly it was also well understood, and deeply felt, that the historic chamber was again the setting for history, that issues of the utmost consequence, truly the fate of nations, were at stake.

The passion of opposing opinion was evident at once, as the youthful John Dyke Acland of Devonshire declared emphatic support of the King's address. True it was that the task of "reducing America to a just obedience" should not be underestimated, he said, but where "the interests of a great people" were concerned, "difficulties must be overcome, not yielded to."

Acland, a headstrong young army officer, was ready to serve in America himself (and would), and thus what he said had unusual force, if not perfect historic validity. "Recollect the strength, the resources, and above all the spirit of the British nation, which when roused knows no opposition."

Let me remind you of those extensive and successful wars that this country has carried on before the continent of America was known. Let me turn your attention to that period when you defended this very people from the attacks of the most powerful and valiant nation in Europe [France], when your armies gave law, and your fleets rode triumphant on every coast. Shall we be told then that this people [the Americans], whose greatness is the work of our hands, and whose insolence arises from our divisions, who have mistaken the lenity of this country for its weakness, and the reluctance to punish, for a want of power to vindicate the violated rights of British subjects — shall we be told that such a people can resist the powerful efforts of this nation?

At about the time the chandeliers were being lighted in the House, John Wilkes, Lord Mayor of London, champion of the people and the homeliest man in Parliament, stood to be heard, and to let there be no doubt that he was John Wilkes.

"I speak, Sir, as a firm friend to England and America, but still more to universal liberty and the rights of all mankind. I trust no part of the subjects of this vast empire will ever submit to be slaves." Never had England been engaged in a contest of such import to her own best interests and possessions, Wilkes said.

We are fighting for the subjection, the unconditional submission of a country infinitely more extended than our own, of which every day increases the wealth, the natural strength, the population. Should we not succeed . . . we shall be considered as their most implacable enemies, an eternal separation will follow, and the grandeur of the British empire pass away.

The war with "our brethren" in America was "unjust . . . fatal and ruinous to our country," he declared.

There was no longer any question whether the Americans would fight, conceded Tory Adam Ferguson, but could anyone doubt the strength of Great Britain to "reduce" them? And this, he said, must be done quickly and decisively, as an act of humanity. Half measures would not do. Half measures could lead only to the horrors of civil war.

In response, George Johnstone, a dashing figure who had once served as governor of West Florida, delivered one of the longest, most vehement declamations of the night, exclaiming, "Every Machiavellian policy is now to be vindicated towards the people of America."

Men are to be brought to this black business hood-winked. They are to be drawn in by degrees, until they cannot retreat. . . . we are breaking through all those sacred maxims of our forefathers, and giving the alarm to every wise man on the continent of America, that all his rights depend on the will of men whose corruptions are notorious, who regard him as an enemy, and who have no interest in his prosperity.

Johnstone praised the people of New England for their courage and fortitude. There was a wide difference, he said, between the English officer or soldier who merely did his duty, and those of the New England army, where every man was thinking of what further service he could perform. No one who loved "the glorious spirit of freedom" could not be moved by the spectacle of Bunker Hill, where "an irregular peasantry" had so bravely faced "the gallant Howe" leading the finest troops in the world. "Who is there that can dismiss all doubts on the justice of a cause which can inspire such conscious rectitude?"

Alexander Wedderburn, the Solicitor General, belittled the very idea of standing in the way of the King and called for the full-scale conquest of America. "Why then do we hesitate?" he asked.

Because an inconsiderable party, inconsistent in their own policies, and always hostile to all government but their own, endeavor to obstruct our measures, and clog the wheels of government? Let us rather second the indignant voice of the nation, which presses in from all quarters upon the Sovereign, calling loudly for vigorous measures. . . . Sir, we have been too long deaf. We have too long shown our forbearance and long-suffering. . . . Our thunders must go forth. America must be conquered.

As the night wore on, Lord North, the stout, round-shouldered Prime Minister, remained conspicuously silent in his front-bench seat, his large, nearsighted eyes and full cheeks giving him the look, as the wit Horace Walpole said, of a blind trumpeter. North was much liked — moderate, urbane, and intelligent. He had made his career in the Commons and, with his affable manner, had acquired few if any enemies among his political opponents. When attacked, he took no offense. He could be a markedly persuasive speaker but was equally capable, when need be, of remaining silent, even napping a bit.

From years of experience North had also learned to count votes in advance, and he knew now, as did nearly everyone present, that the decided majority of the Commons, like the people at large, stood behind the King.

Perhaps the most telling moment of the

whole heated session came near midnight, when another army officer, but of an older generation than John Dyke Acland, rose to speak. Colonel Isaac Barré was a veteran of the French and Indian War who had come home from the Battle of Quebec badly disfigured. He had been hit in the head by a musket ball that blinded him in one eye and left his face twisted into a permanent sneer. Further, it had been Isaac Barré, in a past speech in defense of the Americans, who had first called them "Sons of Liberty," and the name had taken hold.

He had lost one eye, the colonel reminded his listeners, but the one good "military eye" he had left did not deceive him. The only way to avert "this American storm" was to reach an accommodation just as soon as possible.

Between them, Edmund Burke and young Charles James Fox filled the next several hours. Burke, in customary fashion, took his time. Nearly all that he said, he and others had said before, but he saw no harm in repetition, or any need for hurry. He held the floor for nearly two hours, a large part of his speech devoted to the disgrace of British forces cooped up in Boston by those said to be an undisciplined rabble.

There were no ringing lines from Burke this time, little at all for the newspapers to quote. Possibly he did not wish to outshine Fox, his protégé, who spoke next and who, at twenty-six, was already a dazzling political star.

Born to wealth and position, Fox was an unabashed fop, a dandified "macaroni," who at times appeared in high-heeled shoes, each of a different color, and happily spent most nights drinking or gambling away his father's fortune at London's best clubs. But his intellect and oratorical gifts were second to none. He always spoke spontaneously, never from notes or a prepared text. Fox, it would be observed, would as soon write down what he was going to say as pay a bill before it came due.

He attacked immediately and in searing fashion, calling Lord North the "blundering pilot" who had brought the nation to a terrible impasse. If Edmund Burke had failed to provide a memorable line for the night's efforts, Fox did at once:

Lord Chatham, the King of Prussia, nay, Alexander the Great, never gained more in one campaign than the noble lord has lost — he has lost a whole continent.

It was time for a change in the administration, time for new policies. The present ministers were enemies of freedom.

I cannot consent to the bloody consequences of so silly a contest about so silly an object, conducted in the silliest manner that history or observation has ever furnished an instance of, and from which we are likely to derive nothing but poverty, disgrace, defeat, and ruin.

Once Fox finished, North stood at his place and calmly allowed he had no wish to remain a day in office were he to be judged inactive, inattentive, or inconsiderate.

North was not a man enamored with war. He had nothing of the look or temperament of a war leader. Privately he was not at all sure it would be possible to vanquish the Americans, and he worried about the cost. To General Burgoyne he had written, "I would abandon the contest were I not most intimately convinced in my own conscience that our cause is just and important." George III relied on him, calling him "my sheet anchor," and it was, and would remain, North's role to explain and defend the King and administration policies and decisions before the Commons.

The intention now, he affirmed, was to send a powerful sea and land force across the Atlantic. But with these forces would also go "offers of mercy upon a proper submission." How "proper submission" was to be determined, or who was to bear such offers, he did not say. As time would show, however, the real purpose of such peace gestures was to speed up an American surrender.

"This will show we are in earnest, that we are prepared to punish, but are nevertheless ready to forgive. This is, in my opinion, the most likely means of producing an honorable reconciliation."

On that note the debate ended.

In the House of Lords, where work had wound up at midnight, the opposition to the King's address, and thus to all-out war in America, was defeated by a vote of more than two to one, 69 to 29.

In the House of Commons, their impassioned speeches notwithstanding, the opposition was defeated by an even greater margin, 278 to 108.

By the time the vote in the Commons had concluded, it was four in the morning.

One of those members of the House of Commons who had refrained from speaking, and who felt extremely pleased with the outcome, was the gentleman-scholar Edward Gibbon. A supporter of Lord North, Gibbon never spoke on any issue. But in private correspondence from his London home, he had been assuring friends that "some[thing] will be done" about America. The power of the empire would be "exerted to the utmost," he wrote. "Irish papists, Hanoverians, Canadians, Indians, etc. will all in various shapes be employed."

Gibbon, who was then putting the final touches to the first volume of his masterpiece, *History of the Decline and Fall of the Roman Empire*, now felt even more confident about the course of history in his own time. "The *conquest* of America is a *great* work," he wrote.

Soon after, in early November, King George III appointed a new Secretary for the American colonies, Lord George Germain, a choice that left little doubt, if any remained, that the King, too, considered the conquest of America serious work to which he was seriously committed.

Germain was to replace the Earl of Dartmouth, whose attitude toward the war seemed at times less than wholehearted. He was a proud, intelligent, exceedingly serious man of sixty, tall, physically impressive, and, notably unlike the King and Lord North, he was a soldier. He had served in the Seven Years' War in Germany and with good reputation, until the Battle of Minden, when, during a cavalry attack, he was accused of being slow to obey orders. He was not charged with cowardice, as his critics liked to say. At a court-martial called at his own insistence, he was found guilty only of disobedience. But his military career ended when the court declared him unfit for further service.

As a politician in the years since, he had performed diligently, earning a high reputation as an administrator. In his new role he would direct the main operations of the war and was expected to take a firm hand. To many he seemed the perfect counterpart to the obliging, unassertive North.

For the "riotous rebels" of America, he had no sympathy. What was needed, Germain said, was a "decisive blow." The King thought highly of him.

Chapter Two

RABBLE IN ARMS

His Excellency General Washington has arrived amongst us, universally admired. Joy was visible on every countenance.

— General Nathanael Greene

I

"Here we are at loggerheads," wrote the youthful brigadier general from Rhode Island, appraising the scene at Boston in the last days of October 1775.

I wish we had a large stock of [gun]powder that we might annoy the enemy wherever they make their appearance. . . . but for want thereof we are obliged to remain idle spectators, for we cannot get at them and they are determined not to come to us.

At age thirty-three, Nathanael Greene

was the youngest general officer in what constituted the American army, and by conventional criterion, an improbable choice for such responsibility. He had been a full-time soldier for all of six months. Unlike any of the other American generals, he had never served in a campaign, never set foot on a battlefield. He was a foundryman by trade. What he knew of warfare and military command came almost entirely from books.

Besides, he was a Quaker, and though of robust physique, a childhood accident had left him with a stiff right leg and a limp. He also suffered from occasional attacks of asthma.

But Nathanael Greene was no ordinary man. He had a quick, inquiring mind and uncommon resolve. He was extremely hardworking, forthright, good-natured, and a born leader. His commitment to the Glorious Cause of America, as it was called, was total. And if his youth was obvious, the Glorious Cause was to a large degree a young man's cause. The commander in chief of the army, George Washington, was himself only forty-three. John Hancock, the President of the Continental Congress, was thirty-nine, John Adams, forty, Thomas Jefferson, thirty-two, younger even than the young Rhode Island general. In such times many were being cast in roles seemingly beyond their experience or capacities, and Washington had quickly judged Nathanael Greene to be "an object of confidence."

He had been born and raised in Kent County, Rhode Island, on a farm by Potowomut Creek, near the village of Warwick, approximately sixty miles south of Boston. He was the third of the eight sons of a prominent, industrious Quaker also named Nathanael, and the one, of all the sons, his father counted on most to further the family interests. These included the home-farm, a general store, a gristmill, a sawmill, a coasting sloop, and the Greene forge, all, as was said, in "constant and profitable operation." The forge, the most thriving enterprise, which produced anchors and chains and employed scores of men, was one of the leading businesses in the colony, and the Greenes, as a result, had become people of substantial means. The fact that the patriarch owned a sedan chair was taken as the ultimate measure of just how greatly the family had prospered.

Because education did not figure prominently in his father's idea of the Quaker way, young Nathanael had received little schooling. "My father was a man [of] great piety," he would explain. "[He] had an excellent understanding, and was governed in his conduct by humanity and kind benevolence. But his mind was overshadowed with prejudices against literary accomplishments." With his brothers, Nathanael had been put to work at an early age, on the farm at first, then at the mills and forge. In time, determined to educate himself, he began reading all he could, guided and encouraged by several learned figures, including the Rhode Island clergyman Ezra Stiles, one of the wisest men of the time, who would later become the president of Yale College.

Nathanael read Caesar and Horace in English translation, Swift, Pope, and Locke's *Essay Concerning Human Understanding*. On visits to Newport and Boston, he began buying books and assembling his own library. Recalling their youth, one of his brothers would describe Nathanael during lulls in the clamor of the foundry, seated near the great trip-hammer, a leather-bound volume of Euclid in hand, calmly studying.

"I lament the want of a liberal education. I feel the mist [of] ignorance to surround me," he wrote to a like-minded friend. He found he enjoyed expressing himself on paper and had a penchant in such correspondence for endless philosophizing on the meaning of life. Yet for all this no thought of a life or occupation other than what he knew seems to have crossed his mind until the threat of conflict with Great Britain.

The description that would come down the generations in the family was of a "cheerful, vigorous, thoughtful" young man who, like his father, loved a "merry jest or tale," who did comic imitations of characters from *Tristram Shandy*, and relished the company of young ladies, while they, reportedly, "never felt lonely where he was." Once, accused by a dancing partner of dancing stiffly, because of his bad leg, Nathanael replied, "Very true, but you see I dance strong."

His defects were perceived to be a certain "nervous temperament" and susceptibility to poor health, impetuousness, and acute sensitivity to criticism.

Full-grown, he was a burly figure, about five feet ten inches tall, with the arms and shoulders of a foundryman, and handsome, though an inoculation for smallpox had left a cloudy spot in his right eye. A broad forehead and a full, "decided" mouth were considered his best features, though a soldier sent to deliver a message to the general would remember his "fine blue eyes, which struck me with a considerable degree of awe, that I could scarcely deliver my message."

In 1770, when Nathanael was still in his twenties, his father had put him in charge of another family-owned foundry in the neighboring village of Coventry, beside the Pawtuxet River, and on a nearby hill Nathanael built a house of his own. Following the death of his father late that same year, he took charge of the entire business. By 1774, when he met and married pretty, flirtatious Katherine Littlefield, who was fourteen years his junior, he was perceived to be a "very remarkable man."

It was then, too, with war threatening, that he turned his mind to "the military art." Having ample means to buy whatever books he needed, he acquired a number of costly military treatises few could afford. It was a day and age that saw no reason why one could not learn whatever was required — learn virtually anything — by the close study of books, and he was a prime example of such faith. Resolved to become a "fighting Quaker," he made himself as knowledgeable on tactics, military science, and leadership as any man in the colony.

"The first of all qualities [of a general] is courage," he read in the *Memoirs Concerning the Art of War* by Marshal Maurice de Saxe, one of the outstanding commanders of the era. "Without this the others are of little value, since they cannot be used. The second is intelligence, which must be strong and fertile in expedients. The third is health."

He took a leading part in organizing a militia unit, the Kentish Guards, only to be told that his stiff leg disqualified him from being an officer. To have it declared publicly that his limp — his "halting" — would be a "blemish" on the company was, as he wrote, a "mortification" beyond any he had known.

If unacceptable as an officer, he would willingly serve in the ranks. Shouldering an English musket he had bought at Boston from a British deserter, he marched as a private in company drills for eight months, until it became obvious that for a man of such knowledge and ability, it would be best to forget about the limp.

Almost overnight he was given full command of the Rhode Island regiments. Exactly how this came about remains unclear.

One of his strongest admirers and mentors was Samuel Ward of Rhode Island, a delegate to the Continental Congress, who was also the uncle of Nathanael's wife Katherine and presumably used his influence. But that Nathanael had so willingly marched in the ranks could only have favored him strongly among his fellow volunteers when it came to choosing a commander.

General Greene had been at Boston since early May of 1775, at the head of what was called the Rhode Island Army of Observation, applying himself every waking moment, at times sleeping only a few hours a night. Thus far no one had found cause to complain about his youth or inexperience.

Whatever he lacked in knowledge or experience, he tried to make up for with "watchfulness and industry," he would later confide to John Adams.

As commander of the "Army of Observation," encamped at the American citadel on Prospect Hill, he tried to take in everything, to observe and appraise the situation as realistically as possible. While the American army controlled the land around Boston, the British, strongly fortified in the city and on Bunker Hill, had control of the sea and could thereby supply their troops and send reinforcements. (Only weeks before, in September, reinforcements of five regiments had arrived.) The task at hand, therefore, seemed clear enough: to confine the King's men in Boston, cut them off from supplies of fresh provisions, and keep them from coming out to gain what one of their generals, Burgoyne, called "elbow room."

If it ever came to a fight, the American army had scarcely any artillery, and almost no gunpowder, yet to Greene the greater weakness and worry was the continuing disorderly state of the army itself. As he wrote to his friend Samuel Ward at the Continental Congress, the prospect was deeply disturbing, "when you consider how raw and undisciplined the troops are in general, and what war-like preparations are going on [in] England."

At the start of the siege there had been no American army. Even now it had no flag or uniforms. Though in some official documents it had been referred to as the Continental Army, there was no clear agreement on what it should be called in actual practice. At first it was referred to as the New England army, or the army at

Boston. The Continental Congress had appointed George Washington to lead "the army of the United Colonies," but in correspondence with the general, the President of Congress, John Hancock, referred to it only as "the troops under your command." Washington, in his formal orders, called them the "Troops of the United Provinces of North America." Privately he described them as the "raw materials" for an army.

To the British and those Loyalists who had taken refuge in Boston, they were simply "the rebels," or "the country people," undeserving the words "American" or "army." General John Burgoyne disdainfully dubbed them "a preposterous parade," a "rabble in arms."

In April, when the call for help first went out after Lexington and Concord, militia and volunteer troops from the other New England colonies had come by the thousands to join forces with the Massachusetts regiments — 1,500 Rhode Islanders led by Nathanael Greene, 5,000 from Connecticut under the command of Israel Putnam. John Stark's New Hampshire regiment of 1,000 had marched in snow and rain, "wet and sloppy," "through mud and mire," without food or tents, seventy-five miles in three and a half days. The Massachusetts regiments, by far the strongest of the provincial troops, possibly numbered more than 10,000.

By June a sprawling, spontaneous, high-spirited New England army such as had never been seen was gathered about Boston. Washington, arriving in the first week of July, was told he had 20,000 men, but no one knew for certain. No count had been taken until he made it a first order of business. In fact, there were 16,000, of which fewer than 14,000 were fit for duty. More than 1,500 were sick, another 1,500 absent.

In a regular army such a count could have been accomplished in a matter of hours, Washington noted disapprovingly. As things were, it took eight days. The enemy's total strength was believed to be 11,000. In reality, there were perhaps 7,000 of the King's men in Boston, or roughly half the number under Washington's command.

In a formal address from the Massachusetts Provincial Congress, Washington had been warned not to expect "regularity and discipline" among the men. The youth of the army had little or no experience with military life. Nor were they "possessed of the absolute necessity of cleanliness." Beyond that Washington found them to be men of a decidedly different sort than he had expected, and he was not at all pleased.

The lay of the land about Boston was also different from anything in the general's military experience. In the simplest terms, as he drew in his own rough map, the setting was one of three irregular peninsulas at the head of Boston Harbor, with the peninsula of Boston in the middle, that of Charlestown (and Bunker Hill) just to the north, and Dorchester close by to the south. But as Boston was connected to the mainland only by a narrow, half-mile causeway, or neck, it was more like an island than a peninsula. And thus, by barricading the Neck, it had been relatively simple to keep the British "bottled up" in Boston, just as the British had built their own barricades at the Neck to keep the Americans from coming in.

The British still held Charlestown, which was largely in ruins, and Bunker Hill, which was their citadel and a formidable advantage. Neither side had yet moved to fortify the even higher ground of the Dorchester peninsula overlooking the harbor.

With its numerous green hills falling away to blue water, it was a particularly beautiful part of the world and especially in summer. Washington thought it "very delightful country," and more the pity that it should be a theater of war. A British officer described it as "country of the most charming green that delighted eye ever gazed on." Views sketched from the uplands of Charlestown by one of the British engineers, Captain Archibald Robertson, show how many broad, open fields and meadows there were, and how modest was the skyline of Boston, its church spires more like those of a country village. They might have been sketches of Arcadia.

Had a seagull's-eye view been possible, one could have seen the whole American army and its fortifications strung out in a great arc of about ten miles around the landward side of Boston, from the Mystic River on the northeast to Roxbury to the south, with British redcoats camped on the slopes of the Boston Common and manning defenses at the Neck and within the town and on Bunker Hill. A lofty beacon pole rose from the crest of Beacon Hill, and at the center of the town, the Province House, headquarters for the British command, could be readily identified by its large, octagonal cupola and distinctive gold weather vane of an Indian with bow and arrow.

In the harbor off Long Wharf were British ships lying at anchor — and three were ships of the line, ships of fifty guns or more — while over to the right of the Dorchester peninsula, at the narrow entrance to the Inner Harbor, on Castle Island, stood the old fort Castle William, also occupied by the British.

The main concentration of American troops was at Prospect Hill to the north. Others were encamped a few miles farther inland, at the pretty little college town of Cambridge on the Charles River, and close to the Neck at Roxbury, where the white spire of the Roxbury meetinghouse rose from the top of still another prominent hill. At Cambridge troops were encamped mainly on the Common, though most of the town and the red-brick buildings of Harvard College had also been taken over.

Needing more than his rough sketch of the terrain, Washington had assigned a talented nineteen-year-old lieutenant, John Trumbull, the son of the governor of Connecticut, to do a series of maps and drawings. For one sketch of the British defenses at the Neck, young Trumbull had crawled through high grass almost to the enemy line.

For their part, the British had assigned an experienced cartographer, Lieutenant Richard Williams, who, with the help of a small crew, moved his surveyor's transit and brass chains from one vantage point to the next, taking and recording careful sightings. The result was a beautifully delineated, hand-colored map showing "the True Situation of His Majesty's Army and also those of the Rebels." All fortifications were clearly marked, all landmarks neatly labeled, including "Mount Whoredom," Boston's red-light district. Lieutenant Williams had been appalled to find prostitution so in evidence in what was supposedly the center of Puritanism — "There's perhaps no town of its size could turn out more whores than this could," he noted in his journal — and accuracy demanded that this, too, be shown on the map.

Not the least of Washington's problems was that he had command of a siege, yet within his entire army there was not one trained engineer to design and oversee the building of defenses. Still, he ordered larger and stronger defenses built, and the work went forward. "Thousands are at work every day," wrote the Reverend William Emerson of Concord after touring the lines. " 'Tis surprising the work that has been done. . . . 'Tis incredible." It had been the Reverend Emerson who declared the morning of April 19, as British regiments advanced on Concord, "Let us stand our ground. If we die, let us die here!"

With telescopes from Prospect Hill and other vantage points, the army kept constant watch on the regulars in Boston, just as the regulars kept watch on the army. ("It seemed to be the principal employment of both armies to look at each other with spyglasses," wrote the eminent Loyalist Peter Oliver, former chief justice of the province.)

Washington knew little about Boston. He had been there only once and but briefly twenty years before, when he was a young Virginia colonel hoping for advancement in the regular army. And though each side dispatched its spies, he put particular emphasis on "intelligence" from the start, and was willing to pay for it. Indeed, the first large sum entered in his account book was for $333.33, a great deal of money, for an unnamed man "to go into Boston . . . for the purpose of conveying intelligence of the enemy's movements and designs."

58

The fear that the British were preparing an attack was ever present. "We scarcely lie down or rise up, but with expectation that the night or the day must produce some important event," wrote one of Washington's staff.

It was in the first week of August, at the end of his first month as commander, when Washington learned how much worse things were than he knew. A report on the supply of gunpowder at hand revealed a total of less than 10,000 pounds, and the situation was not expected to improve soon. Very little gunpowder was produced in the colonies. What supplies there were came mainly by clandestine shipments from Europe to New York and Philadelphia by way of the Dutch island St. Eustatius in the Caribbean. At present, there was powder enough only for about nine rounds per man. According to one account, Washington was so stunned by the report he did not utter a word for half an hour.

The sprawling American encampments bore little resemblance to the usual military presence. Tents and shelters were mainly patched-together concoctions of whatever could be found. Each was "a portraiture of the temper and taste of the person that encamps in it," wrote clergyman Emerson.

Some are made of boards, some of sailcloth, and some partly of one and partly of the other. Others are made of stone and turf, and others again of brick and others brush. Some are thrown up in a hurry and look as if they could not help it — mere necessity — others are curiously wrought with doors and windows.

A notable exception was the encampment of Nathanael Greene's Rhode Islanders. There, "proper tents" were arranged row on row like "the regular camp of the enemy . . . everything in the most exact English taste," recorded Emerson approvingly. On the whole, however, he thought "the great variety" of the camps most picturesque.

Others were considerably less charmed. The drunken carousing to be seen, the foul language to be heard were appalling to many, even among the soldiers themselves. "Wickedness prevails very much," declared Lieutenant Joseph Hodgkins of Ipswich, Massachusetts.

A veteran of Bunker Hill and a cobbler by trade, Hodgkins was thirty-two years old and a man, like many, who had already seen a good deal of trouble and sorrow in his life. His first wife and four of their five children had all died of disease before the war began. To the remaining child and to his second wife, Sarah Perkins, and the two children born of this second marriage, he was a devoted father and husband. Greatly concerned for their welfare and knowing her concern for him, he wrote to Sarah at every chance. But for now, as he told her, he had no time to be "pertickler" about details.

A British ship's surgeon who used the privileges of his profession to visit some of the rebel camps, described roads crowded with carts and wagons hauling mostly provisions, but also, he noted, inordinate quantities of rum — "for without New England rum, a New England army could not be kept together." The rebels, he calculated, were consuming a bottle a day per man.

To judge by the diary of an officer with the Connecticut troops at Roxbury, Lieutenant Jabez Fitch, who enjoyed a sociable drink, there was considerably more besides plain rum to be had. "Drank some grog," he recorded at the close of one day, after a stop at a nearby tavern; "the gin sling passed very briskly," reads another entry. "In the morning I attended the alarm post as usual . . . then down at Lt. Brewster's tent to drink Ens. Perkins' cherry rum, came back and eat breakfast. . . ." He imbibed wine and brandy sling, and on an expedition "up into Cambridge town," after a stop to sample "some flip" (a sweet, potent mix of liquor, beer, and sugar), he made for another tavern, the Punch Bowl, "where there was fiddling and dancing in great plenty. . . . I came home a little before daylight in."

Lieutenant Fitch was one of a number of veterans of the French and Indian War, an easygoing Norwich, Connecticut, farmer and the father of eight children. He enjoyed soldiering and felt so sure his fourteen-year-old son would, too, that he had brought the boy along with him. Lieutenant Fitch, an early member of the Sons of Liberty, had been one of the first to answer the call for reinforcements for Boston. Little seemed ever to bother him, though he did object to soldiers "dirty as hogs." Much of his free time he spent writing in his diary or to his wife. The sound of British shells overhead was like that of a flock of geese, he wrote, and "has done more to exhilarate the spirits of our people than 200 gallons of New England rum."

For all its lack of ammunition, tents, and uniforms, the army was amply fed. Fresh produce in abundance and at low prices rolled into the camps all through summer and early fall. The men could count on meat or fish almost every day. Jabez Fitch wrote of enjoying fresh eggs, clams, apples, peaches, and watermelons, a "very good" breakfast of "warm bread and good camp butter with a good dish of coffee," "a hearty dinner of pork and cabbage." As yet, no one was complaining of a shortage of food.

There had been sickness aplenty from the start, deadly "camp fever," which grew worse as summer went on. Anxious mothers and wives from the surrounding towns and countryside came to nurse the sick and dying. "Your brother Elihu lies very dangerously sick with a dysentery . . . his life is despaired of," wrote Abigail Adams from nearby Braintree to her husband John in Philadelphia. "Your mother is with him in great anguish." Captain Elihu Adams, a farmer with a wife and three children, was one of several hundred who died of illness.

"Camp fever" or "putrid fever" were terms used for the highly infectious, deadly scourges of dysentery, typhus, and typhoid fever, the causes of which were unknown or only partially understood. Dysentery had been the curse of armies since ancient times, as recorded by Herodotus. Typhus, characterized by high fever, severe headaches, and delirium, was carried by lice and fleas, which were a plague amid the army. (One soldier recorded seeing a dead body so covered with lice that it was thought the lice alone had killed the man.) Typhoid fever, also characterized by a raging fever, red rash, vomiting, diarrhea, and excruciating abdominal pain, was caused by the bacillus *Salmonella typhosa* in contaminated food or water, usually the result of too little separation between sewage and drinking water.

And it was not the troops alone who suffered from camp fever. Many of those who came to nurse them were sickened, or carried the disease home, and thus it lay waste to one New England town after another. Of the parishioners of a single church in Danbury, Connecticut, more than a hundred would die of camp fever by November.

"Infectious filth" was understood to be

the killer. Cleanliness in person, clean cooking utensils, clean water and unspoiled meat and produce were seen as essential to the prolonged health of the army, and this was among the chief reasons for constant insistence on discipline and order, and especially with so many thousands encamped in such close company.

As it was, open latrines were the worst of it, but there was also, as recorded in one orderly book, a "great neglect of people repairing to the necessaries." Instead, they voided "excrement about the fields perniciously." The smell of many camps was vile in the extreme.

New England men were also averse to washing their own clothes, considering that women's work. The British included women in their army — wives and other so-called camp followers, some of whom were prostitutes — who did the washing, but that was not the way with the New Englanders.

The troops were in good spirits, but had yet to accept the necessity of order or obedience. Many had volunteered on the condition that they could elect their own officers, and the officers, in turn, were inclined out of laziness, or for the sake of their own popularity, to let those in the ranks do much as they pleased. Many officers had little or no idea of what they were supposed to do. "The officers in general," remembered John Trumbull, "[were] quite as ignorant of military life as the troops."

Washington had declared new rules and regulations in force, insisting on discipline, and he made his presence felt by reviewing the defenses on horseback almost daily. "New lords, new laws," observed Pastor Emerson. "New orders from his Excellency are read to the respective regiments every morning after prayers. The strictest government is taking place."

Those who broke the rules were subjected to severe punishment or disgrace. They were flogged, or made to ride the "wooden horse," or drummed out of camp. One man was whipped for "making a disturbance in the time of public worship," another for desertion. Another received twenty "stripes" for striking an officer, another, thirty for damning an officer. But change was maddeningly slow in coming.

As scathing as any eyewitness description was that provided by a precocious young New Englander of Loyalist inclinations named Benjamin Thompson, who, after being refused a commission by Washington, served in the British army, later settled in Europe, renamed himself Count Rumford, and ultimately became one of the era's prominent men of science. Washington's army, wrote Thompson, was "the most wretchedly clothed, and as dirty a set of mortals as ever disgraced the name of a soldier. . . . They would rather let their clothes rot upon their backs than be at the trouble of cleaning 'em themselves." To this "nasty way of life" Thompson attributed all the "putrid, malignant and infectious disorders" that took such a heavy toll.

His Loyalist bias notwithstanding, Thompson's portrayal was largely the truth. Such British commanders as Burgoyne and Percy were hardly to be blamed for dismissing Washington's army as "peasantry," "ragamuffins," or "rabble in arms." Except for Greene's Rhode Islanders and a few Connecticut units, they looked more like farmers in from the fields than soldiers.

That so many were filthy dirty was perfectly understandable, as so many, when not drilling, spent their days digging trenches, hauling rock, and throwing up great mounds of earth for defense. At one point early in the siege there were 4,000 men at work on Prospect Hill alone. It was dirty, hard labor, and there was little chance or the means ever to bathe or enjoy such luxury as a change of clothes.

Few of the men had what would pass for a uniform. Field officers were all but indistinguishable from the troops they led. Not only were most men unwashed and often unshaven, they were clad in a bewildering variety of this and that, largely whatever they, or others at home, had been able to throw together before they trudged off to war. (One Connecticut woman was reported to have "fitted out" five sons and eleven grandsons.) They wore heavy homespun coats and shirts, these often in tatters from constant wear, britches of every color and condition, cowhide shoes and moccasins, and on their heads, old broad-brimmed felt hats, weathered and sweat-stained, beaver hats, farmer's straw hats, or striped bandannas tied sailor-fashion. The tricorn, a dressier hat, was more likely to be worn by officers and others of higher status, such as chaplains and doctors. Only here and there might an old regimental coat be seen, something left over from the French and Indian War.

The arms they bore were "as various as their costumes," mainly muskets and fowling pieces (in effect, shotguns), and the more ancient the gun, it seemed, the greater the owner's pride in it. The most common and by far the most important was the flintlock musket, a single-shot, smooth-bore, muzzle-loading weapon that threw a lead ball weighing about an ounce and which could inflict terrible damage. The average musket measured 5 feet and weighed about 10 pounds. Though not especially accurate, it could be primed, loaded, fired, and rapidly reloaded and fired again. A good musket man could get off three to four rounds per minute, or a shot every fifteen seconds.

The trouble now was that so many of the men, accustomed to firearms since childhood, used them any way they saw fit, almost any time they pleased — to start fires, for example, or blast away at wild geese.

In order that officers could be distinguished from those in the ranks, Washington directed that major generals wear purple ribbons across their chests, brigadiers, pink ribbons. Field officers were to be identified by different-colored cockades in their hats. Sergeants were to tie a red cloth to their right shoulders. Washington himself chose to wear a light blue ribbon across his chest, between coat and waistcoat. But then there was never any mistaking the impeccably uniformed, commanding figure of Washington, who looked always as if on parade.

The day he officially took command at Cambridge, July 3, had been marked by appropriate martial fanfare, "a great deal of grandeur," as Lieutenant Hodgkins, the Ipswich cobbler, recorded, "one and twenty drummers and as many fifers a beating and playing round the parade [ground]." A young newly arrived doctor from Barnstable, James Thacher, assigned to the army's hospital at Cambridge, described seeing the commander-in-chief for the first time:

> His Excellency was on horseback, in company with several military gentlemen. It was not difficult to distinguish him from all others. His personal appearance is truly noble and majestic, being tall and well proportioned. His dress is a blue coat with buff colored facings, a rich epaulet on each shoulder, buff underdress, and an elegant small sword, a black cockade in his hat.

The great majority of the army were farmers and skilled artisans: shoemakers, saddlers, carpenters, wheelwrights, blacksmiths, coopers, tailors, and ship chandlers. Colonel John Glover's regiment from Marblehead, who were destined to play as important a part as any, were nearly all sailors and fishermen.

It was an army of men accustomed to hard work, hard work being the common lot. They were familiar with adversity and making do in a harsh climate. Resourceful, handy with tools, they could drive a yoke of oxen or "hove up" a stump or tie a proper knot as readily as butcher a hog or mend a pair of shoes. They knew from experience, most of them, the hardships and setbacks of life. Preparing for the worst was second nature. Rare was the man who had never seen someone die.

To be sure, an appreciable number had no trade. They were drifters, tavern lowlife, some, the dregs of society. But by and large they were good, solid citizens — as "worthy people as ever marched out of step," as would be said — married men with families who depended on them and with whom they tried to keep contact as best they could.

It was the first American army and an army of everyone, men of every shape and size and makeup, different colors, different nationalities, different ways of talking, and all degrees of physical condition. Many were missing teeth or fingers, pitted by smallpox or scarred by past wars or the all-too-common hazards of life and toil in the eighteenth century. Some were not even men, but smooth-faced boys of fifteen or less.

One of the oldest and by far the most popular, was General Israel Putnam, a hero of the Battle of Bunker Hill, who at fifty-seven was known affectionately as "Old Put." Rough, "thick-set," "all bones and muscles," and leathery, with flowing gray locks and a head like a cannonball, he was a Pomfret, Connecticut, farmer who had survived hair-raising exploits fighting the French and Indians, shipwreck, even a face-to-face encounter with a she-wolf in her den, if the stories were to be believed. Old Put also spoke with a slight lisp and could barely write his name. But, as said, Old Put feared nothing.

At the other extreme was little Israel Trask, who was all of ten. Like the son of Lieutenant Jabez Fitch, Israel had volunteered with his father, Lieutenant Jonathan Trask of Marblehead, and served as messenger and cook's helper.

John Greenwood, a fifer — one of the more than 500 fifers and drummers in the army — was sixteen, but small for his age and looked younger. Born and raised in Boston, he had grown up with "the troubles" always close to home. A young apprentice living in his house had been one of those killed in the Boston Massacre. Thrilled by the sound of the fifes and drums of the regulars occupying the city, John had somehow acquired "an old split fife," upon which, after puttying up the crack, he learned to play several tunes before being sent to live with an uncle in Falmouth (Portland), Maine. In May 1775, hearing the news of Lexington and Concord, he had set off on foot with little more than the clothes on his back, his fife protruding from a front pocket. All alone he walked to Boston, 150 miles through what was still, much of the route, uninhabited wilderness. Stopping at wayside taverns, where troops were gathered, he would bring out the fife and play "a tune or two," as he would later recall.

They used to ask me where I came from and where I was going to, and when I told them I was going to fight for my country, they were astonished such a little boy, and alone, should have such courage. Thus by the help of my fife I lived, as it were, on what is usually called free quarters nearly upon the entire route.

After reaching the army encampments, he was urged to enlist, with the promise of $8 a month. Later, passing through Cambridge, he learned of the battle raging at Bunker Hill. Wounded men were being laid out on the Common. "Everywhere the greatest terror and confusion seemed to prevail." The boy started running along the road that led to the battle, past wagons carrying more casualties and wounded men struggling back to Cambridge on foot. Terrified, he wished he had never enlisted. "I could positively feel my hair stand on end." But then he saw a lone soldier coming down the road.

. . . a Negro man, wounded in the back of his neck, passed me and, his collar being open and he not having anything on except his shirt and trousers, I saw the wound quite plainly and the blood running down his back. I asked him if it hurt him much, as he did not seem to mind it. He said no, that he was only to get a plaster put on it and meant to return. You cannot conceive what encouragement this immediately gave me. I began to feel brave and like a soldier from that moment, and fear never troubled me afterward during the whole war.

In response to concerns in Congress over how much of the army was in fact made up of old men and boys, as well as Negroes and Indians, General William Heath reported:

There are in the Massachusetts regiments some few lads and old men, and in several regiments, some Negroes. Such is also the case with the regiments from the other colonies. Rhode Island has a number of Negroes and Indians. The New Hampshire regiments have less of both.

General John Thomas, who commanded the Massachusetts troops at Roxbury, also responded:

The regiments at Roxbury, the privates, are equal to any I served with [in the] last war, very few old men, and in the ranks very few boys. Our fifers are many of them boys. We have some Negroes, but I look upon them in general equally serviceable with other men, for fatigue and in action; many of them have proved themselves brave.

Like most southerners, Washington did not want blacks in the army and would soon issue orders saying that neither "Negroes, boys unable to bear arms, nor old men" were to be enlisted. By year's end, however, with new recruits urgently needed and numbers of free blacks wanting to serve, he would change his mind and in a landmark general order authorize their enlistment.

While no contemporary drawings or paintings of individual soldiers have survived, a fair idea of how they looked emerges from the descriptions in notices posted of deserters. One George Reynolds of Rhode Island, as an example, was five feet nine and a half inches tall, age seventeen, and "carried his head something on his right shoulder." Thomas Williams was an immigrant — "an old country man" — who spoke "good English" and had "a film in his left eye." David Relph, a "saucy fellow," was wearing a white coat, jacket and breeches, and ruffled shirt when last seen.

Deserted from Col. Brewer's regiment, and Capt. Harvey's company [said a notice in the Essex, Connecticut, *Gazette*], one Simeon Smith of Greenfield, a joiner by trade, a thin-spared fellow, about 5 feet 4 inches high, had on a blue coat and black vest, a metal button on his hat, black long hair, black eyes, his voice in the hermaphrodite fashion, the masculine rather predominant. Likewise, Mathias Smith, a small smart fellow, a saddler by trade, gray headed, has a younger look in his face, is apt to say, "I swear! I swear!" And between his words will spit smart; had on a green coat, and an old red great coat; he is a right gamester, although he wears something of a sober look; likewise John Daby, a long hump-shouldered fellow, a shoemaker by trade, drawls his words, and for comfortable says comfable. He had a green coat, thick leather breeches, slim legs, lost some of his fore teeth.

For every full-fledged deserter there were a half-dozen others inclined to stroll off on almost any pretext, to do a little clam digging perhaps, or who might vanish for several weeks to see wives and children, help with the harvest at home, or ply their trades for some much-needed "hard money." Sometimes they requested a furlough; as often they just up and left, only to come straggling back into camp when it suited. It was not that they had no heart for soldiering, or were wanting in spirit. They simply had had little experience with other people telling them what to do every hour of the day. Having volunteered to fight, they failed to see the sense in a lot of fuss over rules and regulations.

It was midsummer by the time the first troops from outside New England began showing up, companies of riflemen from Pennsylvania, Maryland, and Virginia, "hardy men, many of them exceeding six feet in height," noted Dr. James Thacher, who was himself short and slight.

One Virginia company, led by Captain Daniel Morgan, had marched on a "beeline" for Boston, covering six hundred miles in three weeks, or an average of thirty miles a day in the heat of summer.

Mostly backwoodsmen of Scotch-Irish descent, they wore long, fringed hunting shirts, "rifle shirts" of homespun linen, in colors ranging from undyed tan and gray to shades of brown and even black, these tied at the waist with belts carrying tomahawks. At a review they demonstrated how, with their long-barreled rifles, a frontier weapon made in Pennsylvania and largely unknown in New England, they could hit a mark seven inches in diameter at a distance of 250 yards, while the ordinary musket was accurate at only 100 yards or so. It was "rifling" — spiraled grooves inside the long barrel — that increased the accuracy, and the new men began firing at British sentries with deadly effect, until the British caught on and kept their heads down or stayed out of range.

Welcome as they were at first, the riflemen soon proved even more indifferent to discipline than the New Englanders, and obstreperous to the point that Washington began to wish they had never come.

Work on defenses went on steadily, the troops toiling with picks and shovels in all weather, sometimes working through the night when the heat of day was too severe. It was endless, brute labor, but they were remarkably proficient at it — far more so than their British counterparts. As the size and reach of the defenses increased, visitors by the hundreds came to see for themselves. Roads were crowded with spectators to whom the giant ramparts were wondrous works. Nothing on such scale had ever been built by New Englanders before — breastworks "in many places seventeen feet in thickness," trenches "wide and deep," "verily their fortifications appear to be the works of seven years."

The work parties were fired on from time to time. British and American sentries alike were fired on repeatedly. On August 2, as Lieutenant Samuel Bixby of Connecticut recorded in his diary, "One of Gen[eral] Washington's riflemen was killed by the regulars today and then hung! up by the neck!"

His comrades, seeing this, were much enraged and immediately asked leave of the Gen[eral] to go down and do as they pleased. The riflemen marched immediately and began operations. The regulars fired at them from all parts with cannon and swivels, but the riflemen skulked about, and kept up their sharp shooting all day. Many of the regulars fell, but the riflemen lost only one man.

Both sides staged sporadic night raids on the other's lines, or launched forays to capture hay and livestock from nearby harbor islands. The night of August 30, the British made a surprise breakout at the Neck, set fire to a tavern, and withdrew back to their defenses. The same night, three hundred Americans attacked Lighthouse Island, killed several of the enemy, and took twenty-three prisoners, with the loss of one American soldier.

Night was the time for "frolicking," remembered John Greenwood, the fifer, "as the British were constantly sending bombs at us, and sometimes from two to six at a time could be seen in the air overhead, looking like moving stars in the heavens." Some early-morning British bombardments lasted several hours, the British clearly having no shortage of powder. In one furious cannonade from the British works on Bunker Hill, a rifleman lost a leg and a company clerk with Nathanael Greene's Kentish Guards, Augustus Mumford, had his head blown off.

Mumford was the first Rhode Island casualty of the war, and the horror of his death moved Nathanael Greene as nothing had since the siege began. To his wife "Caty," who was pregnant with their first child, Greene wrote that he wished she could be spared such news and any fears she had for his own safety.

British deserters kept crossing the lines, usually at night and alone, but sometimes three or four together. Half-starved and disgruntled, they came from both Boston and from the British ships in harbor, and nearly always with bits of news or descriptions of their travails, word of which would spread rapidly through the camps the next day. One night a lone British lighthorseman swam his horse across. Another night, fifteen men deserted the ships in the harbor.

Then days would follow without incident, one day like another. An officer with a company of Pennsylvania riflemen wrote of nothing to do but pick blueberries and play cricket. "Nothing of note. . . . Nothing important. . . . All quiet," Lieutenant Bixby of Connecticut recorded. On the other side, a British diarist drearily echoed the same refrain, writing, "Nothing extraordinary. . . . Nothing extraordinary," day after day.

Washington kept expecting the British to attack and failed to understand why they would delay, if an end to the rebellion was what they wanted.

By the close of summer, with increasing losses from disease, desertions, and absences of one sort or other, his army was in serious decline. Spirits suffered. The patriotic fervor that had sent thousands rushing to the scene in late April and May was hardly evident any longer.

It was not just that the army was shrinking; it was due to disappear entirely in a matter of months, the troops having signed on to serve only until the end of the year. The Connecticut enlistments would be up even sooner.

It had been the common expectation that the rising of such an armed force as gathered outside Boston would cause the British to think again and reach an accommodation. A short campaign had been anticipated by nearly everyone, including Washington, who had told his wife he would be home by fall.

There were still too few tents, still a shortage of blankets and clothing, and no one had forgotten that winter was on the way. Farmers and soldiers knew about weather. Weather could be the great determiner between failure and success, the great test of one's staying power.

In truth, the situation was worse than they realized, and no one perceived this as clearly as Washington. Seeing things as they were, and not as he would wish them to be, was one of his salient strengths.

He knew how little money was at hand, and he understood as did no one else the difficulties of dealing with Congress. He knew how essential it was to the future effectiveness of the army to break down regional differences and biases among the troops. But at the same time he struggled with his own mounting contempt for New Englanders. Writing to Lund Washington, a cousin and his business manager at home at Mount Vernon, he railed against the Yankees as "exceeding dirty and nasty," nothing like what he had expected. He had only contempt for "these people," he confided in a letter to Congressman Richard Henry Lee, another fellow Virginian. The heart of the problem was an "unaccountable kind of stupidity in the lower class of these people, which believe me prevails but too generally among the officers . . . who are ne[ar]ly of the same kidney with the privates." All such officers desired was to "curry favor with the men" and thereby get reelected.

Still, he allowed, if properly led, the army would undoubtedly fight. And in a letter to General Philip Schuyler, who was in command at Albany, Washington insisted — possibly to rally his own resolve — that they must never lose sight of "the goodness of our cause." Difficulties were not insurmountable. "Perseverance and spirit have done wonders in all ages."

II

On first arriving in Cambridge, Washington had been offered the home of the president of Harvard, Samuel Langdon, for his residence. But finding it too cramped for his needs and those of his staff (his military "family"), the general moved a few days later to one of the largest, most elegant houses in town, a gray clapboard Georgian mansion half a mile from the college on the King's Highway. Three stories tall, with an unobstructed view of the Charles River, it belonged to a wealthy Loyalist, John Vassall, who, fearing for his life and the lives of his family, had abandoned the place, fine furnishings and all, to take refuge in Boston. For Washington, who had a fondness for handsome architecture and river views, the house suited perfectly and would serve as his command headquarters through the siege, with his office established in a drawing room off the front hall.

The house became a hive of activity, with people coming and going at all hours.

It was there that Washington conferred with his highest-ranking officers, convened his councils of war, and, with staff help, coped with numberless problems of organization, issued orders, and labored over correspondence — paperwork without end, letters to Congress, appeals to the governors of the New England states, and the legislature of Massachusetts. There, too, he received or entertained local dignitaries and politicians and their wives, always in elegant fashion, as was both his pleasure and part of the role he felt he must play. And as with everything connected with that role — his uniform, the house, his horses and equipage, the military dress and bearing of his staff — appearances were of great importance: a leader must look and act the part.

To judge by surviving household accounts, Virginia hospitality more than lived up to its reputation at Cambridge. Purchases included quantities of beef, lamb, roasting pig, wild ducks, geese, turtle, and a variety of fresh fish, of which Washington was especially fond; plums, peaches, barrels of cider, brandy and rum by the gallon, and limes by the hundreds, these to fend off scurvy. One entry accounts for payment to a man named

Simon Lovett "for carting a load of liquor from Beverly."

The domestic staff included a steward, two cooks (one of whom was French), a kitchen maid, a washerwoman, eight others whose duties were not specified and included several slaves, plus a personal tailor for the commander, one Giles Alexander. Washington's body servant, a black slave named William ("Billy") Lee, was his steady companion. Riding with Washington on his rounds of the defenses, Billy Lee became a familiar figure, a large spyglass in a leather case slung over one shoulder.

As apparent to all, His Excellency was in the prime of life. A strapping man of commanding presence, he stood six feet two inches tall and weighed perhaps 190 pounds. His hair was reddish brown, his eyes gray-blue, and the bridge of his prominent nose unusually wide. The face was largely unlined, but freckled and sunbeaten and slightly scarred by smallpox. A few "defective teeth" were apparent when he smiled.

He carried himself like a soldier and sat a horse like the perfect Virginia gentleman. It was the look and bearing of a man accustomed to respect and to being obeyed.

He was not austere. There was no hint of arrogance. "Amiable" and "modest" were words frequently used to describe him, and there was a softness in his eyes that people remembered. Yet he had a certain distance in manner that set him off from, or above, others.

"Be easy . . . but not too familiar," he advised his officers, "lest you subject yourself to a want of that respect, which is necessary to support a proper command."

It was a philosophy unfamiliar to most Yankees, who saw nothing inappropriate about a captain shaving one of his soldiers, or rough-hewn General Putnam standing in line for his rations along with everyone else. Nor was it easy for Putnam and others of the older officers to change their ways. On one occasion, surveying the work on defenses by horseback, Putnam paused to ask a soldier to throw a large rock in the path up onto the parapet. "Sir, I am a corporal," the soldier protested. "Oh, I ask your pardon, sir," said the general, who dismounted and threw the rock himself, to the delight of all present.

The Philadelphia physician and patriot Benjamin Rush, a staunch admirer, observed that Washington "has so much martial dignity in his deportment that you would distinguish him to be a general and a soldier from among 10,000 people. There is not a king in Europe that would not look like a *valet de chambre* by his side."

A Connecticut delegate to the Continental Congress, Eliphalet Dyer, who had heartily joined in the unanimous decision to make Washington the commander-in-chief, judged him to be no "harum scarum" fellow. John Adams, who had put Washington's name in nomination for the command, described him in a letter to his wife Abigail as amiable and brave. "This appointment," wrote Adams, "will have great effect in cementing and securing the union of these colonies," and he prophesied that Washington could become "one of the most important characters in the world." After meeting the general herself for the first time, as a guest at one of his social occasions at Cambridge, Abigail wrote to tell her husband he had hardly said enough.

Washington's effect on the troops and young officers was striking. "Joy was visible on every countenance," according to Nathanael Greene, "and it seemed as if the spirit of conquest breathed through the whole army."

I hope we shall be taught to copy his example and to prefer the love of liberty in this time of public danger to all the soft pleasures of domestic life and support ourselves with manly fortitude amidst all the dangers and hardships that attend a state of war.

Joseph Reed, a young man with a long jaw and a somewhat quizzical look in his eyes, was a charming, London-trained Philadelphia lawyer who had been chosen as part of an honorary escort when Washington departed Philadelphia for his new command. Reed had intended to ride only as far as New York, but found himself so in awe of the general that he continued on to Cambridge to become Washington's secretary, despite the fact that he had made no provisions for his wife and three young children or for his law practice. As Reed explained, Washington had "expressed himself to me in such terms that I thought myself bound by every tie of duty and honor to comply with his request to help him through the sea of difficulties."

Few would ever provide a more succinct description of Washington's particular hold on men.

Born in Tidewater Virginia on February 11, 1732 (by the Old Style calendar), George Washington was the great-grandson of John Washington, who had emigrated from Northampton, England, in 1657. His father, Augustine Washington, was a tobacco planter also known for his "noble appearance and manly proportions." His mother, Mary Bell, was widowed when Washington was eleven. Because of the family's reduced circumstances, he had had little education — only seven or eight years of schooling by private tutor, no training in Latin or Greek or law, as had so many prominent Virginia patriots — and, as those close to him knew, he was self-conscious about this.

By steady application he had learned to write in a clear, strong hand and to express himself on paper with force and clarity. He learned to dance — Virginians loved to dance and he was no exception — and he learned to comport himself in the elaborately polite society of the day with perfect manners and polish. (Of the 110 *Rules of Civility and Decent Behavior in Company and Conversation* that he had laboriously copied down as a boy, Rule Number One read: "Every action done in company ought to be with some sign of respect to those who are present.") He enjoyed parties and particularly the company of attractive women. As would be said of British officers, he "liked his glass, his lass, his game of cards," though gambling never became the obsession it was for so many of his counterparts on the British side.

The great teacher for Washington was experience. At age sixteen, he had set out to make his way in the world, as a surveyor's apprentice on an expedition into the wilderness of western Virginia, over the Blue Ridge Mountains, and as years passed he spent more time in the backcountry beyond the Blue Ridge than all but a few from the Tidewater. In addition, surveying proved highly remunerative.

In 1753, at twenty, he had been sent by the governor of Virginia to the wilds of western Pennsylvania, to challenge French claims to the Allegheny River valley, and publication of his diary of the venture, *The Journal of Major George Washington*, made his daring and resourcefulness known throughout the colonies and in Europe. A year later, on his first command, inexperience and poor judgment led to his famous encounter with French troops and Indians at Great Meadows, in the same remote corner of western Pennsylvania — the small, bloody backwoods incident, and first defeat for Washington, that set in motion the conflict that ultimately involved much of the world.

"I heard the bullets whistle; and believe me there is something charming in the sound," he had written in a letter printed later in the *London Magazine*, which could be taken as the bravado of a callow youth, but, as he had found, he was one of those rare few who, under fire, were without fear.

As a provincial officer fighting with the British army during General Edward Braddock's defeat in western Pennsylvania, he had shown conspicuous courage under fire and a marked ability for leadership. If, as a young officer, he seemed at times flagrantly, unattractively ambitious, he had long since overcome that. In 1759, spurned in his desire for a royal commission, he had "retired" at age twenty-seven to the life of a Virginia planter and, that same year, married Martha Dandridge Custis of Williamsburg, an attractive, extremely wealthy widow with two children, to whom he gave full devotion. The children, John Parke Custis and Patsy, were treated quite as though they were his own. Indeed, one of the worst tragedies of

Washington's life had been the death of seventeen-year-old Patsy of an epileptic fit in 1773.

Like other planters of the Tidewater, Washington embraced a life very like that of the English gentry. English by ancestry, he was, in dress, manner, and his favorite pastimes, as close to being an English country gentleman as was possible for an American of the day, and intentionally. His handsome green coach with its brass fittings and leather lining had been custom built in England to his specifications. He ordered his clothes from England, and only the finest English wools and linens and latest fashions would do. He wore English boots, English shoes, and Morocco leather slippers, all made to order for him in London. The books on his shelves, including the military treatises, were published in London. The very glass in the windows through which he viewed his domain was imported English glass.

Only the year before taking command at Cambridge, Washington had commenced an ambitious expansion of his Virginia home, Mount Vernon, which, when completed, would double its size. He was adding a library and building a two-story dining room, or banquet hall, suitable for entertaining on a grand scale. He was a builder by nature. He had a passion for architecture and landscape design, and Mount Vernon was his creation, everything done to his own ideas and plans. How extremely important all this was to him and the pleasure he drew from it, few people ever understood.

He had an abiding dislike of disorder and cared intensely about every detail — wallpaper, paint color, ceiling ornaments — and insisted on perfection. He hated to be away from the project. Even at the distance of Cambridge, with all that weighed on his mind, he worried that things were not being handled as he wished at Mount Vernon and filled pages of instruction for his manager, Lund Washington.

I wish you would quicken Lanphire and Sears [the carpenters] about the dining room chimney piece (to be executed as mentioned in one of my last letters) as I could wish to have that end of the house completely finished before I return. I wish you had done the end of the new kitchen next the garden, as also the old kitchen, with rusticated boards; however, as it is not, I would have the corners done so in the manner of our new church. . . . What have you done with the well? Is that walled up? Have you any acc[oun]ts of the painter?

Second only to his passion for architecture and landscape design was a love of the theater, which again was quite characteristic of Virginians. He had seen his first known theatrical production at age nineteen on a trip with his older brother to Barbados. It was the first and only time Washington had ever been beyond American shores and the place where he was "strongly attacked" by smallpox. Later, at Williamsburg, as a member of the Virginia legislature, he had attended the theater regularly. During a visit to Annapolis, he recorded going to "the play" four nights out of five. In New York later he attended the theater seven times and saw his first production of *Hamlet*.

But of all the theatrical productions he had seen it was *Cato*, by the English author Joseph Addison, the most popular play of the time, that Washington loved best. One line in particular he was to think of or quote frequently in his role now as commander-in-chief: " 'Tis not in mortals to command success, but we'll do more,

Sempronius, we'll deserve it."

Though Washington was often said to be the richest man in America, he probably did not rank among the ten richest. He was very wealthy, nonetheless, and in large part because of his marriage to Martha Custis. His wealth was in land, upwards of 54,000 acres, including some 8,000 acres at Mount Vernon, another 4,000 acres in Virginia's Dismal Swamp, nearly all of which he had acquired for speculation. In addition, he owned more than one hundred slaves, another measure of great wealth, whose labors made possible his whole way of life.

In a popular English novel of the day, *The Expedition of Humphrey Clinker*, Tobias Smollett wrote that to be a country gentleman one was "obliged to keep horses, hounds, carriages, with suitable numbers of servants, and maintain an elegant table for the entertainment of his neighbors." It could have been a description of life at Mount Vernon, with the difference that the servants were black slaves.

Among the Virginia gentry who had taken up fox hunting with an exuberance no less than to be found on the country estates of England, Washington stood out. Thomas Jefferson considered him "the best horseman of his age." That Washington was known to hunt up to seven hours straight, riding as close to the hounds as possible, "leaping fences, and going extremely quick," and always to the end, to be in on the kill, was considered not only a measure of his love of the chase and his exceptional physical stamina, but also of his uncommon, unrelenting determination.

Billy Lee, the body servant, rode with him, rode like the wind by all accounts, and no less fearlessly than his master.

"Found a fox in Mr. Phil Alexander's island which was lost after a chase of seven hours," Washington recorded in his diary at the end of one winter day in 1772, but he did not give up, as shown in his entry for the day following: "Found a fox in the same place again which was killed at the end of 6 hours."

An English sporting writer of a later era would describe fox hunting as "the image of war without its guilt and only half its danger." In some years, according to Washington's own records, the days he devoted to fox hunting added up to a month. He kept precise account of exactly how long each chase lasted, to the minute. Again, he was a man who loved precision in everything.

Stories were told of extraordinary feats of strength — how, for example, Washington had thrown a stone from the bed of a stream to the top of Virginia's famous Natural Bridge, a height of 215 feet. The Philadelphia artist Charles Willson Peale, who had been a guest at Mount Vernon in 1772 while painting Washington's portrait, described how he and several other young men were on the lawn throwing an iron bar for sport, when Washington appeared and, without bothering to remove his coat, took a turn, throwing it "far, very far beyond our utmost limit."

Washington's wealth and way of life, like his physique and horsemanship, were of great importance to large numbers of the men he led and among many in Congress. The feeling was that if he, George Washington, who had so much, was willing to risk "his all," however daunting the odds, then who were they to equivocate. That he was also serving without pay was widely taken as further evidence of the genuineness of his commitment.

There were, to be sure, those in the ranks and among the local populace who had little fondness for Virginia planters and their high-and-mighty airs, or who saw stunning incongruity in the cause of liberty being led by a slavemaster.

It was also a matter of record that Washington had been retired from military life for fifteen years, during which he had not even drilled a militia company. His only prior experience had been in backwoods warfare — a very different kind of warfare — and most notably in the Braddock campaign of 1755, which had been a disaster. He was by no means an experienced commander. He had never led an army in battle, never before commanded anything larger than a regiment. And never had he directed a siege.

Washington was quite aware of his limitations. In formal acceptance of the new command, on June 16, 1775, standing at his place in Congress, he had addressed John Hancock:

> I am truly sensible of the high honor done me in this appointment, yet I feel great distress from a consciousness that my abilities and military experience may not be equal to the extensive and important trust. However, as the Congress desire i[t], I will enter upon the momentous duty, and exert every power I possess in their service and for the support of the glorious Cause.

He knew he might not succeed, and he gave Congress fair warning:

But lest some unlucky event should happen unfavorable to my reputation, I beg it may be remembered by every gentleman in the room that I this day declare with the utmost sincerity, I do not think myself equal to the command I [am] honored with.

To his wife Martha he wrote that "far from seeking this appointment, I have used every endeavor in my power to avoid it, not only from my unwillingness to part with you and the family, but from a consciousness of its being a trust too great for my capacity. . . . it has been a kind of destiny that has thrown me upon this service. . . ."
Yet he had attended Congress in his splendid blue and buff uniform, conspicuously signaling a readiness to take command. If he saw the responsibility as too great for his ability, it was because he had a realistic idea of how immense that responsibility would be. For such a trust, to lead an undisciplined, poorly armed volunteer force of farmers and tradesmen against the best-trained, best-equipped, most formidable military force on earth — and with

so much riding on the outcome — was, in reality, more than any man was qualified for.

But he knew also that someone had to take command, and however impossible the task and the odds, he knew he was better suited than any of the others Congress might have in mind.

Without question, Congress had made the right choice, and not the least of reasons was political. As a Virginian, Washington represented the richest, most populous of the thirteen colonies. He himself had had years of political experience in the Virginia legislature and as a member of the Continental Congress. It was as one of them that the members of Congress knew him best and respected him, not as a general. He knew the ways of politics and factious politicians. He understood how the system worked. For all the delays and frustrations, however severe the tests of patience he was to suffer in his dealings with them and the system, he never forgot that Congress held the ultimate power, that he, the commander-in-chief, was the servant of some fifty-six delegates who, in far-off Philadelphia, unlike Parliament, met in secrecy.

III

In the first days of September, Washington began drawing up plans for two bold moves.

He had decided to carry the war into Canada with a surprise attack on the British at Quebec. A thousand men from the ranks longing for action volunteered at once. Led by an aggressive Connecticut colonel named Benedict Arnold, they were to advance on Quebec across the Maine wilderness, taking a northeastern route up the Kennebec River. Hastily conceived, this "secret expedition" was based on too little knowledge of the terrain, but in small units the men began marching off for Newburyport, north of Boston, from where they would sail by sloop and schooner to the mouth of the Kennebec.

He felt he could detach a thousand troops this way, Washington informed Congress, because he had concluded, from intelligence gathered from spies and British deserters, that the enemy in Boston had no intention of launching an attack until they were reinforced.

His second plan was to end the waiting and strike at Boston, which, it was understood, could mean destruction of the town. British defenses were formidable. In fact, defenses on both sides had been strengthened to the point where many believed neither army would dare attack the other. Also, a siege by definition required a great deal of prolonged standing still and waiting. But standing still and waiting were not the way to win a war, and not in Washington's nature.

"The inactive state we lie in is exceedingly disagreeable," he had confided to his brother John. He wanted a "speedy finish," to fight and be done with it. "No danger is to be considered when put in competition with the magnitude of the cause," he had asserted earlier in a letter to the governor of Rhode Island.

According to his instructions from Congress, he was to take no action of consequence until advising with his council of war, and thus a meeting was scheduled for the morning of September 11, "to know," he informed his generals, "whether in your judgments, we cannot make a successful attack upon the troops in Boston, by means of boats."

On September 10, mutiny broke out among the Pennsylvania riflemen, after several of the worst troublemakers had been confined to the guardhouse. Though the mutiny was put down at once by General Greene and a large detachment of Rhode Island troops, it only added to the sense of an army coming apart, and Washington was visibly shaken.

The council of war convened in his office as scheduled the next morning — three major generals, including the venerable Israel Putnam, and four brigadiers. All were New Englanders but one, Major General Charles Lee, who was Washington's second-in-command and the only professional soldier present. A former British officer and veteran of the French and Indian War, Lee, like Washington, had fought in the ill-fated Braddock campaign and later settled in Virginia. He was a spare, odd-looking man with a long, hooked nose and dark, bony face. Rough in manner, rough of speech, he had nothing of Washington's dignity. Even in uniform he looked perpetually unkempt.

Lee might have been a character out of an English novel, such were his eccentricities and colorful past. He had once been married to an Indian woman, the daughter of a Seneca chief. He had served gallantly with the British army in Spain, and as aide-de-camp to the King of Poland. Like Frederick the Great, he made a flamboyant show of his love for dogs, keeping two or three with him most of the time. A New Hampshire clergyman, Jeremy Belknap, after dining with the general in Cambridge, thought him "an odd genius . . . a great sloven, wretchedly profane, and a great admirer of dogs, one of them a native of Pomerania, which I should have taken for a bear had I seen him in the woods."

Lee was also self-assured, highly opinionated, moody, and ill-tempered (his Indian name was Boiling Water), and he was thought by many to have the best military mind of any of the generals, a view he openly shared. Washington considered him "the first officer in military knowledge and experience we have in the whole army," and it was at Washington's specific request that Congress had made Lee second-in-command.

Whatever opinions Lee had of Washington, he kept to himself, except to remark that he thought the appellation "Excellency" perfectly absurd.

In striking contrast to Lee was Major General Artemus Ward, a heavy-set, pious-looking Massachusetts farmer, storekeeper, justice of the peace, and veteran of the French and Indian War, who had had overall command of the siege of Boston prior to Washington's arrival. Ward was considered "a good man, a thorough New England man," though uninspiring. General Lee privately called him a "fat, old church warden" with "no acquaintance whatever with military matters." But if unspectacular, Ward was competent, thoughtful, and not without good sense, as time would show.

Washington had assigned Lee to command the left wing of the army, Putnam, the center, while Ward was responsible for the right wing, which included Dorchester. As early as July 9, at Washington's first council of war, it had been proposed that the army take possession of Dorchester Heights, but the idea was unanimously rejected. Ward, however, refused to drop the subject. When in August he again recommended that an effort be made to fortify the Heights, again nothing was done.

The brigadiers present now were John Thomas and William Heath of Massachusetts, John Sullivan of New Hampshire, Joseph Spencer of Connecticut, and Nathanael Greene. Thomas was a physician in his early fifties, tall and quiet-spoken. Heath, a much younger man, was a fifth-generation Roxbury farmer, age thirty-eight, who would affably describe himself in a memoir as "of middling stature, light complexion, very corpulent, and bald-headed." Sullivan, a lawyer and politician in his mid-forties, had served with Washington in the Continental Congress, and Spencer, who was older even than Israel Putnam (his troops referred to him as "Granny"), would play almost no part.

Of these New Englanders, all citizen-soldiers, Washington quickly surmised that Thomas, Sullivan, and Greene were the best he had. Thomas was the most commanding in appearance and had served in the French and Indian War. Earlier, his pride hurt that the less experienced Heath was to outrank him, Thomas had talked of resigning, until Washington sent an urgent plea in which, paraphrasing a line from his favorite play *Cato*, he said that in such a cause as they were engaged, "surely every post ought to be deemed honorable in which a man can serve his country."

His council assembled, Washington made the case for an all-out amphibious assault on Boston, by sending troops across the shallow Back Bay in flat-bottomed boats big enough to carry fifty men each. He reminded the generals of what they already knew: that winter was fast approaching and the troops were without barracks and firewood; that men already eager to go home would be extremely difficult to keep on duty once they felt the "severity of a northern winter." When enlistments expired, the disbanding of one army before another was assembled could mean ruin. Gunpowder was still in short supply, but there was enough at hand to mount an attack. Of course, "the hazard, the loss of men in the attempt and the probable consequences of failure" had also to be considered.

There was discussion of these and other points, including the enemy's defenses, after which it was agreed unanimously not to attack, not for the "present at least."

It was a sound decision. The "hazard" was far too great, the chance of disastrous failure all too real. Casualties could have been horrendous. Unless they caught the tide exactly right, the men in the boats could have been stranded on mudflats a hundred yards or more from dry ground and forced to struggle through knee-deep muck while under withering fire. The slaughter could have been quite as horrible as that of the British at Bunker Hill.

In fact, such a headlong attack on their works was exactly what the British generals were hoping for, certain that if the Americans were to be so foolhardy, it would mean the end of the rebellion.

In restraining Washington, the council had proven its value. For the "present at least," discretion was truly the better part of valor.

Washington accepted the decision, but work on the flat-bottomed boats continued, and in a long letter to John Hancock, he made the case for a "decisive stroke," adding, "I cannot say that I have wholly laid it aside." Many in Congress, he sensed, were as impatient as he with the stalemate. "The state of inactivity, in which this army has lain for some time, by no means corresponds with my wishes, by some decisive stroke, to relieve my country from the heavy expense its subsistence must create."

As Washington also reminded Hancock — and thus Congress — his war chest was empty. The fact that the troops had not been paid for weeks did not help morale or alleviate hardships at home. "The paymaster has not a single dollar in hand."

Money at least was on the way. On September 29, $500,000 in Continental bills from Philadelphia were delivered to the headquarters at Cambridge, and in a few days thousands of troops were at last receiving some pay. "I send you eleven dollars," Lieutenant Joseph Hodgkins wrote to his wife Sarah on October 6. His monthly pay was $13.

Asked what they were fighting for, most of the army — officers and men in the ranks — would until now have said it was in defense of their country and of their rightful liberties as freeborn Englishmen. It was to "defend our common rights" that he went to war, Nathanael Greene had told his wife. The British regulars, the hated redcoats, were the "invaders" and must be repelled. "We are soldiers who devote ourselves to arms not for the invasion of other countries but for the defense of our own, not for the gratification of our own private interest, but for the public security," Greene had written in another letter to Samuel Ward. Writing to General Thomas, Washington had said the object was "neither glory nor extent of territory, but a defense of all that is dear and valuable in life."

Independence was not mentioned. Nor had independence been on the minds of those who fought at Bunker Hill or in Washington's thoughts when he took command of the army. En route to Cambridge from Philadelphia, he had been quite specific in assuring the New York Provincial Congress that "every exertion of my worthy colleagues and myself will be equally extended to the reestablishment of peace and harmony between the mother country and the colonies."

But more and more of late there was talk of independence. The Reverend Belknap, from his visits to the camps, concluded that independence had "become a favorite point in the army." A "declaration of independence" was heartily wished for, wrote Nathanael Greene, who was one of the first to say it in writing. "We had as good to begin in earnest first as last."

In late September, the discovery that the surgeon general of the army and head of the hospital at Cambridge, Dr. Benjamin Church, was a spy, the first American traitor, rocked everyone. Church had been one of the local dignitaries who had escorted Washington into Cambridge the day of his arrival. He was as prominent and trustworthy a man as any in the province, it was thought, a member of the Provincial Congress, poet, author, a Harvard classmate of John Hancock, and an outspoken patriot. Yet the whole time he had been secretly corresponding with the British in cipher, and was in their pay.

His treachery had been discovered quite by chance. A mysterious, enciphered letter carried by a young woman of questionable morals had wound up in the hands of a friend of Nathanael Greene, who brought the letter to Greene, who in turn carried it directly to Washington. When the woman was apprehended, she confessed she had been keeping company with Church and said the letter was his. The letter was deciphered and Church exposed. The whole army, indeed all New England and the Congress at Philadelphia, were stunned. Who could say how many other Dr. Churches there might be?

Church, who was tried, convicted, and imprisoned, kept insisting he was innocent. Sent into exile, on a ship bound for the West Indies, he disappeared at sea. Only years later did further evidence come to light proving his guilt.

On October 18, a raw, gloomy Wednesday, a congressional committee of three, including Benjamin Franklin, gathered by a roaring fire in Washington's study and, after lengthy deliberations with the commander and his generals, concluded that if an attack on Boston meant the destruction of the town, they could not approve.

At a meeting of the war council it was decided still again that the risks were too great "under the circumstances," as said Brigadier General Horatio Gates, who had been absent from the previous meeting. Like Charles Lee, Gates was an experienced, former British officer.

"Things hereabouts remain in pretty much the same situation," wrote James Warren, president of the Massachusetts Assembly. "We look at their lines and they view ours. . . . They want courage to attack us and we want powder to attack them and so there is no attack on either side."

On October 24, a post rider from Maine brought news that British ships had attacked and burned the defenseless town of Falmouth. The townspeople had been given advance warning and consequently no one was killed, but the entire population was without homes on the eve of winter. The attack was decried as an outrage, "proof of the diabolical designs" of the administration in London, as Washington said.

At the same time, Washington was dealt a further setback when his bright and by-now-indispensable secretary, Joseph Reed, decided he could no longer delay a return to Philadelphia to see to his affairs and look after his family. "You cannot but be sensible of your importance to me . . . judge you therefore how much I wished for your return," Washington would tell the absent Reed in one of a string of letters. "I miss you exceedingly; and if an express declaration of this be wanting, to hasten your return, I make it most heartily," he wrote another day.

John Adams, who had come to know Reed in Philadelphia, described him as "very sensible," "amiable," even "tender," and Washington felt much the same way. To Reed, as to almost no one, he signed his letters not with the standard "Your Obedient Servant," but "Your Affectionate and Obedient Servant."

The days were turning "cold and blustering," recorded the still uncomplaining Lieutenant Jabez Fitch. The construction of barracks had begun. Washington authorized an order for 10,000 cords of firewood. With epidemic dysentery sweeping through the outlying towns, Dr. Thacher worried over the numbers of ill soldiers in the camps and crowding the hospital. To add further to the miseries of camp life, local farmers were charging ever-higher prices.

Washington fumed over such absence of patriotism, his dislike of New Englanders compounding by the day. Yet the faith of the local populace and their leaders in him remained high. They understood the adversities he faced and they were depending on him, no less than Congress and patriots everywhere were depending on him. As James Warren wrote to John Adams, "He is certainly the best man for the place he is in, important as it is, that ever lived."

Adams, who was acutely sensitive to the differences between New Englanders and Virginians, having experienced firsthand in Congress the distrust many from the middle and southern provinces felt for New Englanders, had become gravely concerned about the damage to the Cause such opinions and prejudices could have should they get out of hand.

Gentlemen in other colonies have large plantations of slaves, and . . . are accustomed, habituated to higher notions of themselves and the distinction between them and the common people than we are. . . . I dread the consequences of this dissimilitude of character, and without the utmost caution on both sides, and the most considerate forbearance with one another and prudent condescension on both sides, they will certainly be fatal.

Nathanael Greene felt certain that Washington only needed time to make himself "acquainted with the genius" of the New England troops.

Meanwhile, Washington put increasing trust in Greene, as well as another impressive young New Englander, Henry Knox, to whom he assigned one of the most difficult and crucial missions of the war.

Colonel Henry Knox was hard not to notice. Six feet tall, he bulked large, weighing perhaps 250 pounds. He had a booming voice. He was gregarious, jovial, quick of mind, highly energetic — "very fat, but very active" — and all of twenty-five.

"Town-born" in Boston, in a narrow house on Sea Street facing the harbor, he was seventh of the ten sons of Mary Campbell and William Knox, Scotch-Irish Presbyterians. When his father, a shipmaster, disappeared in the West Indies, nine-year-old Henry went to work to help support his mother, and was thus, like Nathanael Greene, almost entirely self-educated. He became a bookseller, eventually opening his own London Book Store on Cornhill Street, offering a "large and very elegant assortment" of the latest books and magazines from London. In the notices he placed in the *Boston Gazette*, the name Henry Knox always appeared in larger type than the name of the store.

Though not especially prosperous, the store became "a great resort for British officers and Tory ladies," "a fashionable morning lounge," and its large, genial proprietor became one of the best-known young men in town. John Adams, a frequent patron, remembered Knox as a youth "of pleasing manners and inquisitive turn of mind." Another patron was Nathanael Greene, who not only shared Knox's love of books, but also an interest in "the military art," and it was thus, on the eve of war, that an important friendship had commenced.

Knox read all he could on gunnery and tactics, and, as Greene had joined the Rhode Island Kentish Guards, Knox signed up with the new Boston Grenadier Corps, enjoying everything about it, including the eating and drinking that went on.

At about the same time, Knox suffered an accident which, like Greene's stiff knee, might have precluded service as an officer. On a bird-hunting expedition on Noddle's Island in the harbor, his fowling piece exploded, destroying the third and fourth fingers of his left hand. In public thereafter he kept the hand wrapped in a handkerchief.

To further complicate life, Knox had taken up the patriot cause and fallen in love with the daughter of a prominent Tory. She, too, was a patron of the bookstore, a correspondingly plump, gregarious young woman named Lucy Flucker, whose father, Thomas Flucker, was the royal secretary of the province. "My charmer," he called her, and neither his maimed hand nor his politics deterred her ardor. Despite the objections of her family, they were married. When Lucy's father, in an effort to give his new son-in-law added respectability, arranged for Knox to be offered a commission in the British army, Knox declined.

In the tense days following the bloodshed at Lexington and Concord, the young couple packed what little they could carry and slipped out of Boston in disguise. Lucy was never again to see her mother and father, who would eventually sail for England.

Having settled Lucy safely in Worcester,

Knox reported for service with General Artemus Ward, who assigned him to planning and building fortifications. "Long to see you, which nothing would prevent but the flattering hope of being able to do some little service to my distressed and devoted country," he wrote to her.

Washington first met Knox while inspecting the defenses at Roxbury on July 5, only three days after he had taken command of the army, and apparently he was impressed, while Knox thought Washington everything to be wished for in a commander. "General Washington fills his place with vast ease and dignity, and dispenses happiness around him," Knox wrote. He was called to confer at headquarters, and later, like Nathanael Greene, invited to dine with the general and his guests on several occasions.

It was Henry Knox who first suggested the idea of going after the cannon at far-off Fort Ticonderoga on Lake Champlain, an undertaking so enormous, so fraught with certain difficulties, that many thought it impossible.

The capture of Fort Ticonderoga from the British by Ethan Allen, Benedict Arnold, and a handful of Green Mountain Boys earlier in May had been sensational news, but the fort and its captured artillery were abandoned. When Knox told Washington he was confident the guns could be retrieved and hauled overland to Boston, Washington agreed at once, and put the young officer in charge of the expedition.

Like nearly everyone, Washington enjoyed Knox's company. Probably he also saw something of himself in the large, confident, self-educated young man with the pleasing manners who had lost his father when still a boy and had done so much on his own, and who was so ready to take on a task of such difficulty and potential consequence.

That such a scheme hatched by a junior officer in his twenties who had had no experience was transmitted so directly to the supreme commander, seriously considered, and acted upon, also marked an important difference between the civilian army of the Americans and that of the British. In an army where nearly everyone was new to the tasks of soldiering and fighting a war, almost anyone's ideas deserved a hearing.

By November 16, Knox was on his way, accompanied by his nineteen-year-old brother, William, and with authority to spend as much as $1,000. "Don't be afraid," he wrote to Lucy. "There is no fighting in the [assignment]. I am upon business only."

With the days growing shorter and colder, flocks of wild geese overhead grew in such numbers that orders had to be posted to keep the men from firing at them and wasting precious powder. "Every officer that stands an idle spectator, and sees such a wanton waste of powder, and doesn't do his utmost to suppress the evil, may expect to be reported," declared Nathanael Greene.

So great was the need to conserve powder that the morning gun, a camp ritual, was dispensed with. Spears were issued to the troops to be used in the event of a British attack.

> Every colonel or commanding officer of a regiment [read another of Greene's orders] to appoint thirty men that are active, bold, and resolute to use the spears in the defense of the lines instead of guns.

The first snow fell on November 21, and in the days to follow it was obvious winter had come to stay, with winds as bitter as January and still more snow. The distress within Boston was reportedly extreme. The British were cutting trees and tearing down old houses for firewood. Supplying the besieged city by sea had become increasingly difficult because of winter storms and American privateers. Food was in desperately short supply. The King's troops were said to be so hungry that many were ready to desert at first chance. Some of the redcoats said openly that if there were another action and they could "get off under the smoke," they would choose "the fresh beef side of the question." Men in their ranks were dying of scurvy. Worse, smallpox raged.

Meanwhile, deserters from the American side were telling the British that Washington's army was tired and unpaid, that there was too little clothing to keep warm, and that most of the men longed to go home.

A memorable story of an incident that occurred at about this time may or may not be entirely reliable, but portrays vividly the level of tension among the troops and Washington's own pent-up anger and exasperation. It was told years afterward by Israel Trask, the ten-year-old boy who had enlisted with his father and in whose eyes Washington seemed almost supernatural.

A snowball fight broke out on Harvard

Yard between fifty or more backwoods Virginia riflemen and an equal number of sailors from the Marblehead regiment. The fight quickly turned fierce, with "biting and gouging on the one part, and knockdown on the other part with as much apparent fury as the most deadly enmity could create," according to Trask. Hundreds of others rushed to the scene. Soon more than a thousand men had joined in a furious brawl. Then Washington arrived:

> I only saw him and his colored servant, both mounted [Trask remembered]. With the spring of a deer, he leaped from his saddle, threw the reins of his bridle into the hands of his servant, and rushed into the thickest of the melee, with an iron grip seized two tall, brawny, athletic, savage-looking riflemen by the throat, keeping them at arm's length, alternating shaking and talking to them.

Seeing this, the others took flight "at the top of their speed in all directions from the scene of the conflict." If Trask's memory served, the whole row, from start to finish, lasted all of fifteen minutes and nothing more came of it.

On November 25, the British sent several boatloads of the ragged poor of Boston, some 300 men, women, and children, across the Back Bay, depositing them on the shore near Cambridge for the rebels to cope with.

They were a heartrending sight. Many were sick and dying, "the whole in the most miserable and piteous condition," wrote Washington. According to one explanation, General Howe was making room in Boston for the reinforcements expected to arrive anytime. But it was also said that numbers of the sick had been sent "with [the] design of spreading the smallpox through this country and camp," an accusation Washington refused to believe. But when another 150 desperate people were dispatched from Boston, as smallpox continued unabated there, Washington described the disease as a "weapon of defense they are using against us."

Nearly all his efforts and those of his senior officers were concentrated now on trying to hold the army together. The Connecticut troops, whose enlistments were to expire on December 9, were counting the days until they could start for home. Nothing, it seemed, could change their minds.

A stirring summons to renewed devotion to the cause of liberty, as strong and eloquent an appeal to the men in the ranks, "the guardians of America," as had yet been seen in print, appeared in the *New England Chronicle*, signed simply "A Freeman." Not only did it celebrate the Glorious Cause, but it spoke of a break with Britain soon to come and a future "big with everything good and great," when Americans would decide their own salvation.

Your exertions in the cause of freedom, guided by wisdom and animated by zeal and courage, have gained you the love and confidence of your grateful countrymen; and they look to you, who are experienced veterans, and trust that you will still be the guardians of America. As I have the honor to be an American, and one among the free millions, who are defended by your valor, I would pay the tribute of thanks, and express my gratitude, while I solicit you to continue in your present honorable and important station. I doubt not America will always find enough of her sons ready to flock to her standard, and support her freedom; but experience proves that experienced soldiers are more capable of performing the duties of the camp, and better qualified to face the enemy, than others; and therefore every friend of America will be desirous that most of the gentlemen who compose the present army may continue in the service of their country until "Liberty, Peace, and Safety" are established. Although your private concerns may call for your assistance at home, yet the voice of your country is still louder, and it is painful to heroic minds to quit the field when liberty calls, and the voice of injured millions cries "To arms! to arms!" Never was a cause more important or glorious than that which you are engaged in; not only your wives, your children, and distant posterity, but humanity at large, the world of mankind, are interested in it; for if tyranny should prevail in this great country, we may expect liberty will expire throughout the world. Therefore, more human glory and happiness may depend upon your exertions than ever yet depended upon any of the sons of men. He that is a soldier in defense of such a cause, needs no title; his post is a post of honor, and although not an emperor, yet he shall wear a crown — of glory — and blessed will be his memory!

The savage and brutal barbarity of our enemies in burning Falmouth, is a full demonstration that there is not the least remains of virtue, wisdom, or humanity, in the British court; and that they are fully determined with fire and sword, to butcher and destroy, beggar and enslave the whole American people. Therefore we expect soon to break off all kind of connection with Britain, and form into a Grand Republic of the American United Colonies, which will, by the blessing of heaven, soon work out our salvation, and perpetuate the liberties, increase the wealth, the power and the glory of this Western world.

Notwithstanding the many difficulties we have to encounter, and the rage of our merciless enemies, we have a glorious prospect before us, big with everything good and great. The further we enter into the field of independence, our prospects will expand and brighten, and a complete Republic will soon complete our happiness.

But reenlistments were alarmingly few.

Of eleven regiments, or roughly 10,000 men, fewer than 1,000 had agreed to stay. Some stimulus besides love of country must be found to make men want to serve, Washington advised Congress. Paying the troops a few months in advance might help, he wrote, but again he had no money at hand. By late November, he could report that only 2,540 of his army had reenlisted. "Our situation is truly alarming, and of this General Howe is well apprised. . . . No doubt when he is reinforced he will avail himself of the information."

Washington was a man of exceptional, almost excessive self-command, rarely permitting himself any show of discouragement or despair, but in the privacy of his correspondence with Joseph Reed, he began now to reveal how very low and bitter he felt, if the truth were known. Never had he seen "such a dearth of public spirit and want of virtue" as among the Yankee soldiers, he confided in a letter to Reed of November 28. "These people" were still beyond his comprehension. A "dirty, mercenary spirit pervades the whole," he wrote. "Could I have foreseen what I have and am like to experience, no consideration upon earth should have induced me to accept this command."

For six long months there had been hardly a shred of good news, no single event to lift the spirits of the army, no sign to suggest better days might lie ahead.

The next day, amazingly, came "glad tidings." A privateer, the schooner *Lee*, under the command of Captain John Manley, had captured an enemy supply ship, the brig *Nancy*, off Cape Ann, north of Boston. The ship was loaded with military treasure — a supply of war material such as Congress could not be expected to provide for months to come, including 2,500 stands of arms, cannon, mortars, flints, some forty tons of shot, and 2,000 bayonets — nearly everything needed but powder.

The *Lee* was one of the first of several armed schooners Washington had sent out to prey on enemy shipping. It was a first triumph for his new "navy," and John Manley, a first hero. It was an "instance of divine favor, for nothing surely ever came more apropos," Washington wrote immediately to Joseph Reed.

With the end of enlistments only days away, concern grew extreme. "Our people are almost bewitched about getting home," wrote Lieutenant Hodgkins to his wife

Sarah. "I hope I and all my townsmen shall have virtue enough to stay all winter as volunteers, before we will leave the line without men. For our all is at stake, and if we do not exert ourselves in this Glorious Cause, our all is gone."

"I want you to come home and see us," she wrote. "I look for you almost every day, but I don't allow myself to depend on anything, for I find there is nothing to be depended upon but trouble and disappointments."

"I want to see you very much," she said in other letters, warning him that if he did not "alter" his mind about staying with the army, it would be "such a disappointment that I can't put up with it."

The troops were called repeatedly into formation to be addressed by officers and chaplains. A Connecticut soldier who had decided nothing could keep him from going home, described how his regiment was called out time and again to hear speeches. "We was ordered to form a hollow square," wrote Simeon Lyman in his diary, "and General Lee came in and the first words was, 'Men I do not know what to call you; [you] are the worst of all creatures,' and [he] flung and cursed and swore at us . . . and our lieutenants begged us to stay." But for Simeon Lyman, like nearly all the regiment, December 9 was his last day as a soldier. On Sunday, December 10, he wrote:

In the morning we was ordered to parade before the general's door, and we was counted off and dismissed, and we we[nt] to the lieuten[ant] and he gave us a dram, and then we marched off.

General Lee stood and watched, finding a measure of encouragement only in the response of the troops who remained:

Some of the Connecticutians who were homesick could not be prevailed on to tarry, which means in the New England dialect to serve any longer. They accordingly marched off bag and baggage, but in passing through the lines of the regiments, they were so horribly hissed, groaned at, and pelted that I believe they wished their aunts, grandmothers, and even sweethearts, to whom the days before they were so much attached, [were] at the devil's own palace.

Washington pleaded with Congress and the provincial governments to send more men with all possible speed. And new recruits did continue to arrive, though only in dribs and drabs.

There was still no news from the expedition to Quebec, and no word from Colonel Knox. When General Schuyler at Albany wrote to bemoan his tribulations, Washington responded, "Let me ask you, sir, when is the time for brave men to exert themselves in the cause of liberty and their country, if this is not?" He understood the troubles Schuyler faced, "but we must bear up against them, and make the best of mankind as they are, since we cannot have them as we wish."

Earlier in the fall, Washington had written to his wife Martha to say he would welcome her company in Cambridge, if she did not think it too late in the season for such a journey. Six hundred miles on dreadful roads by coach could be punishing even in fair weather, and especially for someone unaccustomed to travel, no matter her wealth or status.

On December 11, after more than a month on the road, Martha Washington arrived, accompanied by her son John Custis, his wife Eleanor, George Lewis, who was a nephew of Washington, and

Elizabeth Gates, the English wife of General Gates. Joseph Reed, who had looked after the generals' ladies during their stop in Philadelphia, offered the thought, after seeing them on their way, that they would be "not a bad supply . . . in a country where wood is scarce."

Sarah Mifflin, the wife of Colonel Thomas Mifflin, a young aide-de-camp, also arrived. The handsome colonel belonged to one of Philadelphia's most prominent families, and with his beautiful, stylish wife added a distinct touch of glamour to Washington's circle, while Elizabeth Gates caused something of a sensation, going about Cambridge in a mannish English riding habit.

Martha Washington, who had never been so far from home or in the midst of war, wrote to a friend in Virginia that the boom of cannon seemed to surprise no one but her. "I confess I shudder every time I hear the sound of a gun. . . . To me that never see anything of war, the preparations are very terrible indeed. But I endeavor to keep my fears to myself as well as I can."

In the meantime, after much debate, the Congress at Philadelphia had passed a directive to Washington to destroy the enemy forces in Boston, "even if the town must be burnt." John Hancock, whose stone mansion on Beacon Hill overlooking the Common was one of the prominent features on the skyline, had spoken "heartily" for the measure.

Work on fortifications continued without letup, and despite freezing winds and snow, the work improved. Washington kept moving the lines nearer and nearer the enemy. A newly completed bastion at Cobble Hill, below Prospect Hill and fully a half mile nearer to Boston, was described in the *Providence Gazette* as "the most perfect piece of fortification that the American army has constructed during the present campaign."

On December 24, a storm swept across the whole of the province. In the vicinity of Boston, temperatures dropped to the low twenties, and a foot of snow fell. Christmas Day, a Monday, was still bitterly cold, but clear, and the troops continued with their routine as on any day.

On December 30, several British ships arrived in the harbor, presumably bringing reinforcements.

"This is the last day of the old enlisted soldiers' service," wrote a greatly distressed Nathanael Greene to Congressman

Samuel Ward the following day, December 31. "Nothing but confusion and disorder reign."

We have suffered prodigiously for want of wood. Many regiments have been obliged to eat their provisions raw for want of firing to cook, and notwithstanding we have burned up all the fences and cut down all the trees for a mile around the camp, our suffering has been inconceivable. . . . We have never been so weak as we shall be tomorrow.

On New Year's Day, Monday, January 1, 1776, the first copies of the speech delivered by King George III at the opening of Parliament back in October were sent across the lines from Boston. They had arrived with the ships from London.

The reaction among the army was rage and indignation. The speech was burned in public by the soldiers and had stunning effect everywhere, as word of its contents rapidly spread. Its charges of traitorous rebellion, its ominous reference to "foreign assistance," assuredly ended any hope of reconciliation or a short war. It marked a turning point as clear as the advent of the new year.

"We have consulted our wishes rather than our reason in the indulgence of an idea of accommodation," Nathanael Greene wrote in another fervent letter to Samuel Ward in Philadelphia.

Heaven hath decreed that tottering empire Britain to irretrievable ruin and thanks to God, since Providence hath so determined, America must raise an empire of permanent duration, supported upon the grand pillars of Truth, Freedom, and Religion, encouraged by the smiles of Justice and defended by her own patriotic sons. . . . Permit me then to recommend from the sincerity of my heart, ready at all times to bleed in my country's cause, a Declaration of Independence, and call upon the world and the great God who governs it to witness the necessity, propriety and rectitude thereof.

The effect of the King's speech on Washington was profound. If nothing else could "satisfy a tyrant and his diabolical ministry," he wrote to Joseph Reed, "we were determined to shake off all connections with a state so unjust and unnatural. This I would tell them, not under covert, but in words as clear as the sun in its meridian brightness."

Meanwhile, that New Year's Day, the great turnover of the army commenced, as new regiments arrived and the old departed "by hundreds and by thousands . . . in the very teeth of an enemy," as General Heath noted.

Yet substantial numbers who had been in the lines stayed on, including many who had served since Bunker Hill, like Samuel Webb of Connecticut and young John Greenwood, the fifer. Joseph Hodgkins would stay, for all that he and his wife longed for each other. So would the artist John Trumbull and Dr. James Thacher. Many, like Lieutenant Jabez Fitch of Connecticut, would go home, but reenlist a little later in the new year. How many of the "old army" would fight on is impossible to know, but it may have been as many as 9,000.

At the Cambridge headquarters, Washington declared in his general orders for New Year's Day the commencement of a "new army, which in every point of view is entirely continental." And thus the army, though still 90 percent a New England army, had a name, the Continental Army.

He stressed the hope that "the importance of the great Cause we are engaged in will be deeply impressed upon every man's mind." Everything "dear and valuable to freemen" was at stake, he said, calling on their patriotism to rally morale and commitment, but also expressing exactly what he felt.

With the crash of a 13-gun salute, he raised a new flag in honor of the birthday of the new army — a flag of thirteen red and white stripes, with the British colors (the crosses of St. George and St. Andrew) represented in the upper corner. When the British in Boston saw it flying from Prospect Hill, they at first mistook it for a flag of surrender.

Chapter Three

DORCHESTER HEIGHTS

We are not under the least apprehension of an attack on this place by surprise or otherwise.
— General William Howe

I

That Dorchester Heights could decide the whole outcome at Boston had been apparent to the British from the beginning. Their initial plan, agreed to on June 15, had been to seize the high ground on both the Charlestown and Dorchester peninsulas. But then the rebels had made their surprise move at Charlestown, digging in overnight on Bunker Hill, and it had taken the bloodbath of June 17 to remove them. The morning after the battle, in a council of war at the Province House, headquarters of the commander-in-chief, Thomas Gage, it was proposed by Major General Henry Clinton to move immediately on Dorchester. Possession of the heights was "absolutely necessary for the security of Boston, as they lay directly on our water communications and more seriously annoyed the port of Boston than those of Charlestown," Clinton later wrote, adding that he expected to lead the assault. "I foresaw the consequence, and gave it formally as my opinion at the time, that if the King's troops should be ever driven from Boston, it would be by rebel batteries raised on those heights."

But while Gage had kept Bunker Hill heavily armed with cannon and manned by five hundred troops, he had done nothing about Dorchester. Nor had General Howe since taking charge after Gage's departure for home in October. Nor, indeed, had the Americans. Dorchester Heights remained a kind of high, windblown no-man's-land, neither side unmindful of its strategic importance, but neither side daring to seize and fortify it.

Among those Loyalists in Boston who had closest contact with the British command, it was commonly understood that Dorchester was the key and commonly questioned why nothing was being done. "It had often been wished," wrote Justice Peter Oliver, one of the most prominent

Loyalists, "that this hill had had proper attention paid to it; and it had been repeatedly mentioned that it was of the last necessity to secure such a position; but the general answers were that there was no danger from it, and that it was to be wished that the rebels would take possession of it, as they could be dislodged."

Of greater and more immediate interest to the British command was the prospect of abandoning Boston altogether, of packing up and sailing away. As things stood, it was clearly no place to launch an offensive operation. New York should be made the "seat of war," Gage had stressed in correspondence with the administration in London, and Howe and the others were of the same opinion.

Brigadier General James Grant had said months earlier that Boston should be abandoned while there was still time. "We cannot remain during the winter in this place, as our situation must go on worse and that of the rebels better every day," Grant had insisted in a long letter from Boston to Edward Harvey, Adjutant General of the British army in London, on August 11.

Grant, a grossly fat, highly opinionated Scot, who had served in the French and

Indian War, had an extremely low opinion of Americans. (It was he who had boasted to Parliament that with 5,000 men he could march from one end of the American continent to the other.) The only step that made sense, he wrote, was to burn Boston and move on to New York. Besides, he wanted to turn the fleet loose to burn every principal town along the New England coast. "Lenity is out of the question."

Such were the delays in communication across the ocean that by the time General Howe received orders from London to "abandon Boston before winter" and "remove the troops to New York," it was too late — winter had arrived. Besides, there were too few ships at hand to transport the army and the hundreds of Loyalists about whom Howe was greatly concerned, knowing what their fate could be if they were left behind.

Seeing no reasonable alternative, Howe would wait for spring when he could depart at a time and under conditions of his own choosing. He expected no trouble from the Americans. "We are not under the least apprehension of an attack on this place from the rebels by surprise or otherwise," he assured his superiors in London and further stressed the point at a meeting with his general staff on December 3. Should, however, the rebels make a move on Dorchester, then, Howe affirmed, "We must go at it with our whole force."

Quite unlike the man in command of the army encircling the town, the British commander was not impatient for action. On the contrary, William Howe had little inclination ever to rush things. Further, it was taken as a matter of course among professional soldiers that winter was no season for campaigning.

And so the British army settled in for a long Boston winter, seeing to their comforts as best they could under the circumstances.

The notable exception was Major General John Burgoyne, "Gentleman Johnny," an officer of distinguished record and occasional playwright who had added welcome color to the social life of the British officers and their ladies. Impatient with "supineness," as he said, and ambitious for a command of his own, Burgoyne had sailed for England in early December.

Winter in America was a trial British soldiers could never get used to, any more than they could adjust to the incessant clamor of frogs on spring nights or American mosquitoes or the absence of decent beer. The harsh winter winds and driving snows of the bay area inflicted misery indiscriminately on both armies, of course, but for the King's men, unaccustomed to such a climate, the punishment was all but unbearable. A young Irish nobleman, Captain Francis Lord Rawdon, wrote of the suffering of his men encamped on Bunker Hill in early December, their tents "so shattered" they could as well have slept on the open ground — "and we hear with some envy of several little balls and concerts which our brethren have had in Boston." Soldiers froze to death standing watch. Even when the troops moved to winter quarters a few weeks later, keeping warm seemed nearly impossible.

The open sea remained the only lifeline for fuel and food for the town, but with the severity of storms on the North Atlantic, and American privateers operating offshore in increasing numbers despite the weather, fewer and fewer supply ships were getting through. ("The rebels have the impudence to fit out privateers," wrote an indignant British officer, snug in his quarters, but the day would come, he knew, when "we shall give the scoundrels a hearty thrashing and put an end to this business.")

British Admiral Samuel Graves, whose responsibility it was to patrol the coastline against privateers, described snowstorms at sea between Cape Ann and Cape Cod as defying the most resolute of men.

This sort of storm is so severe that it cannot even be looked against, and by the snow freezing as fast as it falls, baffles all resistance — for the blocks become choked, the tackle encrusted, the ropes and sails quite congealed, and the whole ship before long one cake of ice. . . . Indeed, if the severity of the winters be such in this climate that the sentinel on shore is frequently found frozen to death upon his post, though relieved every half hour, the reader may frame some idea of what the seamen of a watch, especially in small vessels, must suffer.

With firewood selling for $20 a cord in Boston, more and more trees were cut down, including the old elm at the corner of Essex and Orange streets, known as the Liberty Tree, which provided fourteen cords. A hundred or more houses were pulled apart. Old barns, old wharves, and derelict ships were chopped up, almost anything that would burn. On orders from General Howe, Old North Church was demolished for firewood.

Only a fraction of Boston's former, peacetime population remained, thousands having long since fled the town. But others, Loyalists, had sought refuge there, and Loyalists were conspicuous, if not necessarily more numerous than those inhabitants who had chosen to stay in the hope of protecting their property, or because they were too poor or helpless to do anything else. A few, like the town's selectmen, had been forbidden to leave. In all, there were now about 4,000 civilians under siege, at least half of whom were women and children, and they, too, no less than the redcoat army, were hurting from shortages of all kinds, the poor inevitably suffering most.

Food remained extremely scarce and dear. Young Lord Rawdon described his famished troops as looking like skeletons. Even inferior cuts of horse meat brought good prices. To put a stop to increasing instances of plunder by the troops, Howe initiated punishments more severe even than the standard for the British army. In fact, the new year of 1776 began in Boston with the public whipping of a soldier and his wife who had been caught with stolen goods.

For the British officers, however — the "redcoat gentry," as Washington called them — life was not entirely unpleasant. They had appropriated Old South Church for a riding ring — Old South Church being odious to them because town meetings had been held there. (Pews were torn out, dirt spread on the floor. According to the diary of Deacon Timothy Newell, one particularly beautiful, hand-carved pew was taken away to serve as a hog sty.) Evening entertainments were numerous. "We have plays, assemblies, and balls, and live as if we were in a place of plenty," wrote an officer. "In the midst of these horrors of war, we endeavor as much as possible to forget them," explained the wife of another officer in a letter to a friend at home.

Writing again to General Harvey, James Grant said, "We must get through a disagreeable winter the best way we can. I do all in my power to keep the ball up — I have all ranks of officers at dinner, give them good wine, laugh at the Yankees and turn them into ridicule when an opportunity offers."

Boston having no theater, Faneuil Hall, sacred to Boston patriots as "the cradle of liberty," was converted on General Howe's wish into a "very elegant playhouse" for amateur productions of Shakespeare and original farces, with officers and favored Loyalists taking parts. Sally Flucker, the sister of Henry Knox's wife, Lucy Flucker, for example, took a lead part in a production of *Maid of the Oaks*, a satire by General Burgoyne.

On the evening of January 8, uniformed officers and their ladies packed Faneuil Hall for what was expected to be the event of the season, a performance of a musical farce said also to have been written by Burgoyne. Titled *The Blockade*, it was off to a rollicking start from the moment the curtain rose. A ridiculous figure, supposed to be George Washington, stumbled on stage wearing an oversized wig and dragging a rusty sword. At the same moment, across the bay, Connecticut soldiers led by Major Thomas Knowlton launched a surprise attack on Charlestown, and the British responded with a thunderous cannon barrage. With the roar of the guns, which the audience at Faneuil Hall took to be part of the show, another comic figure, a Yankee sergeant in farmer garb, rushed on stage to say the rebels were "at it tooth and nail over in Charlestown." The audience roared with laughter and "clapped prodigiously," sure that this, too, was part of the fun.

> But soon finding their mistake [wrote an eyewitness] a general scene of confusion ensued. They immediately hurried out of the house to their alarm posts, some skipping over the orchestra, trampling on the fiddles, and, in short, everyone making his most speedy retreat, the actors (who were all officers) calling out for water to get the paint and smut off their faces, women fainting, etc.

Reportedly, it was General Howe himself who shouted, "Turn out! Turn out!"

The British commander, an easygoing, affable man who had never been averse to taking his pleasures when he could, was openly enjoying himself through the winter with his own elegant dinners, extended evenings at the faro table, and conspicuously in the company of a stunning young woman about whom there was much talk. The lady, who was to become known as Billy Howe's Cleopatra, was Elizabeth Lloyd Loring, the wife of Joshua Loring, Jr., a member of a prominent Loyalist family whom Howe had hired to run the commissary for rebel prisoners. In the words of a contemporary Loyalist chronicler of the war, "Joshua had a handsome wife. The general . . . was fond of her. Joshua had no objections. He fingered the cash, the general enjoyed madam."

William Howe had been a professional soldier from the time he finished school at Eton and at age seventeen received a commission in the Duke of Cumberland's Light Dragoons. Two older brothers had also chosen military careers and distinguished themselves. The oldest, George Augustus Lord Howe, had fought and died in America in the French and Indian War and was remembered in New England as one of the bravest, best-loved British officers of the time. The other brother, Richard — Admiral Lord Howe — had begun his career in the Royal Navy at fourteen. Like William, he was a member of Parliament and much admired by the King.

The Howe brothers belonged to one of England's most eminent families. They were rich, accomplished, and extremely well connected. Their mother, still a force in London society, was said to be the illegitimate daughter of King George I. Both men were staunch Whigs and had a decided resemblance, a rather gloomy, dark look, with dark eyes, heavy lids, and a swarthy complexion. But the general was the taller, at about six feet, the heavier, and a man of fewer words. In Parliament he rarely spoke. To Horace Walpole, Billy Howe was "one of those brave silent brothers [who] was reckoned sensible, though so silent that nobody knew whether he was or not." Nor was it clear how much real heart the general had for the war in America, given his earlier comments about having no wish to serve in it.

William Howe's ability and courage were indisputable. As a heroic young lieutenant colonel in the French and Indian War, he had led a detachment of light infantry up the steep embankments of Quebec in the first light of dawn to make way for the army of General James Wolfe to defeat the French under Montcalm on the Plains of Abraham. Wolfe had called William Howe the best officer in the King's service. At Bunker Hill, assuring his troops he would not ask them "to go a step further than where I go myself," he had marched in the front line. When the men fell back, after the slaughter of the first assault, he led them up the hill twice again. After one blinding volley during the third assault, he had been the only man in the front line still standing.

But for all his raw courage in the heat and tumult of war, Billy Howe could be, in the intervals between actions, slow-moving, procrastinating, negligent in preparing for action, interested more in his own creature comforts and pleasures.

That he had been stunned by the terrible cost of British victory at Bunker Hill there is no question. "The success is too dearly bought," he had written to his brother the admiral. Still, he was a soldier, a gifted strategist, and a fighter. He liked to tell his troops, "I do not in the least doubt but that you will behave like Englishmen and as becomes good soldiers," and he expected no less of himself. He would be a good soldier always, whenever put to the test. He meant business, and at forty-five, or approximately the same age as George Washington, he had far greater experience than Washington, a far more impressive record, not to mention better-trained, better-equipped troops, and ships of the Royal Navy riding at anchor in the harbor.

He also had the ostensible advantage of experienced subordinate officers, professionals all, several of whom had marked ability. When, in the previous spring, Howe, Clinton, and Burgoyne had sailed from England for the war in America, they truly represented the pick of the King's officers. All three were men of proven courage and commitment to duty. Like Howe, Clinton and Burgoyne were well-connected, well-schooled aristocrats, and, as major generals, at the threshold of the peak years of their careers. Clinton, Howe's second-in-command, was the least impressive in appearance, a short, fat, colorless man who could be shy and petulant. But he had a keen military mind and the advantage of knowing Americans from boyhood. He had grown up in New York, where his father, Admiral George Clinton, served as governor from 1741 to 1751.

Among those of lesser rank, an outstanding example was John Montresor, an officer of engineers whose years of service and experience would seem to make a mockery of the very idea that someone like Nathanael Greene could be a major general. Montresor, too, had served in the French and Indian War, in the Braddock campaign and at Wolfe's siege of Quebec. In 1760, at age twenty-four, he had led a winter expedition overland from Quebec to New England, and at the war's end worked on fortifications from Boston to Detroit to New York City, where he bought an island, Montresor's Island, in the East River. He was resourceful, energetic, probably the best engineer in the British army, and with experience in America to equal any.

But it was also true that Howe and Clinton disliked one another and did not work well together, and that John Montresor, who was not an aristocrat, was still, at nearly forty, only a captain. If the desperate American need for leaders had thrust young men like Nathanael Greene into positions beyond their experience, the British military system, wherein commissions were bought and aristocrats given preference, denied many men of ability roles they should have played. Had Captain John Montresor been a major general, the outcome of the struggle might have been quite different.

Howe's sources of intelligence, furthermore, were pitiful, virtually nonexistent. As near at hand as the rebels were, the British commander knew almost nothing of their true situation, their perilously thin lines, their lack of gunpowder. Bunker Hill had taught Howe not to underestimate his foe. Still, he had no doubt that the "present unfavorable appearance of things" could be rectified readily enough. All that was wanting was a "proper army" of 20,000.

In mid-January, on orders from London, General Clinton and a small fleet sailed away southward to see what advantage might be gained in the Carolinas, thus reducing the British force at Boston by 1,500 men. And, as pleased as Howe may have been to see Clinton leave, Clinton had at least served as an antidote to Howe's "supineness."

Oddly, Howe seems to have had no interest in the man who led the army aligned against him. In all that he and others of the British command wrote at the time, officially and privately, George Washington was rarely ever mentioned except in passing. There was no apparent consideration of what manner of man he was, what his state of mind, his strengths and weaknesses, might be. Or what he might be up to, given the working of his mind. Perhaps this was indifference, perhaps the measure of an overreaching sense of superiority. Washington, by contrast, was constantly trying to fathom Howe's intentions, his next move. Strange it was that the British commander-in-chief, known for his chronic gambling, seemed to give no thought to how his American opponent might play his hand.

On January 14, two weeks into the new year, George Washington wrote one of the most forlorn, despairing letters of his life. He had been suffering sleepless nights in the big house by the Charles. "The reflection upon my situation and that of this army produces many an uneasy hour when all around me are wrapped in sleep," he told the absent Joseph Reed. "Few people know the predicament we are in."

Filling page after page, he enumerated the same troubles and woes he had been reporting persistently to Congress for so long, and that he would report still again to John Hancock that same day. There was too little powder, still no money. (Money was useful in the common affairs of life but in war it was essential, Washington would remind the wealthy Hancock.) So many of the troops who had given up and gone home had, against orders, carried off muskets that were not their own that the supply of arms was depleted to the point where there were not enough for the new recruits. "We have not at this time 100 guns in the stores of all that have been taken in the prize ship [the captured

British supply ship *Nancy*]," he wrote to Reed. On paper his army numbered between 8,000 and 10,000. In reality only half that number were fit for duty.

It was because he had been unable to attack Boston that things had come to such a pass, he was convinced. The changing of one army to another in the midst of winter, with the enemy so close at hand, was like nothing "in the pages of history." That the British were so "blind" to what was going on and the true state of his situation he considered nearly miraculous.

He was downcast and feeling quite sorry for himself. Had he known what he was getting into, he told Reed, he would never have accepted the command.

I have often thought how much happier I should have been if, instead of accepting of a command under such circumstances, I had taken my musket upon my shoulders and entered the ranks, or, if I could have justified the measure to posterity, and my own conscience, had retired to the back country, and lived in a wigwam. If I shall be able to rise superior to these, and many other difficulties which might be enumerated, I shall most religiously believe that the finger of Providence is in it, to blind the eyes of our enemies; for surely if we get well through this month, it must be for want of their knowing the disadvantages we labor under.

Could I have foreseen the difficulties which have come upon us, could I have known that such a backwardness would have been discovered in the old soldiers to the service, all the generals upon earth should not have convinced me of the propriety of delaying an attack upon Boston till this time.

To add to his worries — and this he did not tell Reed — Washington had learned through "undoubted intelligence" that the British were fitting out ships in the harbor for the embarkation of troops, which he took to mean, given the season of the year, they could only be bound for a destination to the south, and almost certainly it was New York. Generals Lee and Greene were convinced New York would be of such "vast importance" to the enemy that no time could be lost seeing to its defense. Loyalists were numerous in New York; their support for the Crown was already strong. "If the tide of sentiment gets against us in that province," Nathanael

Greene warned, "it will give a fatal stab to the strength and union of the colonies." In Greene's opinion there were but two choices open: defend New York or burn it. General Lee proposed to Washington that he, Lee, be sent immediately to New York to see about defenses.

Though in agreement that time was of the essence, Washington knew that congressional approval was needed and that there must be no ambiguity over whether his authority extended beyond the immediate theater of war. As he would say, he was not fond of "stretching" his powers, and such sensitivity to and respect for the political ramifications of his command were exactly what made him such an effective political general.

Fortunately, he was able to obtain an immediate opinion from John Adams, who was on a brief leave from Congress at his home in Braintree. The importance of New York was beyond question, Adams formally assured the commander in a letter of January 6 delivered to Cambridge that day. New York was "a kind of key to the whole continent," Adams wrote. "No effort to secure it ought to be omitted." On the matter of Washington's authority, Adams courageously gave him full, unambiguous approval for taking action in New York or anywhere else, and the issue was never to be raised again.

"Your commission constitutes you commander 'of all the forces . . . and [you] are vested with full power and authority to act as you shall think for the good and welfare of the service.' "

Thus, on January 8, Washington had dispatched General Lee to New York to put the city "in the best posture of defense."

There was no January thaw in eastern Massachusetts that year, and this meant continued suffering for soldiers without winter clothing, soldiers "sickly" and dying from disease. But with temperatures in the twenties or lower day after day came the increasing likelihood of Back Bay freezing over, and the possibility of an attack on Boston across the ice.

On January 16, two days after his woeful letter to Reed, Washington convened a council of war with Generals Ward, Putnam, Heath, Spencer, Sullivan, Greene, and Gates present, but also James Warren, head of the Massachusetts Assembly, and John Adams. Washington spoke of the "indispensable necessity of making a bold attempt" on Boston. The council listened, then voiced agreement that a "vigorous attempt" should be made, but only when "practicable."

Late the following day, January 17, well after dark, a dispatch rider dismounted at Washington's headquarters carrying the worst news of the war thus far. It was a letter from General Schuyler at Albany. The army Washington had sent across the Maine wilderness under Benedict Arnold to attack Quebec had been defeated. Arnold was badly wounded. General Richard Montgomery, who, with 300 men, had joined in the assault, attacking from Montreal, had been killed. Help was urgently needed. How many others had been killed or wounded at Quebec, how many taken prisoner, no one yet knew.

Washington, as he wrote privately, often felt that the eyes of the whole continent were on him, "fixed with anxious expectation."

When the council of war convened again the first thing the next morning, it was reluctantly concluded that given the "present feeble state" of the army, no troops could be spared for Quebec.

The single glimmer of hope was confirmation from Schuyler, on January 18, that the guns from Ticonderoga were on the way. As it happened, Colonel Knox, who had ridden on ahead, reached Cambridge later that same day.

Knox had been gone for two months and he had fulfilled all expectations, despite rough forest roads, freezing lakes, blizzards, thaws, mountain wilderness, and repeated mishaps that would have broken lesser spirits several times over. He had succeeded with his bold, virtually impossible idea and at exactly the right moment, justifying entirely the trust Washington had placed in him. The story of the expedition would be told and retold for weeks within the army and for years to come.

Departing from Cambridge on horseback on November 16, Knox and his brother William had traveled first to New York City, where they made arrangements for military supplies to be sent back to Boston, then pressed northward up the Hudson Valley, at times making forty miles a day.

They arrived at Fort Ticonderoga on December 5. Built by the French at the start of the French and Indian War in 1755, the limestone fort had been taken by the British in 1759, then by the Americans in May of 1775. It stood at the southern end of Lake Champlain, where Lake

Champlain meets the northern end of Lake George.

The guns Knox had come for were mostly French — mortars, 12- and 18-pound cannon (that is, guns that fired cannonballs of 12 and 18 pounds), and one giant brass 24-pounder. Not all were in usable condition. After looking them over, Knox selected 58 mortars and cannon. Three of the mortars weighed a ton each and the 24-pound cannon, more than 5,000 pounds. The whole lot was believed to weigh not less than 120,000 pounds.

The plan was to transport the guns by boat down Lake George, which was not yet completely frozen over. At the lake's southern end would begin the long haul overland, south as far as Albany before turning east toward Boston across the Berkshire Mountains. The distance to be covered was nearly three hundred miles. Knox planned to drag the guns on giant sleds and was counting on snow. But thus far only a light dusting covered the ground.

With the help of local soldiers and hired men, he set immediately to work. Just moving the guns from the fort to the boat landing proved a tremendous task. The passage down Lake George, not quite forty miles, took eight days. Three boats and their immense cargo set sail on December 9, and for the first hour had a fair wind. After that progress came only with "the utmost difficulty." Indeed, from Knox's hurried, all-but-illegible diary entries, that first hour on the lake appears to have been the only hour of the entire trek that did not bring "the utmost difficulty."

One of the boats, a scow, struck a rock and sank, though close enough to shore to be bailed out, patched up, and set afloat again. Knox recorded days of heavy rowing against unrelenting headwinds — four hours of "rowing exceeding hard" one day, six hours of "excessive hard rowing" on another. In places, the boats had to cut through ice. Knox's brother William wrote at day's end, December 14, of "beating all the way against the wind. . . . God send us a fair wind." Nights ashore were bitterly cold.

"It is not easy to conceive the difficulties we have had," Knox wrote to Washington at the end of the voyage on the lake, in a letter of December 17 that would reach Cambridge only about the time he did.

On his way north to Ticonderoga, Knox had arranged for heavy sleds or sledges to be rounded up or built, forty-two in all, and to be on hand at Fort George at the southern end of Lake George, about thirty-five miles south of Ticonderoga. ("I most earnestly beg you to spare no trouble or necessary expense in getting these," he had told a local officer.) With the sleds and eighty yoke of oxen, he was now ready to push on. "Trusting that . . . we shall have a fine fall of snow. . . . I hope in sixteen or seventeen days to be able to present your Excellency a noble train of artillery."

To his wife, Knox claimed the most difficult part was over, and speculated, "We shall cut no small figure through the country with our cannon."

Still there was no snow. Instead, a "cruel thaw" set in, halting progress for several days. The route south to Albany required four crossings of the Hudson. With ice on the river so thin, the heavy caravan could only stand idly by at Fort George and wait for a change in the weather. When the change came, it was a blizzard. Three feet of snow fell, beginning Christmas Day. Determined to go ahead to Albany on his own, Knox nearly froze to death struggling through the snow on foot, until finding horses and a sleigh to take him the rest of the route.

Eventually, the "precious convoy"

pushed off from Fort George. "Our caval-cade was quite imposing," remembered John Becker, who at age twelve had accompanied his father, one of the drivers on the expedition. They proceeded slowly, laboriously in the heavy snow, passing through the village of Saratoga, then on to Albany, where Knox was busy cutting holes in the frozen Hudson in order to strengthen the ice. (The idea was that water coming up through the holes would spread over the surface of the ice and freeze, thus gradually thickening the ice.)

On New Year's Day, the weather turned warm again. Precious time was wasting, he wrote to Lucy. "The thaw has been so grave that I've trembled for the consequences, for without snow my very important charge cannot get along."

But the temperature plunged again. On January 7, General Schuyler wrote to Washington from his Albany headquarters, "This morning I had the satisfaction to see the first division of sleds with cannon cross the river."

They moved cautiously over the ice, and for several hours it appeared that Knox's holes had done the trick. Nearly a dozen sleds had crossed without mishap, until suddenly one of the largest cannons, an

18-pounder, broke through and sank not far from shore, leaving a hole in the ice fourteen feet in diameter. Undaunted, Knox at once set about retrieving the cannon from the bottom of the river, losing a full day in the effort, but at last succeeding, as he wrote, "owing to the assistance [of] the good people of Albany."

On January 9, the expedition pushed on from the eastern shore of the Hudson, with more than a hundred miles still to go. Snow in the Berkshires lay thick, exactly as needed, but the mountains, steep and tumbled and dissected by deep, narrow valleys, posed a challenge as formidable as any. Knox, with no prior experience in such terrain, wrote of climbing peaks "from which we might almost have seen all the kingdoms of the earth."

"It appeared to me almost a miracle that people with heavy loads should be able to get up and down such hills," reads another of his diary entries.

To slow the descent of the laden sleds down slopes as steep as a roof, check lines were anchored to trees. Brush and drag chains were shoved beneath the runners. When some of his teamsters, fearful of the risks, refused to go any further, Knox spent three hours arguing and pleading until finally they agreed to head on.

News of the advancing procession raced ahead of the lead sleds, and, as Knox had imagined, people began turning out along the route to see for themselves the procession of the guns from Ticonderoga.

"Our armament here was a great curiosity," wrote John Becker of the reception at the town of Westfield. "We found that very few, even among the oldest inhabitants, had ever seen a cannon." Becker, at age twelve, had never known such excitement.

We were the great gainers by this curiosity, for while they were employed in remarking upon our guns, we were, with equal pleasure, discussing the qualities of their cider and whiskey. These were generously brought out in great profusion.

At Springfield, to quicken the pace, Knox changed from oxen to horses, and on the final leg of the journey the number of onlookers grew by the day.

The halt came at last about twenty miles west of Boston at Framingham. The guns were unloaded, Knox, meantime, having sped on to Cambridge.

Knox's "noble train" had arrived intact. Not a gun had been lost. Hundreds of men had taken part and their labors and resilience had been exceptional. But it was the daring and determination of Knox himself that had counted above all. The twenty-five-year-old Boston bookseller had proven himself a leader of remarkable ability, a man not only of enterprising ideas, but with the staying power to carry them out. Immediately, Washington put him in command of the artillery.

To those who rode out from Cambridge to Framingham to look over the guns, it was clear that the stalemate at Boston was about to change dramatically.

II

There was a perceptible quickening of activity at the big gray house that served as headquarters. The pace of the commander's correspondence, the numbers of post riders and uniformed officers coming and going, gave evidence of something in the offing. "My business increases very fast . . . from great changes," Washington wrote to Joseph Reed without providing details. Reed's help was needed more than ever. "It is absolutely necessary . . . to have persons that can think for me as well as execute orders."

The strength of the army was still deficient, the situation so serious, Washington confided, that he was "obliged to use art to conceal it," even from his own officers.

That he was about to take action could be read easily enough between the lines of this and other correspondence that went speeding off in the pouches of fast mail riders. The camps were alive with rumors and speculation. "Great activity and animation are observed among our officers and soldiers who manifest an anxious desire to have a conflict with the enemy," wrote the ever-perceptive Dr. James Thacher, who predicted either a "general assault on the town of Boston, or the erection of works on the Heights of Dorchester, or both."

The bitter cold continued. On January 27, the thermometer dropped to 4 degrees; the low on January 28 was 1 degree, then 2 degrees on January 30. Yet cold as it was, there was still no "ice bridge" sufficient to carry an army. Some mornings Washington went to the bay to jump up and down on the ice himself to test its strength.

He made a personal reconnaissance of the approaches to Dorchester, even to the heights apparently, accompanied by several of his officers, including Henry Knox. According to one possibly apocryphal account, Washington and the others had left their horses and were proceeding on foot when suddenly two mounted British officers coming at a gallop sent them "running and scampering for life."

A week later, a British raiding party crossed the ice to Dorchester and burned several farmhouses.

On February 16, Washington convened his council of war for what he hoped would be unanimous agreement that the time had come to attack. A "stroke well aimed at this critical juncture might put a final end to the war," he argued.

"Perhaps a greater question was never agitated in a council of war," wrote General Gates of the meeting, and whatever "art" Washington may have exercised to conceal the truth of the army's strength from his officers, there was, in fact, little that Gates and the others gathered in the room were not aware of. For weeks the demonstrative Israel Putnam had been bewailing the need for gunpowder. Old Put would not relent, wrote one of Washington's staff. "He is still as hard as ever, crying out for powder — 'powder — ye gods, give us powder!' "

Conspicuous by his absence was Nathanael Greene, who had been stricken with jaundice. He was "as yellow as saffron," and "so weak that I can scarcely walk across the room," he had written his brother, to whom he also gave his own opinion on the proposed attack. The very thought filled him with dread. An assault on a town garrisoned with regular troops could have horrible consequences, Greene wrote, "horrible if it succeeded, and still more horrible if it failed."

The council of war marked the fourth time Washington had called for approval for an attack on Boston, and once again, wisely, the generals said no. Very likely the shattering defeat at Quebec had reinforced the view that any assault on so heavily defended a position was not worth the terrible risk.

There was, however, agreement to another plan. Instead of striking at the enemy where they were well fortified, they would lure the enemy out to strike at them, as had been done at Bunker Hill. From the accounts of spies and British deserters, it was by now known that Howe had sworn he would "sally forth" if ever the Americans tried to occupy Dorchester. And so it was resolved that preparations begin "with a view of drawing out the enemy."

Washington was crestfallen over the decision not to attack. "Behold! Though we had been waiting all the year for this favorable event, the enterprise was thought too dangerous!" he wrote to Joseph Reed. But perhaps he had been wrong, he gracefully conceded. "Perhaps the irksomeness of my situation led me to undertake more than could be warranted by prudence."

But all that was done with. The issue was "now at an end, and I am preparing to take post on Dorchester." From this point on, there would be no holding back.

The preparations were elaborate and mammoth in scale, and Washington threw himself into the effort, demanding that not an hour be lost. Intelligence reports that the British intended to evacuate Boston at first chance did nothing to deter him.

Twin hills comprised the Heights of the Dorchester peninsula, and the distance from these summits to the nearest British lines at Boston Neck was a mile and a half, well within range of a 12- or 18-pound cannon. The distance to where most of the British fleet lay off Long Wharf was greater, almost two miles, which was also within range, though barely.

The plan was to occupy the Heights on a single night, before the British knew what was happening, just as had been done at Bunker Hill. This time, however, there were the guns from Ticonderoga to haul in place, and the Heights of Dorchester were considerably steeper than at Bunker Hill and, at an elevation of 112 feet, nearly twice as high. More seriously, the frozen ground on top was "impenetrable as a rock," in Washington's words, which meant that digging trenches and throwing up breastworks in the usual fashion would be impossible, at least in one night and with no noise.

The solution was a highly sophisticated scheme whereby the fortifications would be fabricated elsewhere out of sight, then, with massed manpower and oxen, hauled, along with the heavy cannon, to the Heights of Dorchester, where all would have to be in place and ready for action before daylight.

A resourceful lieutenant colonel who had directed the work on the fortifications at Roxbury, Rufus Putnam — a farmer and surveyor in normal times, and a cousin of Israel Putnam — had suggested the idea after seeing an unfamiliar term in a text on artillery, *Muller's Field Engineer*, by a British professor named John Muller. Putnam had taken his plan to his superior officer, Colonel Richard Gridley, and to Henry Knox. In turn, the three had gone to see Washington, and in no time hundreds of men were at work building chandeliers, great timber frames that could be filled with "screwed hay" (hay twisted into bales) or compact bundles of branches and brushwood called fascines.

Washington also wanted barrels filled with earth set in rows in front of the parapets, to add to the appearance of strength, but more importantly to stand ready to be rolled down the steep slopes on the advancing enemy. He had "a very high opinion of the defense which may be made with barrels," he told Artemus Ward, stressing that the hoops should be well nailed so the barrels would not break to pieces.

To divert the enemy and drown out the noise of the work parties, Washington planned to precede the operation with night barrages of artillery fire from Roxbury, Cobble Hill, and Lechmere Point, where a number of the guns from Ticonderoga had been newly emplaced.

As critical and dangerous as any part of

the operation would be the crossing of the low-lying causeway of the Dorchester peninsula, which stood in plain view of the British lines at the Boston Neck, less than a mile away. To conceal all movement over the causeway, an extended barrier of hay bales was to be thrown up.

Three thousand men under General Thomas were to take part in fortifying the Heights. Another 4,000 were to stand by at Cambridge for an amphibious attack on Boston, once the British launched their assault on the Heights — amphibious because milder weather had returned and the bay was again largely open water. General Putnam had overall command of the Boston attack. Generals Greene and Sullivan would lead the crossing. On the Charles River at Cambridge, sixty flatboats stood ready.

To bring the army to maximum strength, 2,000 Massachusetts militia were called out, while work details were dispatched to round up wagons, carts, and 800 oxen. At the army's hospital in Cambridge, thousands of bandages were being prepared, and additional beds made ready. Notices in the *Boston Gazette* (published in Watertown since the start of the siege) called for volunteer nurses.

For miles around Boston everybody seemed to know someone, or someone who knew someone, who was in the know about what to expect. Bets were wagered on what would happen and when. In the surrounding towns tension and fear grew by the day.

"It is generally thought that there will be something done amongst you very soon," Sarah Hodgkins wrote from Ipswich to her husband Joseph.

"The preparations increase and something is daily expected, something terrible it will be," wrote Abigail Adams to her "Dearest Friend," who had since returned to Philadelphia. "I have been in a continual state of anxiety and expectation . . . it has been said 'tomorrow' and 'tomorrow' for this [past] month, but when the dreadful tomorrow will be I know not."

As he had often before in his life, Washington eased the stress of waiting by catching up with his correspondence, writing again to Joseph Reed and to a young black poet, Phillis Wheatley, then living in Providence, who had sent him a poem written in his honor: "Proceed, great chief, with virtue on thy side / Thy every action let the goddess guide."

The country had no poets as yet, and

Washington was not known to be inclined to poetry or poetic musings. Yet he, a soldier and planter — a slave master — despite all that bore heavily on his mind, took time now to write to her in his own hand.

"I thank you most sincerely for your polite notice of me," Washington wrote, "and however undeserving I may be of such encomium and panegyrick, the style and manner exhibit a striking proof of your great poetical talents." Should she ever come to Cambridge, he would be "happy to see a person so favored by the muses."

In a letter to a Virginia friend, Washington wrote almost lightly of preparing to "bring on a rumpus" with the redcoats.

The date had been settled. The move on Dorchester would begin after dark on March 4 and be completed by first light the morning of March 5, the anniversary of the Boston Massacre.

How many hundreds, perhaps thousands, understood what was unfolding, even in some detail, no one knew. Yet success depended on secrecy. To this end Washington ordered a stop to all communication with Boston. Generals Heath and Sullivan personally inspected the lines to verify the vigilance of the guards on duty.

On the chance that the enemy got wind of what was happening and moved first to occupy the Heights, certain regiments stood ready to march at a moment's notice.

One of the closest observers of the situation within Boston, Loyalist Peter Oliver, would later write that there was not the least suspicion of what the rebels were up to. But according to the diary of one British officer, a few of the British did find out as early as February 29, from deserters and from a spy referred to only as "Junius," that the rebels intended to "bombard the town from Dorchester." The warnings, however, were not taken seriously.

Washington issued orders to the troops clarifying how very serious the moment was and what was expected of them:

> As the season is now fast approaching when every man must expect to be drawn into the field of action, it is highly necessary that he should prepare his mind, as well as everything necessary for it. It is a noble cause we are engaged in, it is the cause of virtue and mankind, every temporal advantage and comfort to us, and our posterity depends upon the vigor of our exer-

tions. . . . But it may not be amiss for the troops to know that if any man in action shall presume to skulk, hide himself, or retreat from the enemy, without the orders of his commanding officer, he will be *instantly shot down*, as an example of cowardice.

On Saturday evening, March 2, Washington wrote in haste to Artemus Ward that everything must be set and ready to go as planned on Monday night, March 4. After folding and sealing the note, he scrawled on the back, "Remember barrels."

The bombardment of Boston began at midnight Saturday and continued at intervals until morning. The British answered at once with a heavier, louder cannonade. "The house shakes . . . with the roar of the cannon," wrote Abigail Adams at her home ten miles away. "No sleep for me tonight."

Little damage was done by the exchange. It was nearly all noise, just as Washington wished, and the night would have been reckoned a complete success were it not that three of the big mortars burst, due apparently to the inexperience of Henry Knox and his artillerymen.

Sunday night the firing resumed and again the British responded with full crescendo. On the third and crucial night of Monday, March 4, the roar of the guns from both sides became more furious by far.

British captain Charles Stuart described sheets of fire filling the sky. But as he also recorded, "The inhabitants were in a horrid situation, particularly the women, who were several times drove from their houses by shot, and crying for protection." Watching from the American lines, Lieutenant Samuel Webb wrote, "Our shells raked the houses and the cries of the poor women and children frequently reached our ears."

At the first crash of the guns, General Thomas and 2,000 men started across the Dorchester causeway, moving rapidly and silently, shielded from view by the long barrier of hay bales. An advance guard of 800 men, a "covering party" made up largely of riflemen, went first, to fan out along the Dorchester shores in case the British made any attempt to investigate during the night. The main work party of 1,200 men followed immediately after, and then came hundreds of carts and heavy wagons loaded with chandeliers, fascines, hay bales, barrels, and most important of all, the guns from Ticonderoga.

"The whole procession moved on in solemn silence, and with perfect order and regularity, while the continued roar of cannon serves to engage the attention and divert the enemy," wrote Dr. Thacher, who, crossing the causeway with the troops, noted with gratitude the "vast number of large bundles of screwed hay arranged in a line next [to] the enemy . . . to which we should have been greatly exposed while passing."

Progress up the steep, smooth slopes was extremely difficult, yet numbers of the ox teams and wagons made three and four trips.

The night was unseasonably mild — indeed, perfectly beautiful with a full moon — ideal conditions for the work, as if the hand of the Almighty were directing things, which the Reverend William Gordon, like many others, felt certain it was. "A finer [night] for working could not have been taken out of the whole 365," he wrote. "It was hazy below [the Heights] so that our people could not be seen, though it was a bright moonlight night above on the hills."

At Cambridge, on the moonlit Common,

Generals Greene and Sullivan paraded with 4,000 troops in front of the college buildings, ready to move to the river and the shallow draft boats in the event of a signal from the Roxbury church steeple.

Recounting the night's events later, General Thomas would say it was as early as ten o'clock when the fortifications on the Heights were sufficiently ready to defend against small arms and grapeshot. It was also about ten when a British lieutenant colonel, Sir John Campbell, reported to Brigadier General Francis Smith that the "rebels were at work on Dorchester Heights." It was news that called for immediate action. But Smith, a stout, slow-moving, slow-thinking veteran of thirty years' service, chose to ignore it; and from that point on, the work proceeded unnoticed by any other British officers or troops on guard, or by any of the Loyalists in Boston who served as willing eyes and ears for the British.

On the Heights the men toiled steadily with picks and shovels, breaking the frozen ground for earth and stone to fill the chandeliers and barrels. At three in the morning a relief force of 3,000 men moved in, and an additional five regiments of riflemen took up positions near the shore. By the first faint light before dawn, everything was ready, with at least 20 cannon in place.

It was an utterly phenomenal achievement. General Heath was hardly exaggerating when he wrote, "Perhaps there never was so much work done in so short a space of time."

At daybreak, the British commanders looking up at the Heights could scarcely believe their eyes. The hoped-for, all-important surprise was total. General Howe was said to have exclaimed, "My God, these fellows have done more work in one night than I could make my army do in three months."

The British engineering officer, Archibald Robertson, calculated that to have carried everything into place as the rebels had — "a most astonishing night's work" — must have required at least 15,000 to 20,000 men. Howe, in his official account, would be more conservative and put the number at 14,000.

Later that spring, one of the London papers would carry portions of a letter attributed to an unnamed "officer of distinction at Boston":

5th March. This is, I believe, likely to prove as important a day to the British

empire as any in our annals. We under-
went last night a very severe cannonade, which damaged a number of
houses, and killed some men. This
morning at day break we discovered
two redoubts on the hills of Dorchester
Point, and two smaller works on their
flanks. They were all raised during the
night, with an expedition equal to that
of the genie belonging to Aladdin's
wonderful lamp. From these hills they
command the whole town, so that we
must drive them from their post, or
desert the place.

The shock of discovery threw the British
into "utmost consternation." Their immediate response, a thunderous two-hour
cannonade, proved nothing, as their guns
could not be elevated sufficiently to strike
a target so high. Meantime, from his flagship, Admiral Molyneux Shuldham (who
had replaced Admiral Graves) sent an urgent, unequivocal message to William
Howe: not a ship in the harbor could remain unless the rebels were removed from
their position.

It was not that the ships were directly
"under the guns" on the Heights, as some
later accounts gave the impression. At such

a distance of nearly two miles, a direct hit would be a lucky shot. Still the ships were theoretically within range, and lucky shots were known to happen.

Howe could dally no longer. With his generals gathered at the Province House at midmorning, he made his decision: he would attack, as he had vowed he would — and as his pride and honor demanded. He had no intention of staying in Boston, but that now seemed beside the point. Being who he was, he could not possibly accept the prospect of being outdone by the ragtag enemy, even if the carnage that had resulted from such an attack at Bunker Hill was as well known to him as to any man alive.

Two thousand troops were ordered to proceed by ship down the harbor to Castle Island, from where the attack on Dorchester would be launched at nightfall.

Captain Archibald Robertson thought the plan little short of madness and said so to others. Writing in his diary during the course of the day, he called it "the most serious step ever an army of this strength in such a situation took, considering the state the rebels' works are in and the number of men they appear to have under arms." The fate of the whole town was at stake, "not to say the fate of America." These were his sentiments, he declared, and he listed the names of the officers he had spoken to, hoping they could persuade Howe to change his mind and embark from Boston as quickly as possible. But starting about noon, the big transports loaded with troops began pushing off from Long Wharf.

Years later, recalling the morning of March 5 on Dorchester Heights, John Trumbull would write, "We saw distinctly the preparations which the enemy were making to dislodge us. The entire waterfront of Boston lay open to our observation, and we saw the embarkation of troops from the various wharves. . . . We were in high spirits, well prepared to receive the threatened attack."

Dr. Thacher, setting events down in his journal as they unfolded that "anxious" day on the Heights, wrote of the swarms of spectators covering the nearby hills, waiting to see a bloody battle.

Sometime in the course of the day (the exact hour is not known), Washington arrived to survey the defenses and the panorama below. "His Excellency General Washington is present animating and encouraging the soldiers," recorded Thacher, "and they in return manifest their joy, and express a warm desire for the approach of the enemy."

> Each man knows his place, and is resolute to execute his duty [he continued]. Our breastworks are strengthened, and among the means of defense are a great number of barrels, filled with stone and sand, arranged in front of our works, which are to be put in motion and made to roll down the hill, to break the ranks and legs of assailants as they advance. These are the preparations for blood and slaughter! Gracious God! If it be determined in thy Providence that thousands of our fellow creatures shall this day be slain, let thy wrath be appeased, and in mercy grant that victory be on the side of our suffering, bleeding country.

According to the Reverend William Gordon, Washington called on those within the sound of his voice to " 'remember it is the fifth of March, and avenge the death of your brethren.' It was immediately asked what the general said by those that were not near enough to hear, and as soon answered. And so from one to another through all the troops, which added fresh fuel to the martial fire before kindled."

Describing the troops drawn up at Cambridge, waiting for the order to attack, Washington himself said he "never saw spirits higher."

It was about noon when the first of the British troop transports pushed off for Castle Island and proceeded down the harbor with increasing difficulty against strong headwinds. For by early afternoon, what had been an abnormally warm, pleasant day had changed dramatically. The wind had turned southeasterly, blowing "pretty fresh." Then, as foreseen in no one's calculations, the elements took over.

By nightfall, a storm raged, with hail mixed with snow and sleet. By midnight, "the wind blew almost a hurricane." Windows were smashed, fences blown over. Two of the transports bound for Castle Island were blown ashore. The American lieutenant Isaac Bangs, who was among those freezing at their posts on the high ground of Dorchester, called it the worst storm "that ever I was exposed to." Clearly there would be no British assault that night.

The morning after, the winds continued to blow with a fury. The snow and sleet had changed to driving rain. General Heath concluded that "kind Heaven" had stepped in to intervene. As so it seemed to many on both sides, when, that morning, Howe called off the attack and gave orders to prepare to evacuate Boston.

Possibly it was not the storm alone that caused Howe's change of mind. According to Captain Robertson, his pleas to cancel the attack, and the influence of the other officers to whom he had made his case, and John Montresor in particular, had had the desired effect even before the storm reached full force. From what Robertson wrote in the final lines of his diary entry for the day, it would seem that the storm had merely given Howe an easy out.

It is now eight o'clock in the evening. [We] went to headquarters at seven. After waiting some time Captain Montresor came down from the general [and] told me he had been in council and had advised the going off [embarking] altogether, that Lord [General Hugh] Percy and some others seconded him, and that the general said it was his own sentiments from the first, but

191

thought the honor of the troops concerned. So it is agreed immediately to embark everything.

Interestingly, Isaac Bangs, in his account of the day, wondered whether the intent of the whole British expedition to Castle Island was never anything "more than to make a parade" and if the storm was only a "good excuse."

In the view of General James Grant, however, there was never a doubt of Howe's desire to attack. "Indeed, we had often talked over the subject and agreed that if the rebels made that move to their right [to Dorchester], we must either drive them from that post or leave Boston." According to Grant, everything had been prepared, and the plan to attack was "immediately formed, the redoubts to be stormed by the troops in column [and] not to load, that they might be under an absolute necessity of making use of their bayonets."

Howe, in his own official account, was to say, "I determined upon an immediate attack with all the force I could transport." He added, "The ardor of the troops encouraged me in this hazardous enterprise," and this could be the explanation, though an American who saw the British troops waiting on the wharf to embark, commented that "they looked in general pale and dejected, and said to one another it would be another Bunker Hill or worse."

Howe made no mention in his official account of the council of war convened at seven o'clock, or of any second thoughts on his part. The "contrary" winds of the afternoon of March 5, the storm that followed that night, and the "weather continuing boisterous the next day and night" were the deciding factors, Howe wrote, in that they gave the enemy still more time to improve their defenses of the Heights. "I could promise myself little success by attacking them under all the disadvantages I had to encounter; wherefore I judged it most advisable to prepare for the evacuation of the town."

III

No one who was in Boston would forget the days that followed. In less than forty-eight hours, the supposedly invulnerable security of the town had dissolved. Howe's army and the fleet at anchor were in danger of being destroyed at any time. The very survival of the town itself was in question.

In conference and in dispatches to London, the general had stated repeatedly his confidence that the rebels would make no move. Now he and his vaunted regulars had been outsmarted by "the rabble in arms," whom they had so long disparaged and despised. Instead of victory, they faced the humiliation of ignominious retreat.

"Never [were] troops in so disgraceful a situation," wrote one officer. "I pity General Howe from my soul."

Almost from the moment Howe made his announcement the morning of March 6, ordering the army and fleet to prepare to leave, Boston became a scene of utmost frenzy. "Nothing but hurry and confusion, every person striving to get out of this place," wrote an American merchant, John Rowe.

Deacon Timothy Newell, who, like John Rowe, was a patriotic American, had been forbidden, as a town selectman, to leave Boston. "This day," he wrote on March 6, "the utmost distress and anxiety among the refugees and associators [Loyalists]. . . . Blessed by God, our redemption draws near."

Howe, who had received no orders — no word of any kind — from London since

October, had no long-standing plan for a withdrawal of such magnitude, or any comparable past experience to draw upon. "I told General Howe," wrote James Grant, "that I had been in many scrapes but that I never was in so thick a wood with all the branches [like] thorns, but that we must look forward and get out."

It was not just that there were thousands of troops and military stores to transport, but the hundreds of women and children who were with the army. Further, Howe intended to take every Loyalist who chose to go.

The necessary care of the women, sick, and wounded required every assistance that could be given [one man wrote]. It was not like the breaking up of a camp, where every man knows his duty. It was like departing your country, with your wives, your servants, your household furniture, and all your encumbrances.

It seemed everyone had his own dire needs or urgent special request, someone or something to complain about, someone or something to blame for his plight.

There were a sufficient number of transports and other ships at hand, but these all had to be supplied with provisions and water. Equipment of all kinds had to be put aboard. In the meantime, there was very little to eat. Continued storms at sea had prevented nearly all supply ships from even approaching the coast. When a single sloop from the West Indies did make it into the harbor, it was learned that more than seventy food transports, "victualers," and store ships that had been blown off course that winter were tied up and refitting at Antigua. According to some rumors, there was not enough food left in Boston to last three weeks.

High winds kept blowing, churning the harbor, and the rebel guns remained silent. But while the rebels held their fire, they could be seen in plain view on Dorchester Heights, steadily strengthening their position.

All was still comparatively quiet on Friday, March 8, when Deacon Newell and three other selectmen crossed the lines at the Neck under a white flag carrying an unsigned paper stating that General Howe had "no intention of destroying the town, unless the troops under his command are molested during the embarkation." Though clearly intended for Washington, this declaration was not addressed to him, and so it was given no reply. But the word had been passed — if allowed to depart peacefully, the British would spare the town.

Then, the night of March 9, when the rebels were seen moving on to Nook's Hill on Dorchester, a high point of land only a quarter of a mile from the British lines at the Neck, Howe ordered a thunderous all-night bombardment. "Such a firing was never before heard in New England," wrote Isaac Bangs. Four men were killed by a single ball. But that was the only damage done. The next day the men on the hill gathered up 700 cannonballs that had been fired at them.

In town the pell-mell rush and confusion grew worse. The "cathartic" was drastic, as Loyalist Peter Oliver observed. Hogsheads of sugar and salt, barrels of flour for which there was no room on the ships, were being dumped into the harbor, along with smashed-up furniture, wagons, wheelbarrows, even the commander's elegant coach. Cannon for which there was no room were spiked or dumped in the harbor.

Americans watching from a dozen hillsides and promontories around the town could see, as Washington wrote, streets full of "great movements and confusion among the troops night and day . . . in hurrying down their cannon, artillery, and other stores to the wharves with utmost precipitation." Washington was convinced that Howe was making ready to sail for New York.

The alarm and anxiety among the Loyalists was extreme. Leave they must, but no one knew how many there were, or whether there would be room for all, or where they were heading. Not until the morning of March 10 were they told they could begin coming aboard. There was no time for deliberation. Virtually all they owned would have to be left behind.

Those who were already refugees — those who had earlier fled Cambridge, Roxbury, or Milton for the presumed safety of Boston — knew what it was to abandon everything and find themselves dependent on charity. Now Bostonians, too, faced the prospect of forsaking life-long associations and treasured belongings — indeed, their very homeland and entire way of life.

"It is not easy to paint the distress and confusion of the inhabitants on the occasion. I had but six or seven hours allowed to prepare for this measure, being obliged to embark the same day," wrote the Reverend Henry Caner.

As rector of King's Chapel, the first Anglican church in Boston, the Reverend Caner was the leading Church of England clergyman in Massachusetts and a greatly respected figure among all denominations. He had been rector for nearly thirty years and lived alone in a small frame house close to King's Chapel, at the corner of School and Tremont streets. In his account of "goods left in my house at Boston, March 10, 1776," he listed, among other items: "a handsome clock," two mahogany tables, teacups and saucers, "one rich carved mahogany desk and book case [with] glass doors," pictures of the King and Queen "under glass with rich frames," a pair of brass andirons, "a fine harpsichord," 1,000 books, a barn and "appurtenances," a cow and a calf.

The great majority of the Loyalists had never lived anywhere else, or ever expected to live anywhere else. They were disillusioned, disoriented, and not a little resentful. In their allegiance to the King and to the rule of law, they saw themselves as the true American patriots. They had wanted no part of the rebellion — "the horrid crime of rebellion" Justice Oliver called it — and had trusted, not unrealistically, in the wealth and power of the British nation to protect them and put a quick end to what, by their lights, had become mob rule.

A Boston merchant named Theophilus Lillie, who owned a store on Middle Street specializing in English dry goods and groceries, had expressed his views in print in the aftermath of the mob assault on British soldiers that erupted into the Boston Massacre.

Upon the whole, I cannot help saying — although I have never entered into the mysteries of government, having applied myself to my shop and my business — that it always seemed strange to me that people who contend so much for civil and religious liberty should be so ready to deprive others of their natural liberty. . . .

If one set of private subjects may at any time take upon themselves to punish another set of private subjects just when they please, it's such a sort of government as I never heard of before; and according to my poor notion of government, this is one of the principal things which government is designed to prevent.

Dr. Sylvester Gardiner, one of the best-known men in town, would write to a son-in-law:

I found I could not stay in Boston and trust my person with a set of lawless rebels whose actions have disgraced human nature and who have treated all the King's loyal subjects that have fallen in their hands with great cruelty and for no other crime than for their loyalty to the best of Kings and a peaceable submission to the best constituted government on earth. I don't believe there ever was a people in any age or part of the world that enjoyed so much liberty as the people of America did under the mild indulgent government (God bless it) of England and never was a people under a worser state of tyranny than we are at present.

It was said the fleet was bound for Halifax in Nova Scotia, but no one could say for certain. And who knew, in any event, what miseries lay in store for them at sea? Many who wanted desperately to escape had "families they were loath should be separated." Many who chose to stay did so knowing they could expect "ill-usage" at the hands of the rebels.

Conspicuous among those who began crowding the wharves, and who took their turns going aboard the ships on March 10 and in the days that followed, were many who had once figured prominently in the government of the province and in its professional and commercial life. There were leading churchmen like Henry Caner, jurists like Peter Oliver, physicians, educators, and successful merchants. The elderly Nathaniel Perkins was Boston's foremost physician. John Lovell was headmaster of the Boston Latin School. Attorney James Putnam of Worcester had been John Adams's mentor in the law. Foster Hutchinson, jurist and merchant, was the brother of the former royal governor of Massachusetts, Thomas Hutchinson. General Timothy Ruggles, a veteran of the French and Indian War, was a wealthy landowner and outspoken Tory who had been put in command of three companies of Loyal American Associators, as they were known, who had helped patrol the streets during the siege. John Murray and Harrison Gray were prosperous merchants.

A score or more were Harvard graduates, and many were fourth- or fifth-generation Americans bearing some of the oldest names in the province, such as Coffin and Chandler. Benjamin Faneuil, who was departing with a family of three, was the nephew of wealthy Peter Faneuil, whose many benefactions to Boston had included Faneuil Hall.

These were people of wealth and position among the conservative element of Massachusetts, people of distinction by and large, as well as power. But prominent though they were, they were not the majority of those departing with the fleet. Ultimately, 1,100 Loyalists went aboard the ships, and the greater part were from every walk of life — shopkeepers, clerks, minor customs officials, artisans and tradesmen, and their families. According to one study, 382 heads of families were farmers, mechanics, and ordinary tradesmen. William MacAlpine, printer and bookbinder, declared his "first and chief objective was to convey his wife in safety to Scotland."

Among the women listed as heads of families was Hannah Flucker, the mother of Henry Knox's wife Lucy, with a household of six. (Thomas Flucker, Lucy's father, appears to have departed earlier.) Margaret Draper, who joined the exodus with a family of five, had continued to publish the Loyalist newspaper the *Massa-*

chusetts Gazette and Boston Newsletter, after her husband's death in 1774. It was the only newspaper available in Boston during the siege.

Also listed was Dorcas Griffith, who ran a notorious waterfront grog shop and was known to be John Hancock's "discarded" mistress.

Joshua Loring, Jr., was another of those departing, along with the rebel prisoners he was charged with looking after. But his handsome wife Elizabeth is not accounted for, suggesting she may have been provided with more comfortable accommodations aboard the flagship *Chatham* with General Howe.

Many of the crowd were elderly — the Reverend Caner and Dr. Perkins were in their seventies — and many more were children or infants. William Hill, a baker who had supplied bread for the British troops, went aboard with a family of seventeen.

Accommodations on the crowded transports and other ships were wretched. Foster Hutchinson and his large family were assigned to steerage. Wealthy Benjamin Hallowell found himself sharing a cabin with thirty-six others, "men, women, and children, parents, masters, mistresses, obliged to pig together on the floor, there being no berths," until they left the harbor.

Appraising the situation, the royal governor of New Hampshire, John Wentworth, hired a schooner to sail with the fleet and packed fifty people on board.

In the next few days the ships with Loyalists began falling down the harbor with the tide as far as King's Road, below Castle Island, to anchor out of range of the rebel cannon and to provide space for other vessels to tie up at the wharves. And there the exiles sat, rocking with the tide, day after day.

On March 10, Howe had issued a proclamation ordering inhabitants to give up all linen and woolen goods that could be of use to the enemy, and assigned a man named Crean Brush, one of a Loyalist corps, to see that the order was carried out.

Sir [Brush's official commission read]: I am informed there are large quantities of goods in the town of Boston, which, if in the possession of the rebels, would enable them to carry on the war. And, whereas I have given notice to all loyal inhabitants to remove such goods from hence, and all who do not remove them, or deliver them to your care, will be considered abettors of the rebels, you are hereby authorized and required to take into your possession all such goods as answer this description, and to give certificates to the owners that you have received them for their use, and will deliver them to the owners' order, unavoidable accidents excepted. And you are to make inquiry if any such goods be secreted in stores, and you are to seize all such.

In effect, Brush (remembered later as "a conceited New York Tory") was authorized to take whatever he wanted in return for worthless certificates. And once he and his men began plundering the town, gangs with axes, drunken soldiers and sailors rampaged in the streets, breaking open houses and shops at will. "There never was such destruction and outrage committed any day before this," wrote merchant John Rowe. On a visit to Rowe's wharf and warehouse, Brush and his men made off with goods worth more than 2,000 pounds.

"Soldiers and sailors plundering," wrote Deacon Newell on March 13. "Same as above," he recorded the next day.

On March 15, Newell and the other selectmen were summoned to the Province House and told the army would embark that day and that it would be wise for all remaining citizens to stay in their houses. If there were any interference with the King's troops, Howe warned, he would burn the town. But the wind proved "unfavorable" for departure.

Not until Sunday, March 17, St. Patrick's Day, did the wind turn fair and favorable.

The troops began moving out at four in the morning, more than 8,000 redcoats marching through the dark, narrow streets of Boston, as if on parade. By seven the sun was up and ships thronged at the wharves began lifting sail. By nine o'clock all were under way.

"Fine weather and fair wind," wrote Major Stephen Kemble, a Loyalist serving with the British. "The finest day in the world," wrote an exuberant Archibald Robertson.

It was a spectacle such as could only have been imagined until that morning. There were 120 ships departing with more than 11,000 people packed on board — 8,906 King's troops, 667 women and 553 children, and in addition, waiting down the harbor, were 1,100 Loyalists.

"In the course of the forenoon," wrote James Thacher, "we enjoyed the unspeakable satisfaction of beholding their whole fleet under sail, wafting from our shores the dreadful scourge of war." People on shore were cheering, weeping. "Surely it is the Lord's doings and it is marvelous in our eyes," wrote Abigail Adams.

But then the whole fleet came to anchor at King's Road and with the arrival of General Howe's flagship, *Chatham*, every ship-of-war fired a roaring 21-gun salute, and the full 50 guns of the *Chatham* answered in kind — an ear-splitting reminder of royal might.

The first cheers from the American lines had been heard as early as nine that morning, when the men on Prospect Hill and Dorchester Heights saw clearly what was happening. In no time small boys came running across the Neck from Boston to deliver the news that the "lobster backs" were gone at last.

Puzzled that British troops appeared still to be manning the fortifications on Bunker Hill, even as the fleet was getting under way, General Sullivan mounted his horse and cantered off for a closer look, only to discover that they were hay dummies set up by the fleeing redcoats.

It was early afternoon when the first troops from Roxbury — 500 men who had already had smallpox and were thus immune — crossed the Neck and marched into Boston, drums beating, flags flying, and led by Artemus Ward on horseback.

By all rights, it should have been Washington who made the triumphal entry, but in a characteristically gracious gesture he gave the honor to Ward, the "thorough New England man" who had been his predecessor as commander and the first and most persistent in favoring a move on Dorchester Heights — though how much this may have figured in Washington's decision is impossible to know.

Washington remained at Cambridge where he attended Sunday services conducted by the chaplain of Knox's artillery regiment, the Reverend Abiel Leonard of Connecticut, who chose for his text Exodus 14:25: "And they took off their chariot wheels, that they drove them heavily; so that the Egyptians said, Let us flee from the face of Israel; for the Lord fighteth for them against the Egyptians."

Washington rode into Boston the following day, Monday, March 18, and took a close look at the place for the first time, after eight and a half months of studying it through the lenses of his telescope almost every day in every kind of light and from every possible angle. He came without fanfare. His purpose, as he reported to Congress, was to appraise the damage done and see what the enemy had left behind.

The town, although it had "suffered greatly," was not in as bad shape as he had expected, he wrote to John Hancock, "and I have a particular pleasure in being able to inform you, sir, that your house has received no damage worth mentioning." Other fine houses had been much abused by the British, windows broken, furnishings smashed or stolen, books destroyed. But at Hancock's Beacon Hill mansion all was in order, as General Sullivan also attested, and there was a certain irony in this, since the house had been occupied and maintained by the belligerent General James Grant, who had wanted to lay waste to every town on the New England coast. "Though I believe," wrote Sullivan, "the brave general had made free with some of the articles in the [wine] cellar."

The last desperate efforts of the British to destroy whatever could be of use to the

Americans were in evidence everywhere — spiked cannon, shattered gun carriages and wagons. Ships left behind at the waterfront had been scuttled, their masts cut away. And as Dr. Thacher noted with concern, smallpox was "lurking" still in several parts of town.

But the surprise for Washington was how much had not been destroyed or carried off, so great had been the chaos and rush of the enemy in the last days. An inventory of British goods compiled by Thomas Mifflin, now the quartermaster general, listed 5,000 bushels of wheat at the Hancock wharf, 1,000 bushels of beans and 10 tons of hay at the town granary, 35,000 feet of good planks at one of the lumberyards. There were more than a hundred horses left by the British. Indeed, there was nearly everything that was needed but beef, gunpowder, and hard money. Washington estimated the total value at perhaps 40,000 pounds, but after further examination that figure would be raised to 50,000 pounds.

The other surprise was the strength of the enemy's defenses. The town was "amazingly strong . . . almost impregnable, every avenue fortified," he wrote. But if this gave rise to any second thoughts about his repeated desire to send men against such defenses, or the wisdom of his council of war in restraining him, Washington kept such thoughts to himself.

Just as he had shown no signs of despair when prospects looked bleak, he now showed no elation in what he wrote or in his outward manner or comments.

On March 20, Washington put Nathanael Greene temporarily in command of the town, while he returned to Cambridge to concentrate on his next move. Certain that Howe intended to sail for New York, he had already sent five regiments in that direction. But with the British fleet still hovering below Castle Island, he dared not send more, and worried now that Howe's withdrawal might be a trick, that the plan was to come ashore somewhere near Braintree and double back to outflank Dorchester and Roxbury.

On the night of March 20, Boston and the whole south shore were rocked by a tremendous explosion when British engineers Montresor and Robertson blew up Castle William. The morning after, in heavy snowfall, Howe's fleet dropped still further down from the town, to anchor in Nantasket Road off Braintree.

Those on board the ships were as puzzled by Howe's intentions as anyone. "We do not know where we are going, but are in great distress," one Loyalist wrote. They had been cooped up now in the harbor for nearly two weeks. One man, wracked with despair, threw himself overboard and was drowned. But to most on board, any destination would be welcome after what they had been through. "You know the proverbial expression, 'neither hell, hull nor Halifax' can afford worse shelter than Boston," wrote an officer in description of the prevailing mood.

At last, on March 27, ten days after the evacuation of Boston, the fleet was again under way, and this time heading for the open sea. When several Loyalists gathered at the rail of one of the ships expressed confidence that they would be returning soon in triumph, a prominent Boston merchant, George Erving, turned and said solemnly, "Gentlemen, not one of you will ever see that place again," words long remembered by the five-year-old son who stood beside him.

Merchant Erving had sided with the Loyalists primarily because he thought the rebellion would fail. But the success of Washington's army at Boston had changed his mind, as it had for many.

By day's end the fleet had disappeared over the horizon, bound not for New York but for Halifax.

IV

Fast riders carried the news to Providence and Newport, Hartford and New Haven, New York, Philadelphia, then on to Maryland, Virginia, the Carolinas, and Georgia, 1,100 arduous miles from Boston. For all who believed in the American cause, it was the first thrilling news of the war.

"The joy of our friends in Boston, on seeing the victorious and gallant troops of their country enter the town almost on the heels of their barbarous oppressors was inexplicably great," reported the *New Haven Journal.*

"The British," said the *New York Constitutional Gazette*, "were completely disgraced."

Free men under arms had triumphed, with all the world watching, and in the "admirable and beloved" Washington, the country had a hero, as the citizens of Philadelphia and members of Congress read in the *Evening Post* of March 30:

To the wisdom, firmness, intrepidity,

and military abilities of our admirable and beloved general, his Excellency George Washington, Esq.; to the assiduity, skill, and bravery of our other worthy generals and officers of the army; and to the hardiness and gallantry of the soldiery, is to be ascribed, under God, the glory and success of our arms, in driving from one of the strongest holds in America, so considerable a part of the British army.

Congress ordered a gold medal struck in Washington's honor. "The disinterested and patriotic principles which led you to the field have also led you to glory," read a formal letter of gratitude.

Those pages in the annals of America will record your title to be a conspicuous place in the temple of fame, which shall inform posterity, that under your directions, an undisciplined band of husbandmen, in the course of a few months, became soldiers.

"What an occurrence is this to be known in Europe?" wrote Elbridge Gerry of the Massachusetts delegation in Congress. "How are Parliamentary pretensions to be reconciled to facts?" What was especially wondrous was that the British had been driven from Boston by only "about the thirtieth part of the power of America."

It would be six weeks before the news reached London, and on May 6, a storm of criticism and recrimination erupted in Parliament, led by the same ardent Whigs whose real power was no more than it had ever been. In the House of Commons, Colonel Isaac Barre, Lord Cavendish, and Edmund Burke spoke severely against the administration, as Lord North and Lord Germain defended the management of the war.

In the House of Lords, in defense of the ministry, the Earl of Suffolk patiently and correctly explained that abandoning Boston had been the established policy since the previous October.

"Let this transaction be dressed in what garb you please," answered the Duke of Manchester, "the fact remains that the army which was sent to reduce the province of Massachusetts Bay has been driven from the capital, and that the standard of the provincial army now waves in triumph over the walls of Boston."

At the headquarters in Cambridge, the Boston selectmen and a delegation from the legislature of Massachusetts came to offer their gratitude to Washington for saving the town "with so little effusion of human blood," and to shower him with praise. Harvard, in the spirit of the moment, conferred an honorary degree on the man who had had almost no formal schooling.

Responding to such tributes, Washington was duly modest and gracious, and in truth they meant more than he showed. He was happy to "hear from different quarters that my reputation stands fair," he wrote privately to his brother. He hoped it would be remembered also that none of what happened had come easily or predictably.

We have maintained our ground against the enemy under [a] . . . want of powder, and we have disbanded one army and recruited another within musket shot of two and twenty regiments, the flower of the British army, when our strength has been little if any superior to theirs, and at last have beat them in a shameful and precipitate manner, out of a place the strongest by nature on this continent, strengthened and fortified in the best manner and at an enormous expense.

He was proud of the part he had played and wanted to say something about that, at least to his brother, and about the misconceptions he had been obliged to maintain.

I believe I may, with great truth, affirm that no man perhaps since the first institution of armies ever commanded one under more difficult circumstances than I have done. . . . Many of my difficulties and distresses were of so peculiar a cast that in order to conceal them from the enemy, I was obliged to conceal them from my friends, indeed from my own army, thereby subjecting my conduct to interpretations unfavorable to my character.

An attack by Howe on Dorchester Heights had been his "utmost wish," and he could "scarce forbear lamenting the disappointment" he felt. Like others, he attributed the storm of March 5 to the intervening hand of God. He did not "lament or repine at any act of Providence," he told Joseph Reed, for "in great measure" he had become a convert to the view of the poet Alexander Pope that "whatever is, is right."

For the Loyalists who had fled with the

enemy, he had only contempt. "Unhappy wretches! Deluded mortals!" he called them. He had heard of some committing suicide and thought it would be well if more did the same. "By all accounts a more miserable set of beings does not exist."

But then he had little time to dwell on such matters. "I am hurried in dispatching one brigade after another for New York and preparing for my own departure," he informed Reed.

The siege had been the stunning success it was proclaimed, and Washington's performance had been truly exceptional. He had indeed bested Howe and his regulars, and despite insufficient arms and ammunition, insufficient shelter, sickness, inexperienced officers, lack of discipline, clothing, and money. His patience with Congress had been exemplary, and while he had been saved repeatedly by his council of war from his headlong determination to attack, and thus from almost certain catastrophe, he had accepted the judgment of the council with no ill temper or self-serving histrionics.

He had kept his head, kept his health and his strength, bearing up under a weight of work and worry that only a few could have carried.

Having struggled with his festering dislike of New Englanders, he had proven a keen judge of character and ability and pinned his hopes on such untried born-and-bred Yankees as Greene and Knox. Without Knox, there would have been no triumph at Dorchester Heights. Henry Knox, in sum, had saved the day. And while Nathanael Greene had not played so spectacular a part as Knox, the troops under his command were distinguished as the best disciplined in the army, and he himself had emerged as Washington's ideal lieutenant. In Greene and Knox, Washington had found the best men possible, men of ability and energy who, like Washington, would never lose sight of what the war was about, no matter what was to come. All important, too, was the devotion and loyalty these two young officers felt for Washington.

After the "miracle" of Dorchester Heights, Washington was never again to speak ill of New Englanders because they were New Englanders.

He had no illusions about the gravity of what lay ahead. Nor did many of the wisest heads in Congress. The humiliation the

British had been subjected to, John Hancock warned Washington, could well make them an even more formidable foe.

> What may be their views, it is indeed impossible to tell, with any degree of exactness [Hancock wrote]. We have all the reason, however, from the rage of disappointment and revenge, to expect the worst. Nor have I any doubt, that as far as their power extends, they will inflict every species of calamity upon us.

But great political change was in the offing, Washington sensed, as he confided to Joseph Reed in one of the last letters written from his Cambridge headquarters. This he attributed in good part to the pamphlet *Common Sense*, published earlier in the year, the author of which, Thomas Paine, was as yet unknown.

> My countrymen, I know from their form of government and steady attachment heretofore to royalty, will come reluctantly into the idea of independency [Washington wrote], but time and persecution brings many wonderful things to pass, and by private letters which I have lately received from Vir-

ginia, I find *Common Sense* is working a powerful change there in the minds of many men.

"The sun never shined on a cause of greater worth," Paine had written. "Everything that is right or reasonable pleads for separation."

One after another the regiments were departing for New York. An army that had moved not at all for nearly a year was on the march, leaving New England for the first time.

The huge bastions that encircled Boston were left standing, but only a holding force under General Ward remained to keep watch.

To most of the men the prospect of being on the move was extremely welcome. Spirits were higher than they had ever been. The soldier's life, many decided, had much to be said for it after all.

Most of those in the ranks had no idea where they were bound, but were glad to be going. One soldier, John Lapham of Duxbury, wrote to his "Honored Parents" to send a pair of shoes as quickly as possible, "for I expect that I shall march off soon, but whither we shall go I do not

222

know nor can I tell."

Generals Heath and Sullivan and their forces had already departed. General Greene and five regiments followed on April 1. Three days later, on Thursday, April 4, Washington rode off from Cambridge.

Part II

Fateful Summer

The fate of unborn millions will now depend, under God, on the courage and conduct of this army.
— General George Washington
July 2, 1776

Chapter Four

THE LINES ARE DRAWN

I would not be understood that I should choose to march, but as I am engaged in this glorious cause, I am will[ing] to go where I am called.
— Lieutenant Joseph Hodgkins

I

For two weeks and more, the army was on the move, its long, irregular columns winding through the untroubled countryside of lower Massachusetts, Rhode Island, and Connecticut, where open fields and low-lying wooded hills were only now showing the first faint signs of spring.

In scores of market towns and crossroad hamlets the local citizenry came out to cheer and offer food and drink, or just to stand at gateposts and kitchen doorways taking in the spectacle of so many of their countrymen armed and on the march, whole regiments passing for hours at a time. Large armies — large armies of any kind — were an unfamiliar sight to Americans. No army of such size as this had ever been seen before anywhere in the colonies.

And the army was stepping along "with great expedition," as General Heath wrote, with high-ranking uniformed officers like Heath on horseback, stragglers and trains of heavy baggage wagons struggling to keep up. Hurry was the order of the day, every day. He must "hasten his march" to New York, Nathanael Greene had been instructed by Washington. Henry Knox and his artillery were to move "as speedily as possible" by "the directest road thither." Several times Washington referred to his own "extreme hurry."

On April 5, the day the commander paraded into Providence, it seemed all Rhode Island had come to catch sight of him. Two of Greene's regiments served as escort (none were to turn out "except those dressed in uniforms," all "washed, both face and hands clean, their beards shaved, their hair combed and powdered"). At an elegant banquet provided by the "gentlemen of the town" at Hackers Hall, Washington was feted and toasted befitting a national hero.

But at first light the next day he was on his way again, with no time to spare.

John Greenwood, the fifer, would remember everyone moving "at great speed." A five- or six-mile march before breakfast was usual, fifteen to twenty miles a day about average, however seasonably wet and unpredictable the weather or miserable the roads, which, with the frost still coming out of the ground, could be slick with mud even on fair days.

On days of "wet weather" and "very bad traveling," recorded a soldier named Solomon Nash marching with a Massachusetts artillery company, they made only ten to fourteen miles, while moving ten brass field pieces.

Marching did not trouble him anything like he had expected, Lieutenant Joseph Hodgkins wrote to his Sarah after a few days on the road.

> I am willing to serve my country in the best way and manner that I am capable of, and as our enemy are gone from us, I expect I must follow them. . . . I would not be understood that I should choose to march, but as I am engaged in this glorious cause, I am will[ing] to go where I am called.

He had vowed to "march with cheerfulness," and plainly the spirits of the whole army were greatly improved by being on the move and by the warm reception along the way.

"I am a good deal tired of marching," he confessed after crossing into Connecticut, "though we get very good entertainment [hospitality] in general. People are very kind to us." Like the majority of Massachusetts men, Hodgkins had never been so far from home.

Most of the regiments marched only as far as New London. From there they were to proceed by water down Long Island Sound, keeping close to the Connecticut shore to avoid enemy cruisers. But with movement of any kind subject always to the elements — and never more than by water — precious days were lost waiting for favorable winds. Or at great risk ships embarked in the teeth of foul weather. On April 11, Nathanael Greene and his brigade pushed off in a blinding snow squall. Four days later, with still no word from them, Washington, who was by then in New York, reported to Congress that he feared for their lives. As it was, Greene and his men did not reach New York until April 17.

By whatever means they traveled, all seemed to understand what lay ahead. They were going to meet the enemy on the field of battle for the first time. They were headed for "troble," as Hodgkins wrote.

No one knew how many British there might be, yet few let that bother them. An enthusiastic new recruit in the Connecticut ranks, a farm boy named Joseph Plumb Martin, would recall, "I never spent a thought about numbers. The Americans were invincible in my opinion."

As another soldier remembered, there was scarcely a militia man who did not think himself equal to two or three of the British.

Appraising the situation from his new headquarters at No. 1 Broadway, a magnificent town house just back from the Battery at the southernmost tip of New York, Washington had no illusions about the difficulties to be faced. He was gravely, realistically apprehensive about the magnitude of the enemy force en route. He fretted over when their ships might appear, and how, with no naval strength, to defend a city bounded by navigable rivers on two sides and a harbor of a size sufficient to accommodate the largest fleet imaginable.

New York was not at all like Boston, geographically, strategically, and in other ways. At Boston, Washington had known exactly where the enemy was, and who they were, and what was needed to contain them. At Boston the British had been largely at his mercy, and especially once winter set in. Here, with their overwhelming naval might and absolute control of the waters, they could strike at will and from almost any direction. The time and place of battle would be entirely their choice, and this was the worry overriding all others.

General Lee, after appraising the situation in February, had been extremely dubious. "What to do with the city? I own [it] puzzles me. It is so encircled with deep navigable water that whoever commands the sea must command the town," he had succinctly summed up the situation.

Washington, however, expressed no such misgivings. He would later tell Congress he had not a doubt that he could defend the city, and he was eager to do so, for all his anxieties. New York had "vast importance," he wrote, because control of its harbor could mean control of the Hudson River and thus the whole Hudson–Lake Champlain corridor north to Canada, which if seized by the enemy could isolate

New England from the other colonies — which, in fact, was exactly the British intention.

But the decision to make a stand at New York was based more on Washington's political judgment than on military strategy. It was his political sense that Congress and the patriots of New York expected every effort to be made to hold the city, and that anything less would have devastating political effect on the people at large and thus on the American cause, which Washington fervently hoped would soon become the cause of American independence.

Possibly he had discussed the subject of New York with members of Congress the previous year, before leaving to take command at Cambridge. And John Adams's letter of January 6, describing New York as "a kind of key to the whole continent" and affirming that "no effort to secure it ought to be omitted," was anything but ambiguous.

Still, Congress had issued no specific directive to defend the city. The decision was Washington's alone and he promised unequivocally "to exert myself to the utmost to frustrate the designs of the enemy."

At Boston, where the comparatively few Loyalists of Massachusetts had either fled the country or were bottled up with the British, there had never been a serious threat from "internal foes," in Washington's phrase. (The spy Benjamin Church had turned out to be an aberration.) In New York the atmosphere was entirely different. The city remained divided and tense. Loyalist, or Tory, sentiment, while less conspicuous than it had been, was widespread and ranged from the militant to the disaffected to those hesitant about declaring themselves patriots for a variety of reasons, trade and commerce not being the least of them.

Two-thirds of the property in New York belonged to Tories. The year before, in 1775, more than half the New York Chamber of Commerce were avowed Loyalists. When on a Sunday in January 1776 a prominent pastor, the Reverend John Rodgers, preached an impassioned sermon from the pulpit of the Presbyterian Church on Wall Street, exhorting young men to be brave and fight for the cause of their country, he was himself being notably brave in speaking out. "We are involved in the calamities of a civil war," he had said, and so it felt in New York.

The city and Long Island would provide Washington with five regiments by summer and they would be led by officers bearing prominent names — Livingston, Fish, Roosevelt, Remsen, and Cowenhoven, among others — but the numbers of Loyalists still in the city were considerable, and they included men and women from all levels of society.

Across the East River on Long Island, in the villages and the rich outlying farmlands, where the population was still mostly Dutch, Loyalists were a decided majority. Staten Island, at the far end of the harbor, or the Upper Bay, was another Loyalist stronghold. Thus the potential for conspiracy, sabotage, or organized armed resistance was all too real. At the moment, armed Loyalist bands were in hiding in the swamps of Long Island, awaiting the chance to take action.

For months British warships, including the 64-gun *Asia*, had been a formidable presence, anchored in the Upper Bay, reminders that the city was entirely at their mercy. It was only on April 8, just a week before Washington's arrival, that the *Asia* and its entourage withdrew to the outer approaches to the harbor beyond the Narrows, the water passage between Long Island and Staten Island. On board the King's ship *Duchess of Gordon*, William

Tryon, a seasoned soldier-politician who was the royal governor of New York, maintained a headquarters and was believed to be secretly directing Loyalist operations.

At Boston, Washington had benefited greatly from a steady supply of valuable intelligence coming out of the besieged town, while Howe had known little or nothing of Washington's strengths or intentions. Here, with so much of the population still loyal to the king, the situation was the reverse.

Washington's New England army was intact, to be sure — exhausted from its march, as he reported to Congress, but intact and in place. In addition, new battalions had arrived from Connecticut, New Jersey, and Pennsylvania, and still more were expected from Maryland and Delaware. All were urgently needed, but they also compounded the threat of regional animosity and discord, which Washington still feared might tear the army and the country apart. "We have nothing, my dear sir, to depend upon, but the protection of a kind Providence and unanimity among ourselves," he wrote to John Adams from his Broadway headquarters.

Furthermore, as he knew, discipline was hardly improved, and too many of the new troops were raw recruits as unruly as those of the summer before. Some who were lauded as shining examples of patriotism looked hardly fit for battle, like the Connecticut unit comprised entirely of "aged gentlemen."

When they were ordered to New York [reads an old account] this company was the first that reached the place of rendezvous. They were twenty-four in number; and their united ages reached one thousand. They were all married men, and left behind a hundred and fifty-nine children and grandchildren.

Nor did the look and manner of Washington's New England troops necessarily inspire confidence among those from other colonies. In the stilted phrasing of a young captain from Pennsylvania, Alexander Graydon, "The appearance of things was not much calculated to excite sanguine expectations in the mind of the sober observer." To Graydon, who in what he wrote did little to conceal his feelings of superiority, the Yankees were a "miserably constituted," "unwarlike" lot who did "not entirely come up to the ideas we had formed of the heroes of Lexington and

Bunker Hill." Most officers were still indistinguishable from their men. Deportment seemed altogether absent.

Not until the arrival of the men from Marblehead under Colonel John Glover did Captain Graydon see any New England troops that met his approval. "But even in this regiment," he noted, "there were a number of Negroes, which to persons unaccustomed to such associations had a disagreeable, degrading effect."

One further large and important difference between New York and the experience at Boston was also clear: this time there would be little call for councils of war to decide whether or not to fight.

Washington had arrived in the city with no ceremony at midday, Saturday, April 13, and went directly to work at the Broadway headquarters. Some days later, after Martha Washington arrived, they would establish a country residence at a beautiful estate overlooking the Hudson River, the Abraham Mortier house (later known as Richmond Hill) two miles north, beyond the city limits.

But No. 1 Broadway remained the commander's base of operations. Known also as the Kennedy Mansion, it was a famous

New York landmark. It had been built a generation earlier by a Scottish immigrant and successful New York land speculator named Archibald Kennedy and had remained the home of a son, Captain Archibald Kennedy of the Royal Navy, until his recent departure for England. The house fronted on Bowling Green and was considered the height of elegance, with a grand stairway, a banquet hall, and a parlor fifty feet long. A garden to the rear reached down to the shore of the Hudson and from a rooftop platform and cupola, one could see for miles in every direction.

As at Cambridge, Washington insisted on having his military "family" in residence with him and thus on duty all the time.

Unfamiliar with the terrain, Washington set about inspecting the fortifications begun earlier by General Lee, works that had been subsequently carried on under General William Alexander of New Jersey, better known as Lord Stirling, after Congress sent Lee to take command in South Carolina. Lord Stirling was a rich, socially prominent, hard-driving, hard-drinking patriot who at age fifty-eight looked the part of commander and claimed his title as a Scottish earl through his father. The claim was questionable, but sincere on his part and generally accepted by his fellow officers and the troops he led. Washington thought well of him and with good reason.

Lee and Stirling had had too little time and too few troops to do the job. Men of the town had been pressed into labor, including large numbers of slaves, but this was hardly enough. "It will require at least eight thousand men to put this place in any posture of defense," Stirling had stressed.

Washington found the defenses only about half done, and even with the troops he had, he knew more were needed. Crowding the streets of the city, the army seemed an overwhelming multitude. The soldiers themselves were emboldened by their numbers. But only half were fit for duty and Washington worried exceedingly over what the toll from disease would be with the return of warm weather, and from such dissipations as were now readily at hand. Washington had seen enough of New York on prior visits to dislike and distrust the city as the most sinful place in America, a not uncommon view.

Larger than Boston but smaller than Philadelphia, New York had a peacetime population of perhaps 20,000 people crowded into an area of less than a square mile, less than a tenth of the Island of Manhattan — or York Island, as it was then known — which from the Battery to its northern boundary at the Harlem River reached nearly eleven miles. That far larger stretch north of the city, known as the Outward, was a mix of woods, streams, marshes, and great rocky patches interspersed with a few small farms and large country estates, all the way to King's Bridge, where a narrow wooden bridge over the Harlem connected the island to the mainland.

Normally it was a city of thriving commerce, shipbuilding, and seagoing trade, and with much to see and talk about. "The inhabitants are in general brisk and lively," wrote one visitor. The women were "handsome," he recorded — as did others new to the city — though, he added, "it rather hurts a European eye to see so many Negro slaves upon the streets."

Broadway, straight and wide, was the grand thoroughfare lined with shade trees and fine houses and churches. Queen Street, close to the crowded East River wharves, was the bustling business center. City Hall stood on Wall Street, or "in" Wall Street, as people said.

Henry Knox, stopping at New York for the first time on his way to Ticonderoga in November, had admired the "principal streets much wider than ours" and brick houses "better built than in Boston." New Yorkers, however, were another matter, as he reported to his adored Lucy:

The people — why the people are magnificent: in their carriages, which are numerous, in their house furniture, which is fine, in their pride and conceit, which are inimitable, in their profaneness, which is intolerable, in the want of principle, which is prevalent, in their Toryism, which is insufferable.

But the city had greatly changed. It had become an armed camp, and thousands of people — perhaps a third of the population — had fled, fearing it was soon to be the scene of terrible calamity. One would "think the city almost evacuated," wrote a dispirited resident. Business was at a standstill.

Large numbers of troops were quartered in vacant buildings and many of the finest mansions. ("Oh, the houses of New York, if you could see the insides of them!" grieved another resident.) King's College, west of the Commons, one of the largest, handsomest buildings in town, had been taken over as an army hospital, once the library books were removed, lest the soldiers burn them for fuel.

For the troops from New England a roof overhead of any kind seemed the height of luxury, and New York, however changed, a center of wonders. Joseph Hodgkins decided, "This city York exceeds all places that ever I saw," though he found the living "excessive dear."

"They have all the simplicity of ploughmen," a New Yorker wrote of the Yankee soldiers. And according to one local paper, the *New York Packet*, they were unexpectedly well behaved, "their civility to the inhabitants very commendable." They attended prayers "evening and morning regularly," their officers setting the example, the paper noted. "On Lord's day they attend public worship twice, and their deportment in the house of God is such as becomes the place."

But an earnest young Presbyterian chaplain with the New Jersey troops, a graduate of the College of New Jersey at Princeton, Philip Vickers Fithian, found the level of piety alarmingly below his expectations and worried what the consequences might be to the American cause of so many of all ranks so habitually taking the name of the Lord in vain. "But alas, swearing abounds, all classes swear," he noted sadly.

Lieutenant Isaac Bangs of Massachusetts, who in his journal would provide one of the fullest accounts of unfolding events that spring and summer, wrote of his walking tours about town and such sights to be seen as the waterworks and the larger-than-life equestrian statue of King George III, which dominated Bowling Green in front of Washington's headquarters. "The design was in imitation of one of the Roman emperors," Bangs wrote. The King was represented "about a third larger than a natural man," and both horse and rider were "neatly constructed of lead [and] gilt with gold," and "raised on a pedestal of white marble" fifteen feet high.

With twenty or more churches of differing denominations to choose from (something unknown in Massachusetts), the lieutenant attended as many as possible — an "English" church (most likely Trinity Church on Broadway, which was Church of England), a Congregational meeting, a high Dutch church (probably Old Dutch Church on Garden Street), where only Dutch was spoken, and the city's one synagogue, Shearith Israel, on Mill Street. He liked the Dutch church best, he decided, preferring the priest's manifest piety to the "pomp" of the English church, though he understood not a word of the Dutch sermon. On a later Sunday he and a friend attended a Quaker meeting, but after sitting through two hours during which not a word was said, they happily repaired to a nearby tavern.

In his conscientious way, Bangs proceeded to investigate the darker side of city life that so worried his commander, embarking into the section called the Holy Ground, a foul slum and brothel district west of the Commons, much of which was owned by Trinity Church, hence the name. By some estimates as many as five hundred prostitutes plied their trade there. Robinson Street especially was notorious for its rough gin shops and bawdy houses. If there was trouble after dark in New York, it was nearly always in the Holy Ground.

Bangs, a Harvard graduate with training in medicine, had initiated his own tour of inspection out of concern for the health of his men — though also out of curiosity, as he conceded — and was appalled by what he saw.

"When I visited them [the prostitutes] at

first I thought nothing could exceed them for impudence and immodesty, but I found the more I was acquainted with them the more they excelled in their brutality." How any man could desire "intimate connection" with such "creatures" was more than he could comprehend. But so it was, and among officers and soldiers alike, "till the fatal disorder [syphilis] seized them."

On April 22, less than a week after the Continental Army moved into the city, all hell erupted in the Holy Ground. The mutilated bodies of two soldiers were found concealed in a brothel. One of the victims had been "castrated in a barbarous manner," as Bangs recorded. In furious retaliation, gangs of soldiers went on a rampage, tearing to pieces the building where the murders had taken place. Some days later, the remains of "an old whore" were discovered dumped in a privy, "so long dead that she was rotten," as Bangs also recorded.

Washington condemned all such "riotous behavior." Were it to happen again, the perpetrators would be subjected to the severest punishment. If they resisted arrest, they would be "treated as a common enemy," meaning they would be shot dead on the spot.

He ordered a curfew and warned that any soldier found "disguised with liquor" would be punished. Still, it seems, business was business and not to be intruded upon. "Every brutal gratification can be so easily indulged in this place," wrote William Tudor of Boston, Washington's judge advocate, to his fiancée, "that the army will be debauched here in a month more than in twelve at Cambridge."

The whores, the trulls, "these bitchfoxly, jades, hags, strums," as wrote another officer, Colonel Loammi Baldwin, continued "their employ which is become very lucrative." Baldwin, an apple grower from Massachusetts, was one of the officers dispatched to the Holy Ground with military patrols, under orders to deal only with drunken or unruly soldiers — "hell's work," as he said. Since almost no soldiers had uniforms, it was all but impossible to distinguish who among the drunks and brawlers were soldiers and who were not, in dark, shadowed streets lit only by dim oil lamps. Baldwin and his patrol broke up "knots of men and women" fighting, cursing, "crying 'Murder!' " and "hurried them off to the Provost dungeon by half dozens." Some were punished and some "got off clear — hell's work."

Meantime, the army was "growing sickly." Smallpox appeared and several soldiers died. Frightful rumors swept through the city, including one that the British had returned to Boston and taken Dorchester Heights. With more bad news from Canada, Washington was directed by Congress to send reinforcements. When approximately 3,000 men under General Sullivan departed by ship up the Hudson, Washington informed Congress he had to have at least 10,000 more.

Drill went on in the streets and on the Commons. Work on defenses continued under steadily increasing pressure.

General Lee, considered an expert on defense, had concluded that without command of the sea New York could not be held. Still, as he had said, it could be an "advantageous" battlefield. If the British were determined to take the city, they could be made to pay a heavy toll.

Crucial to Lee's plan was the defense of that part of Long Island directly across the East River and particularly the imposing river bluffs near the tiny hamlet called Brooklyn, which was also spelled Breucklyn, Brucklyn, Broucklyn, Brookland, or Brookline, and amounted to no more than seven or eight houses and an old Dutch church that stood in the middle of the Jamaica Road, the main road inland from the Brooklyn ferry landing.

From the New York side of the river, the village was out of sight, three-quarters of a mile back from the partly wooded "noble bluff" known as Columbia Heights or Brooklyn Heights. All one saw looking across from New York, as Washington frequently did, was the steep face of the bluff rising above the river and crowned now by the beginnings of Fort Stirling, and to the right, also on the brow of the bluff, the country house of Philip Livingston, a wealthy New York importer and delegate to the Continental Congress.

When finished, the large square bastion of Fort Stirling, mounting eight cannon, was expected to command the East River and New York just as Dorchester Heights commanded Boston and its harbor. From Brooklyn Heights one looked down on all of New York City, the harbor, the rivers, and the long, low hills of New Jersey beyond. It was one of the grandest panoramas to be seen on the entire Atlantic seaboard.

The East River, no river at all but a saltwater estuary nearly a mile wide, was famously difficult to navigate, with swift, contrary currents and tides of as much as six feet. Because of winds and tides, ferryboats to and from Brooklyn often had great difficulty. Even with three men pulling at the oars, crossing the river could take over an hour.

The Hudson, or North, River was greater still, more than two miles wide, and so, as Lee had acknowledged, impossible to keep closed to the enemy. But with batteries along the New York shore of the Hudson, the British might think twice before risking their valuable ships.

Washington agreed with the general outlines of the plan, including, most importantly, the premise that an effective defense of New York City would depend on the defense of Long Island. If New York was the key to the continent, then Long Island was the key to New York, and the key to the defense of Long Island was Brooklyn Heights. "For should the enemy take possession of N[ew] York when Long Island is in our hands," Lee had written to Washington, "they will find it almost impossible to subsist."

That New York or Long Island, or both, could be a trap, neither of them seems to have seriously considered, or at least acknowledged for the record.

Given the importance of Long Island, Washington put General Greene in command there, and by the first week of May, Greene and his men, with the addition of a Pennsylvania rifle company, were encamped at Brooklyn. In little time there were several thousand troops on Long Island — which seemed a great many, but were less than a third of those in and around New York — and their efforts began to show. As would be said, the experience at Boston had made them "veterans at least of the spade."

In addition to Fort Stirling, three more forts were under construction on the other, or eastern, side of the hamlet of Brooklyn, these intended as a defense of Fort Stirling and Brooklyn Heights. If the British were to come ashore on the broad beaches to the west, in the vicinity of the village of Gravesend — as was widely expected — and attack from the open plains to the south, this line of defense would check their drive for the river.

To the left was Fort Putnam, named for Rufus Putnam, who marked out most of the fortifications. In the middle was star-shaped Fort Greene, mounting six cannon and commanding the Jamaica Road. On the right was Fort Box, named for one of Greene's officers, Major Daniel Box.

Each of these bastions was to be surrounded with a broad ditch and all were to be connected by a line of entrenchments reaching a mile or more. With hundreds of axmen at work, trees were cut to give full sweep to the fire of the cannon, and along most of the line, pointed stakes — pickets — were driven into the ground. Farther still to the right, at an isolated point on the Upper Bay called Red Hook, a fifth defense, Fort Defiance, was being built. From Fort Putnam on the left to Fort Defiance on the right was nearly three miles.

As the days grew longer and steadily warmer, the hard labor continued with unrelenting determination. Any soldier caught leaving the works without proper liberty would do "constant duty" for a week, Greene warned. One Rhode Island officer riding herd on the men, Colonel Ezekiel Cornell, became known as "Old Snarl."

Greene himself was tireless in his efforts. Nothing escaped his notice. He was everywhere on horseback surveying the work, or scouting the lay of the land, making himself familiar with the whole terrain from

Brooklyn to Gravesend, and particularly the densely wooded ridge about a mile and a half to the south known as the Heights of Gowan, which ran like a natural defense between the forts and the broad flatlands to the south.

Earthworks and gun emplacements were also under way on little Governor's Island between the Heights and Red Hook, in the direct path of the entrance to the East River. "We have done a great deal," Washington could claim in early May. "Governor's Island has a large and strong work erected. . . . The point below (called Red Hook) has a small, but exceedingly strong barbette [mounted] battery — and several new works are constructed and many of them almost executed at other places."

Barricades were thrown up within the city itself. In the words of a surviving British intelligence report, "every street facing both North and East Rivers has wooden trunks made across ten feet thick filled with earth, in order to intercept any troops that may attempt a landing."

There were guns along the banks of the Hudson, heavy cannon at old Fort George by the Battery, and more at the Whitehall dock on the East River.

Henry Knox was proud to report that

120 cannon were in place in and about the city and this time ample ammunition was standing by. The one glaring problem was an acute shortage of artillerymen. Knowing how many soldiers in the ranks were without muskets or arms of any kind, Knox persuaded Washington to reassign five or six hundred of them to the artillery. Never mind that they were entirely inexperienced, almost any live body being preferable to nothing.

The daily labors of the artillerymen were hardly less wearisome than those of the troops digging trenches and throwing up earthworks, and potentially a great deal more dangerous, as the diary of the Massachusetts soldier Solomon Nash gives some suggestion.

MONDAY, MAY 13 . . . Fetched one 32 pounder from the fort and placed it to the eastward of the grand battery. . . . Employed in piling up shot.
THURSDAY, MAY 16 . . . Some of us employed . . . in firing our cannon with double charges in them to prove them and they all proved good but two. One of them split at the muzzle and the other at the grand battery burst all in pieces. One piece went 30 or 40 rods

[about 200 yards] and fell upon a house . . . through the roof and all the floors to the last one, which hurt the house very much, but hurt nobody.
WEDNESDAY, MAY 22 . . . Employed in making cartridges. . . .
FRIDAY, MAY 31 . . . Bigger part of our regiment employed in making cartridges. So ends this month.

In early June, Knox and Greene rode together to the rugged uppermost end of York Island to survey a craggy ridge 230 feet above the Hudson, the highest point on the island, as the site for still another major defense, and work soon commenced on what was to be called Fort Washington, intended to keep the British navy from coming up the river. Another fort, to be known as Fort Constitution, was also planned for the opposite side of the Hudson.

The friendship of Knox and Greene that had begun in Knox's Boston bookshop continued to grow, as the two officers found themselves increasingly important in the overall command and nearly always in agreement on matters of consequence. In their admiration of and loyalty to Washington, they were of one heart and both had begun helping Washington in his dealings with Congress.

Greene, in a letter stressing the urgent need for more troops, told John Adams, head of the Board of War, that if Congress were to provide support for those soldiers maimed or killed that this in itself would increase enlistments and "inspire those engaged with as much courage as any measure that can be fixed upon." He wrote, too, of the low morale among officers whose pay was not enough to defray even ordinary expenses. Good officers were "the very soul of an army," Greene wrote. The Congress must not be overconfident. "The fate of war is very uncertain," he warned.

> Suppose this army should be defeated, two or three of the leading generals killed, our stores and magazines all lost, I would not be answerable for the consequences that such a stroke might produce in American politics.

At Adams's request, Knox provided a list of recommended books on military matters, and in a letter to Adams of May 16, Knox expressed in the strongest terms his belief that it was time to declare American independence. Like Washington, like Greene — and like Adams — Knox longed ardently for a separation from Britain, and the sooner the better.

The future happiness or misery of a great proportion of the human race is at stake — and if we make a wrong choice, ourselves and our posterity must be wretched. Wrong choice! There can be but one choice consistent with the character of a people possessing the least degree of reason. And that is to separate — to separate from that people who from a total dissolution of virtue among them must be our enemies — an event which I de[v]outly pray may soon take place; and let it be as soon as may be.

As Martha Washington had joined the commander-in-chief in New York, so Lucy Knox and Caty Greene traveled from New England to be with their husbands, each young woman bringing an infant born within the year — little Lucy Knox and George Washington Greene. An undated invitation sent from Greene's Long Island quarters that spring reads: "Gen Green[e] and Lady present their compliments to

Col. Knox and his Lady and should be glad of their company tomorrow at dinner at 2 o'clock."

II

Through days of toil on defenses, through endless hours taken up with military routine, endless problems of supply and paperwork, and the innumerable day-to-day preoccupations of those trying to carry on with the little that remained of normal civilian life, the thought that the British could appear any time was seldom out of mind. Every soldier, every civilian, it seemed, had one eye cocked on the harbor for the first sign of British sails. Every waking day began with the thought that it could be *the* day.

Washington ordered a signal system set up between Long Island, Staten Island, and New York. On May 18 a rumor flew through the city that the British had been sighted off Sandy Hook in the Lower Bay, and though there was nothing to it, the story carried for days.

The number of sentries at gun emplacements was doubled. They were "not to suffer any person whatever . . . to go into the batteries at night," Washington's order read. "Nor is any person whatever, but generals or field officers of the army, and officers and men of the artillery who have real business there, to be permitted even in daytime."

More orders followed. Soldiers were to "lay upon [sleep with] their arms and be ready to turn out at a minute's notice." To practice the use of their arms, they were each to fire at least two rounds, and practice moving rapidly from their camps into the trenches and fortifications, to become familiar with the ground they would have to cover when the attack came.

According to his own returns, Washington had 8,880 men at hand, 6,923 of whom were fit for duty. At the same time, he received reliable word that no fewer than 17,000 hired German troops were on the way to serve under the British command, and that the full enemy force could number as many as 30,000.

When Washington was called to Philadelphia to consult with Congress, arrangements were made for fast horses to be held ready at intervals along the road, so that if necessary he could get back to New York with "utmost expedition." It was the first time Washington had left the army since taking command. No sooner had he departed, on May 21, leaving General Putnam in charge, than the rumor spread that he had gone to Philadelphia to resign his command. When he returned, on June 6, after an absence of two weeks, it was to a rousing welcome with drums rolling and five regiments parading.

"Through Broadway we marched, round the King's statue," wrote Lieutenant Bangs, jubilant, like all the army, at the commander's presence among them once more.

There was further bleak news from Canada, including word that General John Thomas, who had been sent north with the expectation that he could set things straight there, had died of smallpox.

The one positive development for Washington was that during his stay in Philadelphia he had convinced Joseph Reed to rejoin the army, to serve as the army's adjutant general — its administrative head — with the rank of colonel, in place of General Horatio Gates, who had been sent by Congress to see what he could do about Canada.

Reed returned full of misgivings. He questioned his fitness for the job — "It is so entirely out of my line," he told his wife — and in a few days he was ready to quit again. But Washington's faith in the gifted Reed, and his need for a confidant, were no less than ever. To Washington his return was a godsend.

Suddenly, with the impact of an explosion, news of a Loyalist plot to assassinate the commander-in-chief burst upon the city. A dozen men were arrested, including the mayor of New York, David Matthews, and two soldiers from Washington's own Life Guard. The plot reportedly was to kill Washington and his officers the moment the British fleet appeared.

Patriot mobs took to the streets to hunt down Loyalists. Those they seized were beaten, tarred and feathered, burned with candles, or made "to ride the rail," the cruel punishment whereby a man was forced to straddle a sharp fence rail held on the shoulders of two men, with other men on either side taking a grip on his legs to keep him straight, and thus the victim was paraded through the streets.

"Dear Brother," a New Yorker named Peter Elting wrote approvingly on June 13, "We had some grand Tory rides in this city this week and in particular yesterday. Several of them were handled very roughly, being carried through the streets on rails, their clothes tore from their back and their bodies pretty well mingled with the dust."

A local Moravian pastor, Ewald Shewkirk, writing in his diary of such "very unhappy and shocking scenes," noted also, "Some of the generals, and especially Putnam, and their forces had enough to do to quell the riot and make the mob disperse."

Washington shifted his headquarters to City Hall. Knox and his wife moved into No. 1 Broadway, while Martha Washington remained at the Mortier house beyond the city — all this apparently out of concern for Washington's safety.

What was learned of the plot, in the course of a court-martial of the two soldiers from the Life Guard, was less sensational than first reported, but serious indeed, even if the evidence was thin. According to the accused themselves, the plan had been to recruit other soldiers to sabotage gun emplacements "when the fleet arrives," in return for royal pardons and financial bonuses ("encouragement as to land and houses"). Besides the mayor, the others arrested and imprisoned included two doctors, a shoemaker, a tailor, a chandler, and a former schoolteacher. But only one of the soldiers was convicted, an English immigrant named Thomas Hickey, whose defense was that he had gotten involved only "for the sake of cheating Tories and getting some money from them."

Hickey was hanged before an enormous crowd on June 28, a fate that most in the army approved. ("I wish twenty more were served the same," wrote Joseph Hodgkins.)

That same night Washington learned for the first time that the British had sailed from Halifax bound for New York on June 9, General Howe having departed somewhat earlier on the frigate *Greyhound*. The information came by express rider from the captain of an American schooner that had been captured by the *Greyhound* off Cape Ann, then retaken by an armed American sloop.

The next morning, Saturday, June 29, officers with telescopes on the roof of Washington's headquarters and other vantage points in the city and on Long Island, saw signals flying from the hills of Staten Island. The first of the British fleet had appeared.

In a matter of hours, forty-five ships had dropped anchor inside Sandy Hook in the Lower Bay, ten miles beyond the Narrows. To a Pennsylvania rifleman closer at hand their masts looked like a forest of trimmed pine trees. "I declare that I thought all London was afloat."

Henry and Lucy Knox were at breakfast at No. 1 Broadway when they saw the fleet. It had become their practice to enjoy breakfast beside a large Palladian window on the second floor with a panoramic view of the harbor. But now suddenly the morning was shattered and Lucy Knox was in a state of abject terror.

"You can scarcely conceive of the distress and anxiety which she then had," Knox would write to his brother William. "The city in an uproar, the alarm guns firing, the troops repairing to their posts, and everything in the [height] of bustle. I not at liberty to attend her, as my country cries loudest."

For weeks Knox had been urging Lucy to leave the city, for her own safety and that of their infant daughter. "My God, may I never experience the like feelings again! They were too much, but I found a way to disguise them, for I scolded like a fury at her for not having gone before."

By sunset the enemy ships at anchor down the bay numbered more than one hundred.

Riders galloped off to Connecticut and New Jersey to spread the news and "hurry on the militia." Martha Washington said her goodbyes to her husband and departed the city by carriage with all possible speed, as did Lucy Knox, Caty Greene, and their children, along with hundreds more of the city's inhabitants.

"The great being who watches the hearts of the children of men, knows I value you above every blessing, and for that reason I wish you to be at such a distance from the horrid scenes of war," Knox wrote to Lucy after she reached Connecticut, and lest anyone forget all that was at stake, he reminded her, "We are fighting for our country, for posterity perhaps. On the success of this campaign the happiness or misery of millions may depend."

Further details on the makeup of the enemy armada followed quickly. The ships included the *Centurion* and the *Chatham*, of 50 guns each, the 40-gun *Phoenix*, and the 30-gun *Greyhound* with General Howe on board, in addition to the 64-gun *Asia*. In their combined firepower these five warships alone far exceeded all the American guns now in place on shore. Nathanael Greene reported to Washington that the total fleet of 120 ships had "10,000 troops received at Halifax, beside some of the Scotch Brigade that have joined the fleet on the passage." And as Lieutenant Colonel Samuel Webb of Washington's staff further noted, an additional 15,000 to 20,000 could be expected "hourly" on still more ships from England under the command of General Howe's brother, Admiral Richard Lord Howe.

The whole of New York was "in commotion," wrote Pastor Shewkirk. "On the one hand everyone that could was packing up and getting away; and on the other hand country soldiers from the neighboring places came in from all sides."

On Long Island, one of Nathanael Greene's field officers took time to pen a note to his son back home in Newburyport, Massachusetts. "I am of opinion our hands will be full," wrote Colonel Moses Little, a veteran of Bunker Hill.

In Philadelphia, the same day as the British landing on Staten Island, July 2, 1776, the Continental Congress, in a momentous decision, voted to "dissolve the connection" with Great Britain. The news reached New York four days later, on July 6, and at once spontaneous celebrations broke out. "The whole choir of our officers . . . went to a public house to testify our joy at the happy news of Independence. We spent the afternoon merrily," recorded Isaac Bangs.

A letter from John Hancock to Washington, as well as the complete text of the Declaration, followed two days later:

> That our affairs may take a more favorable turn [Hancock wrote], the Congress have judged it necessary to dissolve the connection between Great Britain and the American colonies, and to declare them free and independent states; as you will perceive by the enclosed Declaration, which I am directed to transmit to you, and to request you will have it proclaimed at the head of the army in the way you shall think most proper.

Many, like Henry Knox, saw at once that with the enemy massing for battle so close at hand and independence at last declared by Congress, the war had entered an entirely new stage. The lines were drawn now as never before, the stakes far higher. "The eyes of all America are upon us," Knox wrote. "As we play our part posterity will bless or curse us."

By renouncing their allegiance to the King, the delegates at Philadelphia had committed treason and embarked on a course from which there could be no turning back.

"We are in the very midst of a revolution," wrote John Adams, "the most complete, unexpected and remarkable of any in the history of nations."

In a ringing preamble, drafted by Thomas Jefferson, the document declared it "self-evident" that "all men are created equal," and were endowed with the "unalienable" rights of "life, liberty, and the pursuit of happiness." And to this noble end the delegates had pledged their lives, their fortunes, and their sacred honor.

Such courage and high ideals were of little consequence, of course, the Declaration itself being no more than a declaration without military success against the most formidable force on earth. John Dickinson of Pennsylvania, an eminent member of Congress who opposed the Declaration, had called it a "skiff made of paper." And as Nathanael Greene had warned, there were never any certainties about the fate of war.

But from this point on, the citizen-soldiers of Washington's army were no longer to be fighting only for the defense of their country, or for their rightful liberties as freeborn Englishmen, as they had at Lexington and Concord, Bunker Hill and through the long siege at Boston. It was now a proudly proclaimed, all-out war for an independent America, a new America, and thus a new day of freedom and equality.

At his home in Newport, Nathanael Greene's mentor, the Reverend Ezra Stiles, wrote in his diary almost in disbelief:

> Thus the Congress has tied a Gordian knot, which the Parl[iament] will find they can neither cut, nor untie. The *thirteen united colonies* now rise into an *Independent Republic* among the kingdoms, states, and empires on earth. . . . And have I lived to see such an important and astonishing revolution?

At a stroke the Continental Congress had made the Glorious Cause of America more glorious still, for all the world to know, and also to give every citizen soldier at this critical juncture something still larger and more compelling for which to fight. Washington saw it as a "fresh incentive," and to his mind it had come not a moment too soon.

On Tuesday, July 9, at six in the evening, on his orders, the several brigades in the city were marched onto the Commons and other parade grounds to hear the Declaration read aloud.

The general hopes this important event will serve as a fresh incentive to every officer and soldier to act with fidelity and courage, [the orders read] as knowing that now the peace and safety of his country depends (under God) solely on the success of our arms: And that he is now in the service of a state possessed of sufficient power to reward his merit, and advance him to the highest honors of a free country.

The formal readings concluded, a great mob of cheering, shouting soldiers and townspeople stormed down Broadway to Bowling Green, where, with ropes and bars, they pulled down the gilded lead statue of George III on his colossal horse. In their fury the crowd hacked off the sovereign's head, severed the nose, clipped the laurels that wreathed the head, and mounted what remained of the head on a spike outside a tavern.

Much of the lead from the rest of the statue would later be, as reported, melted down for bullets "to assimilate with the brains of our infatuated adversaries."

Not since the spring of 1775 had spirits been so high. But the exuberance of the moment, or any thoughts that grand pronouncements and the toppling of symbolic monuments were sufficient to change the course of history, were quickly dashed in dramatic fashion three days later, on July 12. In a surprise move, the British demonstrated for all to see how much the defenders of New York had still to learn, and the larger, ominous truth that without sea power New York was indefensible.

It was a brilliant summer day with a brisk wind out of the southwest, ideal sailing conditions. At approximately three in the afternoon, His Majesty's ships *Phoenix* and *Rose*, in the company of three tenders, cast off their moorings at Staten Island and started up the harbor under full sail, moving swiftly with the favorable wind and a perfect flood tide.

Alarm guns sounded in New York. Soldiers rushed in every direction through streets crowded with panic-stricken people. The cannon at Red Hook and

Governor's Island opened fire, and as the ships swept by lower Manhattan, heading into the mouth of the Hudson, the guns at old Fort George and other shore batteries opened up. Commanding the fire from Fort George was a nineteen-year-old captain of New York artillery, Alexander Hamilton, who had left King's College to serve in the Cause. The ships returned the fire. Cannonballs slammed into houses and came bounding down streets still swarming with people. Washington would write of the extreme distress he felt at the shrieks and cries of women and children running every which way, and at the spectacle of his own men standing at the water's edge gawking helplessly, so awestruck — or terrified — were they by the ferocious barrage let loose by the enemy ships.

Private Joseph Martin, the fifteen-year-old Connecticut recruit, would remember enjoying "a complete view of the whole affair." It was his first experience with the "muttering" of cannon fire, and he "rather thought the sound was musical, or at least grand."

Every battery along the Hudson fired away until cannon smoke lay thick and heavy over the city, and the air reeked of gunpowder.

The British ships, keeping close to the New Jersey shore, proceeded rapidly up the river and were soon out of sight. By five-thirty they had passed the blasts of cannon from Fort Washington, and by evening they were safely anchored thirty miles above the city in the broadest part of the Hudson, the Tappan Zee at Tarrytown, where their mission was to cut off rebel supplies and rouse local Loyalists.

American gun crews had fired nearly 200 shots — more than 150 from the New York batteries alone — and to no apparent effect. (According to the log of the *Rose*, the Americans "shot away our starb[oa]rd fore shroud, fore tackle pendant, fore lift, fore topsail clewlines, spritsail and main topsail braces, one 18 pound shot in the head of our foremast, one through the pinnace, several through the sails and some in the hull.") Knox's guns had proven more deadly to his own men than to the foe. Six American artillerymen were killed, the only fatalities of the day, when their cannon blew up due to their own inexperience or overconfidence, or possibly, as said, because a great many were drunk.

In his ensuing general orders, Washington could barely conceal his disgust over the inexcusable behavior displayed in the face of the enemy, and the shame he felt over officers who, instead of attending to their duty, had stood gazing like bumpkins. To the proud Washington, he and the army had been made a laughingstock.

Such unsoldierly conduct must grieve every good officer, and give the enemy a *mean* opinion of the army, as nothing shows the brave and good soldier more than in case of alarms, coolly and calmly repairing to his post, and there waiting his orders; whereas a weak curiosity at such a time makes a man look mean and contemptible.

Knox wrote privately that while the loss of his six men had been a great misfortune, he consoled himself with the hope that the day's action had taught the rest to be less "impetuous" the next time.

But there was a far larger, more ominous lesson in what had happened. Clearly if two enemy warships with their tenders could pass so swiftly and readily up the Hudson suffering no serious damage from the onshore batteries, then so could ten or twenty warships and transports, or for that matter, an entire British fleet, and by landing an army of 10,000 or more upriver, they could cut off any chance Washington and his forces might have for escape from New York.

To compound Washington's torment, the day's drama closed in late afternoon with the spectacle of the 64-gun HMS *Eagle* steadily advancing up the bay with all canvas spread and the flag of St. George flying at the foretop masthead, signifying it was the flagship of Admiral Lord Howe and that therefore the fleet from England and still more troops could not be far behind. In the gathering dusk of New York, the boom of a Royal Navy salute came rolling across the waters.

III

Morale in the British ranks had never been higher. After the miseries of the winter in Boston and months of bleak isolation at Halifax, then more wearisome weeks at sea, Staten Island in summer seemed a paradise.

"[We] are in very comfortable cantonments amongst a loyal and liberal people, who produce [supply] us in plenty and in agreeable variety all the necessaries of life, most of which we have been long deprived of," wrote a British officer. "We are in the most beautiful island that nature could form or art improve," declared another. "Here," reported a third, "we experience greater luxury than we have done since the commencement of hostilities . . . fresh meat . . . eggs, butter, milk, and vegetables," and all on "reasonable terms."

Captain Archibald Robertson hiked to the nearby hills with his painting kit to do watercolor sketches as he had at Boston. The difference here was the greater scale of everything spread before him — the sweep of the surpassing harbor defined by New York and Long Island in the distance, and the far larger British fleet now riding at anchor in the middle foreground.

The red-coated soldiers found themselves well nourished and welcome on American soil in a way they had never been — indeed, openly greeted "with greatest joy." "We have now a very good supply of salt provisions," summarized still another officer, "a great quantity of rum, an immense quantity of ammunition of all kinds, and what is best of all, the very people who we suspected would oppose us are coming over to us in great numbers." Hardly a day passed without distraught Loyalists or American deserters turning up, filled with tales of woe, many of them having crossed at night by boat from Long Island or New York.

Ambrose Serle, a patriotic young Englishman and fluent writer who served as a civilian secretary to Admiral Howe, recorded in his journal how his heart went out to the Loyalists. "It excited one's sympathy to see their poor meager faces," he wrote of several who had escaped from Long Island, "and to hear their complaints of being hunted for their lives like game into the woods and swamps, only because they would not renounce their allegiance to their King and affection for their country."

For deserters there was considerably less sympathy and little or no trust. There was "no believing these poor deluded wretches," wrote Colonel Charles Stuart, summing up what most British officers felt. General James Grant thought no American could be trusted, Loyalists any more than the rest. "The inhabitants of this island," Grant concluded from his observations, "hate the rebel army because they have been oppressed by them. . . . But from the confession and conversation of our most loyal subjects of Staten Island, I am quite confirmed in my opinion that we have not a friend in America."

This, however, was not the view of the more astute General Howe, who saw immediately in the Loyalists an advantage he had been denied at Boston. "I met with Governor Tryon on board of ship at the Hook, and many gentlemen, fast friends to [the] government attending him, from whom I have had the fullest information on the state of the rebels," Howe had reported to Lord Germain, on July 7, just days after landing at Staten Island.

News of the Declaration of Independence served only to underscore "the villainy and the madness of these deluded people," an outraged Ambrose Serle observed. "A more impudent, false, and atrocious proclamation was never fabricated by the hands of man."

Soldiers in his Majesty's ranks talked of "the sporting season" about to begin. The lust for the hunt was stronger than ever, their officers happily took note. All rebels were fair game. "The troops hold them very cheap," wrote Serle, "and long for an opportunity of revenging the cause of their countrymen who fell at Bunker Hill."

Lord Rawdon, a veteran of Bunker Hill and of the siege of Boston who had taken delight in the hatred his men felt for Yankees, was cheered now by the number of soldiers being court-martialed for rape, this being perfect proof, he wrote, of their improved diet and of what a "spirited" lot they were.

> The fair nymphs of this isle are in wonderful tribulation, as the fresh meat our men have got here has made them as riotous as satyrs. A girl cannot step into the bushes to pluck a rose without running the most imminent risk of being ravished, and they are so little accustomed to these vigorous methods that they don't bear them with the proper resignation, and of consequence we have most entertaining courts-martial every day.

Yet the courts-martial were themselves proof that such conduct was no laughing matter to the British command, and in fact those convicted faced punishment far more severe than what was customarily dispensed in the American army.

Writing earlier to the Earl of Huntingdon, the handsome Lord Rawdon had expressed the hope that "we shall soon have done with these [American] scoundrels, for one only dirties one's fingers by meddling with them. I do not imagine they can possibly last out beyond this campaign, if you give us the necessary means of carrying on the war with vigor." Now, with "the necessary means" gathering in such heartening numbers on Staten Island, he eagerly anticipated the moment when the "Yankee psalm-singers," as he loved to call them, crossed paths with the likes of the newly arrived Scottish Highlanders armed with their murderous broadswords.

Through telescopes a dozen or more distant rebel camps could be distinctly seen, and the enemy appeared "very numerous." From what could be learned from Loyalists and deserters, rebel strength in New York and on Long Island was overestimated to be between 30,000 and 35,000. But few if any of the British doubted that the conflict ahead would prove fatal to the rebel army, or that it would be exceedingly bloody.

Among many officers the chief worry was that the Americans might not fight. As one wrote anonymously in a letter published in London's *Morning Chronicle*, "Our only fear is that the rebels will not choose to hazard a general action. . . . If . . . they are determined to act upon the defensive only . . . our work will never be done."

Even before the successful dash of the *Phoenix* and the *Rose* up the Hudson, it had been assumed by many British officers that the assault on New York would be made to the north, and thus the army would advance on the city from the undefended rear, while the Royal Navy let loose with a heavy bombardment from the rivers and harbor. But General Howe was saying little of his plans, except that the wait would continue until full reinforcements had arrived. The general, too, was enjoying the comparative comforts of Staten Island, as well as the company of the comely Mrs. Loring, and characteristically he appeared to be in no hurry.

To what extent his brother the admiral would influence or even determine strategy henceforth was an open question, and important, since both the admiral and the general had been lately assigned by the King to serve in the oddly ambiguous, potentially conflicting, role of peace commissioners.

The general was known to want a "decisive action" as the surest way to wind things up quickly — which was also the adamant view of George Lord Germain, from whom he took his orders — and unlike some of his officers, he was certain the

Americans would fight. In a letter written before sailing for New York from Halifax, he had said they were undoubtedly spoiling for a fight, that "flushed with the idea of superiority after the evacuation of Boston, [they] may be readier brought to a decisive action," and that nothing was "more to be desired or sought for" as the most effective means "to terminate this expensive war."

Whether the admiral carried an olive branch or a sword was unclear. But his presence on the *Eagle* and the prospect of more men-of-war and transports arriving had a huge effect. The admiral was a renowned fighting sailor, and as the older, less self-indulgent of the brothers — and with an even darker, gloomier cast to his expression — "Black Dick," as he was known affectionately, was thought to be the wiser of the two.

The fact that they were of like mind on most matters military and political, and got along well, seemed to preclude the friction and jealousies between the Royal Navy and the army frequently endemic to such joint operations. Whatever strategy was resolved, the assumption was that the sea and land forces would work in close cooperation and harmony.

★ ★ ★

On Saturday, July 13, General Howe and his staff, joined by Royal Governor Tryon, dined with the admiral in his cabin on board the *Eagle.* The discussion "turned upon military affairs, upon the country, and upon the rebels," and lasted well into the evening.

The next day came another surprise move when Lord Howe sent a picked officer from the *Eagle,* Lieutenant Philip Brown, across the bay to New York under a flag of truce carrying a letter addressed to "George Washington, Esq." Brown was met by Joseph Reed, who on Washington's orders had hurried to the waterfront accompanied by Henry Knox and Samuel Webb.

"I have a letter, sir, from Lord Howe to Mr. Washington," Lieutenant Brown began.

"Sir," replied Reed, "we have no person in our army with that address."

When Brown asked by what title Mr. Washington chose to be addressed, Reed replied, "You are sensible, sir, of the rank of General Washington in our army."

"Yes, sir, we are," answered Brown. "I am sure Lord Howe will lament exceedingly this affair, as the letter is quite of a civil nature and not a military one."

Lord Howe also lamented "exceedingly that he was not here sooner," Brown added, implying that the admiral regretted not arriving in New York before the Declaration of Independence.

Brown returned to the *Eagle* to report the response of the Americans. ("So high is the vanity and the insolence of these men!" huffed Ambrose Serle in his journal.) But the admiral persisted. Three days later, Brown departed again under a white flag, the letter now addressed to "George Washington, Esq., etc., etc." But again it was declined.

The day after the admiral made a third try, this time sending a different messenger, a captain named Nisbet Balfour, to inquire whether General Washington would receive the adjutant general to General Howe, Colonel James Paterson. This time the answer was yes.

Thus exactly at noon, Saturday, July 20, Colonel Paterson arrived at New York and was escorted directly to No. 1 Broadway, where he met Washington with all due formality, with Reed, Knox, and others in attendance.

Washington's guard stood at attention at the entrance. Washington, as Knox wrote, was "very handsomely dressed and made a most elegant appearance," while Paterson conducted himself with what Reed considered "the greatest politeness and attention."

Seated across a table from Washington, Paterson assured him that Lord Howe did not mean to "derogate from the respect or rank of General Washington." Both Lord and General Howe held the "person and character" of General Washington "in highest esteem," Paterson said. But when he took from his pocket the same letter — addressed still to "George Washington, Esq., etc., etc." — and placed it on the table between them, Washington let it lie, pointedly refusing to touch it.

The use of "etc., etc." implied everything that ought to follow, Paterson offered by way of explanation. "It so does," said Washington, "and anything." A letter addressed to a person in a position of public responsibility ought to indicate that station, Washington said, otherwise it would appear mere private correspondence. He would not accept such a letter.

Paterson talked of the "goodness" and "benevolence" of the King, who had appointed Lord and General Howe as commissioners to "accommodate this unhappy dispute." As Reed would write in a report to Congress — a report soon published in the *Pennsylvania Journal* — Washington replied simply that he was "not vested with any powers on this subject by those from whom he derived his authority and power."

It was his understanding, Washington continued, that Lord Howe had come out from London with authority only to grant pardons. If that was so, he had come to the wrong place.

"Those who have committed no fault want no pardon," Washington said plainly. "We are only defending what we deem our indisputable rights."

According to Henry Knox, the English officer appeared as "awestruck as if before something super-natural."

Paterson said he lamented that an "adherence to forms" might "obstruct business of the greatest moment and concern."

The meeting over, as Paterson himself would write, the general "with a great deal of marked attention and civility permitted me to take my leave."

It had been a scene that those in the room would long remember. Washington had performed his role to perfection. It was not enough that a leader look the part; by Washington's rules, he must know how to act it with self-command and precision. John Adams would later describe Washington approvingly as one of the great actors of the age.

To Washington it had been an obligatory farce. He had no faith, no trust whatever in any peace overtures by the British, however properly rendered. He had agreed to take part in such an "interview," one senses, partly to show the British — and his own staff — he could go through the motions quite as well as any officer and gentleman, but more importantly to send a message to the British command absent any ambiguity. And in this he was unmistakably successful.

As Lord Howe would report to Lord Germain on the prospect of an accommodation acceptable to the King, the "interview . . . induced me to change my subscription for the attainment of an end so desirable."

British ships kept arriving, their sails at first tiny glints on the eastern horizon, then growing steadily larger by the hour as they came up through the Narrows. Samuel Webb counted five ships on July 25, eight on July 26. On July 29 another twenty arrived.

A midsummer drought had set in; the heat was fierce. Just as the winter of 1776 had been one of extreme cold, so the summer was one of extreme heat. "No air, and the thermometer at 94 degrees," recorded Ambrose Serle on board the *Eagle*.

Henry Knox, writing to Lucy at his desk at No. 1 Broadway, said he had never worked so hard or felt so done in by the heat.

I generally rise with or a little before the sun and immediately, with part of the regiment attend prayers, sing a psalm or read a chapter [of the Bible]. I dispatch a considerable deal of business before breakfast. From breakfast to dinner I am boiling in a sun hot enough to roast an egg. Indeed, my dear Lucy, I never suffered so much from fatigue in my life.

On August 1, a swarm of forty-five ships carrying Generals Henry Clinton and Charles Cornwallis and some 3,000 troops were sighted off Sandy Hook, newly returned from South Carolina and making "a very fine appearance," in the eyes of the exultant British.

To the Americans the ships and

Clinton's army were as unexpected as "if they had dropped from the clouds."

And still ships kept coming.

On August 4, Nathanael Greene reported that another twenty-one had been counted on the horizon, the whole of Lord Howe's fleet. And as if to underscore the ambiguity of the admiral's mission, transports loaded with troops bore such names as *Good Intent*, *Friendship*, *Amity's Admonition*, and *Father's Good Will*.

"We have had so many arrivals of late," wrote a nearly giddy Ambrose Serle, "that the rebel commanders, we learn, give out to their people that we send ships down in the night, which come up in the course of the next day, as a maneuver to intimidate them."

Joseph Reed, writing to a friend, said that no fewer than a hundred ships had arrived within ten days, and as yet only part of the "foreign" (Hessian) troops had come in. Reed, it appears, was indeed intimidated. For the first time he expressed great misgivings over the wisdom of even trying to defend New York against such a force. "It is a mere point of honor that keeps us here now." He had a different strategy in mind.

"My opinion is," he wrote, "we should

make it a war of posts, prolong, procrastinate, avoid any general action, or indeed any action, unless we have great advantages."

As things were, he saw no advantages. To what degree he was pressing such views on his commander by this time is not known.

Even stalwart, optimistic Henry Knox suffered his own private anguish. "I shrink and tremble at the importance of our present conduct — the weight absolute without alleviation of perhaps posterity on the shoulders of the present army, an army, I am sorry to say, [that] is not sufficiently numerous to resist the formidable attacks which will probably be made," he told his brother in a letter of August 5.

Washington remained determined to make a stand, convinced still that the city must be defended.

On August 12 the sea beyond the Narrows was filled with yet another one hundred ships or more bearing down on New York, a fleet so large that it took all day for them to come up the harbor under full canvas, colors flying, guns saluting, sailors and soldiers on the ships and on shore cheering themselves hoarse.

In addition, another 3,000 British troops and more than 8,000 Hessians had arrived after an arduous three months at sea.

Nothing like it had ever been seen in New York. Housetops were covered with "gazers"; all wharves that offered a view were jammed with people. The total British armada now at anchor in a "long, thick cluster" off Staten Island numbered nearly four hundred ships large and small, seventy-three warships, including eight ships of the line, each mounting 50 guns or more. As British officers happily reminded one another, it was the largest fleet ever seen in American waters. In fact, it was the largest expeditionary force of the eighteenth century, the largest, most powerful force ever sent forth from Britain or any nation.

But it was also true that as big as the biggest ships were — and to Americans who had never seen anything like them, they were colossal — they could have been bigger still. Even the *Asia* and *Eagle* were small compared to other ships in the British fleet. HMS *Victory*, for example, mounted fully 98 guns. Concerned about the difficulties of clearing the shallows of Sandy Hook and negotiating the East River and the Hudson, Admiral Lord Howe had wisely chosen speed and maneuverability over size and more massive firepower.

Still, by the scale of things in the American colonies of 1776, it was a display of military might past imagining. All told, 32,000 troops had landed on Staten Island, a well-armed, well-equipped, trained force more numerous than the entire population of New York or even Philadelphia, which, with a population of about 30,000, was the largest city in America.

Joseph Reed, writing to his wife, expressed what many felt:

> When I look down and see the prodigious fleet they have collected, the preparations they have made, and consider the vast expenses incurred, I cannot help being astonished that a people should come 3,000 miles at such risk, trouble and expense to rob, plunder and destroy another people because they will not lay their lives and fortunes at their feet.

In the tent encampments dotting Staten Island the redcoats were in holiday spirits. But so it was, also, on the American side, among such veterans of the Boston campaign as Jabez Fitch in camp in New York, and Joseph Hodgkins, on Long Island, who had no doubt the troops would give a good account of themselves, whatever was to come.

Their confidence was bolstered in large degree by distorted notions of their own strength. It was true enough that the enemy was "coming in almost every day," wrote Hodgkins to his wife, and they might number as many as 25,000. Yet she need not worry, "for we have 42,000 men now and they are coming in every day." One newspaper said the American army numbered 70,000.

Many of the new arrivals looked the way soldiers were supposed to, in smart uniforms and well armed, and they marched into town full of pride. Delaware, the smallest colony, had sent the largest battalion in the army, "the Delaware Blues," a force of 800 turned out in handsome red-trimmed blue coats, white waistcoats, buckskin breeches, white woolen stockings, and carrying fine, "lately imported" English muskets. The proud Maryland battalion commanded by General William Smallwood was composed of "men of honor, family, and fortune," and, if anything, they were even better armed and more dazzling in scarlet coats lined with buff. Colonel John Glover's tough Massachusetts fishermen wore the blue jackets of sailors, white shirts, white breeches and caps, while their short, stocky, red-haired commander had silver lace trim on his blue broadcloth coat and carried a brace of silver pistols.

But while the incoming stream of reinforcements had become a daily spectacle, desertions were increasing by the day, and signing up new recruits was proving ever more difficult, in part because that summer of 1776 was a bumper year on American farms and men could rightly claim to be needed at home. "Their complaints are without number," the colonel of a Connecticut regiment wrote.

Some have got ten or twelve loads of hay cut, and not a man left to take it up. Some have got a great quantity of grass to cut. Some have not finished hoeing corn. Some, if not all, have got their ploughing to do, for sowing their winter grain. Some have all their families sick, and not a person left to take care of them.

In the oppressive summer heat in New York and on Long Island, camp fever had become epidemic. When Lieutenant Hodgkins allowed to his wife Sarah that "a good many of our people are poorly," that was hardly the half of it. (Hodgkins was worried sick over his youngest child, a two-year-old son and namesake, who, he had learned, was deathly ill at home, and he was no doubt trying to spare her still more worry.) In the regiment in which Jabez Fitch served, 180 men, nearly two-thirds of the regiment, including the commanding officer, Colonel Jedediah Huntington, were too sick for duty. "Sickness prevails greatly in camp," recorded a regimental surgeon, Albigence Waldo, adding that in other camps conditions were worse.

"The vile water here sickens us all," wrote the New Jersey chaplain Philip Fithian, who was himself ill.

One died this morning in our hospital of a dysentery. . . . Two died yesterday in the New England hospital of a dysentery, and thirty more are confined with it and other putrid disorders.

Many also through the camp are much unwell but will not go to [the] hospital. Poor Mr. Donaldson, my old neighbor, is among these. Yesterday he went to the hospital, but crawled back to his tent this morning, and resolves there to die rather than return.

As they had so often at Boston, Washington and his generals insisted on all possible cleanliness. Nathanael Greene, in particular, gave repeated orders that the camp be kept clean, that the vaults — as latrines were known — were covered with fresh earth daily, and new vaults dug weekly.

The general also forbids in the most positive terms [Greene had written in his orders of July 28] the troops easing themselves in the ditches of the fortifications, a practice that is disgraceful to the last degree. If these matters are not attended to, the stench arising from such places will soon breed a pestilence in the camp.

It was thought that anywhere from 3,000 to 6,000 men were sick. "The numbers of his [Washington's] men are daily diminishing," wrote an English visitor who had recently "escaped from the provincials" at New York.

They desert in large bodies, are sickly, filthy, divided, and unruly. Putrid disorders, the small pox in particular, have carried off great numbers. When I left the city there were six thousand in their hospitals, to which use they have converted King's College.

General Heath would later estimate that 10,000 of the army were ill. "In almost every barn, stable, shed, and even under the fences and bushes, were the sick to be seen, whose countenances were but an index of the dejection of spirit and the distress they endured." And those who had not yet been "taken down" lived with the constant dread that their turn could be next.

"These things are melancholy, but they are nevertheless true," Washington reported to John Hancock. "I hope for better."

Under every disadvantage my utmost exertions shall be employed to bring about the great end we have in view, and so far as I can judge from the professions and apparent disposition of my troops, I shall have their support. The superiority of the enemy and the expected attack do not seem to have depressed their spirits.

It had been a long time waiting. By mid-

August it had been more than four months since the army had set off from Boston for New York, and hurry was the order of the day. The British had not arrived until the end of June and then, instead of attacking at once, as Washington expected, they had kept him watching and waiting week after week, as still more of their navy and more troops arrived. Whatever their plans or however little time remained in the "season for action," they seemed, inexplicably, in no hurry whatever.

Washington's quandary over where the British would strike, and how to apportion the strength he had, was no less extreme now than it had been at the start. Greene and Reed, whose judgment he valued most, were certain the enemy would attack Long Island, both because of the numbers of Loyalists there and the broad accessible beaches where troops could readily land under the protection of British ships.

But Washington worried that a landing on Long Island might be a diversion in advance of a full assault on New York. And with no way of knowing, he felt compelled now to violate one of the oldest, most fundamental rules of battle, never to divide your strength when faced by a superior force. He split his army in roughly equal parts on the theory that he could move men one way or the other over the East River according to how events unfolded.

In a long report to Washington dated August 15, Greene stressed a further cause for concern. The new troops coming over to Long Island, besides being undisciplined, inexperienced, poorly armed, and poorly equipped, were "strangers to the ground." They had no familiarity with the lay of the land, a subject Greene considered of greatest importance. "They will not be so apt to support each other in time of action as those who have long been acquainted, and who are not only attached to each other but to the place."

He confirmed that the troops were in "exceeding good spirits," and that, like Washington, he took heart from this. Only at the conclusion did he acknowledge with regret that he was confined to his bed with a raging fever. Greene, the officer who had been the most concerned of all about the health of the troops, was himself stricken at the crucial hour.

At meetings of the British high command, General Henry Clinton had been making a case for an attack at the northern end of York Island, up the Hudson, but in one conference after another found he could get nowhere with William Howe, who had other plans.

On the morning of Sunday, August 18, taking advantage of a strong northeasterly wind, the *Phoenix* and the *Rose* "passed briskly" back down the Hudson to rejoin the fleet. At one point during their sojourn upriver, the Americans had sent a fireship — a ship set ablaze — against the *Phoenix*, but to no avail; and on the return passage, American guns had blasted away as before, "like incessant thunders," and again without much effect.

If anyone among the American command saw the return of the two enemy ships from upriver as a sign of trouble, there is no record of it.

The day after, August 19, Washington had a number of old ships sunk at the mouth of the East River, between the Battery and Governor's Island, in the hope they would stop the British fleet from any attempt at getting between New York and Brooklyn.

Captain William Tudor, the judge advocate, described the whole army as impatient for action. Spade and pick had been so well employed, wrote "Billy" Tudor, that there was "scarce a spot" left undefended. "From the advantage we now possess, I think General Howe must be repulsed whenever he attacks, but should he be able to carry the island, it must be with so prodigious a loss that victory will be ruin." At the least, in other words, it would be Bunker Hill all over again.

On August 20, Washington learned that Nathanael Greene, upon whom he counted more than anyone, had taken a turn for the worse. Knox, in letters to his wife, reported that "poor General Greene" was "dangerously ill," "sick nearly to death." Left no choice, Washington relieved Greene of command, and the stricken general was moved from Brooklyn Heights across the river to the "airy" safety of a house several miles above New York.

In Greene's place, Washington put the headstrong John Sullivan, who had recently returned from Canada and who had nothing like Greene's ability or judgment. Further, Sullivan was, in Greene's expression, a complete "stranger to the ground" on Long Island.

Writing to John Hancock earlier, Washington had offered a candid appraisal of Sullivan as "spirited and zealously attached to the Cause," but also a man touched with a "tincture of vanity" and too great a "desire of being popular." Then, generously and realistically, Washington conceded that everyone in command of the army suffered from a greater, more serious failing, himself included. "His wants," Washington said of Sullivan, "are common to us all; the want of experience to move upon a large scale."

At some point in the course of Wednesday, August 21, Washington scratched off a quick note to John Hancock to say only that he had "nothing special" to communicate.

That same day, at a country estate near Elizabethtown, New Jersey, General William Livingston, a former member of Congress and newly in command of the New Jersey militia, wrote in "utmost haste" to Washington that a spy he had sent to Staten Island had just returned to report that the British were about to attack, both on Long Island and up the Hudson, and that the attack could come any hour, "this night at farthest."

The reply from Washington, written in Joseph Reed's hand, said, "We have made no discovery of any movement here of any consequence."

Chapter Five

FIELD OF BATTLE

Remember officers and soldiers that you are free men, fighting for the blessings of liberty.

— General George Washington

I

On the night of August 21, 1776, a terrifying storm broke over New York, a storm as vicious as any in living memory, and for those who saw omens in such unleashed fury from the elements — those familiar with the writings of the Roman historian Livy, say, or the plays of Shakespeare, of whom there were many — a night so violent seemed filled with portent.

Chroniclers Philip Fithian, Ambrose Serle, and Pastor Ewald Shewkirk called it "a storm like a hurricane," "a most terrible storm," "the most vehement I ever saw," "an uncommon . . . awful scene." A Connecticut officer on Brooklyn Heights, Major Abner Benedict, would describe how, at seven o'clock, a monstrous thundercloud rose in the west. Looming higher and higher, "it was surcharged with electricity, for the lightning was constantly searching it from limit to limit," he wrote. It began to rain. "Then followed a crash louder than a thousand cannon. . . . In a few minutes the entire heavens became black as ink, and from horizon to horizon the whole empyrean was ablaze with lightning." The thunder did not follow in successive peals, but in one "continuous crash."

The storm raged for three hours, yet strangely the cloud appeared to stand still, "and swing round and round," over the city. "The lightning fell in masses and sheets of fire to the earth, and seemed to strike incessantly and on every side."

Houses burst into flame. Ten soldiers camped by the East River, below Fort Stirling, were killed in a single flash. In New York, a soldier hurrying through the streets was struck deaf, blind, and mute. In another part of town three officers were killed by a single thunderbolt. A later report described how the tips of their swords and coins in their pockets had been melted, their bodies turned as black as if roasted.

To Major Benedict the roar and bloodshed of battle were something to be expected. "But there seems hidden meaning, some secret purpose, when the bolt is launched by an invisible arm, and from the mysterious depth of space."

He could not account for the cloud remaining stationary for so long, unless, he speculated, "the vast amount of arms collected in and about the city held it by attraction and drew from it such a fearful amount of electricity."

Before dawn the following day, Thursday, August 22, the sky was clear and cloudless, as if nothing unusual had happened. And with a fresh morning breeze and roll of drums, the long-awaited British invasion of Long Island got under way.

The frigates *Phoenix* (with Lord Howe aboard), *Rose*, and *Greyhound*, and two bomb ketches, the *Carcass* and the *Thunder* (vessels equipped for shore bombardment), swung loose from their moorings and stood down the Narrows to take their positions to cover the landing. Then, at approximately five o'clock, with day beginning to break, an advance corps — 4,000 of the King's elite troops led by Generals Clinton and Cornwallis — pushed off, the men packed aboard scores of flatboats (these built during the time on Staten Island) with British sailors at the oars.

Slowly but steadily, in glorious early sunshine, the invasion force proceeded across three miles of water, until, at precisely eight o'clock, at the flash of a signal gun from the *Phoenix*, all 4,000 troops went ashore on the long, flat, empty beach at Gravesend Bay.

Everything had been carefully prepared, every move of the army and navy carefully coordinated. The landing was as smooth as if it had been rehearsed, and there was no opposition. The comparative few of Colonel Edward Hand's Pennsylvania riflemen posted near the shore had already withdrawn, driving off or killing cattle as they went, and burning wheat fields and farm buildings. The dense columns of smoke rising in the air could be seen in New York eight miles away.

As more troops followed, a naval spectacle of more than ninety vessels filled the Narrows. Wave after wave of soldiers came on, their red coats and polished bayonets gleaming in the bright sunshine. One battalion of blue-coated Hessian grenadiers was ferried over standing in ranks, muskets in hand and in order of battle. By noon a fully equipped army of 15,000 men and forty pieces of artillery had landed and rapidly, smoothly assembled in perfect formation on the adjacent plain. And still more would follow, including the women who were with the army.

Loyalists by the hundreds converged to welcome the invaders, many of them bringing long-hidden supplies of all kinds. The welcome was more effusive even than it had been on Staten Island. Meanwhile, Cornwallis and the advance guard pressed directly inland for six miles to establish a camp at the little Dutch village of Flatbush, near the wooded Heights of Gowan.

It all made a picturesque scene, wrote Ambrose Serle —

> 15,000 troops upon a fine beach . . . [then] forming upon the adjacent plain. . . . Ships and vessels with their sails spread open to dry, the sun shining clear upon them, the green hills and meadows after the rain. . . . Add to all this, the vast importance of the business . . . and the mind feels itself wonderfully engaged.

British sailors who came ashore "regaled themselves with the fine apples, which hung everywhere upon the trees in great abundance," Serle continued. "It was really diverting to see sailors and apples tumbling from the trees together."

But other aspects of the scene were anything but picturesque. A Hessian officer, Lieutenant Johann Heinrich von Bardeleben, described burned-out houses, fields in ashes, roads lined with dead cattle, and old people looking with sadness at what "appeared previously to have been a paradise standing in blooming abundance."

> Our regiment was camped amidst orchards of apple and pear trees. . . . Here, too, the picture of destruction was to be seen on all sides. Almost everywhere there were chests of drawers, chairs, mirrors with gold-gilded frames, porcelain, and all sorts of items of the best and most expensive manufacture.

The Hessian and British troops alike were astonished to find Americans blessed with such abundance — substantial farmhouses and fine furnishings. "In all the fields the finest fruit is to be found," Lieutenant von Bardeleben wrote after taking a walk on his own, away from the path of destruction. "The peach and apple trees are especially numerous. . . . The houses, in part, are made only of wood and the furnishing in them are excellent. Comfort, beauty, and cleanliness are readily apparent."

To many of the English, such affluence as they saw on Long Island was proof that America had indeed grown rich at the expense of Great Britain.

In fact, the Americans of 1776 enjoyed a higher standard of living than any people in the world. Their material wealth was considerably less than it would become in time, still it was a great deal more than others had elsewhere. How people with so much, living on their own land, would ever choose to rebel against the ruler God had put over them and thereby bring down such devastation upon themselves was for the invaders incomprehensible.

Word reached New York early in the day, but Washington was badly misinformed about the size of the enemy force that had come ashore. Told that there were 8,000 or 9,000, he quickly concluded the landing was the feint he had expected, and consequently he dispatched only 1,500 more troops across the East River to Brooklyn, bringing the total American strength on Long Island to something less than 6,000 men. The expectation of another, larger strike by the British at New York or up the Hudson persisted. But then no one seemed to know what was going on.

Lieutenant Jabez Fitch, whose Connecticut regiment was one of those ordered across the river, wrote in his diary of being marched forward at Brooklyn about a mile before being told to halt and wait for further orders.

> While we are waiting we hear many various reports concerning the enemy, some say they are within four miles of us, others, two and a half. Others say they have not advanced more than a mile from where they landed, which is near ten miles. So on the whole we know not what to believe concerning them until we can see them.

Colonel Moses Little, whose information was remarkably accurate, reported to his son that the enemy was within three miles, and said in the same letter, "I have thought fit to send you my will."

Meanwhile, impressive numbers of Connecticut reinforcements had been arriving in New York. Only that day, twelve Connecticut regiments paraded in the city. "Almost one half of the grand army now consists of *Connecticut troops!*" an officer boasted to his wife. The whole army, noted Joseph Reed, was in better spirits than he had ever seen.

Not until the following day, August 23, did Washington confirm in his general orders that the British had come ashore on Long Island. Leaving no doubt about the seriousness of the moment for every man in the army, he appealed to their pride and patriotism and love of liberty.

The hour is fast approaching, on which the honor and success of this army, and the safety of our bleeding country depend. Remember officers and soldiers that you are free men, fighting for the blessings of liberty — that slavery will be your portion, and that of your posterity, if you do not acquit yourselves like men.

Nor should they forget that they faced an enemy who held them in contempt.

Remember how your courage and spirit

have been despised and traduced by your cruel invaders, though they have found by dear experience at Boston, Charlestown, and other places, what a few brave men contending in their own land, and in the best of causes can do, against base hirelings and mercenaries.

They must be "cool but determined." And again, as at Boston, he threatened instant death to any man who showed cowardice.

To General Heath, in command of defenses to the north at King's Bridge, Washington sent a message saying he dared not weaken his forces in New York until he could be certain of the enemy's real intentions.

"I have never been afraid of the force of the enemy," Heath answered. "I am more so of their arts. They must be well watched. They, like the Frenchman, look one way and row the other."

Joseph Reed, who was as close to Washington as anyone, expressed the same extreme concern. "The greatest vigilance is had to prevent a surprise," he wrote, "which we have to fear more than anything."

Washington crossed to Brooklyn that afternoon to confer with General Sullivan.

There had been some minor skirmishing only, he was told, and he returned to New York still more convinced that Howe had yet to commit his full force.

If the British had made no advance on New York with their fleet since landing on Long Island, he reported to Congress, that could very well be because it was not in their power. For days the wind had either been head-on against them or too little when the tide served.

Washington was beset by second thoughts. On August 24, he reshuffled the command at Brooklyn, placing Israel Putnam over Sullivan, a move likely to unsettle the troops who had seen the stricken Greene replaced by Sullivan, and now Sullivan superseded by Putnam all in a matter of days.

Brave, popular "Old Put" might be the man to boost morale, but he had neither the experience nor the temperament to direct so large a force under such conditions and was thus a poor choice, as Washington seems to have realized almost at once.

Putnam and six battalions crossed to Brooklyn early the next day, a Sunday, causing a great stir. "Scarcely were religious services finished," wrote Abner Benedict, "when strains of martial music were heard from the ferry, and not long after column after column came winding up the Heights toward the fort. . . . The general was received with loud cheers, and his presence inspired universal confidence."

The day's orders from Sullivan deplored the disorder and unsoldierly behavior displayed in the camps on the eve of battle. Yet soldiers were here, there, and everywhere, strolling about as if on holiday, some of them miles from the lines. "Carts and horses driving every way among the army," wrote Philip Fithian. "Men marching out and coming in. . . . Small arms and field pieces continually firing. All in tumult."

The contrast between such disorder and flagrant disregard for authority and the perfectly orchestrated landing by Howe's troops could not have been more pronounced.

Arriving at Brooklyn, Washington was outraged by what he saw, and in a letter written later in the day, he lectured Old Put as he might the greenest lieutenant. All "irregularities" must cease at once. "The distinction between a well regulated army and a mob is the good order and discipline of the first, and the licentious and disorderly behavior of the latter."

Seeing things as they were, not as he would wish they were, was known to be one of Washington's salient strengths, and having witnessed firsthand the "loose, disorderly, and unsoldierlike" state of things among the troops at Brooklyn, and knowing how outnumbered they were by the enemy, he might have ordered an immediate withdrawal back to New York while there was still time. But he did not, nor is there any evidence that such a move was even considered.

In New York all the while, more than half the army, including many of his best troops and best officers, like Henry Knox, waited in anxious expectation of an attack there. "We expect the fleet up every tide if the wind serves," wrote a Connecticut colonel, William Douglas.

That same Sunday another 5,000 Hessians crossed the Narrows from Staten Island bringing Howe's total forces on Long Island to 20,000.

Washington returned again to Brooklyn early the following day, August 26, to confer still again with his commanders and appraise the defenses and deployment of troops. Almost certainly he rode beyond Brooklyn to the Heights of Gowan, where from the ridge line he could have seen the white tents of the British spread across the plain at Flatlands. ("General Washington, with a number of general officers went down to view the motion of the enemy," reads one account.) With his telescope, he could well have watched Howe's troops on their daily parade.

The plan was for General Putnam to direct the entire defense from the fortifications on Brooklyn Heights. Generals Sullivan and Stirling and their troops were to be positioned well forward on the "out work" of the wooded ridge, to cover the few main roads or passes through that long, natural barrier.

The Gowanus Road was on the far right, near the Narrows. The Flatbush Road was at the center and thought to be the way the British would come. A third, the Bedford Road, was off to the left. All three were comparatively narrow cuts through the ridge and thus "easily defensible."

The ridge of hills and woods was all that separated the two armies but was seen by the Americans as the ideal forward line of defense, and so to their decided advantage. Joseph Reed, doubtless reflecting Washington's view, deemed it "very important." The fight when it came would surely come there, in the woods, where, it was agreed, Americans fought best.

Stirling was responsible for the Gowanus Road on the right, where about 500 troops were posted. Sullivan had command of both the Flatbush Road at the center, where 1,000 were deployed, and the Bedford Road, on the left flank, where another 800 or so were positioned under Colonel Samuel Miles of Pennsylvania. In the absence of uniforms, every man was to put a sprig of green in his hat as identification.

Washington's specific order to Putnam, who knew almost nothing about Long Island, having visited there only occasionally, was to position his best troops forward and "at all hazards prevent the enemy's passing the wood and approaching the works."

As things stood, a force of fewer than 3,000 soldiers, nearly all of whom had had no experience in battle, were expected to hold a ridge four miles long, while the rest, another 6,000, remained within the Brooklyn forts. In all, the outposts stretched six miles. The terrain was so rugged that units had trouble communicating, and so thickly wooded that in places men were blind to any movement beyond a hundred feet.

Had there been American cavalry to serve as "eyes and ears," or had there been reliable intelligence, the defenders might have had a better chance. But there was neither. The Continental Army had no cavalry. Congress had not considered cavalry necessary, nor had Washington asked for any. And however adamant he was about the value of spies, as circumstances were, he had none.

Nor in the five days since the British landing had anyone been stationed at a fourth, lesser-known pass on the far left, three miles east of the Bedford Road. The Jamaica Pass, as it was called, was narrower even than the others, and thus the easiest to defend. Yet nothing had been said in any of the orders of Sullivan, or Putnam, or Washington expressing concern about the Jamaica Pass or the need to post sufficient troops there.

Having looked things over and conferred with his commanders, Washington approved the plan, including, presumably, a last-minute idea of having the Jamaica Pass patrolled by five young militia officers who had horses.

Washington returned to New York that evening convinced at last that the British would make their "grand push" against

Brooklyn. Or so he wrote to John Hancock. To General Heath he also wrote that by the "present appearance of things" the enemy would make their "capital impression" on Long Island. But then, as if still unable to make up his mind, he cautioned yet again that it might all be "only a feint to draw over our troops to that quarter, in order to weaken us here."

His army, he knew, was ill prepared for what was to come. There was more sickness in the ranks than at any time before. Only a few of his officers had ever faced an enemy on the field of battle. He himself had never commanded an army in battle. His responsibilities, the never-ending "load of business," weighed heavily. The same uncertainties that had vexed him in his first days of command at New York vexed him still. The enemy could not delay much longer. The time for warm-weather campaigning, "the season for action," was fast waning, yet even now he consoled himself with the hope that he had a few more days before the enemy would strike.

It had been a long, anxious day, and in the privacy of his quarters in the Mortier house, Washington turned his mind — turned for relief it would seem — to thoughts of home. Alone at his desk, he wrote a long letter to his manager at Mount Vernon, Lund Washington, filled with thoughts on the marketing of flour and specific directions concerning work on additions to the house. For much of the letter it was as though he had nothing else on his mind.

I wish most ardently you could get the north end of the house covered in this fall, if you should be obliged to send all over Virginia, Maryland, and Pennsylvania for nails to do it with. Unless this is done it will throw everything exceedingly backward — retard the design of planting trees . . . besides keeping the house in a disagreeable littered situation. It is equally my wish to have the chimneys run up. In short I would wish to have the whole closed in (if you were even to hire many workmen of different kinds to accomplish it).

Of the war he wrote that a few more days would likely "bring matters to an issue one way or other." If he did not think the struggle just, nothing on earth could "compensate [for] the loss of all my domestic happiness and requite me for the load of business which constantly presses upon and deprives me of every enjoyment."

What he may have written to his wife Martha that night, or at any point in the course of events to come, is unknown, since she later destroyed all but three of his letters to her, and these survived only by accident. His sleep that night was to be abbreviated, yet the most he would have for days.

General Henry Clinton, not an impressive man in looks or manner, had thus far in the war done little to show that appearances could be deceiving, and that he had, as he knew, marked intelligence and ability. For more than a year he had fared poorly in the service of his King. At Boston, he and William Howe had been continuously at odds, and he had failed most grievously (in his mind) to convince Howe to seize Dorchester Heights before the rebels did. Sent off to South Carolina, he had failed in his mission there. An attack on Fort Sullivan at Charleston in June had been such a humiliating defeat for the British that the campaign had to be abandoned, and largely because Clinton had been too cautious. Then, returning to New York, he had seen all his arguments for an invasion up the Hudson rejected out of hand by Howe.

Clinton knew his failings. He knew he could be difficult, inclined to "speak too freely," that he was touchy and that in discussion his excessive zeal often worked to his disadvantage.

On paper, however, Henry Clinton could be bold and convincing, and he had returned from Charleston greatly changed in outlook. His defeat had convinced him that the war should be waged not to conquer territory but to destroy the rebel army by outflanking it whenever or wherever possible, if not by water, then on land. As a strategist, he knew well how to use a map. "Look at the map," he would proclaim.

Soon after the landing at Gravesend, accompanied by another general, Sir William Erskine, and Lord Rawdon, Clinton had ridden off to reconnoiter the rebel defenses and the few passes through the wooded Heights of Gowan. Told by Loyalist farmers of the little-used Jamaica Pass beyond the Bedford Road, and that it appeared to be unguarded, the three British officers continued on to find that what they had been told was true.

Clinton immediately drew up a plan. This time, however, instead of going to Howe to make the case himself, he asked

General Erskine to take what he had written to the headquarters at Flatlands. It read as follows:

The position which the rebels occupy in our front may be turned by a gorge about six miles from us, through a country in which cavalry may make the avant garde. That, once possessed, gives us the island; and in a mile or two further we shall be on the communications with their works at Brooklyn. The corps which attempts to turn this flank must be in very great force, for reasons too obvious to require detailing. The attack should begin on the enemy's right by signal; and a share [should be] taken in it even by the fleet, which (as the tide will then suit) may get under way and make every demonstration of forcing by the enemy's batteries in the East River, without, however, committing themselves. The efforts to be made by the army will be along the *dos d'ane* at the points of Flatbush, New Utrecht, etc. These [are] the principal [attacks]; many other small ones to cooperate. They should all be vigorous but not too obstinately persisted in, except that which is designed to turn the left of the rebels, which should be pushed as far as it will go. The moment this corps gets possession of the pass above Howard's House [Howard's Tavern], the rebels must quit directly or be ruined. I beg leave also to propose that this corps may begin to move at nightfall, so that everything may be [ready] at its ground by daybreak.

Several days passed. Then on August 26, the same day Washington spent looking things over at Brooklyn, Clinton was sent for and told by Howe that the attack would be made entirely according to his plan and to be prepared to march that night.

General Grant, with two brigades, was to make a "spirited" early-morning diversion close to the Narrows, striking at the enemy's right. General Leopold Philipp von Heister's Hessians, another 4,000 men, would move out from Flatbush to keep the Americans occupied at the center. In the meantime, the main body of the army would move under the cover of dark to be in position at daybreak.

Clinton was to command the advance guard on the night march, General Howe following with the rest of the main force, numbering in all 10,000 men.

★ ★ ★

If asked to describe the common soldiers of the King's army, the redcoats now falling in and dressing their ranks in the gathering dusk at Flatlands, most of the American soldiers who lay in wait for them would probably have said they were hardened, battle-scarred veterans, the sweepings of the London and Liverpool slums, debtors, drunks, common criminals and the like, who had been bullied and beaten into mindless obedience. It was the common American view. The truth was something else.

That the rank-and-file British regular was far better trained, better disciplined, better equipped, and more regularly paid than his American counterpart was beyond question, as the commanders on both sides well appreciated. Further, the redcoats were in far better health over all. Proper sanitation was part of British army life, and discipline in this regard was as strictly enforced as any aspect of the daily routine. Even after their long summer encampment on Staten Island, the British troops, as their officers noted repeatedly, were in excellent health, in striking contrast to the reports of rampant illness among the rebels.

In an effort to explain why the "provincials" would, in their own climate, be so afflicted with "putrid disorders," while his Majesty's troops, who were foreign to the climate, would enjoy near perfect health, the *London Chronicle* said the difference was the great cleanliness of the regulars.

Among the regular troops every private soldier is obliged to put on a clean shirt twice, perhaps three times a week, according to the season and climate; and there are a certain number of officers appointed every day to see that each man washes his own linen, if he had not a woman to do it for him.

While the dregs of society did indeed count among the King's troops, the great majority were young countrymen from rural England, Scotland, and Ireland. They were farmers, unskilled laborers, and tradesmen — blacksmiths, cordwainers, carpenters, bakers, hatters, locksmiths, and weavers — who had been recruited, not pressed into service, drawn by the promise of clothing, food, and steady, if meager, pay, along with a chance at adventure, perhaps even a touch of glory. In their rural or small-town origins they were not greatly different from their American counterparts.

The average British regular was in his late twenties, or about five years older than the average American soldier, but the average regular had served five or six years in the army, or five or six times longer than the average volunteer under Washington. To the British rank-and-file there was nothing novel about being a soldier. The harsh life was their way of life. They carried themselves like soldiers. They had rules, regulations, and traditions down pat. They were proud to serve in His Majesty's army, proud of the uniform, and fiercely proud of and loyal to their regiments.

On a day such as this, on the eve of battle, they would have given close attention to all the particulars of their arms and accoutrements, and each man to his own appearance. Most would be freshly shaved and their uniforms made as presentable as possible. On the move, seen from a distance, they looked glorious in their red coats and crossbelts, marching rank on rank, their huge regimental battle flags flying at the front atop ten-foot poles. Seen up close, however, the red coats, waist-length in front, longer at the back, were often faded and out at the elbows. Cuffs were frayed, knees patched, stockings or marching gaiters often torn beyond mending, try as each man would to look the part.

And with the pride in who and what they were went a very real contempt for, even hatred of, their American foes, whom they saw as cowards and traitors.

But by no means were they all battle-scarred veterans. Some of the older soldiers and officers were veterans of the killing fields of Europe during the Seven Years' War, or the French and Indian War in America, or had survived the retreat from Concord or the Battle of Bunker Hill. The rest, the great majority of the British forces on Long Island, including the Germans, knew only the drill and routine of army life. For as long as the average soldier in Howe's ranks had been in service, it had been longer still, more than ten years, since Britain had last waged war. For most of the redcoats, soldiers and young officers, like nearly all of the Americans, the battle to come was to be their first.

By nightfall everything was ready. At nine came the order to move out. Clinton led a crack brigade of light infantry with fixed bayonets. Cornwallis followed with eight reserve battalions and fourteen pieces of artillery. They in turn were followed by Generals Howe and Percy with another six battalions, more artillery, and baggage wagons. The column of 10,000 stretched more than two miles. At the head of the advance guard rode two mounted officers, Captains William Glanville Evelyn and Oliver DeLancey, Jr., and three Loyalist farmers who knew the way.

The white tents at Flatlands were left standing, campfires burning, all to appear as though nothing were happening.

The night was unseasonably cool. The long column moved with utmost silence and extremely slowly. An exhausted Scottish officer who had had several sleepless nights on duty, described the march as one of the worst he had known and endless. "We dragged on at the most tedious pace," wrote Sir James Murray, "halting every minute just long enough to drop asleep, and to be disturbed again in order to proceed twenty yards in the same manner."

By agreeing to Clinton's plan — by committing a force of such numbers to a night march through unknown country, led like the blind by three local farmers who might or might not be all they professed — William Howe was putting his army at extreme risk. In the event of discovery or sudden, surprise attack by the enemy, his stretched-out column could be chopped to pieces. If all went as planned, the maneuver would look like little more than a classic turning of the enemy's flank, but it took no great stretch of imagination to picture the unforeseen circumstances, the vagaries of chance that could play havoc.

As it was, no one except the commanders knew the details of the plan. Not an officer or a man knew where they were going.

The route was northeast along what was known as the King's Highway, then at the village of New Lots the troops would swing north toward the Heights of Gowan.

The advance guard moved more swiftly, at the same time "sweeping up" any local inhabitants who looked as though they might give the alarm. When the three Loyalist guides warned that the rebels could be waiting at Schoonmaker's Bridge over a little salt creek that emptied into Jamaica Bay, the whole column halted while skirmishers went ahead. But there was no one at the bridge and the army continued on.

Nor was there a sign of the rebels at Howard's Tavern, which stood a few hundred yards from the entrance to the Jamaica Pass. By then it was two in the morning. The tavernkeeper and his fourteen-year-old son were rousted out of bed, closely questioned, and pressed into service as additional guides. The pass, as far as they knew, was unguarded.

Captains Evelyn and DeLancey and other mounted officers rode ahead into the pass, a winding, rocky road through a narrow gorge overhung by trees and little wider than a bridle path.

It was only ten minutes or so after leaving the tavern when the officers came up on five dark figures on horseback, the five Americans on patrol. When the Americans, supposing the British officers to be a party of their own troops, fell in with them, all five were immediately captured without a shot fired or scarcely a sound.

The prisoners were taken to General Clinton, who succeeded in learning from them that they alone were patrolling the pass, and that indeed the pass was entirely unguarded.

When Clinton pressed harder, demanding to know how many rebel troops were at Brooklyn, one of the Americans, Lieutenant Edward Dunscomb, a twenty-two-year-old graduate of King's College, told Clinton indignantly that under different circumstances he would never insult them in such a manner. Called "an impudent rebel" and threatened with hanging, Dunscomb said that General Washington would respond in kind and hang man for man. But Dunscomb's courage made little difference. He and the other prisoners were taken away, and Clinton and the advance guard moved on.

By first light they were through the gorge and at the Bedford Road on the other side of the ridge. The men were told to lie down in the tall grass by the road and get some rest.

For the main body of the army the march through the pass took nearly two hours. (Wherever a tree had to be cleared to make way for the artillery and wagons, it had to be done with saws instead of axes in order to maintain all possible silence.) By the time Howe and the army reached the Bedford Road, the sun was up.

At exactly nine o'clock, with the blasts of two heavy cannon — the prearranged signal for the Hessians at the center and General Grant on the American right to commence their assaults — Howe's army pushed on down the road toward the village of Bedford and to Brooklyn beyond.

Years later, Henry Clinton would remember Howe being extremely apprehensive. "The commander-in-chief seemed to have some suspicion the enemy would attack us on our march, but I was persuaded that, as they [had] neglected to oppose us at the gorge, the affair was over."

Good fortune had accompanied them through the night. Nothing had gone amiss. The troops had marched nine miles in pitch darkness through unfamiliar country and in perfect order. Everything was on schedule and the day, like the day they first came ashore on Long Island, was perfectly beautiful.

II

It was three in the morning when General Putnam was awakened by one of the guards at the Brooklyn headquarters and told the enemy was attacking on the right near the Narrows, at the Gowanus Road.

The British commander, Grant, had decided to occupy the attention of the Americans on that part of the line ahead of schedule. Three hundred British troops had stormed into the Gowanus Pass with a roar of musket fire and the Americans on guard, green militia, fled as fast as they could.

Putnam rushed to Lord Stirling's camp outside the Brooklyn lines to order Stirling to move to meet the enemy and "repulse them," little knowing how many of the enemy there were. Alarm guns sounded, drums rolled as troops fell out at the forts. General Samuel Parsons, who with Stirling shared responsibility for defenses on the Gowanus Road, and who, like Putnam, had been resting at the Brooklyn headquarters, mounted his horse and galloped off to arrive first on the scene. Until the year before, Parsons had been a small-town Connecticut lawyer.

I found by fair daylight, the enemy were through the wood and descending the hill on the north side, on which, with twenty of my fugitive guard being all I could collect, I took post on a height in their front at about half a mile's distance — which halted their column and gave time for Lord Stirling with his forces to come up.

Stirling's forces numbered 1,600 men and included Colonel Huntington's Connecticut regiment, in which Jabez Fitch served, and Colonel Samuel Atlee's Pennsylvania battalion, in addition to Smallwood's Marylanders and Haslet's colorful Delaware battalion, which were thought to be the two best units in the army. But as it happened, both their commanders, James Smallwood and John Haslet, were absent, on court-martial duty in New York.

"A little before day, as we marched towards the enemy two miles from our camp, we saw them," wrote a nineteen-year-old lieutenant with the Delaware troops, Enoch Anderson. In what seemed no time they were in the middle of what Moses Little called "a smart engagement."

The redcoat regiments came on "in regular order," colors flying, field artillery out in front. Stirling drew up his lines and, in the words of another American soldier, offered them "battle in true English taste." The British marched to within two hundred yards, then opened fire with cannon and muskets, "now and then taking off a head," as the same soldier wrote. "Our men stood it amazingly well, not even one of them showed a disposition to shrink." Their orders were to hold their fire until the enemy came within fifty yards. "But when they perceived *we* stood their fire so cool and so resolutely, they declined to come any nearer, although *treble our number.*"

"We gave them a fair fire — every man leveled well," young Enoch Anderson recounted:

I saw one man tumble from his horse — never did I take better aim at a bird — yet I know not that I killed any or touched any. The fire was returned and they killed two of our men dead, none wounded. It became proper for us to retreat and we retreated about four hundred yards and were joined by Captain Atlee's regiment.

Twice within an hour the British assaulted Parson's troops on their high ground, and twice the American lines held. Stirling's men were under steady cannon bombardment, but American cannon answered in kind and in the roar and smoke the American troops never flinched.

In this its first hours of battle with the enemy on an open field, the Continental Army fought valiantly, believing they were holding their own against British regulars. Addressing the troops, Stirling reminded them that it was General Grant who had boasted that with 5,000 men he could conquer all of America. But as they could not know, Grant was pressing his advantage only so much, holding back according to plan. "We had a skirmishing and a cannonade for some hours, which drew their whole attention," Grant would later say.

At the center, where Hessian artillery had been bombarding Sullivan's lines along the ridges since early morning, General von Heister's brigades could be seen drawn up on the plain to the south, but showed no sign of moving. Three Hessian brigades stood waiting in a line nearly a mile long.

Sullivan had ridden out from Brooklyn to take command at the Flatbush Pass. Seeing that the Hessians were not moving and that Stirling was in trouble on the right, he sent some of his regiments to help.

Until nine o'clock the battle seemed to be unfolding about as the Americans had expected, with the enemy attacking, or poised to attack, head-on.

But at nine came the crash of Howe's signal guns, and suddenly Sullivan realized that a whole British army was coming at him from behind and that he was surrounded.

On the plain beyond the ridge, General von Heister gave the order and with drums rolling, the Hessians were in motion.

Leaving his advance guard posted along the ridge to do what they could to hold off the Hessians, Sullivan pulled back his main force and swung around to face the oncoming British ranks. And though vastly outnumbered, the Americans returned the British fire with murderous effect. Officers on both sides feared their men would be cut to pieces, and officers and soldiers on both sides often had no idea what was happening. Nor was it the Americans only who, when faced with annihilation, ran for their lives.

A British light infantry officer who led thirty of Clinton's advance guard into the "very thick" of several hundred American riflemen, saw a third of his men go down in the most ferocious exchange of fire he had ever known. When he and a half dozen redcoats broke for the woods, more rebels sprang up out of nowhere. The fire seemed to come from every direction.

> I called to my men to run to the first wall they could find and we all set off, some into some short bushes, others straight across a field . . . [and] in run-

ning across the field we [were] exposed to the fire of 300 men. We had literally run out in the midst [of them] and they calling to me to surrender. I stopped twice to look behind me and saw the riflemen so thick and not one of my own men. I made for the wall as hard as I could drive and they peppering at me . . . at last I gained the wall and threw myself headlong.

In the turmoil and confusion, Sullivan struggled to hold control and keep his men from panicking. Their situation was desperate; retreat was the only alternative, and in stages of "fight and flight," he led them as rapidly as possible in the direction of the Brooklyn lines.

Those left to hold the ridge had by now been overrun by the Hessians. Green-coated jaegers (literally, huntsmen) and the blue-coated grenadiers with their seventeen-inch bayonets had moved up through the steep woods of the ridge — the "terrible hills" — as swiftly and expertly as any Virginia rifleman. So suddenly did they appear that the Americans had time to get off only a shot or two, or none at all. Some fought back, wielding their muskets and rifles like clubs, before being run through with bayonets. Some pleaded for mercy. "Their fear of the Hessian troops was . . . indescribable," wrote General von Heister. At the very sight of a blue coat, he said, "they surrendered immediately and begged on their knees for their lives." Those who could get away fled back down through the trees and out into the open, only to run headlong into a hail of British fire.

At the same time, the whole left side of the American line collapsed. Thousands of men were on the run, hundreds were captured. Sullivan held back, in an effort to see as many as possible to safety, and amazingly most of the men succeeded in reaching the Brooklyn lines.

Sullivan, however, was captured. An American soldier named Lewis Morris, who himself barely escaped, wrote of Sullivan in a letter home. "The last I heard of him, he was in a cornfield close by our lines, with a pistol in each hand, and the enemy had formed a line each side of him, and he was going directly between them. I like to have been taken prisoner myself."

The precise time of Washington's arrival on the scene at Brooklyn was not recorded, but it is believed he crossed over from New

York at about nine o'clock, or just as Howe's signal guns sounded.

Like General Putnam, Washington, too, had been awakened in the middle of the night with word of Grant's early assault, and at daybreak, still apprehensive of a second, larger attack on New York, Washington had watched with increasing anxiety as five enemy warships — *Roebuck, Asia, Renown, Preston,* and *Repulse* — started for the East River with a favorable wind and tide. It was what he had most feared.

Then miraculously the wind had veered off to the north. The ships, after tacking to and fro, trying to gain headway, at last gave up. Only the *Roebuck* could "fetch high enough" to threaten the battery at Red Hook with a few random shots.

So Long Island it was to be, Washington saw. He immediately ordered more troops to Brooklyn and wasted no time having himself rowed across the river, Joseph Reed at his side.

Private Joseph Martin, one of those in the units ordered to march to the Brooklyn ferry, remembered the cheers of the soldiers as they embarked, and the answering cheers of the spectators who thronged the wharves to watch the excitement. "They all wished us good luck apparently." For his own part, Private Martin could think only of the horrors of war "in all their hideousness."

On reaching the Brooklyn side, he saw, as he never had, the blood and suffering of wounded men. "What were the feelings of most or all the young soldiers at this time, I know not," he would remember, "but I know what were mine."

I saw a lieutenant who . . . ran round among the men of his company, sniveling and blubbering, praying each one if he had aught against him, or if *he* had injured any one, that they would forgive him, declaring at the same time that he, from his heart, forgave them if they had offended him . . . had he been at the gallows with a halter about his neck, he could not have shown more fear or penitence. A fine soldier you are, I thought, a fine officer, an exemplary man for young soldiers! I would have suffered anything short of death rather than have made such an exhibition of myself.

Accounts of Washington's activities as the battle raged are few and somewhat conflicting. He would be remembered out in plain view on horseback watching the clash of armies through a telescope. Stories would be told of him riding among the troops exhorting them to "quit yourselves like men, like soldiers," or saying, "I will fight so long as I have a leg or an arm." One soldier later described him walking the lines to rally the men. Possibly he did all of that. More likely his place was a vantage point on Brooklyn Heights, and in any case what was happening was out of his hands.

By ten o'clock his army had been hopelessly outflanked. The British were within two miles of the Brooklyn lines. Defeated men by the hundreds were streaming in from the battlefield, many blood-spattered and wounded, all exhausted. Officers were missing. Washington was facing disaster and could do nothing but sit astride his horse and watch.

Only on the right did the uproar of cannon and musket fire continue, as the indomitable Stirling and his men fought on against Grant's far greater force, still in the belief that they were holding the line.

Colonel Samuel Atlee, who commanded the Pennsylvanians, would remember actually thinking that the British were going down to defeat: "For the batteries began to play and mowed them down like grass when they retreated, and our army cried out, 'The day is our own!'"

But Grant kept holding back and in the interval, his division of 5,000 had been reinforced by 2,000 marines from the British ships offshore and two companies of New York Loyalists recruited that spring and summer by Governor Tryon.

Stirling had been ordered by Putnam to "repulse" the enemy, and for lack of orders to the contrary, he and his men had held on for nearly four hours. With great pride and no exaggeration, Colonel John Haslet would describe how his "Delawares" stood with "determined countenance," in close array, their colors flying, the enemy's artillery "playing" on them all the while, and the enemy, "though six times their number," not daring to attack.

But they had stayed too long. At eleven o'clock Grant's redcoats hit hard at the center of Stirling's line, as thousands of Hessians struck from the woods to the left. When Stirling at last pulled back, it was too late. More British were coming at him from the rear, on the Gowanus Road, the line of retreat he had been counting on. A full British division led by Cornwallis now stood between him and Brooklyn. The only escape route still open, he saw, was in the direction of Gowanus Bay, now on his left, across a tidal marsh and a creek, which at high tide was about eighty yards wide, and the tide was coming in rapidly.

Stirling ordered his men to "make the best of their way" through the marsh and across the creek. Then, he and Major Mordecai Gist and no more than 250 Marylanders attacked Cornwallis in a headlong, valiant effort to cover the retreat of the others and perhaps even break through the redcoats who had established their line on the Gowanus Road beside a stone farmhouse.

The fighting was the most savage of the day. Driven back by a blaze of deadly fire, Stirling's men rallied and struck again five times. Stirling himself fought "like a wolf." The Marylanders, who until that morning had never faced an enemy, fought no less tenaciously than their commander.

Washington, watching from a Brooklyn hill, is said to have cried out as he saw the Marylanders cut down time after time, "Good God, what brave fellows I must this day lose!"

Giving up at last, Stirling ordered the men to scatter and try to get back to the

Brooklyn lines any way they could.

Of those trying to escape through the marshes, many bogged down in the mud and could get nowhere. Men unable to swim struggled pitifully in the swift tide of the creek and under a hail of musket fire. Some officers swam their horses across. A few of the men who could not swim held back and were captured.

An eighteen-year-old, six-month volunteer with a Pennsylvania unit, Private Michael Graham, who started the day posted with eight others on the ridge at the center of the American lines, had been ordered to retreat. With men running in almost every direction, he found himself mixed in with Stirling's troops in their desperate flight.

It is impossible for me to describe the confusion and horror. . . . [I] entered a swamp or marsh through which a great many of our men were retreating. Some of them were mired and crying to their fellows for God's sake to help them out. But every man was intent on his own safety. . . . At the side of the marsh there was a pond which I took to be a millpond. Numbers, as they came to this pond jumped in, and some were drowned. . . . I got safely into camp.

Out of the eight men that were taken from the company to which I belonged the day before the battle on guard, I only escaped. The others were killed or taken prisoners.

At the time, I could not account for how it was that our troops were so completely surrounded.

Joseph Hodgkins, as he later recounted for his wife, had run pell-mell into the marshes while being fired on the whole way. He hardly knew who was killed or drowned or taken prisoner.

Lord Stirling, finding himself hopelessly surrounded, and determined not to surrender his sword to the British, broke through their fire to a Hessian regiment and gave himself up to General von Heister.

By noon or shortly thereafter the rout was over, the day lost for the Americans. British troops, having advanced so far so rapidly wanted to keep going and carry the attack straight to the Brooklyn works. Numbers of British officers, too, felt it was no time to stop. But Howe ordered a halt.

In his original plan, General Clinton had said that the principal attacks, while vigorous, should not be pushed too far. The only exception was the all-important flanking attack, which, he said, "should be pushed as far as it will go."

Clinton would later write of Howe's decision to halt: "I had at the moment but little inclination to check the ardor of our troops when I saw the enemy flying in such a panic before them." Howe himself, recalling the mood of the men, would later write that "it required repeated orders to prevail on them to desist."

It had been the first great battle of the Revolution, and by far the largest battle ever fought in North America until then. Counting both armies and the Royal Navy, more than 40,000 men had taken part. The field of battle ranged over six miles, and the fighting lasted just over six hours. And for the Continental Army, now the army of the United States of America, in this first great test under fire, it had been a crushing defeat.

"O Doleful! Doleful! Doleful!" scrawled Chaplain Philip Fithian in his diary, expressing only the obvious.

To the British it was a "glorious day" — "a cheap and complete victory" in the terse summation of General Grant. "You will be glad," Grant wrote to General

Harvey, "that we have had the field day I talked of in my last letter. If a good bleeding can bring those Bible-faced Yankees to their senses, the fever of independency should soon abate."

Everything had gone like "clockwork." Clinton's overall plan had succeeded "beyond our expectations," reported Lord Percy to his father. "Our men behaved themselves like British troops fighting in a good cause." In the opinion of Sir James Murray, no soldiers had ever behaved with greater spirit.

In one thing only had they failed, thought Ambrose Serle. "They could not run so fast as their foes, many of whom indeed were ready to run over each other."

In his own official reports, William Howe left no doubt about the magnitude of the victory and was no less generous than others in his praise of the army:

The behavior of both officers and soldiers, *British* and *Hessians,* was highly to their honor. More determined courage and steadfastness in troops have never been experienced, or a greater ardor to distinguish themselves, as all those who had an opportunity have amply evinced by their actions.

Howe reported his losses to be less than 400 — 59 killed, 267 wounded, and 31 missing. The Hessians had lost a mere 5 killed and 26 wounded.

Rebel losses, on the other hand, numbered more than 3,000, Howe claimed. Over 1,000 prisoners had been taken, while another 2,000 had been killed, wounded, or drowned.

The disparity of the losses as reported by Howe was greatly exaggerated, however. Washington, unable to provide an exact count, would later estimate in a report to Congress that about 700 to 1,000 of his men had been killed or taken prisoner.

General Parsons, who had succeeded in avoiding capture, wrote that in the course of the battle the number of American dead he and his men had collected, taken together with "the heap the enemy had made," amounted to 60, and while the total loss was still impossible to know, Parsons judged the number of killed would be "inconsiderable."

Some of the other officers who had been in the thick of the fight were convinced that the British had suffered more men killed than had the Americans, but that the British took the most prisoners.

Very few on the American side were

ready to acknowledge just how severe a defeat it had been. In fact, American losses, though far less than what Howe had reported, were dreadful. As close as can be estimated about 300 Americans had been killed and over 1,000 taken prisoner, including three generals, Sullivan, Stirling, and Nathaniel Woodhull. Sullivan and Stirling were to be treated with marked courtesy by their captors, would even dine with Lord Howe on board the *Eagle*. But Woodhull died of wounds a few weeks later.

Among the swarms of prisoners in British hands were Captain Samuel Atlee and Lieutenant Jabez Fitch. Atlee was marched under guard to General Howe's headquarters at Bedford, where he and other prisoners were subjected to "the most scurrilous and abusive language, both from officers, soldiers, and camp-ladies, everyone . . . demanding of the guard why we were taken, why we were not put to the bayonet."

Jabez Fitch, who had fought through the long day and surrendered only after being surrounded, was confined with "a great number of prisoners" in a barn, where he did all he could to comfort his friend and company commander, Captain John

Jewett, who had been bayoneted twice, in the chest and stomach, and was in excruciating pain. "I sat with him most of the night, and slept but very little," Fitch wrote. "The capt[ain] . . . was sensible of his being near his end, often repeating that it was hard work to die."

The father of ten children, Jewett made Fitch promise to describe the circumstances of his death to his wife. Later, Fitch would write to tell her that her husband had received his mortal wounds with a bayonet "after he was taken prisoner and stripped of his arms and part of his clothes."

Accounts of British, Scottish, and Hessian soldiers bayoneting Americans after they had surrendered were to become commonplace. There were repeated stories of Hessians pinning Americans to trees with their bayonets. A letter said to have been written by an unnamed British officer appeared in the *Massachusetts Spy* describing how readily surrendered Americans were "dispatched."

The Hessians and our Highlanders gave no quarters [the letter read], and it was a fine thing to see with what alacrity they dispatched the rebels with their bayonets after we had surrendered them so that they could not resist. . . . You know all stratagems are lawful in war, especially against such vile enemies to their King and country.

Numbers of individual Americans were indeed severely beaten after surrendering, or, like Captain Jewett, run through with bayonets, as reliable accounts attest, but no mass atrocities were committed. The letter in the *Massachusetts Spy* — a letter quoted repeatedly — was very likely a fake, fabricated as propaganda. Nor was there truth to an account in a London paper of Hessians burying five hundred American bodies in a single pit.

Some American prisoners, including Jabez Fitch, recorded acts of genuine civility and kindness on the part of their captors. Even the infamous General Grant, wrote Fitch, "was so good as to make us a present of a side of mutton."

For their British and Hessian captors, and particularly for the Hessians, the prisoners were great curiosities, a first chance to see close up what the rebel foe looked like. "They could not have been taken as soldiers as they had no uniforms, but only torn blouses of all colors," wrote one as-

tonished Hessian. Lieutenant von Bardeleben, too, was surprised to see how badly
clothed the Americans were. Most, he
wrote, "have nothing but a wretched
farmer's costume and a weapon. Most of
their officers are no better dressed and
until recently were only ordinary manual
laborers."

Writing in his diary in a code, Lieutenant von Bardeleben also recorded that
some of his fellow officers "shed their
ideas of being heroes. The prisoners who
knelt and sought to surrender were
beaten."

For most of the prisoners still worse
treatment lay in store, when confined and
starved in old jails, church crypts, and vile
British prison ships anchored in the
harbor.

In the remaining hours of the day, after
the guns grew silent, the Americans inside
the Brooklyn defenses, expecting the
British to attack full force, waited tensely
hour after hour as nothing happened. All
afternoon and into the night, pitiful cries
could be heard from wounded men who
lay among the unburied dead on the battlefield. Stragglers who had escaped capture kept coming into the lines almost by

the hour, bedraggled single soldiers or clusters of three or four, many badly wounded. ("And the distressed wounded came crying into the lines!" wrote Philip Fithian.) The morning after, Mordecai Gist and nine others crossed into the camps. They were the only ones of the valiant Marylanders to have made it back.

III

On the morning of Wednesday, August 28, the situation faced by Washington and the army was critical. Having been outsmarted and outfought, they were now hemmed in at Brooklyn in an area about three miles around, their backs to the East River, which could serve as an escape route only as long as the wind cooperated. With a change in the wind, it would take but a few British warships in the river to make escape impossible. Brooklyn was a trap ready to spring.

Yet early that morning Washington ordered still more of his army over from New York, almost as though he did not comprehend how perilous his position was.

Two Pennsylvania regiments and Colonel John Glover's Massachusetts troops — approximately 1,200 men — crossed the river and marched into the Brooklyn entrenchments with considerable show. Possibly it was this, the show, that Washington wanted, and if so, he succeeded. The sight of the new troops, wrote the Pennsylvania officer Alexander Graydon, brought a marked change. "The faces that had been saddened by the disasters of yesterday assumed a gleam of animation on our approach, accompanied with a murmur . . . that 'These were the lads that might do something.' "

In command of the fresh Pennsylvania brigades was handsome, self-assured Thomas Mifflin, formerly of Washington's staff at Cambridge and now, at thirty-two, a brigadier general. Mifflin immediately volunteered to survey the outermost defenses and report back to Washington, little expecting the part he was soon to play.

Joseph Hodgkins, so exhausted from the battle that he could hardly hold his head up, nonetheless took time to write home to report that "through the goodness of God," he was still in one piece. Like everyone, he expected at any moment to be in action again. "The enemy are within a mile and a half of our lines," he noted.

The weather had changed dramatically

from the day before. Under darkening skies, the temperature dropped ten degrees.

Riflemen in the outermost defenses were ordered to keep up a steady fire at the enemy, if only to raise spirits, and the British fired back steadily on into the afternoon when the clouds opened in a cold, drenching downpour, the start of a northeastern storm that brought still further misery to the defeated army.

> Afternoon, at three, an alarm [gun] in the midst of a violent rain [wrote Philip Fithian]. Drums heavily calling to arms. Men running promiscuously and in columns to the lines. All the time the rain falling with an uncommon torrent. The guns of the whole army are wetted. And after the alarm was over, which was occasioned by the regulars coming in a greater body than usual to drive our riflemen, our troops fired off their guns quite till evening, so that it seemed indeed dangerous to walk within our own lines — for we could from every part hear perpetually firing, and continually hear the [cannon] balls pass over us.

The storm and the roar of the guns continued into the night. Across the river in New York, Pastor Ewald Shewkirk wrote of the boom of cannon at Brooklyn intermixed with flashes of lightning and the roar of thunder.

The following day, Thursday, August 29, the storm continued, heavy rains fell. Troops without tents also had little or no food. Fires were nearly impossible to keep going for cooking or warmth. Private Martin got by with biscuits he had had the foresight to stuff into his knapsack before leaving New York, biscuits "hard enough to break the teeth of a rat," as he wrote. Anyone who had a bit of raw pork to gnaw felt privileged. Nearly all were hungry and soaked to the skin. In places in the trenches men stood in water up to their waists. Muskets and cartridges were almost impossible to keep dry. Soldiers, unable to stay awake any longer, fell asleep standing upright in the rain or sitting without cover in the mud.

Washington, who had had little or no sleep, sent off a brief, somewhat incoherent report to Congress at four-thirty in the morning, saying his people were much "distressed." Of the defeat of the day before he said only that there had been "engagement" with the enemy and that he had heard nothing from General Sullivan or Lord Stirling. "Nor can I ascertain our loss." Nor did he report that in the night the British had started "advancing by approaches," as it was known. Instead of risking an open assault, they were digging trenches toward the American lines and throwing up embankments that already were no more than six hundred yards from Fort Putnam.

Yet for all the miseries it wrought, the storm was greatly to Washington's advantage. Under the circumstances, any ill wind from the northeast was a stroke of good fortune. For as long as it held, Lord Howe's ships had no chance to "get up" where they could wreak havoc.

But who knew how long such good fortune might serve? And what if his luck ran out? ("But lest some unlucky event should happen unfavorable to my reputation," he had told Congress when accepting his command, "I beg it may be remembered by every gent[leme]n in the room that I this day declare with the utmost sincerity, I do not think myself equal to the command I [am] honored with.")

He was now advised that the old ships that had been sunk in the East River could not be counted on as a serious barrier against British warships, and especially the smaller ships, which could come up through that part of the East River between Governor's Island and Brooklyn where there were no barriers at all.

With the situation as grim as it could be, no one was more conspicuous in his calm presence of mind than Washington, making his rounds on horseback in the rain. They must be "cool but determined," he had told the men before the battle, when spirits were high. Now, in the face of catastrophe, he was demonstrating what he meant by his own example. Whatever anger or torment or despair he felt, he kept to himself.

Since he first arrived in New York in April, the essence of Washington's policy had been to keep close watch and make decisions according to circumstances. Sometime before noon, having heard General Mifflin's report on the progress made by the British with their "approaches" during the night, as well as the strongly expressed views of Joseph Reed, and having looked things over himself, he made a momentous decision.

A secret and deliberately deceiving urgent message went off to General Heath at King's Bridge. Every flatbottomed boat or sloop, almost any watercraft available, was to be rounded up "without delay" for the reason that "we have many battalions from New Jersey which are coming over to relieve others here." The message was signed by Mifflin.

Washington would later recall emphasizing that there be no "ceremony" in carrying out the order — meaning that whatever boats would serve should be confiscated on the spot.

Heath assigned the roundup to Colonel Hugh Hughes, a New York schoolteacher, who, in pursuit of his mission over the next twenty-four hours, would scarcely ever dismount from his horse.

At four in the afternoon, with still no letup in the rain, Washington called a meeting with his generals at the Livingston mansion, on the brow of Brooklyn Heights overlooking the river.

Mifflin, who had advised Washington that he must either fight or retreat immediately, asked to be the one to propose the retreat, with the understanding that if it were agreed on, he and the Pennsylvania regiment would serve as the rear guard in the outermost defenses, and thus hold the line until the rest of the army had departed. This would be the most dangerous assignment of all and he insisted it be his, Mifflin told Washington, lest by proposing retreat his reputation should suffer.

In the words of the minutes of the meeting: "It was submitted to the consideration of the council whether, under all circumstances, it would not be eligible to leave Long Island and its dependencies [fortifications] and remove the army to New York."

Only one man expressed doubts: General John Morin Scott, a leading New York attorney and ardent patriot-turned-soldier.

"As it was suddenly proposed, *I as suddenly objected to it*," Scott later wrote, "from an aversion to giving the enemy a single inch of ground, *but was soon convinced by the unanswerable reasons for it*."

Of the reasons put forward — ammunition spoiled by heavy rains, the miseries and discouragement of the exhausted troops, the enemy's advancing by approaches, the precarious situation of an army divided in half — the most serious was the looming threat of the British fleet suddenly in command of the East River. As Joseph Reed wrote in explanation, with Lord Howe trying every day to "get up" against the wind, "it became a serious consideration whether we ought to risk the fate of the army, and perhaps America, on defending the circle of about three miles fortified with a few strong redoubts, but chiefly open lines."

The decision was unanimous. Orders went out and by evening the plan was rapidly unfolding.

At Dorchester the year before, Washington had taken advantage of the night to catch Howe by complete surprise. On Long Island, Howe had sent 10,000 men through the night to catch Washington by surprise. The night of Thursday, August 29, it was Washington's turn again.

The orders came at seven. The troops were to be "under arms with packs and everything." It was to be a night attack on the enemy, they were told.

To Alexander Graydon, who was with the Pennsylvania regiments assigned to the rear guard, it seemed a desperate measure, almost suicidal. "Several nuncupative wills were made upon the occasion, uncertain as it was, whether the persons to whom they were communicated would survive, either to prove or to execute them." Graydon concentrated on summoning his own courage.

At about nine o'clock the troops with the

least experience, along with the sick and wounded, were ordered to start for the Brooklyn ferry landing, on the pretext that they were being relieved by reinforcements. But of this the soldiers nearer the front lines knew nothing. "The thing was conducted with so much secrecy," wrote another of the Pennsylvanians, Lieutenant Tench Tilghman, "that neither subalterns or privates knew that the whole army was to cross back again to New York." Nor were the officers told.

Alexander Graydon kept thinking what "extreme rashness" it was to order an attack, given the condition of the men and their rain-soaked arms. The more he thought, the more puzzled he became, until suddenly it "flashed upon my mind that a retreat was the object, and that the order for assailing the enemy was but a cover to the real design." The fellow officers to whom he confided his thoughts "dared not suffer themselves to believe it."

Others elsewhere in the forts and defenses began thinking that a night escape had to be the true intent, and to weigh the risks involved. As one particularly clearheaded officer, Major Benjamin Tallmadge of Connecticut, would later write, putting himself in Washington's place:

To move so large a body of troops, with all their necessary appendages, across a river full a mile wide, with a rapid current, in face of a victorious well-disciplined army nearly three times as numerous as his own, and a fleet capable of stopping the navigation, so that not one boat could have passed over, seemed to present most formidable obstacles.

The rain had stopped at last, but the northeast wind that had kept the river free of the British fleet was blowing still, and this, with an ebb tide, was proving no less a deterrent to an American retreat.

The first troops ordered to withdraw to the ferry landing found that the river was so rough that no boats could cross. The men could only stand and wait in the dark. According to one account, General Alexander McDougall, who was in charge of the embarkation, sent Washington a message saying that with conditions as they were, there could be no retreat that night.

It was about eleven o'clock when, as if by design, the northeast wind died down. Then the wind shifted to the southwest and a small armada of boats manned by more of John Glover's Massachusetts sailors and fishermen started over the river from New York, Glover himself crossing to Brooklyn to give directions.

Glover's men proved as crucial as the change in the wind. In a feat of extraordinary seamanship, at the helm and manning oars hour after hour, they negotiated the river's swift, contrary currents in boats so loaded with troops and supplies, horses and cannon, that the water was often but inches below the gunnels — and all in pitch dark, with no running lights. Few men ever had so much riding on their skill, or were under such pressure, or performed so superbly.

As the boats worked back and forth from Brooklyn, more troops were ordered to withdraw from the lines and march to the ferry landing. "And tedious was the operation through mud and mire," one man remembered.

Wagon wheels, anything that might make noise, were muffled with rags. Talking was forbidden. "We were strictly enjoined not to speak, or even cough," wrote Private Martin. "All orders were given from officer to officer and communicated to the men in whispers."

They moved through the night like specters. "As one regiment left their station on guard, the remaining troops moved to the right and left and filled up the vacancies," wrote Benjamin Tallmadge, recalling also that for many of the men it was their third night without sleep. Washington, meanwhile, had ridden to the ferry landing to take personal charge of the embarkation.

The orderly withdrawal of an army was considered one of the most difficult of all maneuvers, even for the best-trained soldiers, and the fact that Washington's ragtag amateur army was making a night withdrawal in perfect order and silence thus far, seemed more than could be hoped for. The worst fear was that by some blunder the British would discover what was afoot and descend with all their superior force.

Those in greatest jeopardy, the troops in Mifflin's vanguard, were still holding the outer defenses. Waiting their turn to be withdrawn, they kept busy creating enough of a stir and tending campfires to make it appear the army was still in place, knowing all the while that if the enemy were to become the wiser, they stood an excellent chance of being annihilated.

In the event of a British attack, they were supposed to fall back and rally at the old Dutch church in the middle of the road in the village of Brooklyn. As the hours passed, there was no mistaking the sound of British picks and shovels digging steadily toward them in the darkness.

The full garrison at Fort Stirling on Brooklyn Heights also had orders to stay through the night, as cover against an attack by enemy ships.

At about two in the morning a cannon went off. No explanation was ever given. "If the explosion was within our lines," Alexander Graydon later speculated, "the gun was probably discharged in the act of spiking it."

For the rest of his life, Graydon could never recall that night without thinking of the scene in Shakespeare's *Henry V* of the long night wait before the Battle of Agincourt, in which, as Graydon wrote, "is arrayed, in appropriate gloom, a similar interval of dread suspense and awful expectation."

It was approximately four o'clock and still dark when a young officer on horseback, Major Alexander Scammell, came riding through the outer defenses looking for General Mifflin.

Scammell was twenty-nine years old and well liked. A Harvard graduate and an attorney in civilian life, he was quick-witted, charming, six feet two inches tall, and had been serving as an aide-de-camp to General Sullivan.

Scammell told Mifflin the boats were ready at the river landing and that Washington was anxiously waiting for the arrival of the last remaining troops. Mifflin said Scammel had to be mistaken. He could not imagine that Washington meant his own vanguard. Scammel insisted he was not mistaken, saying he had ridden from the extreme left where he had ordered all the troops he met to march for the ferry, that they were then on the move, and that he would continue on to give the same orders.

Mifflin then ordered General Edward Hand to form up the regiment and move out as soon as possible.

But Scammell was mistaken. He had misunderstood Washington. The order was a blunder of exactly the kind that could spell disaster.

The troops left the trenches and started for the river "without delay," until just beyond the Dutch church, within a half mile of the landing, where the column halted.

Washington, astride his horse in the middle of the road, demanded to know what was going on. General Hand was explaining when Mifflin rode up. Faces were hard to see in the dark, but Hand would remember Washington exclaiming, "Good God! General Mifflin, I am afraid you have ruined us!"

Mifflin responded "with some warmth" that he was only obeying Washington's orders as delivered by Major Scammell.

Washington said it was a "dreadful mistake," that they had come too soon, that things were in "much confusion at the ferry," and they must turn at once and go back to their posts.

For the weary troops who had held the lines through the night, counting the hours until they could be relieved and escape with the others, and who waited now in the dark, it was a moment of extreme difficulty, "trying business to young soldiers," as Alexander Graydon wrote. "Whoever has seen troops in a similar situation, or duly contemplates the human heart in such trials well knows how to appreciate the conduct of these brave men on this occasion."

They returned to the lines as ordered, and in the words of General Hand "had the good fortune to recover our stations and keep them for some hours longer, without the enemy perceiving what was going forward."

At the ferry landing all this time troops

and supplies and artillery were being loaded aboard one boat after another as quickly as humanly possible and sent on their way. Everyone worked furiously. A Connecticut soldier manning one of the boats would remember making eleven crossings in the course of the night.

But the exodus was not moving fast enough. Some of the heavy cannon, mired in mud, were impossible to move and had to be left behind. Time was running out. Though nearly morning, a large part of the army still waited to embark, and without the curtain of night to conceal them, their escape was doomed.

Incredibly, yet again, circumstances — fate, luck, Providence, the hand of God, as would be said so often — intervened.

Just at daybreak a heavy fog settled in over the whole of Brooklyn, concealing everything no less than had the night. It was a fog so thick, remembered a soldier, that one "could scarcely discern a man at six yards distance." Even with the sun up, the fog remained as dense as ever, while over on the New York side of the river there was no fog at all.

At long last Mifflin and the rear guard and the troops at Fort Stirling were summoned. "It may be supposed we did not linger," wrote Alexander Graydon.

Major Tallmadge, who with his regiment was among the last to depart on the boats, would write later that he thought he saw Washington on the ferry stairs staying to the very end.

Graydon estimated that it was seven in the morning, perhaps a little later, when he and his men landed in New York. "And in less than an hour after, the fog having dispersed, the enemy was visible on the shore we had left [behind]."

In a single night, 9,000 troops had escaped across the river. Not a life was lost. The only men captured were three who had hung back to plunder.

IV

Friday, August 30th. In the morning, to our great astonishment, found they had evacuated all their works on Brookland . . . with not a shot being fired at them . . . neither could our shipping get up for want of wind, and the whole escaped . . . to New York.

The immediate reaction of the British was, as Major Stephen Kemble recorded in his diary, one of utter astonishment. That the rebel army had silently vanished in the night under their very noses was almost inconceivable. The surprise for the British was no less than it had been the morning of March 5, at Boston, when they awakened to see the guns of Ticonderoga on Dorchester Heights. The great difference now was a feeling of relief, not dread. All at once the whole of Brooklyn and its elaborate defenses were theirs for the taking and the rebels were on the run.

"We cannot yet account for their precipitate retreat," wrote General Grant. Like many of the British, Grant failed to understand how the Americans, having labored for months on their massive fortifications, could so readily abandon them.

General Howe had performed most admirably and deserved his success, Grant thought. The lesson of Brooklyn, Grant decided, was that if pushed the Americans would never face the King's troops again.

Lord Percy agreed. "They feel severely the blow of the 27th," he wrote to his father, "and I think I may venture to assert that they will never again stand before us in the field. Everything seems to be over with them, and I flatter myself now that this campaign will put a total end to the war." To Lord Germain as well, he predicted, "This business is pretty near over."

General Clinton, justifiably proud of his role in the triumph, wrote to his sister that he expected to be home by Christmas.

As many officers as could came to see the rebel works and enjoy the view from Fort Stirling. "This and the parts adjacent is the most beautiful and fertile spot I have yet seen in America," recorded Ambrose Serle, who was disturbed only by the reek of the unburied dead still strewn about in the fields.

As for the rebels and their flight, Serle, like many of the British, thought they had "behaved very ill as men."

But there were those, including General Grant, who saw that the Americans had made a daring and superbly executed move. They had "wisely" gotten out when they did, General Clinton would later comment, and "very ably effected the retreat of their whole army." Charles Stedman, an officer under Lord Percy, would later write a widely respected history of the war — one of the few histories by someone who was actually in the war — in which he called the retreat "particularly glorious to the Americans." Further, he saw, as apparently Grant did not, the peril the Americans would have faced in the event of a change in the wind. Had the *Phoenix* and the *Rose*, with their combined 72 guns, fetched up into the East River as they had done before on the Hudson, Stedman emphasized, any chance of escape would have been cut off "most completely."

As commendable as Washington's leadership during the retreat had been, good luck had played a very large part, and wars were not won by withdrawals, however well handled. Nor could a successful evacuation compensate for the losses suffered in dead and wounded and the thousand or more who had been taken prisoner by the enemy.

The Battle of Brooklyn — the Battle of Long Island as it would be later known — had been a fiasco. Washington had proven indecisive and inept. In his first command on a large-scale field of battle, he and his general officers had not only failed, they had been made to look like fools.

Almost from the moment he took command in New York, Washington had put himself in an impossible position. He had failed to recognize that whether the British were to attack Manhattan or Long Island, he was in a trap either way. General Lee had seen clearly that "whoever commands the sea must command the town," and from the moment Washington chose to ignore that warning, he was in trouble.

Dividing his army, he had counted on his ability to respond to circumstances as need be, as though moving his forces back and forth over the East River would always be his choice to make. On the very eve of the British attack on Long Island, he was still baffled over whether it was the real thing and, if so, what he ought to do.

For the British everything went as planned, from the landing at Gravesend Bay to the night march of 10,000 men through the Jamaica Pass to the battle itself. For Washington almost nothing went as planned. The assumption that the British would make an all-out frontal assault at Brooklyn, as at Bunker Hill, and as they had seemed ready to repeat at Dorchester Heights, was the heart of the American strategy, and it was largely wishful thinking. So quickly, so completely was Washington outmaneuvered, the battle was virtually over before it began. It was as though in all his anguish over where and how he might be outflanked by water, he forgot that it could happen on land.

How a man so characteristically insistent

that things be done just so, who took such care about details, could have let the Jamaica Pass stand unguarded is impossible to explain — and particularly when he had spent the full day at Brooklyn, August 26, studying the situation.

Washington never accounted for his part in what happened at the Battle of Long Island, and for many the brilliant success of the night escape would serve both as proof of his ability and a way to ease the humiliation and pain of defeat. The Americans could also rightly claim that they had been vastly outnumbered by a far-better-trained army, and that given the odds against them, they had, in several instances, shown exemplary courage and tenacity.

General Putnam was blamed for not ordering Stirling to withdraw sooner. Sullivan was blamed for knowing too little about the terrain. Putnam and Sullivan were both faulted for leaving the Jamaica Pass unattended. Colonel Samuel Miles, the one supposed to be in charge of the left flank, later claimed to have had a hunch the enemy would make use of Jamaica Pass, yet he had done nothing about it. Stirling, for all his bravery, was criticized for trying to fight the British on the open field in their own fashion.

Many, including Henry Knox, would insist that had Nathanael Greene, with his familiarity with every detail of the Heights of Gowan, been present, the British would have met stiff opposition at the Jamaica Pass and things would have gone differently. Possibly they could have. Greene's illness and consequent absence was without question one of Washington's severest blows.

Washington would hold Sullivan largely to blame, for too little vigilance at the Jamaica Pass, thus implying that in his view Greene would never have allowed a British surprise to succeed there.

But in fact a British victory had been certain all day, no matter what the Americans did. The struggle might have lasted longer, the cost to the British might have been greater, but outnumbered by such superior troops and without control of the sea, Washington and his army never really had a chance — and this quite apart from the far greater experience of the British command.

General Howe's decision not to continue the attack the afternoon of the battle would be a subject of endless speculation and debate. Among Howe's severest critics was Captain John Montresor, who, the morning of August 30, had been the first to discover that the Americans had vanished in the night. To Montresor there was no question that Howe should have pressed the attack and that to have failed to do so was a grievous mistake. "Never pursues his victories" was Montresor's curt assessment of William Howe.

General Clinton, too, seemed to feel that with the Americans "flying in such a panic" Howe had as good a chance as he would ever have to finish them off and end the war at a stroke. But Clinton would never say so when questioned. Rather he would write that had he been in Howe's position, he, too, would have "judged it prudent" to hold back.

In testimony before Parliament, General Cornwallis would refuse to say that the Brooklyn lines could have been taken by an immediate attack, and said that at the time he never heard anyone claim they could have been.

The Americans had wanted another Bunker Hill. Howe, remembering Bunker Hill, had no desire to squander lives with another bloody frontal attack on an army dug in on a hill, if, with a little patience, that same hill could be taken by less costly means. "It was apparent the lines must have been ours at a very cheap rate by regular approaches," he would say in explanation. "I could not risk the loss that might have been sustained in the assault."

Had Howe pressed on the afternoon of the 27th, the British victory could have been total. Or had the wind turned earlier, and the British navy moved into the East River, the war and the chances of an independent United States of America could have been long delayed, or even ended there and then.

When news of the battle, together with Howe's exaggerated estimates of American losses, at last reached London, it caused a sensation. A victory so grand, said the press, "fully controverted" all the "full-mouthed predictions" of the opponents of the war. Edmund Burke, Charles Fox, and others in Parliament opposed to the war were as downcast as prominent Tories were jubilant. News to "enliven our countenances," the Tory historian Edward Gibbon called it.

All Britain was in "an ecstasy which I cannot express," a friend wrote to Henry Clinton. Bells were rung in London and in rural hamlets, windows lighted with candles. The King was reported to have paused during a stroll in Kew Gardens to express his "great satisfaction" with the report of General Howe, upon whom he was to confer the Order of Bath.

In Congress the defeat was spoken of privately as an "unfortunate beginning" at best, and more candidly as a "disaster." But there was no panic.

Elsewhere in the country early reports of the battle were taken at first as "Tory news." Afterward, great anxiety, if not panic, set in. "All in solicitude," recorded the Reverend Ezra Stiles at his home in Newport. "Tories rejoicing. Sons of Liberty dejected."

Newspapers put heavy emphasis on Washington's daring night retreat, calling it renewed cause for confidence in the army and in Washington most of all. The escape from Brooklyn was "a masterpiece," read a report in the *New England Chronicle*. "The manner in which our retreat was performed," reported the *Virginia Gazette*, "reflects the highest credit upon our commander-in-chief, and the officers in general."

While one writer in the *New England Chronicle* declared, "Providence favored us," another in the *Massachusetts Spy* assured his readers that the defeat on Long Island and consequent distress were "loud speaking testimonies of the displeasure and anger of Almighty God against a sinful people."

We have thought God was for us, and had given many and signal instances of his power and mercy in our favor, and had greatly frowned upon and disappointed our enemies; and verily it has been so. But have we repented and given him the glory? Verily no. His hand seems to be turned and stretched out against us — and strong is his hand.

In New York the gloom of defeat hung heavy. The high spirits of the soldiers that had been counted on for so long to compensate for, even overcome, whatever advantages the enemy might have, were gone. The army that had crossed in the night from Brooklyn was, in the light of day on August 30, a sorry sight to behold — filthy, bedraggled, numb with fatigue, still soaked to the skin, many of them sick and emaciated. The army that had gone off to Brooklyn cheering was no more.

"It was a surprising change," Pastor

Shewkirk noted in his diary, "the merry tones on drums and fifes had ceased. . . . It seemed a general damp had spread, and the sight of scattered people up and down the streets was indeed moving."

They had been swiftly, overwhelmingly defeated. "A hard day this, for us poor Yankees" was young Enoch Anderson's unadorned summing up of the Battle of Brooklyn.

But as resounding as the British victory had been, it was not a decisive victory. The war had not been ended at a stroke by a superior force of professional soldiers. Washington and his 9,000 troops had survived to fight another day.

For the first twenty-four hours in New York, nearly all were collapsed in sleep, including the commander-in-chief. Not until Saturday, August 31, could Washington summon the strength even to notify Congress of the escape. He had been "entirely unfit to take pen in hand," he explained. "Since Monday scarce any of us have been out of the lines till our passage across the East River was effected yesterday morning, and for forty-eight hours preceding that I had hardly been of[f] my horse and never closed my eyes."

Presently he was "much hurried and engaged in arranging and making new dispositions of our forces," he said. He would save for another letter the extremity of the concern he felt.

Part III

The Long Retreat

These are the times that try men's souls.
— Thomas Paine, *The Crisis*
December 1776

Chapter Six
FORTUNE FROWNS

We want great men who, when fortune frowns, will not be discouraged.
— Colonel Henry Knox

I

"I have only time to say I am alive and well," Joseph Reed reported to his wife Esther. His spirits, however, were but "middling."

The justice of our cause, the hope of success, and every other circumstance that can enliven us, must be put into the scale against those of a contrary kind, which I allow to be serious. . . . My honor, duty, and every other tie held sacred among men, call upon me to proceed with firmness and resolution. . . . My country will, I trust, yet be free, whatever may be our fate who are cooped up, or are in danger of being so, on this tongue of land, where we ought never to have been.

It was "a mere point of honor which keeps us here," he had written earlier to a friend. Now, in the dismal aftermath of defeat, the idea of risking the fate of America in defense of New York seemed so senseless that submitting to the "dispensations of Providence," as he said, was about the only recourse left.

The army that had shown such remarkable discipline and unity through the long night of the escape from Brooklyn had rapidly become engulfed with despair, turned surly and out of hand. Gangs of soldiers roamed the streets of New York breaking into houses and taking whatever they wanted. Even Lord Stirling's mansion, at the corner of Broad and Beaver streets, was wantonly ransacked.

Joseph Hodgkins, already as downcast as he had ever been over the defeat, learned in a letter from his wife of the death of their small, ailing son. It was "heavy news," he told her. He was trying hard not to be discouraged over the way the war was going.

But only consider a minute, we have been all this summer digging and building of forts to cover our heads and now we have been obliged to leave them and now we are here and not one shovel full of dirt to cover us. . . . I don't write this to discourage you or to increase you[r] trouble, but only to let you know as near as I can of our circumstances.

Still concerned for her, he wrote again the next day to assure her he himself had suffered no real damage thus far. "I had my sleeve button shot out of my sleeve and the skin a little grazed, but through mercy, received no other hurt." There was no mention of giving up and coming home.

But others by the hundreds were doing just that, many walking off with their arms and ammunition. (One soldier was found lugging a cannonball, to give to his mother, he explained, to use to pound mustard seed.) Entire Connecticut militia units were departing en masse, saying they had had enough. The roads in Connecticut and New Jersey were filled with soldiers heading home. Probably one in four carried disease, and those who did not spread their own corrosive discouragement.

Men in the ranks complained they had been "sold out." Some were openly saying they longed for the return of General Lee. Washington's leadership was in question. Colonel John Haslet wrote to Caesar Rodney, a delegate to Congress, "I fear General Washington has too heavy a task, assisted mostly by beardless boys."

Henry Knox, whose faith in Washington never faltered, wrote to his wife that the pressing need was for great men "who when fortune frowns will not be discouraged." If there was a grievous flaw in how things were being run, it was the "stupid parsimony" of the Congress.

Washington had concluded his general orders for September 2 with a call for steadfastness and valor in the defense of New York: "Now is the time for every man to exert himself and make our country glorious or become contemptible." But by all signs his words had little effect. Indeed, in a letter to Congress written that same day, Washington portrayed much of the army as plainly "contemptible."

The militia, instead of calling forth their utmost efforts to a brave and manly opposition, in order to repair our losses, are dismayed, intractable, and impatient to return. Great numbers of them have gone off, in some instances almost by whole regiments.

Worse, their example had "infected" others to the point that he no longer had confidence in the army as a whole and for the first time questioned whether New York had become a lost cause.

He needed to know from Congress whether, in the event he had to abandon the city, it should be left to "stand as winter quarters for the enemy" — meaning, should it be burned? "They would derive great conveniences from it, on the one hand, and much property would be destroyed on the other." The question, he wrote, allowed "but little time for deliberation."

The letter went immediately off to Philadelphia, where, as it happened, General John Sullivan arrived that same day, September 2, having been temporarily paroled by Lord Howe to deliver a peace overture to Congress. Washington, who took a dim view of Sullivan's mission, had nonetheless given his approval, feeling it was not for him to withhold whatever Howe had to say. As Sullivan reported, His Lordship, being "desirous of an accommodation with America," wished to meet "almost any place" with a delegation from Congress.

British troops all the while were advancing on the opposite shore of the East River, heading north in the direction of King's Bridge. Then, in the dark of night, September 3, the first enemy ship, the frigate *Rose*, towing thirty flatboats, started up the river with a north-flowing tide, anchoring ultimately in the mouth of Newtown Creek, directly across from a large cove on the New York side known as Kips Bay.

The day after brought a "mighty movement" of transports and more flatboats up the East River, while two more frigates, the *Repulse* and the *Pearl*, sailed into the Hudson.

In Philadelphia, Congress resolved that in the event General Washington found it necessary to withdraw from New York, there must be "no damage" done to the city, as Washington was informed in a letter from John Hancock. And as if to underscore how little the members of Congress comprehended the actual situation, it was further stated that they had "no doubt of being able to recover" the city, should the enemy "obtain possession of it."

Where the British would strike was as uncertain as it had been from the start. What Washington feared most was an attack from the rear, in the vicinity of King's Bridge, and having convinced himself that this was Howe's intention, he began moving troops there. General Heath warned that the enemy might land on the coast of Westchester County, beyond the Harlem River. Everything depended on reliable intelligence, Washington told Heath, and he had none. He urged Heath to "leave no stone unturned" or spare any expense in finding out all he could as soon as possible.

"We think (at least I do) that we cannot stay," Joseph Reed wrote again to his wife, "and yet we do not know how to go, so that we may be properly said to be between hawk and buzzard."

Reed, who seemed older and wiser than his years, had tried always to take a large, philosophical view of life's travails, and this, in combination with a natural cheerfulness and a strong, analytical mind, had put him at the head of the legal profession in Philadelphia while still in his early thirties. But it was a struggle now for him to offer even a fragment of hope. It was the sluggards and skulkers, the tavern patriots and windy politicians, who evoked a wrath he could not contain.

When I look round, and see how few of

the numbers who talked so largely of death and honor are around me, and that those who are here are those from whom it was least expected . . . I am lost in wonder and surprise. . . . Your noisy sons of liberty are, I find, the quietest in the field. . . . An engagement, or even the expectation of one, gives a wonderful insight into character.

Though an observer only through the Battle of Brooklyn, Reed had been with Washington throughout. For six days there had not been time even for a change of clothes, and, like Washington, he had had no sleep for several nights. Whether he could continue to bear up under the strain and fatigue, as Washington seemed able to do, remained to be seen.

Esther, as she wrote, hoped he would come home to be with her at the birth of their fourth child.

It was thought that the American army, spread now from the Battery to King's Bridge, numbered 20,000, but with men deserting in droves, it was difficult to tell. Perhaps a quarter of the men were sick, and officers, as well as men in the ranks, often feigned sickness.

One of the most seriously ill had recov-

ered, however, and with immediate consequences. On September 5, Nathanael
Greene returned to duty and promptly
submitted to Washington an emphatic,
closely reasoned argument for abandoning
New York at once. If illness had denied
him the chance to play a part at Brooklyn,
he had by no means let his mind drift from
the fate of the army, or all that was at
stake. While others, like Reed, were of the
same mind, Greene alone committed his
views to paper.

I think we have no object on this side of
King's Bridge. Our troops are now so
scattered that one part may be cut off
before the others can come to their
support. In this situation suppose the
enemy should run up the North River
several ships of force and a number of
transpo[rts] at the same time, and effect
a landing between the town and middle
division of the army. Another party
from Long Island should land right opposite. These two parties form a line
across the Island and entrench themselves. The two flanks of this line could
be easily supported by the shipping.
The center, fortified with the redoubts,
would render it very difficult, if not im-

possible, to cut our way through. . . .
Should this event take place, and by the
by I don't think it very improbable,
your Excellency will be reduced to that
situation which every prudent general
would wish to avoid, that is of being ob-
ligated to fight the enemy to a disadvantage or submit.

It had been agreed, Greene continued,
that without the possession of Long Island,
New York could not be held. The army,
dispersed as it was from one end of York
Island to the other, could not possibly stop
an attack, and another such defeat as at
Brooklyn could be ruinous. " 'Tis our business to study to avoid any considerable
misfortune." Besides, two-thirds of the city
belonged to Tories. There was no sound
reason to run any great risk in its defense.

"I give it as my opinion that a general
and speedy retreat is absolutely necessary
and that the honor and interest of America
require it."

Further, he would burn the city. Once
taken by the British, it could never be recovered without a naval force superior to
theirs. Left standing, it would guarantee
them abundant housing, wharves, and a
market for their every need. Greene could

not conceive of a single benefit to the American cause that could come from preserving New York, and he urged Washington to summon a war council.

By the time the council convened, on September 7, at Washington's headquarters at the Mortier house north of town, the letter from John Hancock had arrived saying Congress wanted no damage done to New York.

It was agreed by the council that if the British were to bring up their fleet and open fire, the city was untenable. Greene, Reed, Israel Putnam, and several others called for a total and immediate withdrawal from all of York Island. This, they argued, would deprive the enemy of the advantage of their sea power, "put nothing to the hazard," and keep the army together.

But they were overruled by the majority, as Washington promptly reported to Congress. What Washington said at the meeting is not known, as no record survived, though it appears he thought the directive from Congress was an egregious mistake and that Nathanael Greene had the right idea. In a letter to Lund Washington he would later write, "Had I been left to the dictates of my own judgment,

New York should have been laid in ashes."

To Congress on September 8, Washington expressed his fear of being outflanked again by the enemy. "On every side there is a choice of difficulties," he wrote. And with every decision went the possibility that his army would not fight. It was a fear that never left him. Young, inexperienced soldiers who were so greatly outnumbered ought never be drawn into an open conflict, he wrote.

"We should on all occasions avoid a general action or put anything to the risk unless compelled by a necessity."

Yet he seemed unable to make up his mind. "On the other hand, to abandon a city which has been by some deemed defensible and on whose works much labor has been bestowed, has a tendency to dispirit the troops and enfeeble our cause." Strong posts at Fort Washington and on the opposite side of the Hudson would secure the Hudson corridor. A retreating army was always "encircled with difficulties," and "declining an engagement subjects a general to reproach."

But then he held out the possibility that some "brilliant stroke" might save the cause, though who knew what that might be.

It did not help that the men were badly

fed and unpaid — many had seen no pay for two months — while across the East River the British were well supplied with fresh provisions from the farms of Long Island, "a pleasing circumstance," as Ambrose Serle noted, "both for the health and spirit of the troops." The Hessians especially claimed they had never fared so well.

At Philadelphia, after days of debate, Congress decided to send a delegation of three — Benjamin Franklin, John Adams, and Edward Rutledge — to meet with Lord Howe. The three men departed on September 9.

On September 10, advancing British forces crossed from Long Island to occupy Montresor's Island at the mouth of the Harlem River.

Nathanael Greene pressed Washington to reconvene the war council. The situation was "so critical and dangerous" that a decision must be made, Washington read in a joint statement signed by Greene and six other general officers, this written September 11, the day the three-man congressional delegation crossed from New Jersey to Staten Island to confer with Lord Howe.

The Staten Island meeting lasted several

hours, during which Lord Howe did most of the talking. "It is desirable to put a stop to these ruinous extremities, as well for the sake of our country as yours," said the resplendently uniformed admiral. Was there no way of "treading back this step of independency?" There was not, he was told, and the meeting came to nothing, as expected.

But it had at least brought a pause to enemy movements. The British had suspended operations during what could have been a golden opportunity to attack, as one perfect, late-summer day followed another.

Washington's war council met again on September 12 and this time resolved to abandon the city. The main part of the army was to move north to King's Bridge as rapidly as possible, while some 4,000 troops under General Putnam remained to hold off an attack. The sick were to be moved first. Cannon and tons of supplies and ammunition had to be hauled from the city, a mammoth undertaking. Every available horse and wagon was pressed into service.

On the afternoon of Friday the 13th, the British were on the move again. Clearly some "grand military exertion" was under way, in Joseph Reed's words. The warships *Roebuck* and *Phoenix*, and the frigates *Orpheus* and *Carysfort* — four ships mounting 148 cannon — proceeded up the East River with six troop transports, to anchor in Bushwick Creek. Fired on "briskly" by American batteries, the ships received no serious damage, nor bothered even to return the fire.

On Saturday the 14th, Washington received another directive from John Hancock. After further consideration, Congress had now decided to leave the timing of an evacuation of New York entirely to the commander-in-chief. He and the army were to remain not "a moment longer" than he thought necessary.

Washington replied at once:

We are now taking every method in our power to remove the stores, etc. . . . they are so great and so numerous that I fear we shall not effect the whole before we meet with some interruption. . . . Our sick are extremely numerous and we find their removal attended with the greatest difficulty.

Yet by late afternoon the larger part of the army had moved north to King's

Bridge and Harlem Heights. Washington and his staff would depart from the Mortier house that night and head north.

Surveying the shore of Kips Bay with his telescope, from the deck of the *Roebuck*, General Henry Clinton could see entrenchments "lined with men whose countenance appeared respectable and firm," as he later wrote. The invasion of New York was about to begin, and Clinton was again to lead the attack.

Kips Bay was not his choice. He had adamantly opposed the plan, insisting that the Harlem River and King's Bridge were the key to victory. If York Island was a bottle, then Harlem was the neck. Close it off, Clinton argued, and Washington and his rebel army would be trapped, the war won.

Though overruled, Clinton continued to press his opinions almost to the last hour. Even if the landing at Kips Bay were to succeed, he said, it would still be necessary to drive the rebels from Harlem and from King's Bridge.

General Howe and his brother the admiral were not unmindful of Clinton's logic, but the captains of the ships in the East River feared the infamously treach-

erous currents at Hell Gate, at the conflu-
ence of the East River and the Harlem.

William Howe issued a final order to the
troops saying an attack on the enemy was
"shortly intended," and recommending
"an entire dependence upon their bayonets, with which they will ever command
that success which their bravery so well deserves." There was no ringing call for valor
in the cause of country or the blessings of
liberty, as Washington had exhorted his
troops at Brooklyn, only a final reminder
of the effectiveness of bayonets.

The invasion was set for Sunday the
15th. Had Howe and the rest of his command known more, and waited one more
day, the American evacuation would have
been complete, and they could have
walked into New York without a worry.

On the opposite shore, at Kips Bay, Private Joseph Martin was among the Connecticut troops posted in shallow trenches
to help secure the retreat of the rest of the
army. As night came on, sentinels by the
water's edge reported regularly on the half
hour, "All's well." From one of the British
ships, Private Martin heard a voice answer,
"We will alter your tune before tomorrow
night."

II

According to the official roster, the Connecticut brigade commanded by Colonel William Douglas numbered 1,500 men. But a third or more were sick, and only about half of those fit for duty were manning the trenches by Kips Bay. They had been awake all night and had had little or nothing to eat in twenty-four hours. Many were the greenest of green American troops, farm boys who had joined the ranks only the week before. Some who had no muskets carried homemade pikes fashioned from scythe blades fixed to the ends of poles.

Colonel Douglas, a New Haven shipmaster and merchant who had fought gallantly at Brooklyn, thought New York untenable. Still, in the expression of the time, he was a thorough soldier. "I think if we will stand by each other, and not run like cowards, with God's blessing, [we] may keep them off," he had written to his wife.

In the course of the night, five British frigates had maneuvered into position off Kips Bay, and in the gray half-light before dawn Douglas and his men could see their dark hulls anchored in a row, broadside to the shore about two hundred yards out, so close that they loomed much larger and more menacing than they had ever looked before. Private Martin would remember being able to read the name of the 44-gun *Phoenix* "as distinctly as though I had been directly under her stern."

The sun rose on a warm late-summer morning with clear skies and a fine, southwest breeze. "We lay very quiet in our ditch . . . till the sun was an hour or two high," Martin wrote. "We heard a cannonade at the city, but our attention was drawn toward our own guests."

The distant roar was an exchange of fire on the other side of York Island, as more of the British fleet, taking advantage of the ideal winds and a running tide, moved into the Hudson, making it appear that the attack was to come there.

The five ships off Kips Bay lay "entirely quiet" as the day grew oppressively hot. Then four long columns of enemy flatboats could be seen emerging from Newtown Cove across the river, brimming with red-coated troops. "When they came to the edge of the tide," wrote Martin, "they formed their boats in line . . . until they appeared like a large field of clover in full bloom."

At about ten o'clock, a first wave of more than eighty flatboats pushed off into the river. On board were 4,000 British and Hessian soldiers, crowded shoulder-to-shoulder. Lord Rawdon, who was with General Clinton in the lead boat, later wrote that the Hessians, unaccustomed to "this water business" and fearful of being fired on when packed so closely, began singing hymns, while the redcoats responded in their own fashion, "by damning themselves and the enemy indiscriminately with wonderful fervency."

The crossing went slowly, almost noiselessly, until all at once, the ships standing broadside to Kips Bay went into action, and the quiet of the nearly three weeks since the Battle of Brooklyn came to a thunderous end.

Just three days earlier, at Staten Island, Admiral Lord Howe had spoken solicitously of putting "a stop to these ruinous extremities," if only the Americans would give up "independency." Now, at about eleven o'clock, he lay aside the olive branch in a manner that none of the three members of Congress, or anyone, could have imagined, or that any of those present at Kips Bay would ever forget.

The fury let loose was impossible to conceive, wrote a British midshipman. "So terrible and so incessant a roar of guns few even in the army and navy had ever heard before," recorded Ambrose Serle.

It continued without stop for a full hour, a total of nearly eighty guns pounding point-blank at the shore and shrouding the river with acrid smoke. Joseph Martin, who had made a "frog's leap" into a ditch, thought he might die of the sound alone.

The barrage pulverized the meager breastworks, buried men under sod and sand, and kicked up such dust and smoke that there was no possibility of firing back at the enemy.

When the guns at last ceased, the first wave of flatboats emerged from the drifting smoke into the sunlight and made for shore. By then the Americans had fled as fast as their legs would carry them.

Colonel Douglas had told his men to save themselves and run, but the order was hardly necessary. The fire from the enemy ships, he wrote, was as "hot" as ever could be imagined, "but they mostly overshot us. The brigade was in such a scattered [position] that I could not collect them and I found the whole army on a retreat."

From the lead landing craft, Lord Rawdon saw the rebels break instantly, "happy to escape" to the nearest woods. "We pressed to shore," he wrote, "landed, and formed without losing a single man."

Not all the Americans got away. As another British officer would write, "I saw a Hessian sever a rebel's head from his body and clap it on a pole in the entrenchments."

Clinton and his advance corps pressed inland unopposed for a quarter of a mile, to secure high ground known as Inclenberg. There they halted and waited.

From his new command post on the crest of Harlem Heights, four miles to the north, Washington had heard the roar of cannon at Kips Bay and seen smoke rising in the distance. In an instant he was on his horse and racing south at a gallop, down the post road. Reining up at a cornfield about a mile inland from Kips Bay, he found men "flying in every direction." It was everything he had feared and worse, his army in pell-mell panic, Americans turned cowards before the enemy.

In a fury, he plunged his horse in among them, trying to stop them. Cursing violently, he lost control of himself. By some accounts, he brandished a cocked pistol. In other accounts, he drew his sword, threatening to run men through. "Take the walls!" he shouted. "Take the corn field!"

When no one obeyed, he threw his hat on the ground, exclaiming in disgust, "Are these the men with which I am to defend America?"

When an advance party of Hessians appeared, and the fleeing men refused to make a stand, Washington is said to have flogged some of their officers with his riding crop. A few soldiers turned and fired on the enemy, killing and wounding several. When a number of other Americans surrendered, with their hands uplifted, the Hessians shot or bayoneted them.

Two Continental brigades, a force of more than 2,000 under Generals Samuel Parsons and John Fellows, arrived in support, but at the sight of men fleeing in panic all around, they, too, turned and ran, strewing the ground with muskets, cartridge boxes, canteens, knapsacks, hats, and coats — this at the sight of fewer than a hundred enemy soldiers.

"The demons of fear and disorder," said Joseph Martin, "seemed to take full possession of all and everything that day." All, that is, but Washington, who, in a rage, heedless of his own safety or the chance of being captured, rode to within a hundred yards of the enemy. Only with difficulty were two of his aides able to grab the bridle of his horse and get him to leave the field.

More British troops were landing. By late afternoon, another 9,000 would be ashore at Kips Bay. When word came that the rebels had abandoned New York, a British brigade headed rapidly south and the city was theirs.

They were welcomed with open arms. "Nothing could equal the expressions of joy shown by the inhabitants, upon the arrival of the King's officers among them," wrote Ambrose Serle. "They even carried some of them upon their shoulders about the streets, and behaved in all respects, women as well as men, like overjoyed Bedlamites." At old Fort George on the Battery, a woman pulled down the flag of the Continental Army and trampled it under foot before raising the Union Jack.

Serle had watched the whole scene from Lord Howe's flagship. His contempt for the rebels had never been greater: "Thus this town and its environs, which these blustering gentlemen had taken such wonderful pains to fortify, were given up in two or three hours without any defense, or the least appearance of a manly resistance."

For the remnants of the American army

who had gotten away, it had been a close call. Henry Knox had managed to escape at the last minute only by seizing a boat on the Hudson. Israel Putnam and several thousand of his troops had set off on a forced march up the post road, a route that would have taken them up the east side of the island and straight into the invading British army had Putnam not been convinced by a young aide, twenty-year-old Lieutenant Aaron Burr, to head north by less traveled roads along the Hudson.

Leading his soldiers through the sweltering afternoon, rugged "Old Put" was at his best, riding up and down the long line exhorting them to stay together and keep moving, to get past the British before they had the island sealed off from the East River to the Hudson. At one time the two armies were passing each other less than a mile apart, only a stretch of woods dividing them.

Another young officer who made the march, Captain David Humphreys, would later write of General Putnam:

Having myself been a volunteer in his division and acting adjutant to the last regiment that left the city, I had frequent opportunities that day of be-

411

holding him, for the purpose of issuing orders, and encouraging the troops, flying on his horse covered with foam, wherever his presence was necessary. Without his extraordinary exertions . . . it is probable the entire corps would have been cut to pieces.

Putnam and his exhausted men marched into the main camp at Harlem after dark to rousing cheers. They had been given up for lost. When Knox turned up later, he, too, was greeted with shouts of welcome, even an embrace from the commander-in-chief.

Washington would call the conduct of those who had fled at Kips Bay "shameful," "scandalous," "disgraceful and dastardly." Nathanael Greene wrote of the "miserable disorderly retreat" and described Washington's behavior as he tried to rally the terrified men as close to suicidal. "Fellows's and Parsons's whole brigade[s] ran away from about fifty men," Greene reported to a friend, "and left his Excellency on the ground within eighty yards of the enemy, so vexed at the infamous conduct of the troops that he sought death rather than life."

Washington's anger may also have been

partly with himself, as the attack at Kips Bay had been nearly as great a tactical surprise as the enemy's night march through the Jamaica Pass. He had been made to look a fool by Howe still again.

The Connecticut militia, already in disgrace for deserting in such appalling numbers, were tagged now with cowardice. The Connecticut "runaways" were held to blame for the whole fiasco, which only made worse the hard feelings between the troops of New England and those of the other states that had plagued the army almost from the beginning.

Not all judgments were so harsh, however. Other things had to be weighed in the balance, wrote General Heath. "The wounds received on Long Island were yet bleeding; and the officers, if not the men, knew that the city was not to be defended." A Connecticut chaplain, Benjamin Trumbull, who only a short while before had delivered a rousing sermon calling for courage and heroism in battle, wrote in his diary:

The men were blamed for retreating and even flying . . . but I imag[in]e the fault was principally in the general officers . . . to give the men [a] rational

413

prospect of defense and a safe retreat, should they engage the enemy. And it is probable many lives were saved . . . though it was not honorable. It is admirable that so few men are lost.

In fact, many lives were saved, and even veteran troops would have fled under such a murderous cannonade as at Kips Bay. For the Connecticut men to have stayed would have been truly suicidal.

Henry Knox attributed the failure at both Brooklyn and Kips Bay to inadequate leadership by ill-trained, inexperienced officers, and a woefully overworked commander-in-chief. "The general is as worthy a man as breathes, but he cannot do everything and be everywhere," Knox reflected in a letter to his brother.

We ought to have men of merit in the most extensive and unlimited sense of the word. Instead of which, the bulk of the officers of the army are a parcel of ignorant, stupid men who might make tolerable soldiers but [are] bad officers.

There should be military academies established to "teach the art of war," Knox wrote, "and every other encouragement possible to draw persons into the army that may give luster to our arms."

Again, as on Long Island, the enemy effort had gone like clockwork. But why their commanders had delayed in crossing the island, why they had not pushed straight on to the Hudson, remained a puzzle. Had they advanced another mile or so, they could have cut the island in two, just as Nathanael Greene had predicted, sealing off any chance Putnam and his troops had to escape.

In explanation, a romantic story spread — a story that would become legendary — that a Mrs. Robert Murray, a Quaker and an ardent patriot, had delayed William Howe and his generals by inviting them to afternoon tea at her country home at Inclenberg, later known as Murray Hill. "Mrs. Murray treated them with cake and wine, and they were induced to tarry two hours or more," the story went, and thus Mary Lindley Murray was credited with saving part of the army, perhaps even the cause of liberty. She would be portrayed as a veritable Circe charming the gallant Britons with her feminine wiles. Possibly she did invite the officers to tea, and she may have been extremely charming, but she was also a woman in her fifties and the mother of twelve children.

More to the point, Clinton's delay at Inclenberg was according to plan. His orders had been to hold the line there until General Howe and the rest of the invading force had landed later in the afternoon.

The British, quite understandably, considered the invasion an immense success. Howe had wanted to seize and occupy New York as quickly as possible and at the least cost in bloodshed, and all that had been accomplished. New York, the key to British strategy, was at last in British hands. Howe and his generals were entirely satisfied with the day's work, and by nightfall their troops had crossed the middle of the island to the Hudson and pressed north to within striking distance of the rebel lines by the Harlem River.

But then, the very next day, September 16, to the astonishment of everyone, it would be the Americans' turn to claim success.

Washington, as usual, was up before dawn, drafting correspondence at his spacious new headquarters, the Palladian-style mansion of a departed Loyalist, Colonel Roger Morris, with whom he had once served in the French and Indian War.

The house, about a mile south of Fort Washington, commanded the summit of Harlem Heights — indeed, it stood at the highest elevation on all of York Island. From the balcony of its columned portico, one could see the Hudson on the right, and off to the left, three miles down the Harlem River valley, the old Dutch village of Harlem and the waters of Hell Gate. To the south, on clear days — and they were nearly all clear, dry days that September — one could pick out the distant spires of New York and further still, the hills of Staten Island, twenty miles away.

According to Joseph Reed, who was with Washington, it was still very early when word came that the enemy was advancing, and Washington sent Reed cantering off to investigate.

Washington had been expecting an attack. "I have sent out some reconnoitering parties to gain intelligence if possible of the disposition of the enemy," he had already reported in a letter to Congress that morning. More than a hundred Connecticut Rangers, some of the best soldiers in the army, had left on the mission before dawn, led by one of the best field officers in the army, a strapping Connecticut farmer and veteran of Bunker Hill, Colonel Thomas Knowlton. (It was Knowlton at Bunker Hill who, with Colonel John Stark, had famously held the rail fence in the face of the oncoming British lines, and Knowlton who, during the siege of Boston, had led the night attack on Charlestown that so upset the British officer's production of the Burgoyne farce *The Blockade* at Faneuil Hall.)

Knowlton and his Rangers were to probe for the enemy along the wooded ridges to the south, which rose beyond a narrow, intervening valley known as the Hollow Way. And it was there at daybreak, in the woods of the highlands to the south, that Knowlton and his men ran into the British and a "brisk" skirmish ensued.

Reed arrived just as the enemy attacked, with some four hundred light infantry, thus outnumbering the Americans by nearly four to one.

I went down to our most advanced post [he wrote] and while talking there with the officer of the guard, the enemy's advanced guard fired upon us at about fifty yards distance. Our men behaved well, stood and returned the fire, till, overpowered by numbers, they were obliged to retreat.

Reed raced off to get help from Washington, who had since ridden to the southern reaches of Harlem Heights, where Nathanael Greene's brigades were drawn up, overlooking the Hollow Way. By the time Reed arrived, Knowlton and his men could be seen retreating swiftly down the slopes on the opposite side.

Then out of the far woods and down the hill came the British in pursuit, sounding their bugles, as if on a fox hunt. "I never felt such a sensation before," Reed wrote. "It seemed to crown our disgrace."

What the Virginia fox hunter watching the scene from his saddle may have felt or thought can only be imagined, for he never said. But his response was an immediate decision to make a fight, if only, as he later explained to Patrick Henry, "to recover that military ardor which is of the utmost moment to an army."

Washington ordered a counterattack across the Hollow Way, and sent Knowlton and his men, plus three companies of Virginians led by Major Andrew Leitch, on the encircling move to the left, with Reed as guide. They were to get behind the redcoats and entrap them in the Hollow Way. Greene and Putnam led the main attack, and both were soon in the thick of it.

The enemy had "rushed down the hill with all speed to a plain spot of ground," wrote Joseph Hodgkins, who was back in action with Greene's troops for the first time since Brooklyn. "Then our brigade marched out of the woods. Then a very hot fire began on both sides."

But Knowlton's encircling move ran into trouble when some of his men opened fire too soon, attacking the enemy's flank, instead of getting behind and cutting off their retreat. The fighting grew fierce. Within minutes Knowlton and Major Leitch both fell, mortally wounded.

With the chance to encircle and capture the British gone, Washington threw more of his forces into the main attack, and the British, too, rushed in reinforcements. In little time the British had committed 5,000 men.

The struggle went on for hours, the Americans, for once, holding their own. Slowly the British began to give way. Then the British turned and ran, and the Americans took after them. "[We] drove the dogs near three miles," wrote one of the Connecticut men.

Fearing the enemy might bring up still more strength, and that his men might be running into a trap, Washington called off the attack, which was not easily done. "The pursuit of a flying enemy was so new a scene, that it was with difficulty our men could be brought to retreat," wrote Joseph Reed.

From all that Joseph Hodgkins had seen, and from what others had told him, he reckoned they had killed no fewer than 500 of the enemy and wounded that many or more. "They were seen to carry off several wagon loads. Besides our people buried a good many that they left."

Probably the British and Hessian losses were 90 killed and about 300 wounded. The number of American casualties was far lower, fewer than 100 wounded and 30 killed, but these included Major Leitch and Colonel Knowlton, whose deaths were a heavy blow to the army. To Reed, who had carried the wounded Knowlton from the field, and to Washington, Thomas Knowlton was the "greatest loss."

Reporting to Congress on the Battle of Harlem Heights, Washington referred to it only as "a pretty sharp skirmish" and made no claims to a great victory. But to the troops it was a genuine victory at long last, and an urgently needed lift to their self-respect. They had seen the backs of redcoats on the fly. As Henry Knox wrote, "They find that if they stick to these mighty men, they will run as fast as other people."

Nathanael Greene, who from the first weeks at Boston had never doubted that the army would fight if properly led, wrote proudly to William Ellery, a delegate to Congress from Rhode Island:

> Our people beat the enemy off the ground. . . . Had all the colonies good officers, there is no danger of the troops; never was troops that would stand in the field longer than the American soldiery. If the officers were as good as the men, and had only a few months to form the troops to discipline, America might bid defiance to the whole world.

British prisoners captured in the fight said they had never expected the Americans to attack, and were "never more surprised." Henry Clinton, in accounting for what happened, blamed the "impetuosity" of the light infantry for pursuing the rebels in the first place. For contrary to what Washington thought, the British had had no plans for or any intention of engaging the rebels that day, or anytime soon.

For days the two armies, close as they were, remained perfectly quiet, "as quiet," wrote Lieutenant Tilghman of Washington's staff, "as if they were a thousand miles apart."

The position of the Americans on the rocky heights above the Harlem River was as advantageous as any they had held since the war began, and they labored on steadily to make it still more secure. "If we cannot fight them on this ground, we can on none in America," concluded Joseph Reed. Nor was the point lost on the British commander-in-chief who, with New York in hand, saw no reason to press the attack just yet.

In his own good time William Howe was drawing up plans to outmaneuver the rebels once again, while his brother, Lord Howe, reflected on whether it might be the opportune moment for another peace overture. Increasing numbers of rebel soldiers, all "much dispirited," were crossing the lines to defect, reinforcing the commonly held opinion among the British commanders that the rebellion had run its course.

Meanwhile, others of the British army were finding New York delightful. There were "many fair houses" for quarters. Food was more plentiful than ever. It was the height of the harvest season and the supply of fresh produce from the farms of Long Island seemed limitless. As a bonus, the rebels, in their hurry to leave, had left behind more than 5,000 barrels of flour.

Off-duty British soldiers and officers flocked like tourists to inspect the abandoned rebel fortifications, marveling at their size and number and the work that had gone into them.

"The shore of the Island, from Hell Gate on the East River, quite round by the town, up to Bloomingdale on the North River, an extent of near fourteen miles, is fortified at almost every accessible part, and there is hardly a height without a redoubt or battery on it," wrote Lieutenant Frederick Mackenzie in admiration. Ambrose Serle, after a walking tour of the town, recorded his "astonishment" at the sight of rebel breastworks and embrasures at the end of nearly every street and avenue.

The infinite pains and labor which they must have bestowed, one would have thought, from regret alone, would have inclined them to make some kind of stand. But their fears overpowered their resolution, and they evacuated the object of all their toil in one short hour, without making the least defense or anything like a handsome retreat.

On September 19, against the judgment of most of the British high command, including presumably his brother the general, Lord Howe issued a direct appeal to the people of America, in the form of a proclamation warning that the stubbornness of their representatives in Congress was leading to their downfall and misery. Americans ought to "judge for themselves," he wrote, "whether it be more consistent with their honor and happiness to offer up their lives as a sacrifice to the unjust and precarious cause in which they are engaged," or "to return to their allegiance, accept the blessings of peace," and thus be "secured in the free enjoyment of their liberty and properties."

The proclamation seemed only to irritate everyone on both sides, and was all but forgotten after the night of September 20–21, when fire raged out of control in New York and a large part of the city burned to the ground.

Fire was a constant fear in every town

and city of the time, and never more than when the weather was as hot and dry as it had been that summer. Fire at night was the most terrifying of all.

The fire, it appears from several eyewitness accounts, began shortly after midnight in a "low grogery" called the Fighting Cocks, at Whitehall Slip, at the southern tip of New York.

Driven by a southwesterly wind, the flames turned quickly to wildfire. Choking smoke and fiery-red, windborne flakes of burning shingles filled the air, as the flames swept uptown, across Dock Street, Bridge Street, Stone, Marketfield, and Beaver streets. Seen from the American lines at Harlem, ten miles to the north, it looked as though the very heavens were ablaze.

No warning bells rang, because Washington had ordered every bell in the city carried away to be recast for cannon. British soldiers and others rushed to help, but the heat was so intense, the fire so out of control, that no one could get near it. There were too few buckets and little water at hand. The few fire engines there were proved useless.

Houses were torn down in advance of the flames, but then nothing seemed to check the inferno. Had the wind not shifted to the southeast at about two in the morning, the entire city might have been consumed. As it was, the fire raged up the west side, destroying nearly everything between Broadway and the Hudson, including the infamous Holy Ground, to as far as the open field at King's College. When Trinity Church, at Broadway and Wall Street, burst into flames, its shingled steeple became a vast "pyramid of fire," until it burned to its timbers and crashed to the ground.

"It is almost impossible to conceive a scene of more horror and distress," wrote Frederick Mackenzie, who was among those trying to fight the flames.

The sick, the aged, women, and children, half naked, were seen going they knew not where, and taking refuge in houses which were at a distance from the fire, but from whence they were in several instances driven a second and even a third time. . . . The terror was increased by the horrid noise of the burning and falling houses, the pulling down of such wooden buildings as served to conduct the fire . . . the rattling of above 100 wagons, sent in from the army, and which were constantly employed in conveying to the common such goods and effects as could be saved. The confused voices of so many men, the shrieks and cries of the women and children . . .

Concerned that the burning city could be the prelude to a night attack by the rebels, the Howes held back from sending more soldiers and seamen to fight the blaze until daybreak, and by ten o'clock the fire had burned itself out.

Nearly five hundred houses were destroyed, or approximately a quarter of the city, and in the shock and horror of the moment it seemed certain the disaster was the villainous work of the enemy. Rebel incendiaries had been caught in the act, it was widely reported. One such man, caught with "fire brand" in hand, had been knocked down by a British grenadier and "thrown into the flames" for his reward. Another who was seen cutting off the handles of water buckets was hanged from a signpost by British sailors, then hung up by the heels like a slaughtered animal.

Witnesses reported having seen the fire break out in several different places, not just at Whitehall Slip, and this was taken as proof of arson. But Frederick Mackenzie, who was no less certain than others that the town had been "designedly" set afire, acknowledged in his diary, "There is no doubt . . . that the flames were communicated to several houses by means of the burning flakes of the shingles, which being light, were carried by the wind to some distance and . . . kindled the fire anew."

In a letter to Lord Germain, General Howe charged the deed to unnamed "lurking" villains. "The Yankees [New York Loyalists] are convinced that the New England men set fire to the town; they will never forgive them," wrote General James Grant. Governor William Tryon went further, implying in a letter to Germain that Washington himself had devised the plot and instructed the incendiaries.

More than a hundred suspects were rounded up, but no evidence was found against them. None were brought to trial. All were eventually released. It was never determined, then or later, that the "Great Fire" was anything other than accidental.

Washington, in his report to Congress, called it an accident. Writing privately, however, he allowed to Lund Washington that "Providence, or some good honest fellow, has done more for us than we were disposed to do for ourselves." Beyond that he said no more.

Nor was Washington to say anything about Captain Nathan Hale, who was "apprehended" by the British the day after the fire and, it appears, as part of the roundup of suspected incendiaries.

By several accounts, Hale's capture took place in New York. A report in the *New York Gazette*, a Tory paper, said an unnamed "New England man who had a captain's commission" was seized in the city with "dreadful implements of ruin [firebrands]" and, when searched, "the sum of 500 [pounds] was found upon him." This could refer to Hale, although Frederick Mackenzie noted that "a person named Nathan Hales" was apprehended on Long Island on the night of September 21.

Whatever the circumstances of his capture, Hale admitted to being a spy, and General Howe ordered him hanged without trial.

Hale was twenty-one years old, a handsome, athletic graduate of Yale, a schoolmaster and wholehearted patriot. Raised on a Connecticut farm, he was one of six brothers who served in the war. He had signed up more than a year before, taken part in the Siege of Boston, and lately joined Colonel Knowlton's Rangers. Yet thus far he felt he had rendered no real service to the country, and when Knowlton, on orders from Washington, called for a volunteer to cross the lines and bring back desperately needed intelligence, he had bravely offered to go.

A fellow Connecticut officer, Captain William Hull, who had known Hale in college, tried to talk him out of it, warning that he was by nature "too frank and open for deceit and disguise," and that no one respected the character of a spy. Hale had said only that he would "reflect, and do nothing but what duty demands." The next thing Hull knew, his friend had disappeared.

The mission was doomed from the start, ill-planned and pathetically amateurish, and Hale was a poor choice. He knew nothing of spying. The scars from a powder burn on his face made him readily identifiable, and a Loyalist cousin who knew him well was serving as General Howe's deputy commissary of prisoners.

Hale went under the guise of a Dutch schoolmaster in search of work. Apparently it was from naïvely confiding the truth of his mission to the wrong people that led to his capture.

He was hanged on the morning of September 21, in an artillery park near the Beekman house, a country estate not far from the East River that served as Howe's headquarters.

It was Captain John Montresor, who, only hours afterward, under a white flag, brought word of Hale's fate to the Americans and described what had happened to Hale to his friend Captain Hull. And it was Hull, later, who reported Montresor's account of Hale's last words as he was about to be executed: "I only regret that I have but one life to lose for my country," which was a variation on another then-famous line from the play *Cato*. (One imagines that in delivering the line to his British executioners, Hale, knowing that it was as familiar to them as to him, put the emphasis on the second-to-last word: "I only regret that I have but one life to lose for *my* country.")

On September 26, a British officer wrote in a letter,

We hung up a rebel spy the other day, and some soldiers got out of a rebel gentleman's garden a painted soldier on a board, and hung it along with the rebel, and wrote upon it, General

Washington, and I saw it yesterday beyond headquarters, by the roadside.

Hale's place in the pantheon of American heroes, as the martyr spy of the Revolution, was not to come until years later. For now very little was known or said of his story. Washington, angry or saddened as he may have been, is not known to have mentioned the subject.

American soldiers were deserting as if leaving a sinking ship, thirty or forty at a time, many defecting to the enemy. Disobedience and theft were epidemic. It was far from an army of heroes only. "A spirit of desertion, cowardice, plunder, and shrinking from duty when attended with fatigue or danger, prevailed but too generally," wrote Joseph Reed, who had become so demoralized that even he was on the verge of quitting.

An experience on the battlefield on September 16 had had a searing effect. In the heat of the fight, Reed had seen a soldier running from the enemy. Ordered to stop and go back, the soldier, a Connecticut private named Ebenezer Leffingwell, had raised his musket, taken aim from a distance of only a few yards, and pulled the trigger. But the lock only snapped. When Reed grabbed the gun of another soldier and pulled the trigger, it too snapped. Reed drew his sword and, striking twice, wounded Leffingwell on the head, severed a thumb, and forced him to surrender. "I should have shot him, could I have got my gun off," Reed said at Leffingwell's court-martial on September 19.

Leffingwell, who confessed he had been running away, was found guilty of cowardice and of "presenting his firelock at his superior officer." He was sentenced to be executed before the assembled troops the following day. But at Reed's urging, Washington pardoned Leffingwell at the last moment, after Leffingwell had kneeled to be shot. The next such offender would "suffer death without mercy," warned Washington.

"To attempt to introduce discipline and subordination into a new army must always be a work of much difficulty," Reed wrote to his wife, "but where the principles of democracy so universally prevail, where so great an equality and so thorough a leveling spirit predominates, either no discipline can be established, or he who attempts it must become odious and detestable, a position which no one will choose."

Washington was no less a commanding presence than ever, and except for his raging outburst at Kips Bay, he seemed imperturbable, entirely in control. In truth, he was as discouraged as he had ever been in his life, and miserably unhappy. It was all he could do to keep up appearances.

"Unless some speedy, and effectual measures are adopted by Congress, our cause will be lost," he told John Hancock in a long, foreboding letter dated September 25.

Like Greene, like Knox and Reed, Washington knew the problem with the army was not so much the men in the ranks as those who led them. The war was to be no "work of a day," he warned, and must be carried on "systematically." Good officers were mandatory, and the only means to obtain good officers was to establish the army on a permanent footing. There must be an end to short-term enlistments. Officers must be better paid, better trained. Soldiers must be offered a good bounty, adequate clothing and blankets, plus the promise of free land.

Inflamed by passions, stirred by patriotism, men will "fly hastily and cheerfully to arms," Washington continued, but to expect "the bulk of an army" to serve on selflessly, come what may, once the first emotions subsided, would be "to look for what never did, and, I fear, never will, happen." Even among officers, those who acted with true "disinterestedness" were "no more than a drop in the ocean," wrote this most disinterested and selfless of officers.

To place any dependence on militia is, assuredly, resting upon a broken staff. Men just dragged from the tender scenes of domestic life — unaccustomed to the din of arms — totally unacquainted with every kind of military skill, which being followed by a want of confidence in themselves when opposed to troops regularly trained, disciplined, and appointed, superior in knowledge, and superior in arms, makes them timid and ready to fly from their own shadows.

He wrote of the "lust after plunder" among the men, of regimental surgeons taking bribes to certify sickness or infirmities that would qualify for discharges. He understood the fear there was in Congress and among the people of a standing army, but he thought the evils imagined were remote. On the other hand, were there to be no standing army, the cause of independence faced ruin.

He wanted rules and regulations adopted, punishments made more severe. As it was, for the most "atrocious offenses," the maximum was thirty-nine lashes, and these, he had found, were seldom layed on as they should be, but more as "sport." It was punishment of a kind that, for a bottle of rum, many "hardened fellows" were quite willing to undergo.

But as Washington had no way of knowing, Congress had already acted on most of what he wanted, due largely to the efforts of John Adams as head of the Board of War and in floor debate. Every soldier who enlisted for the "duration" of the war was to receive $20 and one hundred acres of land. New Articles of War, drawn up by Adams and based largely on the British Articles of War, went far to ensure justice for the individual soldier, provided stiffer punishments for major offenses (up to one hundred lashes), and increased the number of crimes for which the penalty was death. Adams also proposed for the first time the creation of a military academy, as Knox had urged, but nothing came of the motion.

Writing to Lund Washington on September 30, Washington was even more candid about his miseries. "Such is my situation that if I were to wish the bitterest curse to an enemy on this side of the grave, I should put him in my stead with my feelings." He was "wearied to death" with problems. One regiment had fewer than fifty men left, another, all of fourteen fit for duty. "In confidence I tell you that I never was in such an unhappy, divided state since I was born." And the enemy, all the while, was "within stone's throw."

Then, as he had before, and as though such a giant shift of mind was perfectly natural, he turned to the subject of Mount Vernon. He was concerned about the fireplaces:

That in the parlor must, I should think, stand as it does; not so much on account of the wainscotting, which I think must be altered (on account of the door leading into the new building), as on account of the chimney piece and the manner of its fronting into the room. The chimney in the room above ought, if it could be so contrived, to be an angle chimney as the others are: but I would not have this attempted at the expense of pulling down the partition. The chimney in the new room should be exactly in the middle of it — the doors and everything else to be exactly answerable and uniform. In short, I would have the whole executed in a masterly manner.

If all could not be as he wished with the army, if all could not be "exactly answerable and uniform" or "executed in a masterly manner," concerning the war he was expected to wage and win, then he would at least have it so at his distant, beloved home.

The crystal days of late September and early October in New York followed one after another, with lucent skies and stands of maple and sumac just beginning to turn color. The East River had become a spectacle of British ships of every kind lining nearly its entire length. The Hudson, in the sharp light of the season, sparkled like an inland sea. In all, it could not have been a more beautiful setting for the strange, extended intermission in a war that many hoped might be put to rest for the winter, not to resume until spring, and then, preferably, not too early.

On the morning of October 9, any such

hopes ended. Three of the British warships, *Phoenix*, *Roebuck*, and *Tartar*, weighed anchor and with the advantage of a flood tide and a brisk southwesterly wind, proceeded up the Hudson to force passage beyond Forts Washington and Constitution, where, at enormous effort, the Americans had tried to block the river from shore to shore with sunken hulks and a submerged chain of spike-studded logs.

The guns of the forts high above the river opened fire. The ships answered with a pounding barrage, and by holding close to the eastern shore, where the river was deepest, they sailed straight, if slowly, through to safe anchorage upriver at the broad Tappan Zee, off Tarrytown.

Washington had observed the whole sorry scene. "To our surprise and mortification, they ran through without the least difficulty, and without receiving any apparent damage from our forts, though they kept up a heavy fire from both sides," he wrote. Again, no end of time and labor devoted to defense had come to nothing.

In fact, the British had suffered nine seamen killed and considerable damage to their ships, while showing once more in spectacular fashion that the Hudson was undeniably theirs to employ as they wished.

The day could have led to a decisive change in American strategy. If the purpose of the forts was to deny the British navy use of the river, then all the effort and risk of holding the forts should have been reconsidered at once. Clearly the forts had been shown to be useless.

Yet Washington raised no questions then, and Nathanael Greene declared confidently, at day's end, that the army was so strongly positioned in the forts that there was "little more to fear this campaign." Instead of a lesson learned, the day marked the onset of one of the greatest American blunders of the war, and what was to be a painful humiliation for Washington and Greene.

The British plan, once again, was to outflank the rebels, and again by water. Early on October 12, in an unexpected morning fog, a massive armada got under way on the East River.

With Admiral Lord Howe in command, 150 ships set sail upstream, through the dangerous Hell Gate channel "in very thick fog" — a mariner's nightmare — and into Long Island Sound, and all without mishap. It was a stunning feat of seamanship. By noon an advance force of 4,000 troops led by Henry Clinton had landed at Throg's Neck (also known as Frog's Neck), a marshy point of land on the shoreline of Westchester County, due east of the American lines at Harlem Heights and King's Bridge.

Throg's Neck had been Lord Howe's choice and proved to be a poor one for the army. What appeared to be a peninsula on the map was more an island connected to the mainland only at low tide. When the British tried to advance over a causeway, a small detachment of American riflemen, crouched behind log piles, held them in check, and when more American support moved in, after more British troops had landed, General Howe decided to reembark once sufficient supplies arrived and still more reinforcements were at hand, which consumed another four days. ("Tweedledum business," an exasperated Henry Clinton called it.) But the reinforcements Howe expected were worth the wait — 7,000 newly arrived Hessians under the command of the extremely able General Wilhelm von Knyphausen. And when Howe moved, he moved with astonishing speed, landing this time a short way up the sound, at Pell's Point, a part of the mainland.

At the first report of the Throg's Neck landing, Washington knew the Harlem Heights bastion had become a trap. The British were up to "their former scheme of getting to our rear," he wrote. They had only to strike inland toward King's Bridge. The army must withdraw as soon as possible. He would concentrate his forces at safer ground eighteen miles to the north at White Plains, the seat of Westchester County.

Through prisoner exchanges, Lord Stirling and General Sullivan had rejoined the army, in what seemed the nick of time. Both were warmly welcomed by Washington and assigned commands.

On October 14, the gaunt, odd-looking figure of General Charles Lee reappeared, dogs and all, and immediately resumed his place as second-in-command. Lee was the subject of much talk, raising spirits in the ranks and in Congress. Always popular in Congress, he had become even more so since the defeat of Clinton's expedition to South Carolina, where Lee had had overall command of the American forces. While Washington's ability had become subject to question, as one failure followed another,

Lee's reputation had never been higher. Some in Congress saw him as a potential savior.

For his part, Lee recklessly told General Gates that he thought Washington was only compounding his troubles by tolerating such "absurd interference" by the "cattle" in Congress in his conduct of the war, and that Washington was remiss for not "menacing 'em" with threats of resignation. (Were Washington to resign, of course, it would be Lee who succeeded him.)

Washington well knew the quirks and vanity of his old military friend and was glad to have him back. As a gesture of appreciation, he gave Fort Constitution a new name, Fort Lee.

At a council of war on October 16, it was decided that Fort Washington and its garrison should be, in the words of the brief minutes, "retained as long as possible." The passage of ships on the Hudson was no longer the issue — the obstructions in the North River had proved insufficient — still, "communication" across the river to New Jersey had to be maintained.

Besides Washington and Lee, the general officers present included Heath, Sullivan, Stirling, and Mifflin. Colonel Knox was also present, but General Greene was not. According to the minutes, there was only one dissenting voice, and it was General George Clinton, not Lee, as he later implied.

The week before, Congress had resolved that, if "practicable," every effort be made to "obstruct effectually" navigation on the Hudson at Fort Washington, but whether this was known in advance of the council of war, or had any bearing on the decision, is not clear.

All of York Island was finally to be evacuated. The entire American army would march off, except for 1,000 men left to hold Fort Washington.

Officially it was to be called "an alteration of our position," not a retreat. The commander's orders for October 17 read, in part, as follows:

As the movements of the enemy make an alteration of our position necessary . . . tents are to be struck and carefully rolled, the men to take the tent poles in their hands, two men out of a company, with a careful subaltern, to go with the baggage and not leave it on any pretense. No packs (unless of sick men), chairs, tables, benches, or heavy lumber [are] to be put on the wagons. No person, unless unable to walk, is to presume to get upon them. The wagons [are] to move forward before the regiments . . . Every regiment under marching orders, to see they have their flints and ammunition in good order and complete.

The exodus was soon under way, the army crossing the narrow bridge at King's Bridge and heading north along the west bank of the little Bronx River. The sick were the greatest burden. With teams and wagons in short supply, the trek was slow and difficult, the men themselves, in many cases, hauling the baggage wagons and cannon.

Private Joseph Martin would remember lugging a cast-iron kettle the size of a milk pail until his arms were nearly dislocated. During a rest, he put it down, and, as he wrote, "one of the others gave it a shove with his foot, and it rolled down against a fence, and that was the last I ever saw of it. When we got through the night's march, we found our mess was not the only one that was rid of their iron bondage."

As the first of Washington's army struggled toward White Plains, the British made their swift landing at Pell's Point. Again an advance force of 4,000 British and Hessian troops went ashore in the early morning and, this time, were unopposed. They moved directly inland a mile or more and might have kept going had it not been for the intrepid John Glover and his men. The date was October 18.

From a hilltop before dawn, Glover had seen through a telescope what looked like upwards of two hundred ships. "Oh! The anxiety of mind I was in then for the fate of the day. . . . I would have given a thousand worlds to have had General Lee, or some experienced officer present to direct, or at least to approve what I had done," Glover later wrote.

Acting on his own, he rushed forward with some 750 men who fought tenaciously from behind stone walls, inflicting heavy casualties and stalling the enemy advance for a full day before forced to fall back.

Colonel Loammi Baldwin, the Massachusetts apple grower who, with his small regiment, joined in the fight, later claimed the men stayed as calm as if shooting ducks. He thought the enemy dead numbered at least 200, which was undoubtedly an exaggeration. But even if he was wrong by half, the British lost more men killed at

Pell's Point than in the Battle of Brooklyn. By Glover's calculations, American casualties numbered 8 dead, 13 wounded.

Such ferocity as the Americans had shown appears to have stunned Howe, leading him to conclude that, with stone walls lining every road and adjacent field, more deadly fire could be waiting at any turn. Had the British kept moving inland with speed, they might have caught Washington's retreating army head-on.

As it was, the British advance — along the shore as far as Mamaroneck, then inland toward White Plains — was slow and extremely cautious, seldom more than a few miles a day and against little or no resistance.

Probably Howe saw no more need to hurry now than he had before, and in fact, he did not expect to cut the rebel retreat. Rather, in eighteenth-century military fashion, he hoped to maneuver Washington onto the open field, and then, with his superior, professional force, destroy the Yankee "rabel" in one grand, decisive victory. Even after reaching White Plains, Howe took another few days to be sure all was ready.

At last, on October 28, ten days after landing at Pell's Point, William Howe sent

13,000 redcoats and Hessians up the main road to White Plains. It was early morning and yet another sparkling fall day. Washington, determined to avoid any test of strength on an open field, was well dug in on high ground in back of the village, his lines reaching more than a mile in length. For a brief time, it looked as though Howe intended to attack head-on, as the Americans hoped he would. British field guns opened fire, and Howe's army marched in perfect order in two columns straight for where Washington commanded at the center. "The sun shone bright, their arms glittered, and perhaps troops never were shown to more advantage than these now appeared," wrote General Heath of the oncoming foe.

Suddenly, one column wheeled sharply left in the direction of a higher hill on the American right, on the other side of the Bronx River. Chatterton's Hill was thickly wooded on its slopes but had open fields above, and it dominated the American lines. "Yonder is the ground we ought to occupy," Charles Lee had reportedly told Washington, but only at the last hour had troops been rushed to defend Chatterton's Hill and these were mainly militia.

The British artillery moved to closer

range. Cannon roared on both sides. "The air and hills smoked and echoed terribly," wrote a Pennsylvania soldier. "The fences and walls were knocked down and torn to pieces, and men's legs, arms, and bodies mingled with cannon and grapeshot all round us."

Washington ordered more men to the top of Chatterton's Hill. The British and Hessians forded the river, and the Hessians, part of the newly arrived 7,000 led by Colonel Johann Rall, launched the uphill charge. The militia broke and ran, and while the reinforcements, including Colonel Haslet's Delaware troops and Smallwood's Marylanders, fought bravely, they had to give way at the last.

The Battle of White Plains was the battle of Chatterton's Hill and the British and the Hessians carried the day. But it was at a cost of more than 250 casualties, twice what the Americans suffered. Nor was it a victory that achieved anything.

The day after, October 29, Howe decided to pause again, to wait for still more reinforcements. The day after that, October 30, it poured rain. On the morning of November 1, Howe found that overnight Washington and his army had pulled back half a mile to a stronger position on high ground across the Bronx River.

For two more days the two armies waited and watched. "The enemy are determined on something decisive," Henry Knox wrote to his brother, "and we are determined to risk a general battle on the most advantageous terms."

When, on the night of November 3, American sentinels reported the rumbling of enemy carriages in the dark, it was assumed another attack was imminent. There was more stirring among the British ranks the next day, and the Americans braced themselves. But on the morning of November 5, to the complete surprise of the Americans, the whole of the British army was in motion, heading off in another direction, southwest toward the Hudson and King's Bridge.

III

"Opinions here are various," Joseph Reed confided to his wife, following a council of war during which he had kept the minutes.

Some of the generals thought the British were headed for Fort Washington, or were bound for the Hudson to board ships and proceed upriver to attack from the rear.

"Others, and a great majority, think that, finding this army too strongly posted, they have changed their whole plan . . . intending to penetrate the Jerseys and so move on to Philadelphia."

Who had said what or the most in the course of the meeting, Reed did not mention. In his own opinion, however, it was too late in the season for any British movements of consequence, other than a few "excursions" into New Jersey perhaps, to revive the "drooping" spirits of the many Loyalists there.

Washington doubted that Howe would close the campaign "without attempting something more," as he wrote to John Hancock. Almost certainly Howe was headed for New Jersey.

Nearing the close of the letter, Washington added a further worry: "I expect the enemy will bend their force against Fort Washington and invest it immediately," he said, the term "invest" meaning to surround and lay siege, not necessarily to attack all-out.

Like most of the army he led, Washington was still exhausted and dispirited. To some who were closest at hand he seemed a little bewildered and unsuitably indecisive. Reed in particular, as he would later reveal, was having second thoughts about Washington's capacity for leadership.

Increasingly worried over Fort Washington, the commander pondered whether to pull the troops out while there was yet time. In a letter to Nathanael Greene from White Plains dated November 8, Washington had reasoned, as he might well have earlier:

If we cannot prevent vessels passing up [the Hudson], and the enemy are possessed of the surrounding country, what valuable purpose can it answer to attempt to hold a post from which the expected benefit cannot be had. I am therefore inclined to think it will not be prudent to hazard the men and stores.

Yet he left the decision to Greene. "But as you are on the spot, [I] leave it to you to give such orders as to evacuating . . . as you judge best."

Central to all that had to be taken into consideration was the Hudson River, which loomed as large in everyone's calculations as it had for nearly a year, from the time Washington first dispatched Charles Lee south from Cambridge to take charge of fortifying New York — the Hudson, key to the whole British strategy.

Would the British decide to take care of the unfinished business of Fort Washington on this side of the river? Or would they cross over and strike into New Jersey? Or might they do both? And what in any case should be done?

Howe and his army were known to have reached Dobbs Ferry on the Hudson, less than ten miles above King's Bridge, and were now moving south.

Once again, Washington decided to divide his army, and this time four ways. Seven thousand troops, much the largest part of the army, were to remain east of the Hudson under General Lee, to check any British move on New England. General Heath and another 3,000 were to guard the Hudson Highlands at Peekskill, New York, thirty miles to the north. Washington, with what was left of the army — only 2,000 men or so — would cross to the other side of the river, where, it was expected, he would be joined by New Jersey and Pennsylvania reinforcements. Nathanael Greene was to maintain his same position on the river, with overall command of the troops at Fort Washington and Fort Lee.

Washington and his 2,000 left White

Plains on November 10. At midmorning, November 12, at Peekskill, he crossed the Hudson and headed directly south for New Jersey, reaching Fort Lee on November 13 — all told, a sixty-five-mile march in three days.

For the better part of two days he and Greene conferred. Greene, who had yet to fight a battle, remained optimistic, convinced that Fort Washington could be held, and especially as he had more than doubled the number of troops at the fort, bringing the total force there to more than 2,000.

It was a remarkable reversal of roles. Washington, who in September had refused to abandon New York, seemed ready now to do so. Greene, in September, had seen no reason to remain a day longer on York Island, and had he had his way, the whole present crisis would have been avoided. Yet it was Greene now who wanted to make a stand on the last bit of the island still in American hands, arguing that it would keep communications open across the river, tie up British troops that might otherwise join in an attack on New Jersey (and ultimately Philadelphia), and lead possibly to another slaughter of the enemy as at Bunker Hill. Further, Greene reasoned, one more retreat could be devastating to the army's already demoralized state.

Despite its formidable presence high over the river, its steep, rock-bound approaches, Fort Washington was, in several ways, not the impregnable bastion it seemed. An irregular pentagon in plan, it covered about four acres, its walls made of piled-up earth. There were no barracks for the troops, and there was no water supply, other than what could be hauled up from below — hardly what was needed in the event of a long siege with winter approaching.

Nonetheless, its commander, Colonel Robert Magaw, thought the fort could hold out until the end of December, and Greene agreed.

In his letter to Greene from White Plains, Washington had said he was "inclined to think" it prudent to abandon the fort, but left the decision to Greene, who was "on the spot." Now that he himself was on the spot, Washington still could not decide what to do and so again, in effect, he let the decision be Greene's.

"His Excellency General Washington has been with me for several days . . . but finally nothing concluded on," Greene wrote to Henry Knox.

"The movements and designs of the enemy are not yet understood," Washington reported to John Hancock.

To the British captain Frederick Mackenzie it was all-but-perfect campaigning weather. There had been a frost nearly every night, but it disappeared once the sun was up. The only thing lacking was a stiff breeze to accommodate the navy. "No wind for some days past," he recorded in his diary, "so that if it was intended to send any number of ships up the North River, it could not have been effected." The entry, dated November 7, affirmed that General Howe had by then established headquarters just six miles above King's Bridge, and that the next move would "probably be against Fort Washington." But then Captain Mackenzie never doubted that "reduction" of the fort was "the first object," and like others, he felt more confident than ever of success, for a fund of timely and accurate intelligence had unexpectedly fallen into British hands. If Washington failed still to understand British "designs," the British now knew quite a lot about the American situation, or at least a great deal more than they might have.

On November 2, when Howe's army was

still at White Plains, an American staff officer named William Demont (whom Mackenzie referred to as William Diamond), turned traitor, defecting to the British from Fort Washington and bringing with him copies he had made of plans of the fort and the placement of cannon, as well as accounts of the mounting discontent and animosity between the rebels from New England and those from the South.

Only days before a packet of letters written by Washington, Reed, and others of Washington's staff wound up in British hands, after being left unguarded at an inn at Trenton by a careless post rider bound for Philadelphia. In one letter Washington complained bitterly of the lack of discipline in the army and wrote with scorn of the "dreaming, sleepy-headed" officers he had to contend with. Another letter, written by Lieutenant Colonel Robert Hanson Harrison of Washington's staff, provided the far more important revelation that Washington was dividing his army.

The purloined letters and the plan of Fort Washington provided by Demont's treachery may not have greatly altered the course of events to follow. But the British rightfully considered them a windfall, as both Mackenzie's diary and that kept by

Ambrose Serle attest. Washington's decision to divide the army was taken as a clearest possible sign of weakness. "It is easy to see whither all this tends, and what will be the probable consequence of such a division," wrote Serle, who as Lord Howe's secretary had been the first to see the letters. If the rebels could not "find spirit to act under the encouragement of their present numbers, there is little reason to believe that their courage will increase upon a reduction of their strength." The letters, thought Mackenzie, were certain to be "of much service to General Howe."

The British by this time had doubtless picked up sufficient information from deserters to know a considerable amount about the state of things at Fort Washington, but having the plans and Demont's account were of importance all the same, if only as confirmation.

Be that as it may, the famously cautious William Howe, who, supposedly, would never risk a frontal attack on a heavily fortified rebel position, because of the painful lesson learned at Bunker Hill, was about to disprove that theory, and with the full agreement of his commanders.

Frederick Mackenzie had total confidence in the attack, predicting further, "from the general appearance of matters," that as soon as Fort Washington was taken, Howe would move on to New Jersey. The fact that the rebel troops from New Jersey and Pennsylvania that Washington counted on for help had never materialized was also well known to the British, and this, thought Mackenzie, left little "to prevent our arrival at Philadelphia."

By November 12, the day Washington crossed the Hudson, Howe's army was within four miles of King's Bridge. The plan was for a four-part assault, with the Hessians playing the major role.

The plan began to unfold at midday, November 15, when Howe sent Colonel James Paterson under a white flag to deliver a message to the American commander at Fort Washington, Colonel Magaw. Paterson was the same British officer who, in July, had carried letters to Washington from Lord Howe proffering the possibility of peace. This time he bore an ultimatum: surrender the fort or face annihilation.

Told he had two hours to make up his mind, Magaw responded at once with a written reply:

Sir, if I rightly understand the purport

of your message . . . 'this post is to be immediately surrendered or the garrison put to the sword.' I rather think it is a mistake than a settled resolution in General Howe to act a part so unworthy [of] himself and the British nation, but give me leave to assure his excellency that actuated by the most glorious cause that mankind ever fought in, I am determined to defend this post to the very last extremity.

Howe had no intention of carrying out his threat of slaughter. The ultimatum was designed to play on the fears and distress of the rebels. Magaw's bold response was written in the belief that he and his men could indeed hold out, or if need be, escape across the Hudson after dark.

When word of the ultimatum, and of Magaw's answer, reached Fort Lee later that afternoon, Nathanael Greene dispatched a rider to tell Washington, who, earlier, had ridden to Hackensack, six miles away, where his army had pitched camp.

Washington dashed back, arriving at Fort Lee at nightfall. Finding that Greene and Israel Putnam had been rowed across

461

the river to meet with Magaw and appraise the situation, Washington followed in a small boat.

Halfway across, he met Greene and Putnam, who were on their way back, and there, at midriver in the dark, Greene and Putnam gave an encouraging report. The troops were in "high spirits and would make a good defense." And thus, "it being late at night," in Washington's words, the three returned to Fort Lee.

The same night, as went unobserved by the Americans, the British brought a fleet of thirty flatboats up the river with oars muffled, past Fort Washington, into Spuyten Duyvil Creek, and down the Harlem, to be ready for morning.

At first chance, early Saturday, November 16, Washington, with Greene, Putnam, and another of his generals, Hugh Mercer of Virginia, again crossed the Hudson, "to determine," as Greene wrote, "what was best to be done." No sooner had their boat pushed off than the sound of heavy cannon carried over the water, and off in the distance, to the left of Fort Washington, they could see the attack had begun.

Landing on the opposite shore, down-river from the fort, the four generals scrambled up the steep slopes to the crest, to a point near the Morris house.

"There we all stood in a very awkward situation," wrote Greene. "As the disposition [of the troops] was made and the enemy advancing, we durst not attempt to make any new disposition." Somehow, they still could not see the disaster in store. "Indeed, we saw nothing amiss," Greene wrote.

Concerned for Washington's safety, the three generals urged him to leave and go back over the river. Greene volunteered to stay, as in turn did Putnam and Mercer. But Washington thought it "best" that they all go.

The assault came from three directions, after a prolonged pounding of the fort's outer defenses by British cannon. Four thousand Hessians came down from the north, over the bridge at King's Bridge, led by General von Knyphausen, who had requested the honor of leading the main attack.

The Hessians were professionals hired to perform a duty, and this was to be their day to show themselves superior in a profession they took extreme pride in. (During the time he had been held prisoner, Lord Stirling had heard Hessian officers remark that they had never considered it their duty to inquire which of the two sides in the American controversy was right.)

A force of British troops under Cornwallis, plus a battalion of Highlanders, struck from the east, crossing the Harlem River in the flatboats that had been brought up during the night. The third force of some 3,000 men, both British and Hessians, came up from the south, led by Lord Percy.

By ten o'clock General Howe had committed 8,000 troops to the assault, nearly four times the number of those defending Fort Washington.

The farthest reach of the fort's outer defenses was about five miles, north and south, and Knyphausen's Hessians faced the steepest, roughest terrain and withering fire from Virginia and Maryland riflemen positioned among the rocks under Colonel Moses Rawlings. It was the scene of the most ferocious fighting of the day, and the Hessians were dauntless. The rock slopes they scaled would have been a rough struggle even had no one been firing at them. One of their officers, Captain Andreas Wiederhold, would describe attacking up "this almost inaccessible rock," and yet, "every obstacle was swept aside . . . the precipitous rocks scaled."

A Hessian soldier, John Reuber, wrote in his journal, "We were obliged to drag ourselves by the beech-tree bushes up the height where we could not really stand."

At last, however, we got about on top of the hill where there were trees and great stones. We had a hard time of it there together. Because they now had no idea of yielding, Col. Rall gave the word of command thus: "All that are my grenadiers, march forwards!" All the drummers struck up the march, the hautboy-players [oboe players] blew. At once all that were yet alive shouted, "Hurrah!" Immediately all were mingled together, Americans and Hessians. There was no more firing, but all ran forward pell-mell upon the fortress.

General Grant, who disliked the Hessians almost as much as he disliked Americans, wrote with unalloyed admiration of how they "surmounted every difficulty," and after gaining the heights kept on "at a trot . . . and if General Knyphausen had not stopped Colonel Rall, I am convinced he would have been in the fort in five minutes."

The other sides of the attack advanced accordingly, with some of the American defenders putting up little resistance, while others fought tenaciously. Alexander Graydon, who commanded a company facing the assault by Lord Percy from the south, described how 150 men with a single 18-pound cannon held off 800 of the British.

When Percy's attacking troops captured the Morris house, it was, according to Graydon, only fifteen minutes after Washington and his generals made their exit.

But courage was not enough. The Americans were too few to hold such extended lines. The only recourse was to retreat to the fort with all speed. A seventeen-year-old private from York, Pennsylvania, John Adlum, described running such a distance uphill that he had hardly breath enough to keep going. "As I was a good deal fatigued and the firing had in a great measure ceased, I walked to the fort very leisurely," he wrote.

Before I was near the fort the British began to fire at it with a field piece with round shot, at the men who were standing in huddles between the fort and the lines within the abbitis that was round the fort. When I arrived at this work, I sat upon it looking at the enemy who were firing at us with the field piece and not more than four hundred yards of us, or from where I was then sitting, when at length a ball took off a part of two men's heads and wounded another. I then went into the fort.

By one o'clock nearly all the defending force had been driven inside the fort, where there was scarcely room for them.

An hour or so later, the Hessian commander, Knyphausen, demanded surrender. Colonel Magaw said he needed time to decide, and asked for half an hour. General Howe arrived and ordered the Americans to surrender immediately, and with no terms other than a promise of their lives.

It was three o'clock when Magaw capitulated, and about four when the entire garrison of 2,837 Americans marched out of the fort between two lines of Hessians and lay down their arms.

In a disastrous campaign for New York in which Washington's army had suffered one humiliating, costly reverse after another, this, the surrender of Fort Washington on Saturday, November 16, was the most devastating blow of all, an utter catastrophe. The taking of more than a thousand American prisoners by the British at Brooklyn had been a dreadful loss. Now more than twice that number were marched off as prisoners, making a total loss from the two battles of nearly four thousand men — from an army already rapidly disintegrating from sickness and desertions and in desperate need of almost anyone fit enough to pick up a musket.

(As Frederick Mackenzie recorded, the British were astonished to find how many of the American prisoners were less than fifteen, or old men, all "indifferently clothed," filthy, and without shoes. "Their odd figures frequently excited the laughter of our soldiers.")

The crushing defeat at Fort Washington, the capture of its garrison, plus quantities of arms, tools, tents, blankets, and some 146 brass and iron cannon, had been accomplished by the British and Hessians in a matter of hours. And it need never have happened.

Fifty-nine Americans had been killed and 100 or more wounded. The British lost 28 killed and over 100 wounded. Hessian losses were heavier, 58 killed and more than 250 wounded.

Bad as it was, it could have been even worse. In the view of both General Grant and Colonel Mackenzie, an all-out slaughter of Americans had been avoided only because General Knyphausen stopped Colonel Rall and his Hessians from entering the fort. "They had been pretty well pelted [in the battle], were angry and would not have spared the Yankees," Grant wrote. "The carnage would then have been dreadful," wrote Mackenzie, "for the rebels were so numerous they had not room to defend themselves with effect, and so frightened they had not the power."

What lay ahead of the Americans taken prisoner was a horror of another kind. Nearly all would be held captive in overcrowded, unheated barns and sheds, and on British prison ships in the harbor, where hundreds died of disease.

Washington is said to have wept as he watched the tragedy unfold from across the river, and though this seems unlikely, given his well-documented imperturbability, he surely wept within his soul. He had faced ruin before, but never like this.

To his brother Jack he would write, "I am wearied almost to death with the retrograde motions of things."

Nathanael Greene, in an anguished letter to Henry Knox, said, "I feel mad, vexed, sick, and sorry. Never did I need the consoling voice of a friend more than now. Happy should I be to see you. This is a most terrible event. Its consequences are justly to be dreaded."

Both Washington and Greene had been badly mistaken in their judgment. Both worried over what would become of their reputations. Indeed, it would be hard to say which of them was the most sensitive to what others thought of them, and criticism of both was to be severe, and especially among those who had been taken prisoner. Alexander Graydon, writing more than a generation later, could still barely contain his disdain for the decisions that had been made.

Most immediate and blistering was the reaction of Charles Lee. By his own account, Lee became so furious over the news of Fort Washington he tore out some of his hair. "I must entreat that you will keep what I say to yourself, but I foresaw, predicted, all that has happened," Lee wrote to Dr. Benjamin Rush, an influential member of Congress, who, Lee knew, would never keep it to himself. Lee claimed his last words to Washington were, "Draw off the garrison, or they will be lost."

"Had I the powers, I could do you much good," he told Rush not very subtly, "but I am sure you will never give any man the necessary power."

"Oh, General," Lee admonished Washington in a letter, "why would you be over-persuaded by men of inferior judgment to your own?" — thereby inviting the commander to blame it all on Nathanael Greene.

Washington had failed to override Greene's judgment and make a clear decision of his own, and, as commander-in-chief, he was, of course, ultimately responsible. Greene's responsibility for what happened ceased with Washington's arrival at Fort Lee on November 13, three days before the attack. Washington never blamed himself for the loss of Fort Washington, but then he never openly blamed Greene either, which he could have. He said only that he had acted on the judgment of others.

Nor, importantly, did he fire Greene, or shuffle him off to some meaningless, out-of-the-way command. He undoubtedly thought less of the young general than he had before. Still, he knew Greene's strengths. Only weeks before, Greene had demonstrated both rare foresight and a marked gift for organization when he recommended to Washington, and Washington agreed, that a series of supply depots be established across New Jersey, along what might, of necessity, become the army's path of retreat, should the British make a drive toward Philadelphia.

Washington needed Greene. He knew that Greene, like Knox, would never give up, never walk away, any more than he would, or lose sight of what the war was about, any more than he would. Washington would repay loyalty with loyalty, and this, after so many bad decisions, was one of his wisest decisions ever.

Only one American hero was to emerge from what happened at Fort Washington. She was Margaret ("Molly") Corbin, the wife of a Pennsylvania soldier, John Corbin, who had gone into battle at her husband's side, and when he was killed, stepped into his place, to load and fire a cannon, until she fell wounded, nearly losing one arm. After the surrender, she was allowed by her captors to return home to Pennsylvania.

The usually unhurried William Howe

made his next move with hardly a pause. Three nights later, he sent 4,000 British and Hessian troops under the cover of darkness and drenching rain across the Hudson to land upstream from Fort Lee at a point called Closter. There, led by Cornwallis, they scaled the Palisades, climbing a steep, almost perpendicular footpath, and once on top, advanced on Fort Lee. It was a daring attack very like the one Howe himself, as a young officer, had led up the steep slopes of Quebec early on the morning of the British triumph there in the French and Indian War.

Warning of the attack reached Fort Lee in advance, possibly from a local farmer, possibly from a British deserter — accounts differ. Washington rushed to the scene from Hackensack and shouted orders to abandon the fort at once. Everything was to be left behind, guns, stores, hundreds of tents, even breakfast cooking on the fire. When the British arrived, they found the place deserted, but for a dozen men who had gotten into the rum supply and were all drunk.

Washington and his army fled in haste down the road and over the Hackensack River farther into New Jersey.

Chapter Seven

DARKEST HOUR

I hope this is the dark part of the night,
which is generally just before day.
— General Nathanael Greene

I

The retreat of George Washington and his battered little army, southward across New Jersey, began the morning of November 21. They were headed for a crossing point called Acquackanonk on the Passaic River, five miles away, retreat being their only choice and rivers offering the one possible defense against the oncoming foe in "dead flat" country, as Washington described it, with no stone walls. Once over the Passaic, they pushed on another twenty miles down the west bank of the river to the little port town of Newark.

Heavy rains had left the narrow road sloppy with mud, and the men were in tatters, many without shoes, their feet wrapped in rags. Washington rode at the rear of the column, a point long remembered by a newly arrived eighteen-year-old Virginia lieutenant named James Monroe. "I saw him . . . at the head of a small band, or rather in its rear, for he was always near the enemy, and his countenance and manner made an impression on me which I can never efface."

By young Monroe's estimate, Washington had at most 3,000 men, yet his expression gave no sign of worry. "A deportment so firm, so dignified, but yet so modest and composed, I have never seen in any other person."

Washington had set the army on the road in the early morning but not before getting off an urgent request to General Lee at North Castle, New York, in which he had made his worries and troubles abundantly clear. The men were "broken and dispirited." They had no tents, no baggage, no entrenching tools. (Every pick and shovel had been left behind at Fort Lee.) As things were, he dared not risk contact with the enemy, Washington wrote, and "so must leave a very fine country open to their ravages."

He urged Lee to cross the Hudson with

his brigades and join forces before it was too late. New Jersey was too rich a prize to give up without even the "appearance" of a fight. Were New Jersey to fall, it could have devastating effect on Pennsylvania.

To be certain Lee understood what he wanted, Washington said it again. "I would have you move over by the easiest and best [swiftest] passage."

Yet it was a request only, not an order.

The letter had been dictated to Joseph Reed and sent off by express rider in a dispatch case into which Reed put a letter of his own to Lee. But of this Washington was told nothing.

Reed's letter was a stunning indictment of Washington. At best, it could be taken as a desperate indiscretion; at worst, an underhanded act of betrayal.

His commander's indecision over whether to abandon New York and again at Fort Washington had left Reed badly shaken. His confidence in Washington was shattered. But instead of confiding his feelings to Washington, he secretly poured them out to Lee, leaving no doubt as to who he thought should be leading the army in its hour of need.

He wished "most earnestly" to have Lee "where the principal scene of action is laid," Reed wrote, seconding what Washington had said. Then, claiming he had no wish to flatter Lee, he went on to do just that and to make his main point.

I do not mean to flatter or praise you at the expense of any other, but I confess I do think it is entirely owing to you that this army, and the liberties of America, so far as they are dependent on it, are not totally cut off. . . . You have decision, a quality often wanted in minds otherwise valuable. . . . Oh! General, an indecisive mind is one of the greatest misfortunes that can befall an army. How often have I lamented it this campaign. All circumstances considered, we are in a very awful and alarming situation — one that requires the utmost wisdom and firmness of mind. As soon as the season will admit, I think yourself and some others should go to Congress and form the plan of the new army.

Washington worried about the health of his men. He worried about rumors of a British invasion to the south of Newark at Perth Amboy, at the mouth of the Raritan River, where New Jersey and Staten Island were separated by only a narrow channel.

In less than two weeks, on December 1, the enlistments of 2,000 of his troops would be up, the men free to go. It was the same nightmare prospect he had faced at Boston exactly a year before, and with the misery of the men greater now than ever, and morale suffering, there seemed every chance that his army would evaporate before his eyes.

Privately, Washington talked with Reed about the possibility of retreating to western Pennsylvania if necessary. Reed thought that if eastern Pennsylvania were to give up, the rest of the state would follow. Washington is said to have passed his hand over his throat and remarked, "My neck does not feel as though it was made for a halter." He talked of retreating to the mountains of Augusta County, in western Virginia. From there they could carry on a "predatory war," Washington said. "And if over-powered, we must cross the Allegheny Mountains." He knew, as the enemy had little idea, just how big a country it was.

The problem was not that there were too few American soldiers in the thirteen states. There were plenty, but the states were reluctant to send the troops they had to help fight the war, preferring to keep them close to home, and especially as the war was not going well. In August, Washington had had an army of 20,000. In the three months since, he had lost four battles — at Brooklyn, Kips Bay, White Plains, and Fort Washington — then gave up Fort Lee without a fight. His army now was divided as it had not been in August and, just as young Lieutenant Monroe had speculated, he had only about 3,500 troops under his personal command — that was all.

Desperate for help, he sent Reed off to Burlington, New Jersey, on the eastern bank of the Delaware River, upstream from Philadelphia, to impress upon the governor of New Jersey, William Livingston, the urgent need for reinforcements. As it was, New Jersey militia were not turning out in any numbers that could make a difference.

General Mifflin was dispatched on a similar mission to Philadelphia, to alert Congress to the "critical state of our affairs," and do everything possible to round up Pennsylvania troops and send them on with all speed.

These were two critical undertakings, and in the choice of Reed, his closest confidant, and the very able Mifflin, the Philadelphian who had shown such valor in command of the rear guard at Brooklyn, Washington felt confident he was sending two of the best men he had, and that this would not be lost on any who listened to what they had to say.

The first report from Mifflin was bitterly disappointing. His fellow Pennsylvanians were "divided and lethargic," Mifflin wrote, "slumbering under the shade of peace and in the full enjoyment of the sweets of commerce." From Reed, Washington heard nothing.

It rained heavily on November 22, the day the army reached Newark, and rain fell through that night and again the next day. "The sufferings we endured are beyond description — no tent to cover us at night — exposed to cold and rains day and night," one soldier would remember. Colonel Samuel Webb, writing at the time, said it was impossible to describe conditions as they were. "I can only say that no lads ever showed greater activity in retreating than we have. . . . Our soldiers are the best fellows in the world at this business." Webb, who had only just recovered from wounds received at White Plains, served still on Washington's staff.

But of greatest importance, as time would tell, was the impression made on Thomas Paine, the author of *Common Sense*, who had recently volunteered to serve as a civilian aide on Greene's staff. Greene, with his love of literature and political philosophy, had taken a great liking to the brilliant Paine, an impoverished English immigrant, who, like Greene, had been raised a Quaker, and whose pamphlet, *Common Sense*, since its appearance early in the year, had become more widely read than anything yet published in America. Greene called him Common Sense. ("Common Sense and Col. Snarl, or Cornell, are perpetually wrangling about mathematical problems," Greene had reported to his wife during less troubled times before the fall of Fort Washington.)

Sick at heart over the suffering and despair he saw, but inspired by the undaunted resolution of many around him, Paine is said to have committed his thoughts to paper during the retreat, writing at night on a drumhead by the light of a campfire. He himself, however, said it was not until later, at Philadelphia, that in a "passion of patriotism," he began what he called *The Crisis*, with its immortal opening lines:

These are the times that try men's souls. The summer soldier and the sunshine patriot will, in this crisis, shrink from the service of their country; but he that stands it now, deserves the love and thanks of man and woman.

On November 24, Washington sent off another message to General Lee saying he must come by a "safe and secure route," and asking that he bring a particular 24-pound cannon, "provided it can be done without great inconvenience."

With Loyalists more prevalent in New Jersey than in any other of the thirteen states, and American deserters continuing to go over to the enemy, Washington's plight was well known to the British command.

"The fact is," wrote Lord Rawdon, "their army is broken all to pieces, and the spirit of their leaders and their abettors is all broken. . . . I think one may venture to pronounce that it is well nigh over with them."

Since the fall of Fort Washington there had been a major shift in British plans. General Clinton was reassigned. He was to sail with an expedition of 6,000 troops to take Rhode Island, or more specifically Newport. For in the time when the fortunes of the rebel army were going steadily from bad to worse, rebel privateers off the New England coast had been attacking British supply ships with increasing success, and Admiral Lord Howe was in need of a secure, ice-free winter roadstead in the vicinity for some of his fleet.

Clinton thought ill of the Rhode Island expedition. He had argued that it be postponed and that instead he and his forces land at Perth Amboy and thus outflank and destroy the crippled rebels in one sweeping, concentrated effort before the onset of winter snow. Or, Clinton proposed, he could carry his attack directly to Philadelphia, by sailing up the Delaware. "This, in all probability," he later wrote, "would have dispersed the Congress, and . . . deranged all their affairs."

It was a critical moment in the management of the war, with Clinton and William Howe once more opposed on how best to proceed. Clinton continued to see Washington's army as the heart of the rebellion, and the envelopment of the army, therefore, as the most expeditious strategy. Howe wanted to keep the Americans on the run, and continue to clear the board, so to speak — to clear New Jersey and Rhode Island of the rebel forces just as he had cleared New York, and by such conquests of vital territory bring the deluded American people and their political leaders to their senses and end their demonstrably futile rebellion.

Clinton was overruled, and though unconvinced, he departed dutifully for Rhode Island, where his expedition seized Newport without opposition and the predominantly Quaker inhabitants seemed quite happy to live in peace under his protection. But it was a conquest of little importance. As would be said, its effect on the course of the war was about what it would have been had Clinton's forces occupied the town of Newport on the Isle of Wight.

Difficulties between Clinton and William Howe, the friction of the two contrasting personalities, had grown steadily worse. At White Plains, in an outburst of frustration and anger, Clinton had told General Cornwallis he could not bear to serve under Howe, and this Cornwallis had chosen to tell Howe. Thus it was with considerable relief that Howe saw Clinton sail off from New York, just as when Clinton had departed Boston for South Carolina.

In Clinton's place, Howe put Cornwallis,

knowing he had a far more reasonable man to deal with and a highly energetic and effective field commander.

Like Howe — indeed, like Clinton — Charles Cornwallis was a true eighteenth-century English aristocrat, a shining representative of Britain's ruling class, born to wealth, position, and influence. Schooled at Eton, he had decided in his youth on a military career, in which he had distinguished himself ever since. At age thirty-seven, he was at his professional prime but, unlike Howe, a man with no bad habits or inclinations to self-indulgence, and if not as intellectually gifted as Clinton, he had no peevish or contrary side.

Tall and somewhat overweight, as was the fashion, he carried himself well and was considered handsome, except for a cast in one eye. (In fact, he had lost sight in one eye as a result of a boyhood accident.) He was devoted to his ailing wife, whom he missed dreadfully, and devoted to his men — "I love that army," he had once declared — and their devotion to him was notable. He was the most popular British general serving in America, known to be strict but fair, and genuinely concerned for the well-being of his troops. Repeatedly in the year's campaign — at

Brooklyn, Kips Bay, Fort Washington, and in his stunning surprise capture of Fort Lee — he had shown himself to be enterprising and aggressive. Thus far, he had done everything right.

On November 23, two days after the capture of Fort Lee, Cornwallis had met there with General Howe (who, having been made a Knight of the Bath by the King, was now Sir William Howe). The two conferred for several hours, going over the map of New Jersey and reviewing plans.

Howe gave orders to Cornwallis to pursue the rebels as far as New Brunswick, or Brunswick as it was then known, another fifty miles south of Newark, on the Raritan River, and stop there until further orders.

On November 25, after the rains subsided, Cornwallis and an army now numbering 10,000 set off, determined to catch Washington, Cornwallis said, as a hunter bags a fox. But on the rain-drenched roads, in muck ankle-deep or worse, the long columns of redcoats and Hessians with their heavy baggage trains and artillery moved slower even than the Americans had. They were three days reaching Newark.

At nine o'clock on the morning of November 28, the British engineering officer, Captain Archibald Robertson, recorded, "All the army marched in two columns towards Newark, where it was said the rebels would stand." About one o'clock, the British advanced on the town in force, only to find it empty.

Washington had pressed on toward Brunswick and the Raritan. "The enemy gave us not the least interruption upon our march," he wrote to General Heath.

There was word at last from Charles Lee, but only to report his own tribulations with foul weather and men without shoes. He was still at North Castle and made no mention of plans to leave.

Washington replied at once. "My former letters were so full and explicit as to the necessity of your marching as early as possible . . . that I confess I expected you would have been sooner in motion," he said sharply. Yet he was still reluctant to issue a clear order to Lee.

By the time he reached Brunswick the morning of November 29, Washington had been joined by the dauntless Lord Stirling and more than 1,000 reinforcements. They were a first glimmer of hope, though hardly enough. Numbers of Stirling's men, too, were shoeless and without coats or even shirts, and the December 1 expiration of enlistments, when twice that number would be free to leave, was only two days away.

On November 30 at Brunswick, a sealed letter from General Lee to Joseph Reed arrived by express rider. With Reed still absent, Washington tore it open thinking it might be news that Lee and his men were at last on the way. The letter was dated November 24. "My dear Reed," it began.

I received your most obliging, flattering letter — lament with you that fatal indecision of mind which in war is a much greater disqualification than stupidity or even want of personal courage. Accident may put a decisive blunder in the right, but eternal defeat and miscarriage must attend the men of the best parts if cursed with indecision.

Lee went on to explain why he had not started for New Jersey as Washington wished, and apparently he did not intend to do so.

What Washington thought or felt as he read the letter, or how many times he may have reread its first paragraph, no one knows. Clearly Reed, his trusted confidant and supposed friend, and Lee, his second-in-command, had both lost faith in him.

Washington resealed the letter and sent it off to Reed with a note of explanation.

> The enclosed was put into my hands by an express [rider]. . . . Having no idea of its being a private letter . . . I opened it. . . . This, as it is the truth, must be my excuse for seeing the contents of a letter which neither inclination *or* intention would have prompted me to.

He thanked Reed for the "trouble and fatigue" of his journey to Burlington and wished him success in his mission. And that was all.

Possibly, Washington was more hurt than angry. Later he would tell Reed, "I was hurt not because I thought my judgment wronged by the expressions contained in it [the letter], but because the same sentiments were not communicated immediately to myself." Possibly the charge of "fatal indecision of mind" also hurt deeply, because Washington knew it to be true.

Above all, he must have felt profoundly alone, as alone as he had ever been. First

Greene had let him down, now Reed. And who was to say what Lee had in mind, or might do?

At Philadelphia many of the Congress were ill or exhausted or absent. All three of the principal contributors to the Declaration of Independence were no longer present. Thomas Jefferson had gone home to Virginia in September. John Adams was at Braintree. Benjamin Franklin had departed on a mission to France. At times there were not enough delegates for a quorum, and as the news from New Jersey became more bleak, and the British army drew nearer, Philadelphia was beset by an extreme outbreak of the jitters.

The *Pennsylvania Journal* announced "very good intelligence that the British intend to make a push for Philadelphia," and Richard Henry Lee of Virginia, among others, reported "much alarm" in the city and in Congress. Delegate William Hooper of North Carolina, another signer of the Declaration of Independence, described a prevailing "torpor" in Congress. Hooper, however, had no patience with those blaming Washington for every misfortune.

Oh how I feel for Washington, that best of men [he wrote]. The difficulties which he has now to encounter are beyond the power of language to describe, but to be unfortunate is to be wrong and there are men . . . who are villains enough to brand him. There are some long faces here.

Once, during the Siege of Boston, when almost nothing was going right and General Schuyler had written from Albany to bemoan his troubles, Washington had replied that he understood but that "we must bear up against them, and make the best of mankind as they are, since we cannot have them as we wish." It was such resolve and an acceptance of mankind and circumstances as they were, not as he wished them to be, that continued to carry Washington through. "I will not however despair," he now wrote to Governor William Livingston.

On Sunday morning, December 1, with British and Hessian columns advancing on Brunswick, 2,000 of Washington's troops, New Jersey and Maryland militia, their enlistments up, walked away from the war, and without apology. "Two brigades left us at Brunswick," wrote Nathanael Greene, "notwithstanding the enemy are within two hours march and coming on."

Washington sent off still another urgent summons to Lee to come with all speed, "or your arrival may be too late to answer any valuable purpose."

"The enemy are fast advancing," he reported in a hurried dispatch to John Hancock, noting that the time was half past one. "Some of them are in sight."

He ordered the only bridge over the Raritan at Brunswick destroyed, and this had been largely accomplished. But the river was fordable — in some places only knee-deep — and as he also told Hancock, mincing no words, his present force was "totally inadequate" to stop the enemy.

The first of the British artillery arrived at the river, and by late afternoon British and American cannon were exchanging fire, the American guns commanded by young Captain Alexander Hamilton. But again, as at Newark, when the British troops pressed on to the town the next morning, they found that the Americans had taken off.

Washington had decided what must be done. He was heading for Trenton. "It being impossible to oppose them with our present force with the least possible prospect of success," he informed Congress, "we shall retreat to the west bank of the Delaware."

"When we left Brunswick," wrote Nathanael Greene, "we had not 3,000 men — a very pitiful army to trust the liberties of America on." The hour had never looked darker.

The post road, or King's Highway, from Brunswick to Trenton, the main thoroughfare between New York and Philadelphia, was as straight and flat and fine a thirty-mile stretch of road as any in the country, and the retreating army made good time. The retreat was not at a run. It was a forced march, not a rout, as sometimes portrayed. Washington and the main body of the army, marching through the night, reached Trenton on the Delaware the morning of December 2, having left Lord Stirling and two brigades as a rear guard at the little college town of Princeton.

Orders were issued to round up all boats along the east bank of the Delaware and to destroy any that could not be used, to keep them out of enemy hands.

Among the delegates to Congress, the distances from Brunswick to Trenton and Trenton to Philadelphia were well known, and so if Cornwallis was at Brunswick, then he and his army were a mere sixty miles from Philadelphia. "The inhabitants of Princeton and Trenton . . . are evacuated," wrote Massachusetts delegate Robert Treat Paine. "The people left them on Sunday night with panic and precipitation." People in Philadelphia were getting out, too, many taking all the possessions they could carry. "Numbers of families loading wagons," a citizen recorded. "All shops ordered shut . . . people in confusion, of all ranks."

The great question on everyone's mind was where were Lee and his men. It was said they were not far, "close in the rear of the enemy." But no one knew. "I have not heard a word from General Lee since the 26th of last month," John Hancock read in a letter from Washington dated December 3.

II

With his brother Sir William's campaign succeeding splendidly in New Jersey, and the war rapidly losing support among the people there, Admiral Lord Howe decided to make yet another appeal for conciliation. Signed also by Sir William, the new proclamation was their boldest, most generous gesture thus far, they felt. It was issued in the spirit of their obligation, as commissioned by the King, to serve as peace negotiators as well as military commanders, but also because Lord Howe genuinely believed that a negotiated settlement with the Americans was yet possible and vastly preferable to a long-drawn-out conflict. He had no desire to lose any more British lives or to inflict any more destruction and suffering on the Americans than necessary.

The proclamation, dated November 30, was an immediate success. It offered all who, within sixty days, would come forth and take an oath of allegiance to the King — and pledge their "peaceable obedience" — a "free and general pardon," and that they would

reap the benefit of his Majesty's paternal goodness, in the preservation of their property, the restoration of their commerce, and the security of their most valuable rights, under the just and most moderate authority of the crown and Parliament of Britain.

Hundreds, eventually thousands, in New Jersey flocked to the British camps to declare their loyalty. Considering the way the war was going, the size and might of the British army, and the pathetic state of Washington's meager band, it seemed the prudent thing to do. As a farmer near Brunswick named John Bray wrote to a kinsman:

You can come down and receive protection and return home without molestation on the part of the King's troops and you best know the situation of the provincial army. Do advise Cousin Johnny and Thomas and Cousin Thomas Jones, for if they do stay out to the last, they will undoubtedly fare the worst.

Having crossed the Raritan and occupied Brunswick on December 1, Cornwallis called a halt, as he had been ordered by General Howe. For six days — six merciful days for Washington and his army — the British and Hessians made no move, a decision that puzzled, even infuriated many of the British and local Loyalists who saw no reason to let up on the chase.

Called on to explain later, Cornwallis would say his troops were exhausted, footsore, hungry, and in need of rest. More important, it had not seemed at the time that excessive haste was wise or necessary.

There were dangers in too rapid a pursuit. He worried about General Lee, who was variously reported just ahead or coming up from behind. But had it looked like he could catch Washington, Cornwallis said, he would have kept going, whatever the risks, no matter the orders.

Some would see the pause as a horrendous blunder and blame William Howe. Captain Charles Stedman, one of Cornwallis's own officers and the earliest British historian of the war, would speculate that had Cornwallis been allowed "to act at his own discretion . . . he would have pursued the weakened and alarmed enemy to the Delaware, over which, without falling into his hands, they never could have passed." But this assumed that Washington and the army could not have escaped down the east side of the river, which seems unreasonable.

The Hessian officer Johann Ewald, an intelligent and experienced soldier, concluded that Cornwallis had no desire to put his valuable troops in needless jeopardy. On the night of the capture of Fort Lee, when Ewald and his jaegers had started after a column of rebels retreating in "a cloud of dust," Cornwallis had ordered them back. "Let them go, my dear

Ewald, and stay here," Cornwallis had said. "We do not want to lose any men. One jaeger is worth more than ten rebels." By the time of the halt at Brunswick, Ewald wrote, the hope of the whole British command was "of ending the war amicably, without shedding the blood of the King's subjects in a needless way."

Others would say it was for political reasons related to the latest peace move that Cornwallis intentionally let Washington get away. No one would ever prove this, and it seems unlikely, especially since General Howe, sensing that a final blow might now indeed be struck, arrived at Brunswick on December 6 with an additional brigade commanded by General Grant, and ordered the advance to continue at once.

The weather had turned unseasonably warm, ideal for campaigning. A Loyalist newspaper in New York had already set the scene in a report published the day before:

> It is said by some persons who have lately seen the rebel forces that they are the most pitiable collection of ragged, dispirited mortals that ever pretended to the name of an army . . . and that if the weather continues fair but a little

longer, there is no visible impediment to His Majesty's troops in completing a march to the capitol of Pennsylvania.

Everything seemed to the advantage of the conquering army, all was going as wished except for one vexing problem that had been growing steadily worse for several weeks. Marauding and pillaging by redcoats and Hessians had gotten out of hand. "Scandalous behavior for British troops," wrote Major Stephen Kemble, the Loyalist serving with the British army, "and the Hessians outrageously licentious, and cruel to such a degree as to threaten with death all such as dare obstruct them in their depredations." Kemble had recorded this in his diary in early November, before the capture of Fort Washington. "[I] shudder for New Jersey," he had written.

The plenty of New Jersey, the "Garden of America," its broad, fertile, well-tended farms, abundant supplies of livestock, grain, hay, food put up for winter, barrels of wine and beer for the taking, were all too much to resist. On the first night his Hessian troops set foot in New Jersey, Captain Ewald wrote, "All the plantations in the vicinity were plundered, and whatever the soldiers found in the houses was declared booty." Ewald was appalled by what he saw.

> On this march [through New Jersey] we looked upon a deplorable sight. The region is well-cultivated, with very attractive plantations, but all their occupants had fled and all the houses had been or were being plundered and destroyed.

The British blamed the Hessians. ("The Hessians are more infamous and cruel than any," wrote Ambrose Serle, after hearing reports of British plundering.) The Hessians blamed the British. The Americans blamed both the British and the Hessians, as well as the New Jersey Loyalists, and the British and Hessian commanders seemed no more able to put a stop to such excesses than Washington had been. The stories, amplified as many may have been, were a searing part of a war that seemed only to grow more brutal and destructive.

Accounts of houses sacked, of families robbed of all they had, became commonplace. American reports of atrocities were often propaganda, but many were also quite accurate. The *Pennsylvania Journal*, the *Pennsylvania Evening Post*, and the *Freeman's Journal* carried reports of the sick and elderly being abused, of rape and murder. No one was safe, according to the British officer Charles Stedman. "The friend and the foe from the hand of rapine shared alike."

The New Jersey Loyalists were the most villainous of all, Nathanael Greene reported to his wife Caty.

They lead the relentless foreigners to the houses of their neighbors and strip poor women and children of everything they have to eat or wear; and after plundering them in this sort, the brutes often ravish the mothers and daughters and compel the fathers and sons to behold their brutality.

"The enemy's ravages in New Jersey exceed all description," Greene would report to Governor Nicholas Cooke of Rhode Island. "Many hundred women ravished."

At Newark, according to the report of a congressional committee, three women, one of whom was in her seventies, another pregnant, were "most horribly ravished."

Fear and outrage spread across New Jersey and beyond. "Their footsteps are marked with destruction wherever they go," Greene said of the enemy.

What remained of Washington's army, the "shadow army," as Greene called it, was pitiful to behold. "But give me leave to tell you, Sir," Greene would write to John Adams, "that our difficulties were inconceivable to those who were not eye witnesses to them."

British and Hessian forces got under way from Brunswick on December 7 and came on faster than ever, William Howe having decided that, "The possession of Trenton was extremely desirable." With the continuing success of the Proclamation of November 30 and hardly any opposition from the rebels, Howe intended to secure another large part of New Jersey where Loyalists were plentiful, and where, as he also said, Philadelphia was in easy striking distance.

Washington was on his way from Trenton to look things over at Princeton when he received word of the enemy's strength and rapid advance. Immediately he turned back.

"Our retreat should not be neglected for fear of consequences," advised Nathanael Greene, who had also ridden to Princeton earlier in the day. In the trek across New Jersey, Washington had become increasingly dependent on Greene. But it was "beyond doubt" that the enemy was advancing, Greene reported. Lord Stirling expected them by noon. Lee was also said to be "at the heels of the enemy," but Greene cautioned Washington that, whatever happened, Lee ought to be kept under control "within the lines of some general plan or else his operations will be independent of yours."

Washington had already made his decision, and he calmly, deliberately, carried it out. A fleet of boats was standing ready at Trenton. By nightfall, the weary troops and their commander were crossing the Delaware to the Pennsylvania shore, where bonfires had been set ablaze to light the way.

One of those watching from the Pennsylvania side was the artist Charles Willson Peale, who had arrived with a Philadelphia militia unit in answer to Washington's call for help. Peale wrote later of the firelight on the river and shore, of boats laden with soldiers, horses, cannon, and equipment, of men calling out orders. It was "a grand but dreadful" spectacle: "The hallooing of hundreds of men in their difficulties getting horses and artillery out of the boats, made it rather the appearance of Hell than any earthly scene."

The long retreat that had begun in New York and continued from the Hudson to the Delaware was over. Casualties had been few in New Jersey, and its pitiable appearance and miseries notwithstanding, the army, or the semblance of an army, had once again survived.

"With a handful of men we sustained an orderly retreat," wrote Thomas Paine in *The Crisis*, which soon appeared in Philadelphia. No sign of fear was to be seen, he insisted. "Once more we are collected and collecting. . . . By perseverance and fortitude we have the prospect of a glorious issue."

Henry Knox, writing on the morning of December 8, his first letter to his wife in weeks, said she might be surprised to find he was in Pennsylvania. Though physically exhausted, he, like Paine, refused to be downcast. It was "a combination of unlucky circumstances" that had brought things to such a pass, he told her. "We are now making a stand on the side of the Delaware toward Philadelphia."

In truth, men were dreadfully dispirited. Many had given up, in addition to the

2,000 who had refused to sign on again after December 1. Hundreds had deserted. Many of those left were sick, hungry, altogether as miserable as they appeared.

To Charles Willson Peale, walking among them by the light of the next morning on the Pennsylvania shore, they looked as wretched as any men he had ever seen. One had almost no clothes. "He was in an old dirty blanket jacket, his beard long, and his face so full of sores that he could not clean it." So "disfigured" was he that Peale failed at first to recognize that the man was his own brother, James Peale, who had been with a Maryland unit as part of the rear guard.

That the enemy might cross the Delaware at one or several points and move quickly to seize Philadelphia, as they had New York, no one doubted. On Washington's orders every boat not commanded to bring the army across had been destroyed for sixty miles along the east bank of the river, which was no small accomplishment. But broad and swift as it was, the river could remain a barrier to Howe only so long, as Washington warned the members of Congress repeatedly in a series of urgent dispatches.

"From several accounts, I am led to think that the enemy are bringing boats with them," he wrote.

If so, it will be impossible for our small force to give them any considerable opposition in the passage of the river. . . . Under the circumstances, the security of Philadelphia should be our next object.

In another letter to John Hancock, he stated flatly that "Philadelphia beyond all question is the object of the enemy's movements," that "nothing less than our utmost exertions" could stop Howe, and that his own force was too thin and weak to count on.

Washington and his staff had taken up quarters in a brick house directly across the river from Trenton, where he hoped to keep watch on the enemy. His troops were scattered close by the river for nearly twenty-five miles, camped in the woods and brush out of sight from the river, the greater part of them about ten miles to the north of Washington's headquarters.

While Joseph Reed had gotten nowhere with his recruiting efforts in New Jersey, Mifflin's efforts had produced some results. The Philadelphia volunteer militia (or Philadelphia Associators as they were called) that Charles Willson Peale had arrived with numbered 1,000 and marched into camp "in a very spirited manner," as Washington noted approvingly.

On December 10, word came at last that Lee and 4,000 troops commanded by General Sullivan had reached Morristown to the northeast.

"General Lee . . . is on his march to join me," Washington wrote to the governor of Connecticut, Jonathan Trumbull. "If he can effect this junction, our army will again make a respectable appearance, and such as I hope will disappoint the enemy in their plan on Philadelphia."

Everything depended on Lee.

The letter to Trumbull was written December 14, when Washington knew nothing of events of the day before, Friday the 13th — events wholly unexpected and of far-reaching consequences. As time would show, that Friday the 13th had been an exceedingly lucky day for Washington and for his country.

In an inexplicable lapse of judgment, General Lee had spent the previous night of the 12th separated from his troops, stopping at a tavern about three miles away at Basking Ridge, for what reason is not known.

With Lee was a personal guard of fifteen officers and men. The next morning, in low spirits and no apparent hurry, Lee sat at a table in his dressing gown attending to routine paperwork, then took time to write a letter to General Gates for no other purpose than to blame Washington for all his troubles and for the woeful state of affairs in general.

"Entre nous, a certain great man is damnable deficient," Lee told Gates.

> He has thrown me into a situation where I have my choice of difficulties: if I stay in this province, I risk myself and army; and if I do not stay, the province is lost forever. . . . In short, unless something which I do not expect turns up, we are lost.

It was just after ten when a swarm of British cavalry appeared suddenly at the end of the lane. They were a scouting party of twenty-five horsemen commanded by Colonel William Harcourt, who had once served under Lee in Portugal. They had been sent out from Trenton by Cornwallis to gather intelligence on Lee's "motions and situation." At Basking Ridge, a local Loyalist had given them the answer.

From the end of the lane to the tavern was a distance of about a hundred yards. Six of the horsemen, led by Lieutenant Banister Tarleton, came at a gallop. In minutes they had the building surrounded, killed two of the guards, and scattered the rest.

"I ordered my men to fire into the house through every window and door, and cut up as many of the guard as they could," Tarleton later wrote.

Some of those inside fired back. Then the owner of the tavern, a woman named White, appeared at the door. Screaming that Lee was inside, she begged for mercy.

Tarleton shouted that he would burn the building unless Lee gave himself up. In a few minutes Lee appeared and surrendered, saying he trusted he would be treated as a gentleman.

A young American lieutenant who had been inside and managed to escape, James Wilkinson, would later describe how a cheer went up among Lee's captors and a trumpet sounded. Then off they dashed with their prize, the "unfortunate" Lee, hatless, still in his dressing gown and slippers, mounted on Wilkinson's horse, which happened to have been tethered at the door. The astonishing raid had taken no more than fifteen minutes.

News of Lee's capture spread in all directions as fast as the fastest horses could move. The British were jubilant. At Brunswick, where the prisoner was put under lock and key, Harcourt's cavalrymen celebrated by getting Lee's horse (Wilkinson's horse) drunk, along with themselves, as a band played into the night.

A Hessian captain wrote in his journal, "We have captured General Lee, the only rebel general whom we had cause to fear." The hero of the hour, Lieutenant Tarleton, wrote triumphantly to his mother, "This *coup de main* has put an end to the campaign."

When the news reached England it was thought at first to be too improbable, then set off bell-ringing and joyful demonstrations as if a great battle had been won.

Among the British, it was thought that because Lee was a British soldier and gentleman, he was therefore, of course, superior to any raw American provincial who had assumed high rank, but then for the same reason, he was also that much more of a traitor to his King.

To the American officers and troops deployed along the west bank of the Delaware, and all whose hopes were riding on them, the loss of Lee seemed the worst possible news at the worst possible moment.

To Nathanael Greene it was one of a "combination of evils . . . pressing in upon us on all sides." Washington, on first hearing what had happened, called it a "severe blow," then said he would comment no further on "this unhappy accident." Privately he was furious with Lee for having been such a fool. "Unhappy man! Taken by his own imprudence," he told Lund Washington. And privately he must also have breathed a sigh of relief. After the continuing frustrations and anxieties Lee had subjected him to, there must have been a feeling of deliverance for Washington.

The popular, egotistical general who considered the members of Congress no better than cattle and longed for the "necessary power" to set everything straight was no longer a factor. In little time, fearing he might be hanged as a traitor and hoping to ingratiate himself with his old military friend William Howe, Lee would resort to offering his thoughts to Howe on ways the British could win the war.

The same day as Lee's capture, Washington learned that Congress had adjourned in order to move to a safer location at Baltimore. It was abandoning Philadelphia for the first time since convening there for the First Continental Congress in 1774.

Everything seemed to be happening at once. On December 13, at his Trenton headquarters across the river from Washington, William Howe made one of the fateful decisions of the war. He was suspending further military operations until spring. Beginning immediately, he and his army would retire to winter quarters in northern New Jersey and New York. To secure the ground gained in the campaign, he would establish a string of outposts in New Jersey.

There had been a change in the weather. The days had turned much colder. The nights were the coldest yet with a "hard frost" and snow flurries, and this was all Howe had needed to make up his mind, "the weather," as he wrote, "having become too severe to keep the field."

It was commonly understood that eighteenth-century professional armies and their gentlemen commanders did not subject themselves to the miseries of winter campaigns, unless there were overriding reasons to the contrary. Considering all he had accomplished in the year's campaign and knowing the helpless state of the rebel army, Howe saw no cause to continue the fight or to remain a day longer than necessary in a punishing American winter in a place like Trenton.

And there were, besides, compelling reasons to retire to New York City, for quarters for the army, and for the comforts and pleasures that so appealed to the general himself.

Howe departed for New York on Saturday, December 14, joined by Cornwallis, whom he had granted leave to return to England to visit his ailing wife.

General Howe cozily accommodated in New York, as pictured in the minds of many, would rekindle old gossip and give rise to some popular doggerel:

Sir William, he, snug as a flea,
Lay all this time a-snoring;
Nor dreamed of harm, as he lay warm
In bed with Mrs. Loring.

No boats were to be built or hauled overland by the British to cross the Delaware. And for now there was to be no march on Philadelphia. The members of Congress could as well have stayed where they were.

But of this Washington seems to have known little or nothing. Close as he was to the enemy he had almost no idea of what they were doing, no knowledge that Howe and Cornwallis had departed, and that neither he nor Congress were any longer under immediate threat.

"The Delaware now divides what remains of our little force from that of General Howe whose object, beyond all question, is to possess Philadelphia," Washington wrote on December 18, four days after Howe's departure, to James Bowdoin, a member of the Massachusetts Council. Were the river to freeze, Washington feared, the enemy might attack over the ice. "Strain every nerve for carrying out the necessary works," he told Israel Putnam, who was charged with the defense of Philadelphia. "There seems to be the strongest reason to believe the enemy will attempt to pass the river as soon as the ice is sufficiently formed."

Desperate for reliable intelligence — for information of almost any kind — Washington let it be known he was willing to pay for it, at almost any price. In a dispatch to his general officers, he implored them to find a spy who would cross the river and determine whether any boats were being built or coming overland. "Expense must not be spared in procuring such intelligence, and will readily be paid by me." To Lord Stirling, he wrote, "Use every possible means without regard to expense to come with certainty at the enemy's strength, situation, and movements — without this we wander in a wilderness of uncertainties."

As early as December 15, he had received a report from a commander of Pennsylvania militia posted below Trenton, John Cadwalader, saying, "General Howe is certainly gone to New York, unless the whole is a scheme to amuse and surprise." Perhaps Washington found it impossible to believe, or suspected that it was indeed a ruse. Whatever the reason, he seems to have ignored it.

The foe gathered on the other side of the river was the British army no longer, but a holding force of 1,500 Hessians settled in for the winter under the command of Colonel Johann Rall, the veteran officer who had led the fierce Hessian assaults at White Plains and Fort Washington.

Concerned about "the apparent designs" of the enemy — the "wilderness of uncertainties" — Washington moved his headquarters ten miles upstream to Buckingham Township, closer to the main body of the army, where Greene, Stirling, and Knox had their headquarters.

In two weeks, on New Year's Day, all enlistments would expire. And what then? "Our only dependence now is upon the speedy enlistment of a new army," he wrote to Lund Washington. "If this fails, I think the game is pretty near up."

On December 20, in the midst of a snowstorm, General Sullivan rode into Buckingham at the head of Lee's troops, having marched at a pace four times what Lee had set in order to join Washington as soon as possible. But instead of the 4,000 that Washington had been expecting, there were only half that number, and the men were in more wretched condition even than Washington's own ranks. When Lee had complained of his troops having no shoes, it had been no exaggeration for effect. General Heath would later write of seeing Lee's troops pass through Peekskill, many "so destitute of shoes that the blood left on the frozen ground, in many places, marked the route they had taken."

One of those who had made the trek from Peekskill was Lieutenant Joseph Hodgkins. In a letter headed "Buckingham in Pennsylvania, December 20, 1776," Hodgkins reported to his wife Sarah:

We have been on the march since the 29th of last month and we are now within 10 or 12 miles of General Washington's army. We expect to be there tonight. But how long we shall stay there I can't tell. Neither can I tell you much about the enemy, only that they are on one side of the Delaware River and our army on the other.

They had marched about two hundred miles, Hodgkins thought, and the greatest part of the way was dangerous — "the enemy being near," but also because so much of the country was "full of them cursed creatures called Tories."

General Gates, too, arrived, but to Washington's disappointment, he had with him only six hundred men.

Before departing for Baltimore, Congress had named Robert Morris to head the committee to look after affairs in Philadelphia, by now an all-but-abandoned city. Writing to Morris three days before

Christmas, Washington said he thought the enemy was waiting for two events only before marching on Philadelphia — "Ice for a passage, and the dissolution of the poor remains of our debilitated army."

As near as could be determined, Washington now had an army of about 7,500, but that was a paper figure only. Possibly 6,000 were fit for duty. Hundreds were sick and suffering from the cold. Robert Morris and others in and around Philadelphia were doing everything possible to find winter clothes and blankets, while more and more of the local citizenry were signing the British proclamation. Congress had fled. Two former members of Congress, Joseph Galloway and Andrew Allen, had gone over to the enemy. By all reasonable signs, the war was over and the Americans had lost.

Yet for all the troubles that beset him, all the high expectations and illusions that he had seen shattered since the triumph at Boston, Washington had more strength to draw upon than met the eye — in his own inner resources and in the abilities of those still with him and resolved to carry on.

In Greene, Stirling, and Sullivan he had field commanders as good as or better than any. Though Greene, his best, and the very able Joseph Reed had let him down, both had learned from the experience, just as Washington had, and were more determined than ever to prove themselves worthy in his eyes. Greene, as he would confide to his wife, was extremely happy to have again "the full confidence of his Excellency," confidence that seemed to increase "the more difficult and distressing our affairs grow."

Henry Knox, a novice artilleryman no longer, and the steadfast John Glover, could be counted on no matter how tough the going. (In recognition of the part played thus far by the twenty-six-year-old Knox, Washington had already recommended him for promotion to the rank of brigadier general.) Junior officers and soldiers in the ranks, men like Joseph Hodgkins, were battered, weary, ragged as beggars, but not beaten.

Washington himself was by no means beaten. If William Howe and others of like mind thought the war was over and the British had won, Washington did not. Washington refused to see it that way.

With Lee gone and Congress entrusting him with more power, Washington was fully the commander now and it suited him. Out of adversity he seemed to draw greater energy and determination. "His Excellency George Washington," wrote Greene later, "never appeared to so much advantage as in the hour of distress."

His health was excellent. The loyalty of those he counted on was stronger than ever.

On December 24, the day before Christmas, Washington's judge advocate, Colonel William Tudor, who had been with him from the beginning, wrote again, as he often had during the campaign, to tell his fiancée in Boston of his continuing love for her, and to explain why his hopes of returning soon to Boston had vanished. "I cannot desert a man (and it would certainly be desertion in a court of honor) who has deserted everything to defend his country, and whose chief misfortune, among ten thousand others, is that a large part of it wants spirit to defend itself."

Bristol, Pennsylvania, was a small town on the western side of the Delaware, downstream from Trenton, across the river from Burlington, New Jersey. It was from Bristol, where he was helping to organize Pennsylvania militia, that Joseph Reed had written a remarkable letter to Washington dated December 22.

It was time something was done, something aggressive and surprising, Reed wrote. Even failure would be preferable to doing nothing.

> Will it not be possible, my dear General, for our troops or such part of them as can act with advantage to make a diversion or something more at or about Trenton? The greater the alarm, the more likely success will attend the attacks. . . .
>
> I will not disguise my own sentiments that our cause is desperate and hopeless if we do not take the opp[ortunit]y of the collection of troops at present to strike some stroke. Our affairs are hastening fast to ruin if we do not retrieve them by some happy event. Delay with us is now equal to total defeat.

Apparently the letter was unsolicited. What was remarkable was the degree to which it corresponded with Washington's own mind and plans.

In the bleak days after the Battle of Brooklyn, Washington had told Congress, "We should on all occasions avoid a general action or put anything to the risk unless compelled by a necessity." But he had also written of the possibility of some "brilliant stroke" on his part that might save the cause.

On December 14, he had written to Governor Trumbull that a "lucky blow" against the enemy would "most certainly rouse the spirits of the people, which are quite sunk by our misfortunes."

Now, compelled by necessity, his "brilliant stroke" worked out in his mind, he was ready to put almost everything at risk.

With Greene and a few others at the Buckingham headquarters, he had been going over the plan for days, insisting on the strictest secrecy.

But on December 21, Robert Morris had written to say he had heard an attack across the Delaware was being prepared and that he hoped this was true.

Responding now to Reed, Washington confirmed that an attack on Trenton was to begin Christmas night. "For Heaven's sake keep this to yourself, as discovery of it may prove fatal to us . . . but necessity, dire necessity, will, nay must, justify an attempt."

III

On Christmas Eve, Washington called a meeting at Greene's headquarters to go over the final details.

The army was to attack across the Delaware at three places. A force of 1,000 Pennsylvania militia and some 500 veteran Rhode Island troops, led by General John Cadwalader and Joseph Reed, were to cross downriver at Bristol and advance toward Burlington.

A second smaller force of 700 Pennsylvania militia under General James Ewing was to attack directly across the river at Trenton and hold the wooden bridge over Assunpink Creek at the foot of Queen Street, which the enemy might use as an escape route.

The third and much the largest force of 2,400 of the Continental Army led by Washington, Greene, Sullivan, and Stirling would cross the Delaware, nine miles upstream from Trenton, at McKonkey's Ferry.

Once over the river, Washington's army would head south, then halfway to Trenton divide into two columns, one led by Sullivan, taking the River Road, the other, commanded by Greene, taking the Pennington Road farther inland. Four of Knox's cannon were to advance at the head of each column. Washington would ride with Greene.

According to the latest intelligence, the enemy's force at Trenton numbered between 2,000 and 3,000 men.

The first step, the crossing, was set for midnight, December 25, Christmas night. By marching through the night, the two columns were to arrive at Trenton no later than five in the morning. The attack was set for six, an hour before daylight. Officers were to have a piece of white paper in their hats to distinguish them. Absolute secrecy was demanded. A "profound silence" was to be observed, the orders read, "and no man to quit his ranks on pain of death."

Christmas Day the weather turned ominous. A northeast storm was gathering. The river was up, and filled with broken sheets of ice.

In the course of the day, Joseph Reed arrived from Bristol, accompanied by Congressman and physician Benjamin Rush, who, since the adjournment of Congress, had reported to Reed and Cadwalader to volunteer his services. Years later, Rush would recall a private meeting with Washington at Buckingham, during which

Washington seemed "much depressed." In "affecting terms," he described the state of the army. As they talked, Washington kept writing something with his pen on small pieces of paper. When one of them fell to the floor by Rush's foot, he saw what was written: "Victory or Death." It was to be the password for the night.

When Rush, or possibly Reed, warned the general not to expect very much from the militiamen under Cadwalader, Washington scratched out a note that he asked Rush to take to Cadwalader as soon as possible:

> I am determined, as the night is favorable, to cross the river and make an attack on Trenton in the morning. If you can do nothing real, at least create as great a diversion as possible.

The crossing of Washington's force was to be made in big flat-bottomed, high-sided Durham boats, as they were known, normally used to transport pig iron on the Delaware from the Durham Iron Works near Philadelphia. Painted black and pointed at both ends, they were forty to sixty feet long, with a beam of eight feet. The biggest of them could carry as many as forty men standing up, and fully loaded they drew only about two feet, and so could be brought close to shore. The oars — or sweeps — used to propel the boats were eighteen feet long.

Henry Knox was to organize and direct the crossing, and the biggest, most difficult part of the task, as he knew, would be transporting eighteen field cannon and fifty horses or more, including those of the officers. Again, as at Brooklyn, John Glover and his men were in charge of the boats.

Before leaving his headquarters to lead the march, Washington, in what seems to have been a state of perfect calm, wrote to Robert Morris, "I agree with you that it is vain to ruminate upon, or even reflect upon the authors of our present misfortunes. We should rather exert ourselves, and look forward with hopes, that some lucky chance may yet turn up in our favor."

Drums rolled in the camps, and starting about two in the afternoon the army began moving out for the river, each man carrying sixty rounds of ammunition and food enough for three days.

It was nearly dark and raining when the first troops reached McKonkey's Ferry where the boats waited. Henry Knox's unmistakable bass voice could be heard bellowing orders above the rising wind and rain. According to one account, had it not been for the powerful lungs and "extraordinary exertions" of Knox, the crossing that night would have failed.

Knox himself later praised the heroic efforts of Glover and his men, describing how ice in the river made their labor "almost incredible," and the "almost infinite difficulty" they had getting the horses and cannon on board the boats.

The Delaware was not so broad at McKonkey's Ferry as at Trenton or below Trenton, where it became a tidal estuary. Under normal conditions the width of the river at McKonkey's Ferry was about eight hundred feet, but with the water as high as it was that night, the distance was greater by fifty feet or more, and the current strong, the ice formidable, as all accounts attest.

Glover's men used oars and poles to get the big boats across. The troops went standing, packed on board as close as possible.

Washington crossed early and watched the slow process from the New Jersey side. About eleven o'clock, the storm struck, a full-blown northeaster.

Among the most vivid firsthand accounts of the night was that of John Greenwood, the young fifer from Boston, who after the march to New York in April had been sent off to serve in Canada and had only just rejoined Washington's army.

Fifes not being a priority under the circumstances, sixteen-year-old Greenwood carried a musket like every other man and crossed in one of the first boats.

> Over the river we then went in a flat-bottomed scow [he wrote] . . . and we had to wait for the rest and so began to pull down fences and make fires to warm ourselves, for the storm was increasing rapidly. After a while it rained, hailed, snowed, and froze, and at the same time blew a perfect hurricane, so much so that I perfectly recollect, after putting the rails on to burn, the wind and fire would cut them in two in a moment, and when I turned my face to the fire, my back would be freezing. However . . . by turning myself round and round I kept myself from perishing.

As during the escape from Brooklyn, Washington's other daring river-crossing by night, a northeaster was again, decisively, a blessing and a curse — a blessing in that it covered the noise of the crossing, a curse in that, with the ice on the river, it was badly slowing progress when time was of the essence. The plan was to have the whole army over the river no later than midnight, in order to reach Trenton before dawn.

According to Washington, it was three o'clock, three hours behind schedule, before the last of the troops, horses, and cannon were across.

At that point the attack might have been called off, the men sent back over the river, since the entire plan rested on the element of surprise and the chances for surprise now seemed gone. It was a decision that could not be delayed and involved great risk either way.

Washington decided without hesitation. As he would explain succinctly to John Hancock, "I well knew we could not reach it [Trenton] before day was fairly broke, but as I was certain there was no making a retreat without being discovered, and harassed on repassing the river, I determined to push on at all events."

Downstream, as he had no way of knowing, the other part of his plan was failing badly. General Ewing had called off his attack on Trenton because of ice in the river. At Bristol, where ice was piled higher even than at Trenton, Cadwalader and Reed had succeeded in getting some of their troops over to the other side, but then, unable to move their cannon across, they, too, had called off the attack.

"It was as severe a night as I ever saw," wrote an officer with Cadwalader,

and after two battalions were landed, the storm increased so much that it was impossible to get the artillery over, for we had to walk one hundred yards on the ice to get on shore. General Cadwalader, therefore, ordered the whole to retreat again, and we had to stand at least six hours under arms — first to cover the landing, and till all the rest had retreated again — and by this time the storm of wind, rain, hail, and snow with the ice was so bad that some of the infantry could not get back till next day.

Unable to recross the ice with their horses, Reed and another officer chose to stay on the New Jersey side, concealed in the house of a friend.

Thus, of the three planned attacks on

the enemy, only one was moving forward and it perilously behind schedule.

The march south from McKonkey's Ferry was for many the most harrowing part of the night. The storm grew worse, with cold driving rain, sleet, snow, and violent hail. The troops, as Henry Knox wrote, pushed on "with the most profound silence."

For the first half mile or more the dark road from the ferry was a steep uphill climb. After another two miles the road dropped into a ravine and crossed Jacobs Creek.

John Greenwood remembered moving no faster than a child could walk, stopping frequently, and suffering terribly from the cold.

> I recollect very well that at one time, when we halted on the road, I sat down on the stump of a tree and was so benumbed with cold that I wanted to go to sleep. Had I been passed unnoticed, I should have frozen to death without knowing it.

In fact, in the course of the night two of the men did freeze to death.

There was little light to see by. A few

men carried lanterns, and torches were mounted on some of the cannon.

The entire 2,400 on the march kept together for five miles, as far as a little crossroads called Birmingham, where the army divided, Sullivan's column keeping to the right on the River Road, while Washington's and Greene's force veered off to the left on the Pennington Road, both routes slick with ice and snow. The distance to Trenton was the same either way, about four miles. Men and horses kept slipping and skidding in the dark.

A Connecticut lieutenant, Elisha Bostwick, remembered Washington coming along on his horse, telling the men "in a deep and solemn voice" to keep with their officers. "For God's sake keep with your officers."

When his army had marched out of Boston heading for New York and their first field of battle, the commander-in-chief had traveled by coach. Much of the time since, he had conducted the war from established headquarters in elegant houses. And though he had been with the army the night of the escape from Brooklyn and through the retreat across New Jersey, until now he had never been with them as a field commander on the attack.

When handed a message from General Sullivan saying that the men had found their guns too soaked to fire, Washington answered, "Tell the general to use the bayonet."

"None but the first officers knew where we were going, or what we were about," John Greenwood wrote.

This was not unusual, however, as I never heard soldiers say anything, nor ever saw them trouble themselves, as to where they were or where they were led. It was enough for them to know that wherever the officers commanded they must go . . . for it was all the same owing to the impossibility of being in a worse condition than their present one, and therefore the men always liked to be kept moving in expectation of bettering themselves.

The two columns reached their assigned positions outside Trenton at about the same time, a few minutes before eight, an hour after daylight.

Trenton was often referred to as a pretty village, which was an exaggeration. With perhaps a hundred houses, an Episcopal church, a marketplace, and two or three mills and iron furnaces, it was, in peacetime, a busy but plain little place of no particular consequence, except that it was at the head of navigation on the river and a stop on the King's Highway from New York to Philadelphia. There was also a large two-story stone barracks built during the French and Indian War, and the bridge over Assunpink Creek below town.

The principal streets were King Street and Queen Street, which ran parallel toward the river, sloping downhill from the point above town where the Pennington Road and the King's Highway converged. By Washington's plan of attack, this point, the head of King and Queen streets, would decide the day.

But in the early light of December 26, in the white blur of the continuing storm, it was difficult to distinguish much of anything about Trenton.

Most of the townspeople had fled, taking as much as possible of their belongings. In the bare houses and the stone barracks were quartered the 1,500 Hessians who occupied the town. Their commander, Colonel Rall, had established himself in an ample frame house on King Street, the home of an owner of an iron furnace,

Stacy Potts, who was happy to have the colonel as his guest.

Johann Gottlieb Rall was a sturdy, able career soldier, and at age fifty-six a senior among officers. The command at Trenton had been conferred in recognition of his valor at White Plains and Fort Washington. He was a man of limited imagination. He spoke little or no English and had only contempt for the rebel army. His pleasures were a game of cards, a good drink or two, and martial music, which he relished to the point of absurdity, marching himself with his military band at almost any excuse.

Rall would be roundly criticized later by some of his junior officers for being lazy, lax, indifferent to the possibility of surprise attack, and a drunkard. Captain Johann Ewald, as fair-minded as any Hessian officer who served in America, later wrote that many who criticized Rall after his death were not fit to have carried his sword.

Harassed by rebel patrols that kept coming over the Delaware, Rall had established outposts beyond the town and insisted that each night one company sleep with their muskets ready to be called out at a moment's notice, and they were called out, it seemed to some, more often than necessary. If anything, the colonel was thought to be too much on edge. (An officer complained in his diary, "We have not slept one night in peace since we came to this place.")

It was the size of the attack to come, and in such weather, that Rall did not anticipate, and in this he was not alone.

Before departing for New York, General Howe had put James Grant in overall command of the string of outposts in New Jersey. Grant was at Brunswick, twenty-five miles from Trenton. On December 24, he received "certain intelligence" that the rebels were planning an attack on Trenton. While he did not think them "equal to the attempt," he alerted Rall, telling him to be on guard. Rall received the message at five o'clock the afternoon of the 25th.

Not long after, a dozen Hessians on guard on the Pennington Road beyond town were fired on in the dark by an American patrol, which had quickly withdrawn. Rall himself rode out through the storm to look things over and concluded that this was the attack he had been warned about. On such a night, he assumed nothing more would happen.

Later in the evening Rall attended a

small Christmas gathering at the home of a local merchant and was playing cards when, reportedly, a servant interrupted to deliver still another warning message that had been delivered to the door by an unknown Loyalist, and this Rall is said to have thrust into his pocket.

It is not known what time he returned to his quarters or whether, as later said, he had had too much to drink.

The attack began just after eight o'clock. The Americans under Nathanael Greene came out of the woods and across a field through driving snow about half a mile from town. They were moving fast, at what was called a "long trot." The Hessians on guard on the Pennington Road had trouble at first making out who they were and how many there were. "The storm continued with great violence," Henry Knox wrote, "but was in our backs, and consequently in the faces of the enemy."

The Americans opened fire. The Hessians waited for them to get closer, then fired and began quickly, smoothly falling back into town, exactly as they had been trained to do when retreat was the only choice. Washington thought they performed particularly well keeping up a steady retreating fire.

As Greene's and Sullivan's columns converged on the town, Washington moved to high ground nearby on the north where he tried to keep watch on what was happening.

His 2,400 Americans, having been on their feet all night, wet, cold, their weapons soaked, went into the fight as if everything depended on them. Each man "seemed to vie with the other in pressing forward," Washington wrote.

In town the Hessians came rushing out of their houses and barracks into the streets. Drums beat, the band played, officers shouted orders in German, and as fast as the Hessians began forming up, Knox's artillery were in position at the head of King and Queen streets.

The cannon opened fire with deadly effect down hundreds of yards on each street, and in minutes — "in the twinkling of an eye," Knox said — cleared the streets.

When the Hessians retreated into the side streets, they found Sullivan's men coming at them with fixed bayonets. For a brief time, a thousand or more Americans and Hessians were locked in savage house-to-house fighting.

It was all happening extremely fast, in wild confusion and swirling snow made more blinding by clouds of gunpowder smoke. "The storm of nature and the storm of the town," wrote Nathanael Greene, "exhibited a scene that filled the mind during the action with passions easier conceived than described."

When the Hessians rolled out a field gun midway on King Street, a half dozen Virginians led by Captain William Washington (a distant cousin of the commander) and Lieutenant James Monroe rushed forward, seized it, and turned it on them.

Colonel Rall, who had been rousted from his bed and was quickly on horseback and in command in the midst of the fray, ordered a charge. Men were being hit all around him. The line faltered. He ordered a retreat into an orchard at the southeast edge of town. Then Rall, too, was hit and fell from his horse. Mortally wounded, he was picked up and carried to the Potts house.

The Hessians in the orchard, finding themselves surrounded, lay down their arms and surrendered.

It had all happened in forty-five minutes or less. Twenty-one Hessians had been killed, 90 wounded. The prisoners taken numbered approximately 900. Another 500 had managed to escape, most of them by the bridge over Assunpink Creek.

Incredibly, in a battle of such extreme savagery, only four Americans had been wounded, including Captain Washington and Lieutenant Monroe, and not one American had been killed. The only American fatalities were the two soldiers who had frozen to death during the night on the road.

"After having marched off the prisoners and secured the cannon, stores, etc.," wrote Knox, "we returned to the place nine miles distant, where we had embarked." Thus after marching through the night a second time, back to McKonkey's Ferry, the army crossed the Delaware once again back to the Pennsylvania side of the river.

Not since taking command the summer of 1775 had Washington ever addressed the army with such words of praise, affection, and gratitude as he did in his general orders for the following day, December 27. And never had he greater reason. It had been their triumph, he wanted them to know.

"The general, with the utmost sincerity

and affection, thanks the officers and soldiers for their spirited and gallant behavior at Trenton yesterday," he began. "It is with inexpressible pleasure that he can declare that he did not see a single instance of bad behavior in either officers or privates."

In appreciation of such "spirited behavior" he would see that all who had "crossed the river" would receive, in cash, a proportionate part of the total value of the cannon, arms, horses, and "everything else" captured at Trenton.

Allegedly there had been some less-than-stellar behavior, which either Washington did not see or chose to ignore given the spirit of the moment. With the battle over, a number of soldiers reportedly broke into the Hessian rum supply and got roaring drunk.

Far more, however, would be said later and repeated endlessly of Hessians who supposedly, on the morning of the attack, were still reeling drunk or in a stupor from having celebrated Christmas in the Germanic tradition. But there is no evidence that any of them were drunk. John Greenwood, who was in the thick of the fight, later wrote, "I am willing to go upon oath that I did not see even a solitary drunken soldier belonging to the enemy."

Major James Wilkinson, the young officer who had been present at the capture of General Lee and who also fought at Trenton and later wrote an account of the battle, made no mention of anyone being drunk.

What Wilkinson did record, memorably, was riding to Washington with a message just after the Hessians had surrendered. "On my approach," he wrote, "the commander-in-chief took me by the hand and observed, 'Major Wilkinson, this is a glorious day for our country.'"

They all felt something of the kind. They knew they had done something big at last. "The troops behaved like men contending for everything that was dear and valuable," Knox wrote to Lucy. Nathanael Greene told his wife, "This is an important period to America, big with great events."

Writing to Governor Trumbull earlier, Washington had prophesied that some "lucky blow" would "rouse the spirits of the people," but he could hardly have imagined how stunning the effect of the news of Trenton would be on the morale of the country.

In a matter of days, newspapers were filled with accounts of Washington's crossing of the Delaware, the night march and the overwhelming success of the surprise attack, the numbers of prisoners taken, the cannon, arms, swords, horses, even the number of drums and trumpets from Colonel Rall's military band. But fast post riders and word of mouth spread the story more rapidly still.

John Adlum, the seventeen-year-old private from York, Pennsylvania, who had been captured at Fort Washington and was among the fortunate prisoners — mostly officers — confined to houses in New York and allowed some freedom of movement, wrote later of how he heard the news of Trenton. The owner of a grocery store had pulled him into a back room and kept shaking his hand and trembling with such emotion he was unable to speak.

"I looked at him and thought him crazy or mad," Adlum wrote, "but as soon as he could give utterance to his word he says to me, 'General Washington has defeated the Hessians at Trenton this morning and has taken 900 prisoners and six pieces of artillery!'"

I did not wait to hear anything more said, but dropped the basket and ran out into the street and passed two [British] sentinels that I had given the countersign on my way to the store. Though they challenged me, I did not stop, but ran as fast as I could to my quarters. . . . By the time I got home I was quite out of breath and ran into the room where the officers were sitting around the table. Several of them asked what's the matter, and as soon as I could recover breath to speak I spoke with considerable emphasis: "General Washington has defeated the Hessians at Trenton this morning and has taken 900 prisoners and six pieces of artillery."

"Who told you so?"

I could not tell as I did not know the gentleman's name, but I told them it was where I purchased the groceries. . . . At which some of the officers laughed and asked me various questions, while others did not say a word and looked very serious, as if doubting the news, and others thought it too good to be true.

Washington was extolled as he had been at Boston, as a hero and savior. "It appears to us that your attack on Trenton was . . . [a] success beyond expectation," wrote Robert Morris from Philadelphia on behalf of the Executive Committee of Congress, and this was entirely befitting "a character which we admire and which we have long wished to appear in the world with that brilliancy that success always obtains and which members of Congress know you deserve."

From Baltimore, addressing Washington on behalf of the entire Congress, John Hancock said that the victory at Trenton was all the more "extraordinary" given that it had been achieved by men "broken by fatigue and ill-fortune."

But troops properly inspired, and animated by a just confidence in their leader will often exceed expectation, or the limits of probability. As it is entirely to your wisdom and conduct, the United States are indebted for the late success of your arms.

To General James Grant, Howe's commander of the New Jersey outposts, and thus the one who bore the responsibility for what had happened, Trenton was an "unlucky," "cursed" affair, quite beyond comprehension. " 'Tis an infamous business. I can not account for the misbehavior of the Hessians," Grant wrote to General

Harvey. He had been sure, Grant told Harvey, that the Hessians at Trenton were "as safe as you are in London."

How Colonel Rall could have failed to act upon the warning he had been given was more than Grant could understand. But then Rall had died of his wounds and would have no chance to speak in his own defense.

In New York, William Howe responded to the news of Trenton by taking immediate action. Cornwallis, his leave canceled, was ordered to return at once to New Jersey with an army of 8,000.

Washington had been weighing his next move and worrying over how possibly to keep his army together. His decision, given the way events had turned and his own nature, was not surprising. He would go after the enemy once again.

Thinking that Washington was still in New Jersey, General Cadwalader, in a bold move, had crossed the Delaware downstream at Bristol, and General Mifflin was joining him with more recruits.

On December 29, Washington, Greene, Sullivan, Knox, and their troops were on the move, marching through a six-inch snowfall, to cross the Delaware at

McKonkey's Ferry and nearby Yardley's Ferry, an undertaking that was as harrowing as the crossing of Christmas night. At Yardley's Ferry, where Greene's troops crossed, the river was iced over, just thick enough for the men to pick their way warily across, but too thin for horses and cannon. At McKonkey's, it was only with the greatest difficulty that Washington and the rest were able to get over. Amazingly, Knox and Glover succeeded this time in transporting some 40 cannon and their horses, twice what had been managed Christmas night.

At Trenton, Washington drew up his forces on a low ridge along the south side of Assunpink Creek, with the Delaware on their left flank, a patch of woods to the right. It was December 30. The following day, the last day of 1776, he made a dramatic appeal to the veteran troops of the Continental Army to stay with him.

Having no authority whatever to do so, he offered a bounty of ten dollars for all who would stay another six months after their enlistments expired that day — a considerable sum for men whose pay was six dollars a month.

"I feel the inconvenience of this advance," Washington would later tell Congress. "But what was to be done?" To Robert Morris he said more bluntly, "I thought it no time to stand on trifles."

One of the soldiers would remember his regiment being called into formation and His Excellency, astride a big horse, addressing them "in the most affectionate manner." The great majority of the men were New Englanders who had served longer than any and who had no illusions about what was being asked of them. Those willing to stay were asked to step forward. Drums rolled, but no one moved. Minutes passed. Then Washington "wheeled his horse about" and spoke again.

"My brave fellows, you have done all I asked you to do, and more than could be reasonably expected, but your country is at stake, your wives, your houses, and all that you hold dear. You have worn yourselves out with fatigues and hardships, but we know not how to spare you. If you will consent to stay one month longer, you will render that service to the cause of liberty, and to your country, which you can probably never do under any other circumstance."

Again the drums sounded and this time the men began stepping forward. "God Almighty," wrote Nathanael Greene, "inclined their hearts to listen to the proposal and they engaged anew."

In the last hours before New Year's Day, Washington would learn that on December 27, by the vote of Congress, he had been authorized to "use every endeavor," including bounties, "to prevail upon the troops . . . to stay with the army. . . ." Indeed, for a period of six months the Congress at Baltimore had made him a virtual dictator.

"Happy it is for this country," read part of the letter transmitting the resolution, "that the general of their forces can safely be entrusted with the most unlimited power, and neither personal security, liberty, nor property be in the least degree endangered thereby."

In his letter of reply to the members of Congress, Washington wrote:

Instead of thinking myself freed from all civil obligations by this mark of their confidence, I shall constantly bear in mind that as the sword was the last resort for the preservation of our liberties, so it ought to be the first thing laid aside when those liberties are firmly established.

"The year 1776 is over. I am heartily glad of it and I hope you nor America will ever be plagued with such another," Robert Morris wrote to Washington on New Year's Day. But the campaign was not over just yet.

By January 1, 1777, Cornwallis and his army had reached Princeton. On January 2, Cornwallis left part of his force there, and with 5,500 strong, set off down the road to Trenton, ten miles away.

There had been a sudden thaw and the mud of the road slowed the march.

Colonel Edward Hand and the Pennsylvania riflemen sent to check the enemy advance fought with deadly effect but could only fall back against such a force. By dusk the Americans were retreating back through Trenton, down Queen Street toward the bridge over the Assunpink, and it was only Knox's cannon from across the creek that held the British at bay.

"The enemy pushed our small party through the town with vigor . . . [then] advanced within reach of our cannon, who saluted them with great vociferation and some execution," Knox wrote. British artillery answered and Cornwallis ordered three successive attacks on the bridge, only to be driven back each time.

Dr. Benjamin Rush, who had arrived with Cadwalader's brigades to help establish a field hospital, wrote later of this his first direct encounter with war. Indeed, Rush was one of the very few signers of the Declaration of Independence yet to see the reality of the war firsthand.

The American army retired and left the British in possession of Trenton. The scene which accompanied and followed this combat was new to me. The first wounded man that came off the field was a New England soldier. His right hand hung a little above his wrist by nothing but a piece of skin. It had been broken by a cannon ball. I took charge of him and directed him to a house on the river which had been appropriated for a hospital. In the evening all the wounded, about 20 in number, were brought to this hospital and dressed by Dr. [John] Cochran, myself, and several young surgeons who acted under our direction. We all lay down on some straw in the same room with our wounded patients. It was now for the first time war appeared to me in its awful plenitude of horrors. I want words to describe the anguish of my soul, excited by the cries and groans and convulsions of the men who lay by my side.

In the last light of day Cornwallis and his commanders had convened to decide whether to carry the attack across the Assunpink still again, or to wait for daylight. "If Washington is the general I take him to be," one of them, Sir William Erskine, is alleged to have commented, "he will not be found in the morning." Cornwallis is said to have replied that they would "bag him" in the morning.

It was an understandable decision. Night attacks could be extremely costly and there seemed no reason not to wait.

The British engineer Captain Archibald Robertson thought the Americans had positioned themselves extremely well. "We . . . durst not attack them," Robertson recorded in his diary. "They were exactly in the position Rall should have taken when he was attacked, from which he might have retreated towards Borden's Town [downstream on the Delaware] with very little loss."

It had turned cold again. The British troops slept that night on the frozen ground and without campfires in order to keep watch on the rebels and their fires across the creek.

But when morning came, the Americans were gone. Leaving a small force to keep the fires burning and make the appropriate noises of an army settling in for the night, Washington and some 5,500 men, horses, and cannon had stolen away in the dark. But instead of heading south to Bordentown as would be expected, he struck off on a wide, daring sweep on little-known back roads to attack Cornwallis's rear guard at Princeton.

They marched east to Sandtown, then north-northeast to Quaker Bridge by mud roads frozen as hard as rock. Fields along the way were covered with hoarfrost, and with a few dim stars overhead the night was not as dark as it might have been. But for men with scant clothing and broken shoes, or no shoes, it was again an extreme ordeal.

Washington's plan, as at Trenton, was again to divide his force, with Greene's column going off to the left, Sullivan's column to the right.

The battle broke out at sunrise, Friday, January 3, when Greene's vanguard and British forces ran into each other by chance two miles out from Princeton. General Hugh Mercer with several hundred men went off to the left to destroy a bridge on the King's Highway, to stop any enemy retreat from the town in that direction. Mercer and his men arrived just as the British commander at Princeton, Colonel Charles Mawhood, and two regiments were setting off from Princeton to join Cornwallis at Trenton.

For the British the appearance of the Americans at that hour and in such numbers was totally unexpected. "They could not possibly suppose it was our army, for that, they took for granted, was cooped up near Trenton," Knox would write. "I believe they were as much astonished as if an army had dropped perpendicularly upon them. However, they had not much time for consideration."

Both sides opened fire, and in a battle that quickly escalated on the sweeping open fields and orchard of William Clarke's farm, the fighting turned as furious as any of the war, the dead and bleeding strewn everywhere.

Mercer, who had dismounted when his horse was hit in the midst of a British bayonet attack, fought with his sword until he was clubbed to the ground, then bayoneted repeatedly — bayoneted seven times — and left for dead. Colonel John Haslet, who tried to rally the brigade, was killed instantly by a bullet in the head.

More Americans rushed forward, many of them Pennsylvania militia with little or no training, who refused to yield, as Washington, Greene, and Cadwalader rode among them to lead the way. The sight of Washington set an example of courage such as he had never seen, wrote one young officer afterward. "I shall never forget what I felt . . . when I saw him brave all the dangers of the field and his important life hanging as it were by a single hair with a thousand deaths flying around him. Believe me, I thought not of myself."

"Parade with us, my brave fellows," Washington is said to have called out to them. "There is but a handful of the enemy, and we will have them directly!"

More Americans descended on the enemy's flanks and Mawhood and his redcoats were soon in full flight toward Trenton. ("A resolution was taken to retreat," remembered one of Mawhood's junior officers, "i.e., run away as fast as we could.") Washington, unable to resist, spurred his horse and took after them, shouting, "It's a fine fox chase, my boys!"

The ferocious battle on the Clarke farm, the deciding action of the day, had lasted all of fifteen minutes.

By the time Washington had reigned in his horse and called off the pursuit, another part of the army had entered the town, where some 200 of the British garrisoned there had barricaded themselves inside the large stone main building of the college, Nassau Hall. When Captain Alexander Hamilton and his artillerymen fired a few rounds into the building, the redcoats gave up.

The American dead numbered 23, including Colonel Haslet and General Mercer, who suffered nine days before dying of his wounds. Mercer, a doctor and pharmacist in civilian life who came from Fredericksburg, Virginia, not far from Mount Vernon, had been a favorite of Washington's.

But losses were greater in British dead and wounded, and the Americans had taken three hundred prisoners. The British, though greatly outnumbered, had put up a fierce fight. But for Washington and the army it was another stunning, unexpected victory.

Washington's impulse was to push on to Brunswick, to destroy enemy supplies there and capture a British pay chest of 70,000 pounds, and thereby, he speculated, end the war. But his exhausted army was in no shape for another forced march of nineteen miles or another battle, and Greene, Knox, and others talked him out of it, warning of the danger of losing all they had gained "by aiming at too much."

Thus, the army marched north to Somerset Courthouse and, in the days that followed, on to the comparative security of the hilly, wooded country near the village of Morristown for the duration of the winter.

The campaign of 1776 had ended with a second astonishing victory. Had Washington been born in the days of idolatry, declared the *Pennsylvania Journal*, he would be worshiped as a god. "If there are spots on his character, they are like the spots on the sun, only discernible by the magnifying powers of a telescope."

As Nathanael Greene wrote to Thomas Paine, "The two late actions at Trenton and Princeton have put a very different face upon affairs."

But as thrilling as the news of Princeton was for the country, coming so quickly after the triumph at Trenton, it was

Trenton that meant the most, Trenton and the night crossing of the Delaware that were rightly seen as a great turning point. With the victory at Trenton came the realization that Americans had bested the enemy, bested the fearsome Hessians, the King's detested hirelings, outsmarted them and outfought them, and so might well again.

Among some of the British command, and some skeptical Americans, what happened at Trenton was seen as only a minor defeat, an aggravating affair, but of no great consequence when compared to such large-scale British victories of 1776 as the Battle of Brooklyn or the taking of Fort Washington. Trenton was a "skirmish," an "engagement," not a battle.

But some on the British side grudgingly conceded that the "rabble" must henceforth be regarded with new respect. Colonel William Harcourt, the cavalry officer who had led the capture of Charles Lee, wrote in a letter to his father that though the Americans remained ignorant of military order and large-scale maneuver, they had shown themselves capable of great cunning, great industry, and spirit of enterprise. And while it had been "the fashion in this army to treat them in the most contemptible light, they are now become a formidable enemy."

Measured by the size of its importance to those fighting for the Cause of America, those everywhere in the country who saw Washington and his army as the one means of deliverance of American independence and all that was promised by the Declaration of Independence, Trenton was the first great cause for hope, a brave and truly "brilliant" stroke.

From the last week of August to the last week of December, the year 1776 had been as dark a time as those devoted to the American cause had ever known — indeed, as dark a time as any in the history of the country. And suddenly, miraculously it seemed, that had changed because of a small band of determined men and their leader.

A century later, Sir George Otto Trevelyan would write in a classic study of the American Revolution, "It may be doubted whether so small a number of men ever employed so short a space of time with greater and more lasting effects upon the history of the world."

Closer to the moment, Abigail Adams wrote to her friend Mercy Otis Warren, "I am apt to think that our later misfortunes have called out the hidden excellencies of our commander-in-chief." " 'Affliction is the good man's shining time,' " she wrote, quoting a favorite line from the English poet Edward Young.

Mercy Warren, the wife of James Warren and an author, would write in her own history of the American Revolution that there were perhaps "no people on earth in whom a spirit of enthusiastic zeal is so readily kindled, and burns so remarkably, as among Americans."

The energetic operation of this sanguine temper was never more remarkably exhibited than in the change instantaneously wrought in the minds of men, by the capture of Trenton at so unexpected a moment. From the state of mind bordering on despair, courage was invigorated, every countenance brightened.

With the new year, news arrived from England that on October 31 in London, His Majesty King George III had once again ridden in splendor from St. James's Palace to Westminster to address the opening of Parliament on the still-distressing war in America.

Nothing could have afforded me so much satisfaction [said the King] as to have been able to inform you . . . that my unhappy people [in America], recovered from their delusion, had delivered themselves from the oppression of their leaders and returned to their duty. But so daring and desperate is the spirit of those leaders, whose object has always been dominion and power, that they have now openly renounced all allegiance to the Crown, and all political connection with this country . . . and have presumed to set up their rebellious confederacies for independent states. If their treason be suffered to take root, much mischief must grow from it.

Another military campaign would be undertaken in America.

The same Whig leaders in Parliament spoke out as they had before, ardently denouncing the "wicked war." Lord Germain, in response, said the army in America would be reinforced. And as it had before, in what seemed the long-ago October of 1775, the Parliament approved the King's policy by an overwhelming margin.

When, in March 1777, the news of

Trenton reached England, it was said (in the *London General Evening Post* and elsewhere) that the defeat of the Hessians, while "disagreeable," was "more than counter-balanced" by the capture of General Lee. Lord Germain saw at once that the importance of the news was the effect it would have on American opinion. Still, he had no doubt that the rebel army was all but finished.

In New Jersey the fighting would continue sporadically as winter wore on. The war itself would continue, endlessly it seemed to many. In all, it would be another six and a half years before the Treaty of Paris ending the war was signed in 1783.

Some who had been with the army and Washington at the beginning, like Joseph Hodgkins, would serve several more years before deciding they had done their duty. Some, like Private Joseph Martin, would serve to the end.

In the campaign in the South that set the stage for the last major battle, at Yorktown, Virginia, Nathanael Greene would prove the most brilliant American field commander of the war. Washington felt that if anything were to happen to him — were Washington to be captured or killed —

Greene should become the commander-in-chief.

Of all the general officers who had taken part in the Siege of Boston, only two were still serving at the time of the British surrender at Yorktown, Washington and Greene. Henry Knox, who had become a brigadier general after the Battle of Trenton, and who fought in every battle in which Washington took part, was also present at Yorktown. Greene and Knox, the two young untried New Englanders Washington had singled out at the beginning as the best of the "raw material" he had to work with, had both shown true greatness and stayed in the fight to the finish.

Financial support from France and the Netherlands, and military support from the French army and navy, would play a large part in the outcome. But in the last analysis it was Washington and the army that won the war for American independence. The fate of the war and the revolution rested on the army. The Continental Army — not the Hudson River or the possession of New York or Philadelphia — was the key to victory. And it was Washington who held the army together and gave it "spirit" through the most desperate of times.

He was not a brilliant strategist or tactician, not a gifted orator, not an intellectual. At several crucial moments he had shown marked indecisiveness. He had made serious mistakes in judgment. But experience had been his great teacher from boyhood, and in this his greatest test, he learned steadily from experience. Above all, Washington never forgot what was at stake and he never gave up.

Again and again, in letters to Congress and to his officers, and in his general orders, he had called for perseverance — for "perseverance and spirit," for "patience and perseverance," for "unremitting courage and perseverance." Soon after the victories of Trenton and Princeton, he had written: "A people unused to restraint must be led, they will not be drove." Without Washington's leadership and unrelenting perseverance, the revolution almost certainly would have failed. As Nathanael Greene foresaw as the war went on, "He will be the deliverer of his own country."

The war was a longer, far more arduous, and more painful struggle than later generations would understand or sufficiently appreciate. By the time it ended, it had taken the lives of an estimated 25,000 Americans, or roughly 1 percent of the population. In percentage of lives lost, it was the most costly war in American history, except for the Civil War.

The year 1776, celebrated as the birth year of the nation and for the signing of the Declaration of Independence, was for those who carried the fight for independence forward a year of all-too-few victories, of sustained suffering, disease, hunger, desertion, cowardice, disillusionment, defeat, terrible discouragement, and fear, as they would never forget, but also of phenomenal courage and bedrock devotion to country, and that, too, they would never forget.

Especially for those who had been with Washington and who knew what a close call it was at the beginning — how often circumstance, storms, contrary winds, the oddities or strengths of individual character had made the difference — the outcome seemed little short of a miracle.

Acknowledgments

Material for this book has been gathered at more than twenty-five libraries, archives, special collections, and historic sites here in the United States, and in the United Kingdom, at the British Library and the National Archives. I am greatly indebted to the staffs of all of them and wish to thank the following in particular for their many courtesies and help:

William Fowler, Peter Drummey, Brenda Lawson, and Anne Bentley of the Massachusetts Historical Society; Philander Chase, Frank Grizzard, Jr., and Edward Lengel, editors of *The Papers of George Washington* at the University of Virginia; James C. Rees, Carol Borchert Cadou, Linda Ayres, and Barbara McMillan of Mount Vernon; Gerard Gawalt, Jeffrey Flannery, James Hutson, Edward Redmond, and Michael Klein of the Library of Congress; Richard Peuser of the National Archives; John C. Dann, Brian

Leigh Dunnigan, Barbara DeWolfe, and Clayton Lewis of the William L. Clements Library, Ann Arbor, Michigan; Jack Bales, Roy Strohl, and Tim Newman of the Simpson Library, University of Mary Washington; Ellen McCallister Clark, Jack D. Warren, Sandra L. Powers, Lauren Gish, and Emily Schulz of the Society of the Cincinnati, Washington, D.C.; Andrea Ashby-Leraris of Independence National Historic Park, Philadelphia; Roy Goodman and Robert Cox of the American Philosophical Society, Philadelphia; David Fowler, Greg Johnson, and Kathy Ludwig of the David Library of the American Revolution, Washington Crossing, Pennsylvania; Michael Bertheaud of the Washington Crossing Historic Park; Cathy Hellier and John Hill of Colonial Williamsburg; James Shea and Anita Israel of the Henry Wadsworth Longfellow House, Cambridge, Massachusetts; Vincent Golden of the American Antiquarian Society, Worcester, Massachusetts; Jan Hilley and Ted O'Reilly of the New-York Historical Society; Leslie Fields of the Pierpont Morgan Library, New York; Rick Statler of the Rhode Island Historical Society; Greg and Mary Mierka of the Nathanael Greene Homestead, Coventry, Rhode Island;

Martin Clayton, the King's Map Collection, Windsor Castle; Mr. and Mrs. Oliver Russell, Ballindalloch Castle, Banffshire, Scotland; Bryson Clevenger, Jr., of the Alderman Library, University of Virginia; Helen Cooper of the Yale University Art Gallery; and Eric P. Frazier of the Boston Public Library.

Peter Drummey, the incomparably knowledgeable Librarian of the Massachusetts Historical Society, and Major General Josiah Bunting III, soldier, scholar, author, and generous friend, were good enough to read the manuscript and offer valuable suggestions. And so, too, was Philander Chase, senior editor of *The Papers of George Washington*, whose insights into the life and character of Washington and close reading of and comments on the manuscript helped immeasurably.

Sean P. Hennessey and his associates at the National Park Service in Charlestown, Massachusetts, gave me a superb tour of Bunker Hill and Dorchester Heights; Martin Maher of the New York City Parks Department took me the length and breadth of Brooklyn on a memorable all-day survey of the events that took place there August 27, 1776; and on another expedition, John Mills, superintendent of the

Princeton Battlefield State Park, guided me along the route of the famous night march to Trenton, beginning at the point where Washington and the army crossed the Delaware, then through the battles of both Trenton and Princeton. For their time, their illuminating commentary and infectious enthusiasm for their subjects, I thank them all.

For the privilege of visiting the birthplace of Nathanael Greene at East Greenwich, Rhode Island, I am ever grateful to its present owner, Thomas Casey Greene, who, as a direct descendant, knows much about the general not to be found in the usual texts.

Over the years I have benefited repeatedly from the friendship and the insights of historians Richard Ketchum, Thomas Fleming, Don Higginbotham, and David Hackett Fischer, each the author of landmark works on the Revolutionary War.

For their interest and a great variety of thoughtful suggestions and favors, I thank William Paul Deary, Philip A. Forbes, Wendell Garrett, Richard Gilder, J. Craig Huff, Jr., Father Michael Greene, Tim Greene, Daniel P. Jordan, Michael Kammen, Ravi Khanna, William Martin, Sally O'Brien, Doug Smith, Matthew Stackpole,

Renny A. Stackpole, Clarence Wolf, and John Zentay.

Thomas J. McGuire has read so much about the realities of soldiering in the Revolution that it is almost as though he fought in it himself. He was a great help from the start of my efforts, supplying a wealth of material from his own wide-ranging research and abundant knowledge.

Gayle Mone helped with correspondence, typed the manuscript, and assisted superbly and tirelessly in the work of the Bibliography and Source Notes.

Mike Hill, my research assistant on this and previous books, has been a mainstay. His expertise and enterprise, his amazing stamina and unfailing good cheer, are beyond compare.

Again, I proudly acknowledge the parts played by my editor Michael Korda and my literary agent, Morton L. Janklow. I am ever grateful for their support and counsel, not to say the pleasure of their company. And again I thank my lucky stars for copy editors Gypsy da Silva and Fred Wiemer, for Amy Hill, who designed the book, and Wendell Minor, who designed the jacket. I think it is no exaggeration to say they are the best in the business.

As always, I thank my family, who know

how much help and support they have given me and how much I appreciate all they have done.

To my wife Rosalee, to whom the book is dedicated, I owe the most by far. She is editor-in-chief. Her spirit never flags. She holds a steady course in all seasons.

David McCullough
West Tisbury, Massachusetts
November 29, 2004

Source Notes

ABBREVIATIONS USED

LOC Library of Congress
MHS Massachusetts Historical Society,
     Boston, Mass.
NYHS New-York Historical Society,
     New York, N.Y.
PGW *The Papers of George Washington,*
     Revolutionary War Series, Vols.
     I–VIII, W. W. Abbott, Philander D.
     Chase, and Dorothy Twohig, eds.
     (Charlottesville: University Press of
     Virginia, 1985–1998).
PNG *The Papers of General Nathanael*
     Greene, Vols. I, II, X, Richard K.
     Showman and Dennis Conrad, eds.
     (Chapel Hill: University of North
     Carolina Press, 1976, 1980, 1998).

1. SOVEREIGN DUTY

60,000 people: London Public Advertiser, October 27, 1775.

"mob": Oliver Andrew, ed., *The Journal of Samuel Curwen, Loyalist*, I (Cambridge, Mass.: Harvard University Press, 1972), 82.

"the whitest hand": Ibid., 42.

King's procession: London Public Advertiser, October 27, 1775.

royal coach: Royal Mews in London, England, where actual coach is still housed.

"superb": Fact Sheet, "Gold State Coach," Golden Jubilee Media Centre, London, Eng.

nearly a million souls: Kirstin Olsen, *Daily Life in 18th-Century England* (Westport, Conn.: Greenwood Press, 1999), 57.

plain food: Christopher Hibbert, *George III: A Personal History* (New York: Basic Books, 1998), 53.

Socially awkward: Ibid., 18–19, 80.

farms: Ibid., 197.

Handel: Ibid., 75.

loved architecture: Ibid., 178.

"unaffected good nature": Ibid., 79.

"Sir, they may talk": Ibid., 61.

appears to have been porphyria: Ibid., 267.

"George, be a King": Barbara W. Tuchman, *March of Folly: From Troy to Vietnam* (New York: Ballantine Books, 1984), 138.

"I have no doubt": George III to Lord North, July 5, 1775, in John Fortescue, ed., *Correspondence of King George the Third,* III (London: Macmillan, 1927–1928), 233.

"Suppose the colonies": Peter Force, *American Archives,* 4th series, Vol. I (Washington, D.C., 1846), 1682–1683.

conciliation with America: Paul Langford, ed. *Writings and Speeches of Edmund Burke,* III (Oxford, Eng.: Clarendon Press, 1996), 102–169.

"I was ordered": Bellamy Partridge, *Sir Billy Howe* (London: Longmans, Green & Co., 1932), 7.

had taken command: Mark M. Boatner, III, ed., *Encyclopedia of the American Revolution* (New York: David McKay, 1966), 1167.

"rabble": John Rhodehamel, ed. *The American Revolution: Writings from the War of Independence* (New York: Library of America, 2001), 123.

"We must persist": George III to Lord North, July 26, 1775, in John Fortescue, ed., *Correspondence of King George the Third,* III (London: Macmillan, 1927–1928), 235.

"foreign war": Lord North to George III, July 26, 1775, in John Fortescue, ed.,

Correspondence of King George the Third,
III (London: Macmillan, 1927–1928),
234.

1,000 casualties: Howard H. Peckham, ed.
Toll of Independence (Chicago: University of Chicago Press, 1994), 4.

"A few of the men": New England Essex and
Gazette, December 14, 1775.

"melancholy, disease, and death": Margaret
Wheeler Willard, ed., *Letters on the
American Revolution: 1774–1776*
(Boston: Houghton Mifflin, 1925),
190.

"almost lost for want of fresh provisions":
Ibid., 200.

"It is inconceivable": Henry Pelham to John
Singleton Copley, May 15, 1775, *Letters and Papers of John Singleton Copley
and Henry Pelham, 1739–1776* (Boston:
Massachusetts Historical Society,
1914), 324.

"the devil's drawing-room": Tobias Smollett,
Adventures of Roderick Random
(London: Hutchinson & Company,
1904), 119.

"vicious indulgence": Sir George Otto
Trevelyan, *The American Revolution,* I
(New York: Longmans, Green & Co.,
1926), 21, n. 1.

"unnatural, unconstitutional": Solomon

Lutnick, *The American Revolution and the British Press, 1775–1783* (Columbia: University of Missouri Press, 1967), 59.

"all the gaudy trappings": *The Crisis*, 1775, Nos. 4, 6.

"What, in God's name": Margaret Wheeler Willard, ed., *Letters on the American Revolution: 1774–1776* (Boston: Houghton Mifflin, 1925), 205.

recalled General Thomas Gage: Allen French, *The First Year of the American Revolution* (Boston: Houghton Mifflin, 1934), 319–320.

"distressing America": George III to Lord North, October 15, 1775, in John Fortescue, ed., *Correspondence of King George the Third*, III (London: Macmillan, 1928), 269.

crowds greater: London Gazetteer and News Daily Advertiser, October 27, 1775.

"looks spoke peace": *London Public Advertiser*, October 27, 1775.

"The present situation of America": William Cobbett, *The Parliamentary History of England from the Earliest Period to the Year 1803*, XVIII (London: T. C. Hansard, 1813), 695.

"anxious to prevent": Ibid., 696.

"When the unhappy and deluded multitude":

Ibid., 696–697.

"as peaceably as he went": London Public Advertiser, October 27, 1775.

"We will support": William Cobbett, *The Parliamentary History of England from the Earliest Period to the Year 1803,* XVIII (London: T. C. Hansard, 1813), 706.

"big with the most portentous": Ibid., 708–709.

"wild and extravagant": Ibid., 709.

"no longer be trusted": Ibid., 714.

"How comes it that the colonies": Peter Force, *American Archives,* 4th series (Washington, D.C.: M. St. Clair and Peter Force, 1837–1846), 12.

"amicably adjusted": William Cobbett, *The Parliamentary History of England from the Earliest Period to the Year 1803,* XVIII (London: T. C. Hansard, 1813), 710.

"reducing America to a just obedience": Ibid., 730.

"Let me remind you": Ibid., 730–731.

"We are fighting": Ibid., 735.

"reduce": Ibid., 739.

"Men are to be brought": Ibid., 734–750.

"the glorious spirit of freedom": Ibid., 752.

"Because an inconsiderable party": October 26, 1775, Peter Force, *American Ar-*

chives, 4th series (Washington, D.C.: M. St. Clair and Peter Force, 1837–1846), 41.

blind trumpeter: Peter D. G. Thomas, *Lord North* (New York: St. Martin's Press, 1976), 1.

napping a bit: Peter Force, *American Archives*, 4th series (Washington, D.C.: M. St. Clair and Peter Force, 1837–1846), 41.

"Sons of Liberty": Mark M. Boatner, III, ed., *Encyclopedia of the American Revolution* (New York: David McKay, 1966), 1017.

"military eye": William Cobbett, *The Parliamentary History of England from the Earliest Period to the Year 1803,* XVIII (London: T. C. Hansard, 1813), 767.

held the floor for nearly two hours: London Gazetteer and News Daily Advertiser, October 28, 1775; *London Chronicle,* October 26–28, 1775.

"macaroni": L. G. Mitchell, *Charles J. Fox* (Oxford, Eng.: Oxford University Press, 1992), 13.

"blundering pilot": William Cobbett, *The Parliamentary History of England from the Earliest Period to the Year 1803,* XVIII (London: T. C. Hansard, 1813), 769.

"I cannot consent": John Drinkwater, *Charles James Fox* (New York: Cosmopolitan Book Corp., 1928), 130.

no wish to remain: William Cobbett, *The Parliamentary History of England from the Earliest Period to the Year 1803,* XVIII (London: T. C. Hansard, 1813), 770.

"I would abandon the contest": F. J. Huddleston, *Gentleman Johnny Burgoyne* (Garden City, N.Y.: Garden City Publishing, 1927), 71.

"my sheet anchor": Peter D. G. Thomas, *Lord North* (New York: St. Martin's Press, 1976), 89.

"offers of mercy": William Cobbett, *The Parliamentary History of England from the Earliest Period to the Year 1803,* XVIII (London: T. C. Hansard, 1813), 771.

House of Lords: Ibid., 726.

House of Commons: Ibid., 772.

"some[thing] will be done": Edward Gibbon to J. B. Holroyd, August 1, 1775, in *The Letters of Edward Gibbon,* II, J. E. Norton, ed. (New York: Macmillan, 1956), 82.

"The conquest of America": Ibid., 91.

"decisive blow": Piers Mackesy, *The War for America: 1775–1783* (London: Longmans, Green & Co., 1964), 46.

2. RABBLE IN ARMS

"Here we are at loggerheads": Nathanael Greene to Samuel Ward, October 23, 1775, in *PNG,* I, 139–140.

asthma: Theodore Thayer, *Nathanael Greene: Strategist of the American Revolution* (New York: Twayne Publishers, 1960), 26.

on a farm: Author's visit to Nathanael Greene homestead.

"constant and profitable operation": George Washington Greene, *Life of Nathanael Greene,* I (Freeport, N.Y.: Books for Libraries Press, 1962), 5.

"My father was a man": Nathanael Greene to Samuel Ward, October 9, 1772, in *PNG,* I, 49.

Locke's Essay: Theodore Thayer, *Nathanael Greene* (New York: Twayne Publishers, 1960), 21.

Euclid: Ibid., 24.

"I lament the want": George Washington Greene, *The Life of Nathanael Greene,* I (Freeport, N.Y.: Books for Libraries Press, 1962), 47.

"cheerful, vigorous, thoughtful": Ibid., 25.

imitations of characters: Theodore Thayer, *Nathanael Greene* (New York: Twayne Publishers, 1960), 24.

"Very true, but you see": George Washington Greene, *The Life of Nathanael Greene,* I (Freeport, N.Y.: Books for Libraries Press, 1962), 27.

cloudy spot in his right eye: Theodore Thayer, *Nathanael Greene* (New York: Twayne Publishers, 1960), 26.

"The first of all qualities": Marshal Maurice de Saxe, *Reveries on the Art of War,* Brig. Gen. Thomas R. Phillips, ed. (Harrisburg, Pa.: The Military Service Publishing Co., 1944), 117.

"halting": Nathanael Greene to James Varnum, October 31, 1774, in *PNG,* I, 75–76.

"watchfulness and industry": Nathanael Greene to John Adams, July 14, 1776, in *PNG,* I, 254.

"Army of Observation": George Washington Greene, *Life of Nathanael Greene,* I (Freeport, N.Y.: Books for Libraries Press, 1952), 79.

"when you consider how raw": Nathanael Greene to Samuel Ward, October 23, 1775, in *PNG,* I, 140.

"the army of the United Colonies": Congress to George Washington, June 19, 1775, in *PGW,* I, 7.

"the troops under your command": John Hancock to George Washington, July 5,

1775, in *PGW,* I, 64.

"*raw materials*": George Washington to Philip Schuyler, July 28, 1775, in *PGW,* I, 189.

"*rabble in arms*": Sir George Otto Trevelyan, *The American Revolution,* I (New York: Longmans, Green & Co., 1926), 298.

1,500 Rhode Islanders: Allen French, *The First Year of the American Revolution* (Boston: Houghton Mifflin, 1934), 77.

"*wet and sloppy*": Journal of Simeon Lyman, *Collections of the Connecticut Historical Society,* VIII, 131.

"*through mud and mire*": Lois K. Stabler, ed., *Very Poor and of a Lo Make: The Journal of Abner Sanger* (Portsmouth, N.H.: Historical Society of Cheshire County, 1986), 37.

"*regularity and discipline*": Massachusetts Provincial Congress to George Washington, July 3, 1775, in *PGW,* I, 52–53.

"*possessed of the absolute necessity*": Ibid., 53.

own rough map: Washington's map of the Boston area, in *PGW,* I, 186–187.

"*very delightful country*": George Washington to Samuel Washington, July 20, 1775, in *PGW,* I, 135.

"*country of the most charming green*": Allen

French, *The First Year of the American Revolution* (Boston: Houghton Mifflin, 1934), 164.

John Trumbull: Theodore Sizer, ed., *The Autobiography of Colonel John Trumbull* (New Haven, Conn.: Yale University Press, 1953), 21–22.

"the True Situation": Map drawn by Lieutenant Richard Williams, Boston, October 1775, MHS.

"Mount Whoredom": Walter Muir Whitehill, *Boston: A Topographical History* (Cambridge, Mass.: Belknap Press, 1968), 7–8.

"There's perhaps no town": Journal of Lieutenant Richard Williams, MHS.

"Thousands are at work": Amelia Forbes Emerson, ed., *Diaries and Letters of William Emerson, 1743–1776* (Boston: Thomas Todd, 1972), 79.

" *'Tis surprising the work":* Ibid.

"Let us stand our ground": David Hackett Fischer, *Paul Revere's Ride* (New York: Oxford University Press, 1994), 204.

"It seemed to be the principle": John Rhodehamel, ed., *The American Revolution: Writings from the War of Independence* (New York: Library of America, 2001), 51.

account book was for $333.33: John C.

Fitzpatrick, ed., *George Washington Accounts of Expenses* (Boston: Houghton Mifflin, 1917), 6.

"We scarcely lie down": Thomas G. Frothingham, *History of the Siege of Boston, and of the Battles of Lexington, Concord, and Bunker Hill* (New York: Da Capo Press, 1970), 23.

"Some are made of boards": Amelia Forbes Emerson, ed., *Diaries and Letters of William Emerson, 1743–1776* (Boston: Thomas Todd, 1972), 80.

"the regular camp of the enemy": Ibid.

"Wickedness prevails very much": Joseph Hodgkins to Sarah Hodgkins, September 20, 1775, in Herbert T. Wade and Robert A. Lively, eds., *This Glorious Cause: The Adventures of Two Company Officers in Washington's Army* (Princeton, N.J.: Princeton University Press, 1958), 174.

cobbler by trade: Ibid., 8.

"pertickler": Ibid., 174.

"for without New England rum": Henry Steele Commager and Richard B. Morris, eds., *The Spirit of 'Seventy-Six: The Story of the American Revolution as Told by Participants,* I (Indianapolis: Bobbs-Merrill, 1958), 152.

"Drank some grog": "Diary of Jabez Fitch,

Jr.," *Proceedings of the MHS,* 2nd series, IX (1894–1895), 47.

"the gin sling": Ibid., 55.

"In the morning I attended": Ibid., 62.

"up into Cambridge town": Ibid., 76.

"dirty as hogs": Ibid., 52.

"has done more to exhilarate": Ibid., 45.

"very good": Ibid., 57.

"a hearty dinner": Ibid., 59.

"Your brother Elihu": Abigail Adams to John Adams, August 10, 1775, in *Adams Family Correspondence,* I (Cambridge, Mass.: Belknap Press, 1963), 272.

"Camp fever": Kenneth F. Kiple, ed., *Cambridge World History of Human Disease* (Cambridge, Eng.: Cambridge University Press, 1992), 1071–1076; Anton Sebastian, *Dictionary of the History of Medicine* (New York: Parthenon Publishers, 1999), 268.

dead body so covered with lice: Journal of Simeon Lyman, *Collections of the Connecticut Historical Society,* VIII, 123.

Danbury, Connecticut: Charles Royster, *A Revolutionary People at War: The Continental Army and American Character, 1775–1783* (Chapel Hill: University of North Carolina Press, 1979), 132.

"Infectious filth": George H. Guttridge, ed.,

The Correspondence of Edmund Burke, III (Cambridge, Eng.: Cambridge University Press, 1961), 293.

"great neglect": Herbert T. Wade and Robert A. Lively, eds., *This Glorious Cause* (Princeton, N.J.: Princeton University Press, 1958), 33.

"The officers in general": Theodore Sizer, ed., *The Autobiography of Colonel John Trumbull* (New Haven, Conn.: Yale University Press, 1953), 18.

"New lords, new laws": William Emerson to his wife, July 17, 1775, in George F. Scheer and Hugh F. Rankin, eds., *Rebels and Redcoats* (New York: Da Capo Press, 1957), 83.

"wooden horse": North Callahan, *Henry Knox: George Washington's General* (South Brunswick, Maine: A. S. Barnes, 1958), 37.

"the most wretchedly clothed": Henry Steele Commager and Richard B. Morris, eds., *The Spirit of 'Seventy-Six,* I (Indianapolis: Bobbs-Merrill, 1958), 153–154.

"fitted out": New England Chronicle and Essex Gazette, September 14, 1775.

Washington himself chose to wear: "Uniforms of the Revolutionary Army," *Proceedings of the MHS,* IV (1858–1860), 152–163.

"a great deal of grandeur": Joseph Hodgkins to Sarah Hodgkins, September 3, 1775, in Herbert T. Wade and Robert A. Lively, eds., *This Glorious Cause* (Princeton, N.J.: Princeton University Press, 1958), 171.

"His Excellency was on horseback": James Thacher, M.D., *Military Journal During the American Revolutionary War, July 1775 to February 17, 1777* (Boston: Richardson & Lord, 1823), 37.

"worthy people": Sir George Otto Trevelyan, *The American Revolution*, II (New York: Longmans, Green & Co., 1899), 187.

Old Put: Allen French, *The First Year of the American Revolution* (Boston: Houghton Mifflin, 1934), 83.

"the troubles": Isaac J. Greenwood, ed., *Revolutionary Services of John Greenwood of Boston and New York, 1775–1783* (New York: De Vinne Press, 1922), 3.

"an old split fife": Ibid., 4.

"They used to ask": Ibid., 6.

"Everywhere the greatest": Ibid., 12.

"a Negro man": Ibid., 12–13.

"There are in the Massachusetts regiments": William Heath to John Adams, October 23, 1775, in *Papers of John*

Adams, III, Robert J. Taylor, ed. (Cambridge, Mass: Belknap Press, 1979), 230.

"The regiments at Roxbury": John Thomas to John Adams, October 24, 1775, in *Papers of John Adams,* III, Robert J. Taylor, ed. (Cambridge, Mass.: Belknap Press, 1979), 329.

"Negroes, boys unable to bear arms": George Washington, General Orders, November 12, 1775, in *PGW,* II, 354.

notices posted of deserters: New England Chronicle and Essex Gazette, July–September 1775.

"Deserted from Col. Brewer's regiment": Ibid., November 2, 1775.

"hardy men": James Thacher, M.D., *Military Journal During the American Revolutionary War, July 1775 to February 17, 1777* (Boston: Richardson & Lord, 1823), 37–38.

"bee-line": Joseph Whitehorne, "Shepardstown and the Morgan-Stevenson Companies," *Magazine of the Jefferson County Historical Society,* LVIII (December 1992), 16–19.

Washington began to wish: George F. Scheer and Hugh F. Rankin, *Rebels and Redcoats* (New York: Da Capo Press, 1957), 86.

"in many places": Thomas G. Frothingham, *History of the Siege of Boston, and of the Battles of Lexington, Concord, and Bunker Hill* (New York: Da Capo Press, 1970), 274.

"His comrades": "Diary of Samuel Bixby," August 2, 1775, *Proceedings of the MHS*, Vol. XIV (1875–1876), 291.

"frolicking": John Greenwood, *The Revolutionary Services of John Greenwood of Boston*, Isaac J. Greenwood, ed. (New York: De Vinne Press, 1922), 21.

"Nothing of note": "Diary of Samuel Bixby," August 3–12, 1775, *Proceedings of the MHS*, Vol. XIV (1875–1876), 293.

"Nothing extraordinary": Stephen Kemble, *Journals of Lieutenant-Colonel Stephen Kemble, 1773–1789, and British Army Orders: General Sir William Howe, 1775–1778; General Sir Henry Clinton, 1778; and General Daniel Jones, 1778* (Boston: Gregg Press, 1972), 55–60.

"exceeding dirty and nasty": Lund Washington to George Washington, August 20, 1775, in *PGW*, I, 336.

"these people": George Washington to Richard H. Lee, August 29, 1775, in *PGW*, I, 372.

"the goodness of our cause": George Wash-

ington to Philip Schuyler, August 20, 1775, in *PGW,* I, 331.

Georgian mansion: Research and discussions with curators and Park Service staff at Longfellow House National Historic Site, Cambridge, Mass.

household accounts: See "George Washington's Revolutionary War Expenses and Accounts, 1775–1776, kept by Ebenezer Austin," LOC.

William (Billy) Lee: James Thomas Flexner, *George Washington in the American Revolution, 1775–1783,* II (Boston: Little Brown, 1967), 60.

"Be easy": George Washington to William Woodford, November 10, 1775, in *PGW,* II, 347.

"Sir, I am a corporal": John C. Dann, ed., *The Revolution Remembered* (Chicago: University of Chicago Press, 1980), 392.

"has so much martial": Benjamin Rush to Thomas Rushton, October 29, 1777, in L. H. Butterfield, ed., *Letters of Benjamin Rush,* I (Princeton N.J.: American Philosophical Society, 1951), 92.

"harum scarum": Paul H. Smith, ed., *Letters of Delegates to Congress, 1774–1789,* I (Washington D.C.: Library of Con-

gress, 1976), 499–500.

"This appointment": John Adams to Abigail Adams, June 11, 1775, in *Adams Family Correspondence,* I (Cambridge, Mass.: Belknap Press, 1963), 215.

"one of the most important": Ibid., June 17, 1775, 216.

hardly said enough: Abigail Adams to John Adams, July 16, 1775, in *Adams Family Correspondence,* I (Cambridge, Mass.: Belknap Press, 1963), 246.

"Joy was visible": Nathanael Greene to Samuel Ward, July 14, 1775, in *PNG,* I, 99.

"expressed himself to me": John F. Roche, *Joseph Reed: A Moderate in the American Revolution* (New York: Columbia University Press, 1957), 66.

"noble appearance": Frank Grizzard, Jr., *George Washington: Biographical Companion* (Santa Barbara, Calif.: ABC-Clio, 2002), 326.

"Every action done": Richard Brookhiser, ed., *George Washington's Rules of Civility* (New York: Free Press, 1997), 27.

"liked his glass": Bellamy Partridge, *Sir Billy Howe* (London: Longmans, Green & Co., 1932), 34.

"I heard the bullets": George Washington to

John Washington, May 31, 1754, in *Papers of George Washington*, Colonial Series, I, W. W. Abbot, ed. (Charlottesville: University Press of Virginia, 1983), 118.

glass in the windows: Author's conversation with Carol Borchert Cadou, curator, Mount Vernon Estate and Gardens, Mount Vernon, Va.

"I wish you would quicken": George Washington to Lund Washington, August 20, 1775, in *PGW,* I, 337.

"strongly attacked": Paul Leicester Ford, *Washington and the Theater* (New York: Dunlap Society, 1899), 7.

Cato: Ibid., 2–21; James Thomas Flexner, *George Washington in the American Revolution, 1775–1783* (Boston: Little, Brown, 1968), 30.

His wealth was in land: Information on George Washington's landholdings from Frank Grizzard, associate editor, *Papers of George Washington.*

"obliged to keep horses": Tobias Smollett, *The Expedition of Humphrey Clinker* (Oxford, Eng.: Oxford University Press, 1966), 321.

"the best horseman": Thomas Jefferson to Dr. Walter Jones, January 21, 1814, LOC.

"Found a fox": Donald Jackson, ed., *Diaries of George Washington*, III (Charlottesville: University Press of Virginia, 1978), 160–191.

"the image of war": R. S. Surtees, *Mr. Sponge's Sporting Tour* (London, The Folio Society, 1950), 10.

"far, very far": Charles Coleman Sellers, *Charles Willson Peale: Early Life*, I (Philadelphia: American Philosophical Society, 1947), 109.

"I am truly sensible": George Washington to Continental Congress, June 16, 1775, in *PGW*, I, 1.

"far from seeking": George Washington to Martha Washington, June 18, 1775, in *PGW*, I, 3–4.

"secret expedition": Instructions to Nathaniel Tracy, September 2, 1775, in *PGW*, I, 405.

"The inactive state": George Washington to John Washington, September 10, 1775, in *PGW*, I, 447.

"speedy finish": George Washington to General Officers, September 8, 1775, in *PGW*, I, 432.

"No danger": George Washington to Nicholas Cooke, August 4, 1775, in *PGW*, I, 221.

"to know": George Washington to General

Officers, September 8, 1775, in *PGW,* I, 432.

Seneca chief: John Richard Alden, *General Charles Lee: Traitor or Patriot?* (Baton Rouge: Louisiana State University Press, 1951), 9.

"an odd genius": Ibid., 83.

Boiling Water: John Shy, *A People Numerous and Armed: Reflections on the Military Struggle for American Independence* (Ann Arbor: University of Michigan Press, 1990), 137.

"the first officer": George Washington to John Washington, March 31, 1776, in *PGW,* III, 570.

"a good man": William Cooper to John Adams, April 22, 1776, in *Naval Documents of the American Revolution,* IV, William Bell Clark, ed. (Washington, D.C.: U.S. Department of the Navy, 1969), 1192.

"fat, old, church warden": Christopher Hibbert, *Redcoats and Rebels: The American Revolution Through British Eyes* (New York: Avon, 1990), 70.

"of middling stature": William Heath, *Heath's Memoirs of the American War* (New York: A. Wessels Co., 1904), 15.

"surely every post": George Washington to

John Thomas, July 23, 1775, in *PGW,* I, 160.

"severity of a northern winter": George Washington, Council of War, September 11, 1775, in *PGW,* I, 450.

"the hazard": Ibid., 451.

"decisive stroke": George Washington to John Hancock, September 21, 1775, in *PGW,* II, 28–29.

"I send you eleven dollars": Joseph Hodgkins to Sarah Hodgkins, October 6, 1775, Herbert T. Wade and Robert A. Lively, eds., *This Glorious Cause* (Princeton, N.J.: Princeton University Press, 1958), 178.

"defend our common rights": Nathanael Greene to Catharine Greene, June 2, 1775, in *PNG,* I, 83.

"We are soldiers": Nathanael Greene to Samuel Ward, July 4, 1776, in *PNG,* I, 98.

"neither glory": George Washington to John Thomas, July 23, 1775, in *PGW,* I, 160.

"every exertion": George Washington to New York Provincial Congress, June 26, 1775, in *PGW,* I, 41.

"become a favorite point": Nathanael Greene to Samuel Ward, October 23, 1775, in *PNG,* I, 140.

Dr. Benjamin Church: Clifford K. Shipton, ed., *Sibley's Harvard Graduates,* XIII (Boston: Massachusetts Historical Society, 1965), 380–398.

"Things hereabouts remain": James Warren to Samuel Adams, October 23, 1775, in *Warren-Adams Letters,* II, Massachusetts Historical Society Collections (Boston: Massachusetts Historical Society, 1925), 422.

"proof of the diabolical designs": George Washington to William Ramsay, November 10–16, 1775, in *PGW,* II, 345.

"You cannot but be sensible": George Washington to Joseph Reed, November 20, 1775, in *PGW,* II, 407.

"I miss you exceedingly": Ibid., November 28, 1775, 448.

"very sensible": L. H. Butterfield, ed., *Diary and Autobiography of John Adams,* II (Cambridge, Mass.: Harvard University Press, 1961), 131.

"cold and blustering": "Diary of Jabez Fitch, Jr.," November 12, 1775, *Proceedings of the MHS,* 2nd series, IX (1894–1895), 79.

"He is certainly the best": James Warren to John Adams, November 14, 1775, in *Papers of John Adams,* III, Robert J. Taylor, ed. (Cambridge, Mass.:

Belknap Press, 1983), 306.

"Gentlemen in other colonies": John Adams to Joseph Hawley, November 25, 1775, in *Papers of John Adams,* III, Robert J. Taylor, ed. (Cambridge, Mass.: Belknap Press, 1979), 316.

"acquainted with the genius": Nathanael Greene to Samuel Ward, December 18, 1775, in *PNG,* I, 163.

Henry Knox: George F. Scheer and Hugh R. Rankin, eds., *Rebels and Redcoats* (New York: Da Capo Press, 1957), 79–104.

"very fat, but very active": Marquis de Chastellux, *Travels in North America in the Years 1780, 1781, and 1782,* I, Howard C. Rice, ed. (Chapel Hill: University of North Carolina Press, 1963), 112.

seventh of the ten sons: North Callahan, *Henry Knox: George Washington's General* (South Brunswick, Maine: A. S. Barnes, 1958), 16.

"large and very elegant: Ibid., 21.

"of pleasing manners": L. H. Butterfield, ed., *Diary and Autobiography of John Adams,* III (Cambridge, Mass.: Harvard University Press, 1961), 446.

Another patron was Nathanael Greene: North Callahan, *Henry Knox: George Washing-*

ton's *General* (South Brunswick, Maine: A. S. Barnes, 1958), 29–30.

"military art": Ibid., 35.

bird-hunting: Ibid., 26.

Lucy Flucker: Ibid.

"My charmer": Henry Knox to Lucy Knox, December 17, 1775, NYHS.

"Long to see you": Ibid., July 7, 1775.

"George Washington fills": Ibid., July 9, 1775.

"Don't be afraid": Ibid., November 18, 1775.

"Every officer that stands": Nathanael Greene's Orders, November 7, 1775, in *PNG,* I, 149.

"Every colonel": Nathanael Greene's Orders, November 15, 1775, in *PNG,* I, 151.

smallpox raged: Allen Bowman, *The Morale of the American Revolutionary Army* (Washington, D.C: American Council of Public Affairs, 1943), 21.

"I only saw him": John C. Dann, ed., *The Revolution Remembered: Eyewitness Accounts of the War for Independence* (Chicago: University of Chicago Press, 1980), 409.

"the whole in the most miserable": George Washington to Joseph Reed, November 27, 1775, *PGW,* II, 442.

"with [the] design": George Washington to John Hancock, December 4, 1775, in *PGW,* II, 486.

"weapon of defense": Ibid., December 14, 1775, 548.

"Your exertions": Frank Moore, *Diary of the American Revolution,* I (New York: Scribner, 1860), 171–173.

"Our situation": George Washington to John Hancock, November 28, 1775, in *PGW,* II, 446.

"such a dearth": George Washington to Joseph Reed, November 28, 1775, in *PGW,* II, 449–450.

"glad tidings": Ibid., November 30, 1775, 463.

"instance of divine favor": Ibid.

"Our people are almost bewitched": Joseph Hodgkins to Sarah Hodgkins, October 6, 1775, in Herbert T. Wade and Robert A. Lively, eds., *This Glorious Cause* (Princeton, N.J.: Princeton University Press, 1958), 178.

"I hope I and all my townsmen": Ibid., November 25, 1775, 185.

"I want you to come home": Sarah Hodgkins to Joseph Hodgkins, December 10, 1775, in Herbert T. Wade and Robert A. Lively, eds., *This Glorious Cause* (Princeton, N.J.: Princeton University

Press, 1958), 187.

"I want to see you very much": Ibid., May 23, 1775, 203, and June 2, 1775, 204.

"alter": Ibid., November 19, 1775, 184.

"We was ordered": George F. Scheer and Hugh F. Rankin, eds., *Rebels and Redcoats* (New York: Da Capo Press, 1957), 102.

"In the morning": Journal of Simeon Lyman of Sharon, August 10 to December 28, 1775, *Collections of Connecticut Historical Society*, VII, 131.

"Some of the Connecticutians": George G. Scheer and Hugh F. Rankin, eds., *Rebels and Redcoats* (New York: Da Capo Press, 1957), 103.

"Let me ask you": George Washington to Philip Schuyler, December 24, 1775, in *PGW*, II, 599–600.

"not a bad supply": George F. Scheer and Hugh F. Rankin, *Rebels and Redcoats* (New York: Da Capo Press, 1957), 103.

"I confess I shudder": Martha Washington to Elizabeth Ramsay, December 30, 1775, in Joseph E. Fields, ed., *Worthy Partner: The Papers of Martha Washington* (Westport, Conn.: Greenwood Press, 1994), 164.

"even if the town must be burnt": Diary of

Richard Smith, December 22, 1775, in *Letters of Delegates to Congress, 1774–1789*, Paul Smith, ed., II (Washington, D.C.: Library of Congress, 1977), 513.

"the most perfect piece": Providence Gazette, December 23, 1775.

"This is the last day": Nathanael Greene to Samuel Ward, December 31, 1775, in *PNG*, I, 173–174.

sent across the lines from Boston: Allen French, *The First Year of the American Revolution* (Boston: Houghton Mifflin, 1934), 630.

"We have consulted": Nathanael Greene to Samuel Ward, January 4, 1776, in *PNG*, I, 176–177.

"satisfy a tyrant": George Washington to Joseph Reed, February 10, 1776, in *PGW*, III, 288.

"by hundreds": William Heath, *Heath's Memoirs of the American War* (New York: A. Wessels Co., 1904), 43–44.

"new army": George Washington's General Orders, January 1, 1776, in *PGW*, III, 1.

new flag: Allen French, *The First Year of the American Revolution* (Boston: Houghton Mifflin, 1934), 630.

3. DORCHESTER HEIGHTS

"absolutely necessary": Sir Henry Clinton, *The American Rebellion: Sir Henry Clinton's Narrative of His Campaigns, 1775–1782*, William B. Willcox, ed. *(New Haven, Conn.: Yale University Press, 1954)*, 20.

"It had often been wished": John Rhodehamel, ed., *The American Revolution: Writings from the War of Independence* (New York: Library of America, 2001), 120.

"We cannot remain": James Grant to Edward Harvey, August 11, 1775, James Grant Papers, LOC.

"Lenity is out of the question": Ibid.

"abandon Boston before winter": K. G. Davies, ed., *Documents of the American Revolution, 1770–1783*, Colonial Office Series, XI (Dublin: Irish University Press, 1976), 99.

"We are not under": Ibid., 191.

"We must go at it": Sir Henry Clinton memorandum, December 3, 1775, in *The American Rebellion: Sir Henry Clinton's Narrative of His Campaigns*, William B. Willcox, ed. (New Haven, Conn.: Yale University Press, 1954), 23n.

"Gentleman Johnny": David Hackett

Fisher, *Washington's Crossing* (New York: Oxford University Press, 2004), 36.

"so shattered": Francis, Lord Rawdon, to Francis, 10th Earl of Huntingdon, December 13, 1775, in *Report on the Manuscripts of the late Reginald Rawdon Hastings,* III (London: Her Majesty's Stationery Office, 1930–1947), 161.

"and we hear": Ibid., October 5, 1775, 160.

"The rebels have the impudence": Margaret Wheeler Willard, ed., *Letters on the American Revolution: 1774–1776* (Boston: Houghton Mifflin, 1925), 259.

"This sort of storm": Allen French, *The First Year of the American Revolution* (Boston: Houghton Mifflin, 1934), 650.

"redcoat gentry": George Washington to John Washington, October 13, 1775, in *PGW,* II, 161.

Pews were torn out: Henry Steele Commager and Richard B. Morris, eds., *The Spirit of 'Seventy-Six,* I (Indianapolis: Bobbs-Merrill, 1958), 148–149.

"We have plays": Allen French, *The First Year of the American Revolution* (Boston: Houghton Mifflin, 1934), 651.

"In the midst of these horrors": Margaret Wheeler Willard, ed., *Letters on the American Revolution: 1774–1776* (Boston: Houghton Mifflin, 1925), 255.

"We must get through": James Grant to Edward Harvey, November 29, 1775, James Grant Papers, LOC.

"very elegant playhouse": Margaret Wheeler Willard, ed., *Letters on the American Revolution: 1774–1776* (Boston: Houghton Mifflin, 1925), 255.

The Blockade: Allen French, *The First Year of the American Revolution* (Boston: Houghton Mifflin, 1934), 634.

"But soon finding": George F. Scheer and Hugh F. Rankin, *Rebels and Redcoats: The American Revolution Through the Eyes of Those Who Fought and Lived It* (New York: Da Capo Press, 1957), 97.

"Turn out!": Henry Steele Commager and Richard B. Morris, eds., *The Spirit of 'Seventy-Six: The Story of the American Revolution as Told by Participants,* I (Indianapolis: Bobbs-Merrill, 1958), 166.

Billy Howe's *Cleopatra:* Thomas Fleming, *1776: Year of Illusions* (New York: Norton, 1975), 63.

"Joshua had a handsome wife": Thomas Jones, *History of New York During the*

Revolutionary War, I (New York: New-York Historical Society, 1879), 351.

"one of those brave": Richard M. Ketchum, *The Winter Soldiers* (Garden City, N.Y.: Doubleday, 1973), 94.

"to go a step further": Sir George Otto Trevelyan, *The American Revolution,* I (New York: Longmans, Green & Co., 1899), 306.

"The success is too dearly bought": Thomas J. Fleming, *Now We Are Enemies: The Story of Bunker Hill* (New York: St. Martin's Press, 1960), 330.

"I do not in the least": Ibid., 235.

"proper army": Troyer Anderson, *Command of the Howe Brothers During the American Revolution* (New York: Oxford University Press, 1936), 116.

"The reflection upon my situation": George Washington to Joseph Reed, January 14, 1776, in *PGW,* III, 89.

"We have not at this time": Ibid.

"I have often thought": George Washington to Joseph Reed, January 14, 1776, in *PGW,* III, 89–90.

"undoubted intelligence": George Washington to Jonathan Trumbull, January 7, 1776, in *PGW,* III, 51.

"vast importance": Nathanael Greene to Samuel Ward, January 4, 1776, in

PNG, I, 177.

"stretching": George Washington to Joseph Reed, February 26–March 9, 1776, in *PGW,* III, 372.

"a kind of key": John Adams to George Washington, January 6, 1776, in *PGW,* III, 37.

"put the city": George Washington to Charles Lee, January 8, 1776, in *PGW,* III, 53.

"indispensable necessity": George Washington, Council of War, January 16, 1776, in *PGW,* III, 103.

"the eyes of the whole continent": George Washington to John Hancock, February 18–21, 1776, in *PGW,* III, 336.

"present feeble state": George Washington, Council of War, January 18, 1776, in *PGW,* III, 133.

guns Knox: Allen French, *The First Year of the American Revolution* (Boston: Houghton Mifflin, 1934), 655; North Callahan, *Henry Knox: George Washington's General* (South Brunswick, Maine: A. S. Barnes, 1958), 40–41.

"the utmost difficulty": "Ticonderoga Diary of Henry Knox," *New England Historical and Genealogical Register,* XXX (1876), 323.

"rowing exceeding hard": Ibid.

"beating all the way": William Knox to

Henry Knox, December 14, 1775, NYHS.

"It is not easy to conceive": Henry Knox to George Washington, December 17, 1775, in *PGW,* II, 563.

"I most earnestly beg": Henry Knox to Captain Palmer, December 12, 1775, NYHS.

"Trusting that": Henry Knox to George Washington, December 17, 1775, in *PGW,* II, 564.

"We shall cut": Henry Knox to Lucy Knox, December 17, 1775, NYHS.

"cruel thaw": Allen French, *The First Year of the American Revolution* (Boston: Houghton Mifflin, 1934), 655.

"Our cavalcade": John Becker, *The Sexagenary; or, Reminiscences of the American Revolution* (Albany, N.Y.: J. Munsell, 1866), 30.

"The thaw has been so grave": Henry Knox to Lucy Knox, January 5, 1776, NYHS.

"This morning I had the satisfaction": Philip Schuyler to George Washington, January 5–7, 1776, in *PGW,* III, 34.

"owing to the assistance": Henry Knox Diary, January 8, 1776, MHS.

"from which we might almost": Ibid., January 10, 1776.

"It appeared to me": Ibid.

"We were the great gainers": John Becker, *The Sexagenary; or Reminiscences of the American Revolution* (Albany, N.Y.: J. Munsell, 1866), 34.

"noble train": Henry Knox to George Washington, December 17, 1775, in *PGW,* II, 564.

"My business increases": George Washington to Joseph Reed, January 23, 1776, in *PGW,* III, 172–173.

"obliged to use art": Ibid., February 10, 1776, 287.

"Great activity": James Thacher, M.D., January 22, 1776, *Military Journal During the American Revolutionary War, July 1775 to February 17, 1777* (Boston: Richardson & Lord, 1823), 45–46.

two mounted British officers: Allen French, *The First Year of the American Revolution* (Boston: Houghton Mifflin, 1934), 648.

"stroke well aimed": George Washington, Council of War, February 16, 1776, in *PGW,* III, 321.

"Perhaps a greater question": Council of War, February 16, 1776, in *PGW,* III, 323, n. 5.

"He is still as hard as ever": Sir George Otto Trevelyan, *The American Revolution,* I

(New York: Longmans, Green & Co., 1926), 358.

"as yellow as saffron": Nathanael Greene to Jacob Greene, February 8, 1776, in *PNG*, I, 193.

"horrible if it succeeded": Ibid., February 15, 1776, 194.

"Behold!": George Washington to Joseph Reed, February 26–March 9, 1776, in *PGW*, III, 370.

"now at an end": Ibid.

"impenetrable as a rock": George Washington to John Washington, March 31, 1776, in *PGW*, III, 567.

fortifications: Allen French, *First Year of the American Revolution* (Boston: Houghton Mifflin, 1934), 656–657.

"screwed hay": George Washington to Joseph Reed, February 26–March 9, 1776, in *PGW*, III, 371.

"a very high opinion": George Washington to Artemus Ward, March 3, 1776, in *PGW*, III, 409.

"It is generally thought": Sarah Hodgkins to Joseph Hodgkins, in Herbert T. Wade and Robert A. Lively, eds., *This Glorious Cause: The Adventures of Two Company Officers in Washington's Army* (Princeton, N.J.: Princeton University Press, 1958), 193–194.

"The preparations increase": Abigail Adams to John Adams, February 21, 1776, in L. H. Butterfield, ed., *Adams Family Correspondence*, I (Cambridge Mass.: Belknap Press, 1963), 350.

"I have been in a continual state": Ibid., March 2, 1776, 352–353.

"Proceed, great chief": *PGW*, II, 243.

"I thank you most sincerely": George Washington to Phyllis Wheatley, February 28, 1776, in *PGW*, III, 387.

"bring on a rumpus": George Washington to Burwell Bassett, February 28, 1776, in *PGW*, III, 386.

"Junius": Lachlan Campbell, "British Journal from Aboard Ship in Boston Commencing January 1776 and Then Moving to New York," NYHS.

"As the season is now fast approaching": George Washington, General Orders, February 27, 1776, in *PGW*, III, 379.

"Remember barrels": George Washington to Artemas Ward, March 2, 1776, in *PGW*, III, 401.

"The house shakes": Abigail Adams to John Adams, March 2, 1776, in L. H. Butterfield, ed., *Adams Family Correspondence*, I (Cambridge, Mass.: Belknap Press, 1963), 353.

"The inhabitants were in a horrid situation":

Henry Steele Commager and Richard B. Morris, eds., *The Spirit of 'Seventy-Six,* I (Indianapolis: Bobbs-Merrill, 1958), 182.

"Our shells raked the houses": Worthington Chauncey Ford, ed., *Correspondence and Journals of Samuel Blachley Webb, 1772–1775,* I (Lancaster, Pa.: Wickersham Press, 1893), 134.

"covering party": William Gordon to Samuel Wilcon, April 6, 1776, *Proceedings of the MHS,* LX (October 1926–June 1927), 362.

"The whole procession": James Thacher, M.D., March 4, 1776, in *Military Journal During the American Revolutionary War, July 1775 to February 17, 1777* (Boston: Richardson & Lord, 1823), 46.

"vast number of large bundles": Ibid., March 5, 1776, 46–47.

"A finer [night] for working": William Gordon to Samuel Wilcon, April 6, 1776, *Proceedings of the MHS,* LX (October 1926–June 1927), 363.

Recounting the night's events: Allen French, *The First Year of the American Revolution* (Boston: Houghton Mifflin, 1934), 659.

"Perhaps there never was": William Heath, *Heath's Memoirs of the American War*

(New York: A. Wessels Co., 1904), 49.

"My God, these fellows": Allen French, *The First Year of the American Revolution* (Boston: Houghton Mifflin, 1934), 660.

"a most astonishing night's work": Archibald Robertson, March 4, 1776, in *Archibald Robertson: His Diaries and Sketches in America, 1762–1780* (New York: New York Public Library, 1930), 74.

number at 14,000: Allen French, *The First Year of the American Revolution* (Boston: Houghton Mifflin, 1934), 660.

"This is, I believe": *London Chronicle*, May 15, 1776.

"utmost consternation": George Washington to Charles Lee, March 14, 1776, in *PGW,* III, 467.

"the most serious step": Archibald Robertson, March 5, 1776, in *Archibald Robertson* (New York: New York Public Library, 1930), 74.

"We saw distinctly": Theodore Sizer, ed., *The Autobiography of Colonel John Trumbull* (New Haven, Conn.: Yale University Press, 1953), 23.

"Each man knows his place": James Thacher, M.D., March 5, 1776, in

Military Journal During the American Revolutionary War, July 1775 to February 17, 1777 (Boston: Richardson & Lord, 1823), 47.

" 'remember it is the fifth of March' ": William Gordon to Samuel Wilcon, April 6, 1776, *Proceedings of the MHS*, LX (October 1926–June 1927), 363.

"never saw spirits higher": George Washington to Joseph Reed, February 26–March 9, 1776, in *PGW*, III, 374.

"pretty fresh": William Gordon to Samuel Wilcon, April 6, 1776, *Proceedings of the MHS*, LX (October 1926–June 1927), 364.

"that ever I was exposed to": Isaac Bangs, April 1, 1776, in *Journal of Lieutenant Isaac Bangs, April 1–July 29, 1776*, Edward Bangs, ed. (Cambridge, Mass.: John Wilson & Son, 1890), 12.

"kind Heaven": William Heath, *Heath's Memoirs of the American War* (New York: A. Wessels Co., 1904), 50.

"It is now eight o'clock": Archibald Robertson, March 5, 1776, in *Archibald Robertson* (New York: New York Public Library, 1930), 74.

"more than to make a parade": Isaac Bangs, April 1, 1776, *Journal of Lieutenant Isaac Bangs, April 1–July 29, 1776*, Ed-

ward Bangs, ed. (Cambridge, Mass.: John Wilson & Son, 1890), 12.

"Indeed, we had often talked": James Grant to General Harvey, March 26, 1776, James Grant Papers, LOC.

"I determined upon an immediate": K. G. Davies, ed., *Documents of the American Revolution, 1770–1783*, Colonial Office Series, XII (Dublin: Irish University Press, 1976), 82.

"contrary": Ibid.

"Never [were] troops": London *Chronicle*, May 15, 1776.

"Nothing but hurry and confusion": Anne Rowe Cunningham, ed., *Letters and Diary of John Rowe, Boston Merchant, 1759–1762, 1764–1779* (Boston: W. B. Clarke Co., 1903), 301.

"This day": Josef and Dorothy Berger, eds., *Diary of America* (New York: Simon & Schuster, 1957), 112.

"I told General Howe": James Grant to General Harvey, March 26, 1776, James Grant Papers, LOC.

"The necessary care": Thomas G. Frothingham, *History of the Siege of Boston, and of the Battles of Lexington, Concord, and Bunker Hill* (New York: Da Capo Press, 1970), 302.

"no intention of destroying": Ibid., 303.

"*Such a firing*": Isaac Bangs, April 1, 1776, in *Journal of Lieutenant Isaac Bangs, April 1–July 29, 1776*, Edward Bangs, ed. (Cambridge, Mass.: John Wilson & Son, 1890), 13.

"*cathartic*": John Rhodehamel, ed., *The American Revolution* (New York: Library of America, 2001), 122.

"*great movements and confusion*": George Washington to John Hancock, March 7–9, 1776, in *PGW*, III, 424.

"*It is not easy to paint*": James H. Stark, *The Loyalists of Massachusetts and the Other Side of the American Revolution* (Boston: W. B. Clarke Co., 1910), 348.

"*goods left in my house*": Loyalist Claims, Public Records Office, Kew Gardens, London, Eng.

"*the horrid crime of rebellion*": Henry Steele Commager and Richard B. Morris, eds., *The Spirit of 'Seventy-Six*, I (Indianapolis: Bobbs-Merrill, 1958), 350.

"*Upon the whole*": James H. Stark, *The Loyalists of Massachusetts and the Other Side of the American Revolution* (Boston: W. B. Clarke Company, 1910), 311.

"*I found I could not stay*": Catherine S. Crary, *The Price of Loyalty: Tory Writings from the Revolutionary Era* (New

York: McGraw-Hill, 1973), 125.

"first and chief objective": Memoir of William MacAlpine, Loyalist Claims, Public Records Office, Kew Gardens, London, Eng.

Margaret Draper: Lorenzo Sabine, *Biographical Sketches of Loyalists of the American Revolution,* I (Port Washington, N.Y.: Kennicat Press, 1966), 387.

"discarded" mistress: Alfred E. Jones, *The Loyalists of Massachusetts* (London: St. Catherine Press, 1930), xvii.

"men, women, and children": Allen French, *The First Year of the American Revolution* (Boston: Houghton Mifflin, 1934), 665.

"I am informed": Thomas G. Frothingham, *History of the Siege of Boston, and of the Battles of Lexington, Concord, and Bunker Hill* (New York: Da Capo Press, 1970), 306.

"a conceited New York Tory": Ibid., 307.

"There never was such destruction": Anne Rowe Cunningham, ed., *Letters and Diary of John Rowe, Boston Merchant, 1759–1762, 1764–1779* (Boston: W. B. Clarke Co., 1903), 302.

"Soldiers and sailors": Joseph Berger and Dorothy Berger, eds., *Diary of America*

(New York: Simon & Schuster, 1957), 112.

"Fine weather": Journal of Lieutenant Colonel Stephen Kemble, 1783–1789 (Boston: Gregg Press, 1972), 73.

"The finest day": Archibald Robertson, March 17, 1776, in *Archibald Robertson: Diaries and Sketches in America, 1762–1780* (New York: New York Public Library, 1930), 80.

"In the course of the forenoon": James Thacher, M.D., March 8–21, 1776, in *Military Journal During the American Revolutionary War, July 1775 to February 17, 1777* (Boston: Richardson & Lord, 1823), 49.

"Surely it is the Lord's doings": Abigail Adams to John Adams, March 16, 1776, in *Adams Family Correspondence,* I (Cambridge, Mass.: Belknap Press, 1963), 360.

"thorough New England man": William Cooper to John Adams, April 22, 1776, in *Naval Documents of the American Revolution,* IV, William Bell Clark, ed. (Washington, D.C.: U.S. Department of the Navy, 1969), 1192.

"suffered greatly": George Washington to John Hancock, March 19, 1776, in *PGW,* III, 490.

"Though I believe": John Sullivan to John Adams, March 15–19, 1776, in *Papers of John Adams*, IV, Robert J. Taylor, ed. (Cambridge, Mass.: Belknap Press, 1979), 55.

"lurking": James Thacher, M.D., March 22, 1776, *Military Journal During the American Revolutionary War, July 1775 to February 17, 1777* (Boston: Richardson & Lord, 1823), 50.

"amazingly strong": George Washington to Joseph Reed, March 19, 1776, in *PGW*, III, 494.

"We do not know where": *London Chronicle*, May 4–6, 1776.

"You know the proverbial expression": Ibid.

"Gentlemen, not one of you": Clifford K. Shipton, ed., *Sibley's Harvard Graduates: 1756–1760*, XIV (Boston: Massachusetts Historical Society, 1968), 153–154.

"The joy of our friends": *New Haven Journal*, March 27, 1776.

"were completely disgraced": *Constitutional Gazette*, March 30, 1776.

"To the wisdom": *Philadelphia Evening Post*, March 30, 1776.

"Those pages in the annals": John Hancock to George Washington, April 2, 1776, in *PGW*, IV, 16.

"*What an occurrence*": Paul H. Smith, ed., *Letters of the Delegates to Congress,* III (Washington, D.C.: Library of Congress, 1976–1979), 440.

"*Let this transaction be dressed*": Thomas G. Frothingham, *History of the Siege of Boston, and of the Battles of Lexington, Concord, and Bunker Hill* (New York: Da Capo Press, 1970), 323.

"*with so little effusion*": Address from the Boston Selectmen, March 1776, in *PGW,* III, 571.

"*hear from different quarters*": George Washington to John Washington, March 31, 1776, in *PGW,* III, 569.

"*We have maintained*": Ibid., 566.

"*I believe I may*": Ibid., 569.

"*utmost wish*": Ibid., 567.

"*lament or repine at any act*": George Washington to Joseph Reed, February 26–March 9, 1776, in *PGW,* III, 373.

"*Unhappy wretches!*": George Washington to Joseph Reed, April 1, 1776, in *PGW,* IV, 12.

"*By all accounts*": Ibid., 11.

"*I am hurried*": Ibid., 9.

"*What may be their views*": John Hancock to George Washington, March 25, 1776, in *PGW,* III, 532.

"*My countrymen, I know*": George Washington to Joseph Reed, April 1, 1776, *PGW,* IV, 11.

"The sun never shined": Thomas Paine, *"Rights of Man" and "Common Sense"* (New York: Knopf, 1994), 265.

"for I expect that I shall march": John Lapham to his parents, March 17, 1776, published in the *Boston Transcript,* March 17, 1928, Allen French Papers, MHS.

4. THE LINES ARE DRAWN

"with great expedition": William Heath, *Heath's Memoirs of the American War* (New York: A. Wessels Co., 1904), 53.

"hasten his march": George Washington to John Hancock, April 1, 1776, in *PGW,* IV, 7.

"as speedily as possible": George Washington's Orders and Instructions to Henry Knox, April 3, 1776, in *PGW,* IV, 23–24.

"extreme hurry": See, for example, George Washington to Joseph Reed, April 23, 1776, in *PGW,* IV, 115.

"at great speed": John Greenwood, *Revolutionary Services of John Greenwood of Boston and New York, 1775–1783,* Isaac

J. Greenwood, ed. (New York: De Vinne Press, 1922), 25.

"wet weather": Solomon Nash Diary, March 31–April 7, 1776, NYHS.

"I am willing to serve": Joseph Hodgkins to Sarah Hodgkins, March 20, 1776, in Herbert T. Wade and Robert A. Lively, eds., *This Glorious Cause: The Adventures of Two Company Officers in Washington's Army* (Princeton, N.J.: Princeton University Press, 1958), 195.

"I am a good deal tired": Ibid., April 10, 1776, 198.

"troble": Ibid., April 4, 1776, 197.

"I never spent": Joseph Plumb Martin, *A Narrative of a Revolutionary Soldier* (New York: Penguin, 2001), 16.

There was scarcely a militia man: John Adlum, *Memoirs of the Life of John Adlum in the Revolutionary War*, Howard H. Peckham, ed. (Chicago: Caxton Club, 1968), 12.

"What to do with the city?": Charles Lee to George Washington, February 19, 1776, in *PGW*, III, 340.

"vast importance": John Adams to George Washington, January 6, 1776, in *PGW*, III, 37.

"to exert myself to the utmost": George Washington to John Hancock, April 1,

1776, in *PGW,* IV, 7.

"internal foes": George Washington to Philip Schuyler, January 27, 1776, in *PGW,* III, 203.

"We are involved": "Sermon of Rev. John Rodgers, Jan. 14, 1776," *New York Times,* March 16, 2003.

"We have nothing": George Washington to John Adams, April 15, 1776, in *PGW,* IV, 67.

"When they were ordered": Sir George Otto Trevelyan, *The American Revolution,* II (New York: Longmans, Green & Co., 1899), 184.

"The appearance of things": Alexander Graydon, *Memoirs of His Own Time,* John Stockton Littell, ed. (Philadelphia: Lindsay & Blakiston, 1846), 147.

"unwarlike": Ibid., 156.

"not entirely come up": Ibid., 140.

"But even in this regiment": Ibid., 149.

"It will require": Alan Valentine, *Lord Stirling* (New York: Oxford University Press, 1969), 170.

population of perhaps 20,000: Henry P. Johnston, *The Campaign of 1776 Around New York and Brooklyn* (Brooklyn: Long Island Historical Society, 1878), Part 1, 36.

"The inhabitants": I. N. Phelps Stokes, *The*

Iconography of Manhattan Island 1498–1909, I (New York: Arno Press, 1967), 862.

"principal streets": Henry Knox to Lucy Knox, January 5, 1776, NYHS.

"The people": Ibid.

"This city York": Joseph Hodgkins to Sarah Hodgkins, April 24, 1776, in Herbert T. Wade and Robert A. Lively, eds., *This Glorious Cause* (Princeton, N.J.: Princeton University Press, 1958), 199.

"excessive dear": Ibid., May 9, 1776, 201.

"They have all the simplicity": Henry P. Johnston, *The Campaign of 1776 Around New York and Brooklyn* (Brooklyn: Long Island Historical Society, 1878), Part II, 132.

"their civility": I. N. Phelps Stokes, *The Iconography of Manhattan Island, 1498–1909,* I (New York: Arno Press, 1967), 926–927.

"But alas, swearing abounds": Philip Vickers Fithian, July 24, 1776, in *Philip Vickers Fithian: Journal, 1775–1776, Written on the Virginia-Pennsylvania Frontier and in the Army Around New York,* Robert Greenhalgh Albion and Leonidas Dodson, eds. (Princeton N.J.: Princeton University Press, 1934), 194.

"The design was in imitation": Isaac Bangs, April 19, 1776, in *Journal of Lieutenant Isaac Bangs, April 1–July 29, 1776*, Edward Bangs, ed. (Cambridge, Mass.: John Wilson & Son, 1890), 25.

twenty or more churches: Ibid., April 21, April 28, and June 8, 1776, 28, 30, 31, 41.

"pomp": Ibid., April 28, 1776, 31.

Quaker meeting: Ibid., June 30, 1776, 54.

Holy Ground: Ibid., April 25, 1776, 29.

five hundred prostitutes: I. N. Phelps Stokes, *The Iconography of Manhattan Island, 1498–1909*, I (New York: Arno Press, 1967), 862.

"When I visited them": Isaac Bangs, April 19, 1776, in *Journal of Lieutenant Isaac Bangs, April 1–July 29, 1776*, Edward Bangs, ed. (Cambridge, Mass.: John Wilson & Son, 1890), 29.

"castrated in a barbarous manner": Ibid., 30.

"an old whore": Ibid., 31.

"riotous behavior": George Washington, General Orders, April 27, 1776, in *PGW,* IV, 140.

"disguised with liquor": George F. Scheer and Hugh F. Rankin, eds., *Rebels and Redcoats: The American Revolution Through the Eyes of Those Who Fought and Lived It* (New York: Da Capo

Press, 1957), 147.

"these bitchfoxly": Loammi Baldwin to May Baldwin, June 12, 1776, Baldwin Papers, Houghton Library, Harvard University; Henry Steele Commager and Richard B. Morris, eds., *The Spirit of 'Seventy-Six,* I (Indianapolis: Bobbs-Merrill, 1958), 420–421.

"growing sickly": William Heath, *Heath's Memoirs of the American War* (New York: A. Wessels Co., 1904), 56.

"advantageous": Henry P. Johnston, *The Campaign of 1776 Around New York and Brooklyn* (Brooklyn: Long Island Historical Society, 1878), Part I, 57.

ferryboats to and from Brooklyn: I. N. Phelps Stokes, *The Iconography of Manhattan Island, 1498–1909,* I (New York: Arno Press, 1967), 846.

"For should the enemy": Charles Lee to George Washington, February 19, 1776, in *PGW,* III, 339–340.

"veterans at least": Henry P. Johnston, *The Campaign of 1776 Around New York and Brooklyn* (Brooklyn: Long Island Historical Society, 1878), Part I, 78.

"constant duty": Nathanael Greene, General Orders, May 5, 1776, in *PNG,* 1, 212.

"Old Snarl": Henry P. Johnston, *The Campaign of 1776 Around New York and*

Brooklyn (Brooklyn: Long Island Historical Society, 1878), Part I, 79.

"We have done": George Washington to Charles Lee, May 9, 1776, in *PGW,* IV, 245.

"every street": I. N. Phelps Stokes, *The Iconography of Manhattan Island, 1498–1909,* I (New York: Arno Press, 1967), 923.

diary of the Massachusetts soldier: Solomon Nash Diary, NYHS.

"inspire those engaged": Nathanael Greene to John Adams, May 24, 1776, in *PNG,* I, 219.

"the very soul": Ibid., June 2, 1776, 224.

"Suppose this army": Ibid., 226.

"The future happiness": Henry Knox to John Adams, May 16, 1776, in *Papers of John Adams,* IV, Robert J. Taylor, ed. (Cambridge, Mass.: Belknap Press, 1979), 190.

"Gen Green[e] and Lady": Nathanael and Catharine Greene to Henry and Lucy Knox, June 1776, in *PNG,* I, 245.

"not to suffer": George Washington, General Orders, May 20, 1776, in *PGW,* IV, 343.

"lay upon": Ibid., May 7, 1776, 224.

with the "utmost expedition": George Washington to Israel Putnam, May 21,

1776, in *PGW,* IV, 355.

"Through Broadway": Isaac Bangs, June 6, 1776, in *Journal of Lieutenant Isaac Bangs, April 1–July 29, 1776,* Edward Bangs, ed. (Cambridge, Mass.: John Wilson & Son, 1890), 40.

"It is so entirely": Joseph Reed to Esther Reed, June 21, 1776, NYHS.

Loyalist plot: Henry P. Johnston, *The Campaign of 1776 Around New York and Brooklyn* (Brooklyn: Long Island Historical Society, 1878), Part I, 92, n. 2.

"We had some grand": George F. Scheer and Hugh F. Rankin, eds., *Rebels and Redcoats* (New York: Da Capo Press, 1957), 146.

"very unhappy": Ewald Shewkirk Diary, in Henry P. Johnston, *The Campaign of 1776 Around New York and Brooklyn* (Brooklyn: Long Island Historical Society, 1878), Part II, 108.

"I wish twenty more": Herbert T. Wade and Robert A. Lively, eds., *This Glorious Cause* (Princeton, N.J.: Princeton University Press, 1958), 210.

"I declare": George F. Scheer and Hugh F. Rankin, eds., *Rebels and Redcoats* (New York: Da Capo Press, 1957), 148.

"You can scarcely conceive": Henry Knox to William Knox, July 11, 1776, NYHS.

"My God, may I never": Ibid.

"The great being": Henry Knox to Lucy Knox, July 11, 1776, NYHS.

"10,000 troops": Nathanael Greene to George Washington, July 5, 1776, in *PNG*, I, 248.

"hourly": Chauncey Ford Worthington, ed., *Correspondence and Journals of Samuel Blachley Webb, 1772–1775*, I (Lancaster, Pa.: Wickersham Press, 1893), 152.

"in commotion": Ewald Shewkirk Diary, in Henry P. Johnston, *The Campaign of 1776 Around New York and Brooklyn* (Brooklyn: Long Island Historical Society, 1878), Part II, 109.

"I am of opinion": Moses Little to his son, July 6, 1776, in Henry P. Johnston, *The Campaign of 1776 Around New York and Brooklyn* (Brooklyn: Long Island Historical Society, 1878), Part II, 42.

"The whole choir": Isaac Bangs, July 6, 1776, in *Journal of Lieutenant Isaac Bangs, April 1–July 29, 1776*, Edward Bangs, ed. (Cambridge, Mass.: John Wilson & Son, 1890), 56.

"That our affairs": John Hancock to George Washington, July 6, 1776, in *PGW*, V, 219.

"The eyes of all America": Henry Knox to Lucy Knox, July 8, 1776, NYHS.

"We are in the very midst": Charles Francis Adams, ed., *The Works of John Adams*, IX (Boston: Little, Brown, 1856), 391.

"skiff made of paper": John Dickinson, July 1, 1776, in *Letters of Delegates to Congress, 1774–1789*, Paul H. Smith, ed., IV (Washington, D.C.: Library of Congress, 1979), 352.

"Thus the Congress": Frank Bowditch Dexter, ed., *Literary Diary of Ezra Stiles*, II (New York: Scribner, 1901), 21.

"fresh incentive": George Washington, General Orders, July 9, 1776, in *PGW*, V, 246.

"The general hopes": Ibid.

The formal readings: *New York Gazette*, July 22, 1776.

"to assimilate with the brains": Frank Moore, *Diary of the American Revolution*, I (New York: Scribner, 1860), 271.

"a complete view": Joseph Plumb Martin, *A Narrative of a Revolutionary Soldier* (New York: Penguin, 2001), 18.

"shot away our starb[oa]rd": William James Morgan, ed., *Naval Documents of the American Revolution*, V (Washington,

D.C.: U.S. Department of the Navy, 1970), 1038.

"Such unsoldierly conduct": George Washington, General Orders, July 13, 1776, in *PGW,* V, 290.

"impetuous": Henry Knox to Lucy Knox, July 13, 1776, NYHS.

"[We] are in very comfortable": Margaret Wheeler Willard, *Letters on the American Revolution: 1774–1776* (Boston: Houghton Mifflin, 1925), 341; and William Carter, *A Genuine Detail of the Several Engagements, Positions and Movements of Royal and American Armies During the Years 1775 and 1776* (London: Printed for the Author, 1784), 32.

"We have now a very good supply": Margaret Wheeler Willard, ed., *Letters on the American Revolution: 1774–1776* (Boston: Houghton Mifflin, 1925), 345.

"It excited one's sympathy": Ambrose Serle, July 23, 1776, in *The American Journal of Ambrose Serle, 1776–1778,* Edward H. Tatum, Jr., ed. (San Marino, Calif.: Huntington Library, 1940), 40.

"no believing": Charles Stuart to Lord Bute, July 9, 1776, in *A Prime Minister and His Son: From the Correspondence of the Third Earl of Bute and of Lieutenant*

General the Honorable Sir Charles Stuart, The Honorable Mrs. E. Stuart Wortley, ed. (London: John Murray, 1925), 83.

"The inhabitants": James Grant to Edward Harvey, July 9, 1776, James Grant Papers, LOC.

"I met with Governor Tryon": Henry P. Johnston, *The Campaign of 1776 Around New York and Brooklyn* (Brooklyn: Long Island Historical Society, 1878), Part I, 139, n. 1.

"the villainy and the madness": Ambrose Serle, July 12, 1776, in *The American Journal of Ambrose Serle, 1776–1778,* Edward H. Tatum, Jr., ed. (San Marino, Calif.: Huntington Library, 1940), 30.

"A more impudent": Ibid., July 13, 1776, 31.

"The troops hold them": Ambrose Serle, July 13, 1776, in *The American Journal* of *Ambrose Serle, 1776–1778,* Edward H. Tatum, Jr., ed. (San Marino, Calif.: Huntington Library, 1940), 30.

"The fair nymphs": Francis, Lord Rawdon, to Francis, 10th Earl of Huntingdon, August 5, 1776, in *Report on the Manuscripts of the late Reginald Rawdon Hastings,* III (London: Her Majesty's

Stationery Office, 1930–1947), 179–
180.

"we shall soon": Ibid., January 13, 1776,
167.

"Our only fear": Margaret Wheeler Willard,
ed., *Letters on the American Revolution:
1774–1776* (Boston: Houghton Mifflin,
1925), 344–45.

"flushed with the idea": Troyer Steele Anderson, *The Command of the Howe
Brothers During the American Revolution* (New York: Oxford University
Press, 1936), 121.

"Black Dick": George F. Scheer and Hugh
F. Rankin, eds., *Rebels and Redcoats*
(New York: Da Capo Press, 1957),
156.

"turned upon military affairs": Ambrose
Serle, July 13, 1776, in *The American
Journal of Ambrose Serle, 1776–1778,*
Edward H. Tatum, ed. (San Marino,
Calif.: Huntington Library, 1940), 31.

letter addressed to "George Washington":
Henry Knox to Lucy Knox, July 15,
1776, and July 22, 1776, MHS;
Henry P. Johnston, *The Campaign of
1776 Around New York and Brooklyn*
(Brooklyn: Long Island Historical Society, 1878), Part I, 97–98.

"So high is the vanity": Ambrose Serle, July

14, 1776, in *The American Journal of Ambrose Serle, 1776–1778*, Edward H. Tatum, Jr., ed. (San Marino, Calif.: Huntington Library, 1940), 33.

"very handsomely dressed": Henry Knox to Lucy Knox, July 22, 1776, NYHS.

"the greatest politeness": Joseph Reed to Charles Pettit, July 15, 1776, in *Life and Correspondence of Joseph Reed,* 1 (Philadelphia: Lindsay & Blakiston, 1847), 207.

"awe-struck": Henry Knox to Lucy Knox, July 22, 1776, NYHS.

one of the great actors of the age: David McCullough, *John Adams* (New York: Simon & Schuster, 2001), 593.

"interview": K. G. Davies, ed., *Documents of the American Revolution, 1770–1783,* Colonial Office Series, XII (Dublin: Irish University Press, 1976), 179.

"No air": Ambrose Serle, July 28, 1776, in *The American Journal of Ambrose Serle, 1776–1778*, Edward H. Tatum, Jr., ed. (San Marino, Calif.: Huntington Library, 1940), 49.

"I generally rise": Henry Knox to Lucy Knox, August 2, 1776, NYHS.

"a very fine appearance": Edward H. Tatum, Jr., ed., *The American Journal of Ambrose Serle, 1776–1778* (San Ma-

rino, Calif.: The Huntington Library, 1940), 52.

"We have had so many arrivals": Ibid., 54.

"It is a mere point": Joseph Reed to Charles Pettit, August 4, 1776, NYHS.

"My opinion is": Ibid.

"I shrink and tremble": Henry Knox to William Knox, August 5, 1776, NYHS.

harbor under full canvas: Edward H. Tatum, Jr., ed., *The American Journal of Ambrose Serle, 1776–1778* (San Marino, Calif.: Huntington Library, 1940), 62.

"When I look down": Joseph Reed to Esther Reed, August 9, 1776, NYHS.

"coming in almost every day": Joseph Hodgkins to Sarah Hodgkins, July 17, 1776, in Herbert T. Wade and Robert A. Lively, eds., *This Glorious Cause* (Princeton, N.J.: Princeton University Press, 1958), 209.

"the Delaware Blues": Charles M. Lefferts, *Uniforms of the American, British, French, and German Armies of the War of the American Revolution* (New York: New-York Historical Society, 1926), 26.

"Some have got ten": Sir George Otto Trevelyan, *The American Revolution*, II

(New York: Longmans, Green & Co., 1899), 190–191.

"*a good many of our people*": Joseph Hodgkins to Sarah Hodgkins, August 11, 1776, in Herbert T. Wade and Robert A. Lively, eds., *This Glorious Cause* (Princeton, N.J.: Princeton University Press, 1958), 212.

"*Sickness prevails*": John Waldo to his parents, August 3, 1776, in *The New York Diary of Lieutenant Jabez Fitch of the 17th (Connecticut) Regiment from August 2, 1776, to December 15, 1777*, W. H. Sabine, ed. (New York: Colburn & Tegg, 1954), 12.

"*The vile water*": Philip Vickers Fithian, July 19, 1776, in *Philip Vickers Fithian: Journal, 1775–76, Written on the Virginia-Pennsylvania Frontier and in the Army Around New York*, Robert Greenhalgh Albion and Leonidas Dodson, eds. (Princeton, N.J.: Princeton University Press, 1934), 190.

"*One died this morning*": Ibid., July 22, 1776, 193.

"*The general also forbids*": Nathanael Greene, General Orders, July 28, 1776, in *PNG*, I, 268.

"*They desert in large bodies*": I. N. Phelps Stokes, *The Iconography of Manhattan*

Island, I (New York, Arno Press, 1967), 1002.

"In almost every barn": William Heath, *Heath's Memoirs of the American War* (New York: A. Wessels Co., 1904), 61.

"Under every disadvantage": George Washington to John Hancock, August 8–9, 1776, in *PGW,* V, 627.

"season for action": George Washington to John Hancock, September 8, 1776, in *PGW,* VI, 252.

"strangers to the ground": Nathanael Greene to George Washington, August 15, 1776, in *PGW,* VI, 29.

"exceeding good spirits": Ibid., 30.

the Phoenix *and the* Rose*:* William James Morgan, ed., *Naval Documents of the American Revolution,* VI (Washington, D.C.: U.S. Department of the Navy, 1972), 224–225.

"From the advantage": William Tudor to John Adams, August 18, 1776, in *Papers of John Adams,* IV (Cambridge, Mass.: Belknap Press, 1979), 473.

"poor General Greene": Henry Knox to Lucy Knox, August 26, 1776, NYHS.

"spirited and zealously attached": George Washington to John Hancock, June 17, 1776, in *PGW,* V, 21.

"nothing special": George Washington to

John Hancock, August 21, 1776, in
PGW, VI, 97.

"this night at farthest": William Livingston
to George Washington, August 21,
1776, in *PGW,* VI, 99.

"We have made no discovery": George Washington to William Livingston, August
21, 1776, in *PGW,* VI, 100.

5. FIELD OF BATTLE

"a storm like a hurricane": Ewald Shewkirk
Diary, August 21, 1776, in Henry P.
Johnston, *The Campaign of 1776
Around New York and Brooklyn*
(Brooklyn: Long Island Historical Society, 1878), Part II, 113.

"a most terrible storm": Philip Vickers
Fithian, August 22, 1776, in *Philip
Vickers Fithian: Journal, 1775–1776,
Written on the Virginia-Pennsylvania
Frontier and in the Army Around New
York,* Robert Greenhalgh Albion and
Leonidas Dodson, eds. (Princeton,
N.J.: Princeton University Press,
1934), 214.

"the most vehement": Ambrose Serle, August 21, 1776, in *The American Journal
of Ambrose Serle, 1776–1778,* Edward

H. Tatum, Jr., ed. (San Marino, Calif.: Huntington Library, 1940), 71.

"an uncommon": Ewald Shewkirk Diary, August 21, 1776, in Henry P. Johnston, *The Campaign of 1776 Around New York and Brooklyn* (Brooklyn: Long Island Historical Society, 1878), Part II, 113.

"it was surcharged": Thomas W. Field, *Battle of Long Island* (Brooklyn: Long Island Historical Society, 1869), 349.

"But there seems hidden": Ibid., 351.

as if nothing unusual: Ibid., 350.

precisely eight o'clock: William James Morgan, ed., *Naval Documents of the American Revolution*, VI (Washington, D.C.: U.S. Department of the Navy, 1972), 267.

"ships and vessels": Ambrose Serle, August 22, 1776, in *The American Journal of Ambrose Serle, 1776–1778*, Edward H. Tatum, Jr., ed. (San Marino, Calif.: The Huntington Library, 1940), 71–73.

"regaled themselves": Ibid.

"Our regiment": Bruce Burgoyne, *An Anonymous Hessian Diary, Probably the Diary of Lieutenant Johann Heinrich von Bardeleben of the Hesse-Cassel von Donop Regiment* (Bowie, Md.: Heritage

Books, 1998), 54–55.

"While we are waiting": Jabez Fitch, August 22, 1776, in *The New York Diary of Lieutenant Jabez Fitch*, W. H. W. Sabine, ed. (New York: Colburn & Tegg, 1954), 25.

"I have thought fit": Moses Little to his son, August 22, 1776, in Henry P. Johnston, *The Campaign of 1776 Around New York and Brooklyn* (Brooklyn: Long Island Historical Society, 1878), Part II, 43.

"The hour is fast approaching": George Washington, General Orders, August 23, 1776, in *PGW*, VI, 109–110.

"Remember how your courage": Ibid.

"I have never been afraid": William Heath to George Washington, August 23, 1776, in *PGW*, VI, 114.

"The greatest vigilance": Joseph Reed to Esther Reed, August 23, 1776, NYHS.

"Scarcely were religious": Thomas W. Field, *Battle of Long Island* (Brooklyn: Long Island Historical Society, 1869), 351.

"Carts and horses": Philip Vickers Fithian, August 25, 1776, in *Philip Vickers Fithian: Journal, 1775–1776, Written on the Virginia-Pennsylvania Frontier and in the Army Around New York*, Robert Greenhalgh Albion and Leonidas

Dodson, eds. (Princeton, N.J.: Princeton University Press, 1934), 218.

"The distinction between": George Washington to Israel Putnam, August 25, 1776, in *PGW,* VI, 126–127.

"loose, disorderly": Ibid.

"We expect the fleet": William Douglas to his wife, August 23, 1776, in Henry P. Johnston, *The Campaign of 1776 Around New York and Brooklyn* (Brooklyn: Long Island Historical Society), Part II, 68.

"General Washington, with a number": Henry P. Johnston, *The Campaign of 1776 Around New York and Brooklyn* (Brooklyn: Long Island Historical Society, 1878), Part II, 58.

"very important": Joseph Reed to Esther Reed, August 24, 1776, NYHS.

"at all hazards": George Washington to Israel Putnam, August 25, 1776, in *PGW,* VI, 128.

"grand push": George Washington to John Hancock, August 26, 1776, in *PGW,* VI, 129.

"present appearance": George Washington to William Heath, August 26, 1776, in *PGW,* VI, 131.

"load of business": George Washington to Lund Washington, August 26, 1776, in

PGW, VI, 137.

"I wish most ardently": George Washington to Lund Washington, August 26, 1776, in *PGW,* VI, 136.

"could compensate [for] the loss": Ibid., 137.

failed most grievously: Sir Henry Clinton, *The American Rebellion: Sir Henry Clinton's Narrative of His Campaigns, 1775–1782,* William B. Willcox, ed. (New Haven, Conn.: Yale University Press, 1954), 20.

"speak too freely": Sir Henry Clinton to William Phillips, December 12, 1775, in *The American Rebellion,* William B. Willcox, ed. (New Haven, Conn.: Yale University Press, 1954), xviii n.

"Look at the map": Henry Clinton, September 24, 1776, Henry Clinton Papers, Clements Library.

"The position which the rebels": Sir Henry Clinton, *The American Rebellion,* William B. Willcox, ed. (New Haven, Conn.: Yale University Press, 1954), 41.

attack would be made: Ibid.

British troops: See Richard Holmes, *Redcoat: The British Soldier in the Age of the Horse and Musket* (New York: Norton, 2001); J. A. Houlding, *Fit for Service: The Training of the British Army,*

1715–1795 (Oxford, Eng.: Clarendon Press, 1981); and Sylvia R. Frey, *The British Soldier in America* (Austin: University of Texas, 1981).

"Among the regular troops": London Chronicle, October 12–15, 1776.

"We dragged on": Eric Robson, ed., *Letters from America, 1773–1780* (Manchester, Eng.: Manchester University Press, 1951), 33.

"an impudent rebel": Henry P. Johnston, *The Campaign of 1776 Around New York and Brooklyn* (Brooklyn: Long Island Historical Society, 1878), Part I, 178.

"The commander-in-chief": Sir Henry Clinton, *The American Rebellion*, William B. Willcox, ed. (New Haven, Conn.: Yale University Press, 1954), 42.

"I found by fair daylight": Henry P. Johnston, *The Campaign of 1776 Around New York and Brooklyn* (Brooklyn: Long Island Historical Society, 1878), Part II, 235.

"A little before day": Personal Recollections of Captain Enoch Anderson: An Officer of the Delaware Regiments in the Revolutionary War, XVI (Wilmington, Del.: The Historical Society of Delaware, 1896), 21.

"a smart engagement": Moses Little to his son, September 1, 1776, in Henry P. Johnston, *The Campaign of 1776 Around New York and Brooklyn* (Brooklyn: Long Island Historical Society), Part II, 43.

"battle in true English taste": George F. Scheer and Hugh F. Rankin, *Rebels and Redcoats* (New York: Da Capo Press, 1957), 165.

"Our men stood it amazingly well": Henry P. Johnston, *The Campaign of 1776 Around New York and Brooklyn* (Brooklyn: Long Island Historical Society, 1878), Part I, 168.

"I saw one man": *Personal Recollections of Captain Enoch Anderson*, XVI (Wilmington, Del.: Historical Society of Delaware, 1896), 21.

"We had a skirmishing": James Grant to General Harvey, September 2, 1776, James Grant Papers, LOC.

"I called to my men": Letter of Captain William Dancey to his mother, Mrs. Dancey. Dancey, August 30, 1776, Delaware Historical Society.

"Their fear of the Hessian troops": Rodney Atwood, *The Hessians: Mercenaries from Hessen: Kissel in the American Revolution* (Cambridge, Eng.: Cambridge

University Press, 1980), 68.

"The last I heard": George F. Scheer and Hugh F. Rankin, eds., *Rebels and Redcoats* (New York: Da Capo Press, 1957), 167.

"They all wished": Joseph Plumb Martin, *A Narrative of a Revolutionary Soldier* (New York: Penguin, 2001), 22.

"I saw a lieutenant": Ibid., 23.

"quit yourselves": George F. Scheer and Hugh F. Rankin, *Rebels and Redcoats* (New York: Da Capo Press, 1957), 166.

"For the batteries began": Thomas W. Field, *Battle of Long Island* (Brooklyn: Long Island Historical Society, 1869), 365.

"determined countenance": Henry P. Johnston, *The Campaign of 1776 Around New York and Brooklyn* (Brooklyn: Long Island Historical Society, 1878), Part I, 168.

"make the best": Thomas W. Field, *Battle of Long Island* (Brooklyn: Long Island Historical Society, 1869), 396.

"like a wolf": Charles G. Stevenson and Irene Wilson, *The Battle of Long Island* (Brooklyn: Brooklyn Bicentennial Commission, 1975), 14.

"Good God, what brave fellows": George F.

Scheer and Hugh F. Rankin, eds., *Rebels and Redcoats* (New York: Da Capo Press, 1957), 168.

"It is impossible": John C. Dann, ed., *The Revolution Remembered: Eyewitness Accounts of the War for Independence* (Chicago: University of Chicago Press, 1980), 50.

Lord Stirling, finding himself: Thomas W. Field, *Battle of Long Island* (Brooklyn: Long Island Historical Society, 1869), 396–397.

"should be pushed": Sir Henry Clinton, *The American Rebellion*, William B. Willcox, ed. (New Haven, Conn.: Yale University Press, 1954), 41n.

"I had at the moment": Ibid., 43.

"O Doleful!": Philip Vickers Fithian, August 27, 1776, in *Philip Vickers Fithian Journal*, Robert Greenhalgh Albion and Leonidas Dodson, eds. (Princeton, N.J.: Princeton University Press, 1934), 218.

"You will be glad": James Grant to Edward Harvey, September 2, 1776, James Grant Papers, LOC.

"beyond our expectations": Charles Knowles Bolton, ed., *Letters of Hugh Earl Percy from Boston and New York 1774–1776* (Boston: Gregg Press, 1972), 68.

behaved with greater spirit: Eric Robson, ed., *Letters from America, 1773–1780* (Manchester, Eng.: Manchester University Press, 1951), 33.

"They could not run": Ambrose Serle, August 27, 1776, in *The American Journal of Ambrose Serle, 1776–1778,* Edward H. Tatum, Jr., ed. (San Marino, Calif.: Huntington Library, 1940), 79.

"The behavior": K. G. Davies, ed., *Documents of the American Revolution, 1770–1783,* Colonial Office Series, XII (Dublin: Irish University Press, 1976), 218.

"the heap": Henry P. Johnston, *The Campaign of 1776 Around New York and Brooklyn* (Brooklyn: Long Island Historical Society, 1878), Part II, 34.

"the most scurrilous": Thomas W. Field, *Battle of Long Island* (Brooklyn: Long Island Historical Society, 1869), 360.

"a great number": Jabez Fitch, August 27, 1776, in *The New York Diary of Lieutenant Jabez Fitch,* W. H. W. Sabine, ed. (New York: Colburn & Tegg, 1954), 31.

"I sat with him": Ibid., August 28, 1776, 34.

"The Hessians": Henry P. Johnston, *The Campaign of 1776 Around New York and Brooklyn* (Brooklyn: Long Island

Historical Society, 1878), Part I, 186, 206.

"was so good": Jabez Fitch, August 28, 1776, in *The New York Diary of Lieutenant Jabez Fitch*, W. H. W. Sabine, ed. (New York: Colburn & Tegg, 1954), 34.

"They could not have been taken": Bruce E. Burgoyne, ed., *The Hesse-Cassel Mirbach Regiment in the American Revolution* (Bowie, Md.: Heritage Books, 1998), 54.

"And the distressed": Philip Vickers Fithian, August 27, 1776, in *Philip Vickers Fithian Journal*, Robert Greenhalgh Albion and Leonidas Dodson, eds. (Princeton, N.J.: Princeton University Press, 1934), 219.

"The faces": Alexander Graydon, *Memoirs of His Own Time*, John Stockton Littell, ed. (Philadelphia: Lindsay & Blakiston, 1846), 164.

"through the goodness": Joseph Hodgkins to Sarah Hodgkins, August 28, 1776, in Herbert T. Wade and Robert A. Lively, eds., *The Glorious Cause: The Adventures of Two Company Officers in Washington's Army* (Princeton, N.J.: Princeton University Press, 1958), 215.

"Afternoon, at three": Philip Vickers Fithian, August 28, 1776, *Philip Vickers Fithian Journal*, Robert Greenhalgh Albion and Leonidas Dodson, eds. (Princeton, N.J.: Princeton University Press, 1934), 220.

boom of cannon: Ewald Shewkirk Diary, in Henry P. Johnston, *The Campaign of 1776 Around New York and Brooklyn* (Brooklyn: Long Island Historical Society, 1878), Part II, 114.

"hard enough to break": Joseph Plumb Martin, *A Narrative of a Revolutionary Soldier* (New York: Penguin, 2001), 22.

"distressed": George Washington to John Hancock, August 29, 1776, in *PGW,* VI, 156.

"Nor can I ascertain": George Washington to John Hancock, August 29, 1776, in *PGW,* VI, 155.

"get up": Thomas W. Field, *Battle of Long Island* (Brooklyn: Long Island Historical Society, 1869), 396.

"we have many battalions": Henry P. Johnston, *The Campaign of 1776 Around New York and Brooklyn* (Brooklyn: Long Island Historical Society, 1878), Part I, 218.

"ceremony": Ibid., 219, n. 1.

"It was submitted": Council of War, August

29, 1776, in *PGW,* VI, 153.

"As it was suddenly proposed": John Morin Scott to John Jay, September 6, 1776, in Henry P. Johnston, *The Campaign of 1776 Around New York and Brooklyn* (Brooklyn: Long Island Historical Society, 1878), Part II, 37.

"it became a serious consideration": Thomas W. Field, *Battle of Long Island* (Brooklyn: Long Island Historical Society, 1869), 398.

"under arms with packs": Joseph Hodgkins to Sarah Hodgkins, August 31, 1776, in *This Glorious Cause,* Herbert T. Wade and Robert A. Lively, eds. (Princeton, N.J.: Princeton University Press, 1958), 216.

"Several noncupative wills": Alexander Graydon, *Memoirs of His Own Time,* John Stockton Littell, ed. (Philadelphia: Lindsay & Blakiston, 1846), 166.

"The thing was conducted": Tench Tilghman to his father, September 3, 1776, in Henry P. Johnston, *The Campaign of 1776 Around New York and Brooklyn* (Brooklyn: Long Island Historical Society, 1878), Part II, 85.

"flashed upon my mind": Alexander Graydon, *Memoirs of His Own Time,* John Stockton Littell, ed. (Philadel-

phia: Lindsay & Blakiston, 1846), 166–167.

"To move so large a body": "Major Tallmadge's Account of the Battles of Long Island and White Plains," in Henry P. Johnston, *The Campaign of 1776 Around New York and Brooklyn* (Brooklyn: Long Island Historical Society, 1878), Part II, 78.

"And tedious was the operation": Thomas W. Field, *Battle of Long Island* (Brooklyn: Long Island Historical Society, 1869), 519.

"We were strictly": Joseph Plumb Martin, *A Narrative of a Revolutionary Soldier* (New York: Penguin, 2001), 26.

"As one regiment": "Major Tallmadge's Account of the Battles of Long Island and White Plains," in Henry P. Johnston, *The Campaign of 1776 Around New York and Brooklyn* (Brooklyn: Long Island Historical Society, 1878), Part II, 78.

"If the explosion": Alexander Graydon, *Memoirs of His Own Time,* John Stockton Littell, ed. (Philadelphia: Lindsay & Blakiston, 1846), 167.

"is arrayed": Ibid.

Major Alexander Scammell: George F. Scheer and Hugh F. Rankin, eds.,

Rebels and Redcoats: (New York: Da Capo Press, 1957), 170–171.

"without delay": Alexander Graydon, *Memoirs of His Own Time,* John Stockton Littell, ed. (Philadelphia: Lindsay & Blakiston, 1846), 167.

"Good God!": George F. Scheer and Hugh F. Rankin, eds., *Rebels and Redcoats* (New York: Da Capo Press, 1957), 171.

"trying business": Alexander Graydon, *Memoirs of His Own Time,* John Stockton Littell, ed. (Philadelphia: Lindsay & Blakiston, 1846), 168.

"had the good fortune": George F. Scheer and Hugh F. Rankin, eds., *Rebels and Redcoats* (New York: Da Capo Press, 1957), 171.

"could scarcely discern": "Major Tallmadge's Account of the Battles of Long Island and White Plains," in Henry P. Johnston, *The Campaign of 1776 Around New York and Brooklyn* (Brooklyn: Long Island Historical Society, 1878), Part II, 78.

"It may be supposed": Alexander Graydon, *Memoirs of His Own Time,* John Stockton Littell, ed. (Philadelphia: Lindsay & Blakiston, 1846), 168.

saw Washington on the ferry: "Major

Tallmadge's Account of the Battles of Long Island and White Plains," in Henry P. Johnston, *The Campaign of 1776 Around New York and Brooklyn* (Brooklyn: Long Island Historical Society, 1878), Part II, 79.

"And in less than an hour": Alexander Graydon, *Memoirs of His Own Time,* John Stockton Littell, ed. (Philadelphia: Lindsay & Blakiston, 1846), 168.

"In the morning": "Journals of Lieutenant Colonel Stephen Kemble, 1773–1789," *Collections of the New-York Historical Society* (1883), 86.

"We cannot yet account": James Grant to Edward Harvey, September 2, 1776, James Grant Papers, LOC.

"They feel severely": Lord Percy to his father, September 1, 1776, in Charles Knowles Bolton, ed., *Letters of Hugh Earl Percy from Boston and New York, 1774–1776* (Boston: Gregg Press, 1972), 69.

"This business": Ibid., 71.

"This and the parts adjacent": Ambrose Serle, September 1, 1776, in *The American Journal of Ambrose Serle, 1776–1778*, Edward H. Tatum, Jr., ed. (San Marino, Calif.: Huntington Library, 1940), 86.

"behaved very ill": Ibid., August 30, 1776, 84.

"very ably effected": Sir Henry Clinton, *The American Rebellion,* William B. Willcox, ed. (New Haven, Conn.: Yale University Press, 1954), 44.

"particularly glorious": Charles Stedman, *The History of the Origin, Progress, and Termination of the American War,* I (New York: Arno Press, 1969), 197.

"most completely": Ibid., 198.

"Never pursues": "Journals of Captain John Montresor," *Collections of the New-York Historical Society* (1881), 310.

"flying in such a panic": Sir Henry Clinton, *The American Rebellion,* William B. Willcox, ed. (New Haven, Conn.: Yale University Press, 1954), 43.

"judged it prudent": Ibid., 44.

"It was apparent": Troyer Steele Anderson, *The Command of the Howe Brothers During the American Revolution* (New York: Oxford University Press, 1936), 134.

"fully controverted": *London Morning Chronicle,* October 14, 1776.

"enliven our countenances": Edward Gibbon to Dorothea Gibbon, October 24, 1776, in *The Letters of Edward Gibbon,* II (New York: Macmillan, 1956), 117.

"great satisfaction": London Morning Chronicle, October 15, 1776.

"unfortunate beginning": Josiah Bartlett to Nathaniel Folsom, September 2, 1776, in *Letters of Delegates to Congress*, V, Paul H. Smith, ed. (Washington, D.C.: Library of Congress, 1979), 91.

"disaster": John Adams to Abigail Adams, September 4, 1776, in *Adams Family Correspondence*, II, L. H. Butterfield, ed. (Cambridge, Mass.: Harvard University Press, 1963), 118.

"All in solicitude": The Literary Diary of Ezra Stiles: President of Yale College, II Franklin Bowditch Dexter, ed. (New York: Scribner, 1901), 51.

"a masterpiece": New England Chronicle, September 19, 1776.

"The manner": Virginia Gazette, September 14, 1776.

"Providence favored us": New England Chronicle, September 19, 1776.

"We have thought": Massachusetts Spy, October 23, 1776.

"It was a surprising change": Ewald Shewkirk Diary, in Henry P. Johnston, *The Campaign of 1776 Around New York and Brooklyn* (Brooklyn: Long Island Historical Society), Part II, 115.

"A hard day this": Personal Recollections of

Captain Enoch Anderson (Wilmington, Del.: Historical Society of Delaware, 1896), 22.

"entirely unfit": George Washington to John Hancock, August 31, 1776, in *PGW,* VI, 177.

"much hurried": Ibid., 178.

6. FORTUNE FROWNS

"I have only time": Joseph Reed to Esther Reed, September 2, 1776, NYHS.

"a mere point": Joseph Reed to Charles Pettit, August 4, 1776, in *Life and Correspondence of Joseph Reed,* I, William B. Reed, ed. (Philadelphia: Lindsay & Blakiston, 1847), 212.

"dispensations of Providence": Joseph Reed to Esther Reed, September 2, 1776, NYHS.

"But only consider a minute": Joseph Hodgkins to Sarah Hodgkins, September 5, 1776, *This Glorious Cause: The Adventures of Two Company Officers in Washington's Army,* Herbert T. Wade and Robert A. Lively, eds. (Princeton, N.J.: Princeton University Press, 1958), 217.

"I had my sleeve button shot": Ibid., 219.

"I fear General Washington": Henry P. Johnston, *The Campaign of 1776 Around New York and Brooklyn* (Brooklyn: Long Island Historical Society, 1878), Part I, 227–228.

"who when fortune frowns": Henry Knox to Lucy Knox, September 5, 1776, NYHS.

"Now is the time": George Washington, General Orders, September 2, 1776, in *PGW,* VI, 199.

"The militia": George Washington to John Hancock, September 2, 1776, in *PGW,* VI, 199.

"stand as winter quarters": Ibid., 200.

"desirous of an accommodation": Josiah Bartlett to William Whipple, September 3, 1776, in Paul H. Smith, ed., *Letters of Delegates to Congress, 1774–1789,* V (Washington, D.C.: Library of Congress, 1979), 94.

"no damage": John Hancock to George Washington, September 3, 1776, in *PGW,* VI, 207.

"no doubt": Ibid.

"leave no stone": George Washington to William Heath, September 5, 1776, in *PGW,* VI, 224.

"We think": Joseph Reed to Esther Reed, September 6, 1776, in William B.

Reed, ed., *Life and Correspondence of Joseph Reed*, I (Philadelphia: Lindsay & Blakiston, 1847), I, 230–231.

"When I look round": Ibid.

"I think we have": Nathanael Greene to George Washington, September 5, 1776, in *PGW*, VI, 222.

"'Tis our business": Ibid., 223

"I give it as my opinion": Ibid.

"put nothing to the hazard": George Washington to John Hancock, September 8, 1776, in *PGW*, VI, 251.

"Had I been left": George Washington to Lund Washington, October 6, 1776, in *PGW*, VI, 494.

"On every side": George Washington to John Hancock, September 8, 1776, in *PGW*, VI, 248–251.

"We should on all occasions": Ibid.

"On the other hand": Ibid.

"a pleasing circumstance": Ambrose Serle, September 6, 1776, in *The American Journal of Ambrose Serle, 1776–1778*, Edward H. Tatum, Jr., ed. (San Marino, Calif.: Huntington Library, 1940), 94.

"so critical and dangerous": Officers to George Washington, September 11, 1776, in *PGW*, VI, 279.

"It is desirable": Henry Steele Commager

and Richard B. Morris, eds., *The Spirit of 'Seventy-Six,* I (Indianapolis: Bobbs-Merrill, 1958), 453.

"grand military exertion": Joseph Reed to Esther Reed, September 14, 1776, in *Life and Correspondence of Joseph Reed,* William B. Reed, ed. (Philadelphia: Lindsay & Blakiston, 1847), I, 235.

"a moment longer": Paul H. Smith, ed., *Letters of Delegates to Congress,* V, 97, n. 1.

"We are now taking": George Washington to John Hancock, September 14, 1776, in *PGW,* VI, 308–309.

"lined with men": Sir Henry Clinton, *The American Rebellion: Sir Henry Clinton's Narrative of His Campaigns, 1775–1782,* William B. Willcox, ed. (New Haven, Conn.: Yale University Press, 1954), 45.

"an entire dependence": *Diary of Frederick Mackenzie,* I (Cambridge, Mass.: Harvard University Press, 1930), 45.

"We will alter your tune": Joseph Plumb Martin, *A Narrative of a Revolutionary Soldier* (New York: Penguin, 2001), 30.

"I think if we stand": Henry P. Johnston, *The Campaign of 1776 Around New York and Brooklyn* (Brooklyn: Long Island Historical Society, 1878), Part II, 70–71.

"as distinctly as though": Joseph Plumb Martin, *A Narrative of a Revolutionary Soldier* (New York: Penguin), 30.

"We lay very quiet": Ibid., 31.

"When they came": Ibid., 30.

"by damning themselves": Francis, Lord Rawdon, to Francis, Earl of Huntingdon, September 23, 1776, in *Report on the Manuscripts of the late Reginald Rawdon Hastings,* III (London: Her Majesty's Stationery Office, 1930–1947), 183.

"So terrible": Ambrose Serle, September 15, 1776, in *The American Journal of Ambrose Serle, 1776–1778,* Edward H. Tatum, Jr., ed. (San Marino, Calif.: Huntington Library, 1940), 104.

"frog's leap": Joseph Plumb Martin, *A Narrative of a Revolutionary Soldier* (New York: Penguin, 2001), 31.

"but they mostly overshot": Henry P. Johnston, *The Campaign of 1776 Around New York and Brooklyn* (Brooklyn: Long Island Historical Society, 1878), Part II, 71–72.

"happy to escape": Francis, Lord Rawdon, to Francis, Earl of Huntingdon, September 23, 1776, *Report on the Manuscripts of the late Reginald Rawdon Hastings,* III (London: Her Majesty's

Stationery Office, 1930–1947), 184.

"I saw a Hessian": Journal of Bartholomew James, September 15, 1776, in *Naval Documents of the American Revolution,* William James Morgan, ed., VI (Washington, D.C.: U.S. Department of the Navy, 1972), 841.

"flying in every direction": George Washington to John Hancock, September 16, 1776, in *PGW,* VI, 313.

"Take the walls!": George F. Scheer and Hugh F. Rankin, *Rebels and Redcoats* (New York: Da Capo Press, 1957), 182.

"Are these the men": William Heath, *Heath's Memoirs of the American War* (New York: A. Wessels Co., 1904), 70.

"The demons of fear": Joseph Plumb Martin, *A Narrative of a Revolutionary Soldier* (New York: Penguin, 2001), 32.

"Nothing could equal": Ambrose Serle, September 15, 1776, in *The American Journal of Ambrose Serle, 1776–1778,* Edward H. Tatum, Jr., ed. (San Marino, Calif.: Huntington Library, 1940), 104.

"Thus this town": Ibid., 105.

"Having myself been a volunteer": Henry P. Johnston, *The Campaign of 1776 Around New York and Brooklyn*

(Brooklyn: Long Island Historical Society, 1878), Part I, 89.

"disgraceful and dastardly": George Washington to John Hancock, September 6, 1776, in *PGW,* VI, 314.

"Fellow's and Parson's whole brigade": Nathanael Greene to Nicholas Cooke, September 17, 1776, in *PNG,* I, 300.

"The wounds received": William Heath, *Heath's Memoirs of the American War* (New York: A. Wessels Co., 1904), 70.

"The men were blamed": Benjamin Trumbull, "Journal of the Campaign at New York, 1776–1777," *Collections of the Connecticut Historical Society,* VII (1899), 195.

"We ought to have men": Henry Knox to William Knox, September 23, 1776, NYHS.

Mrs. Robert Murray: Henry P. Johnston, *The Campaign of 1776 Around New York and Brooklyn* (Brooklyn: Long Island Historical Society, 1878), Part I, 239.

"Mrs. Murray treated them:" Ibid.

Washington sent Reed cantering: Joseph Reed to Esther Reed, September 17, 1776, NYHS.

"I have sent out": George Washington to John Hancock, September 16, 1776, in

PGW, VI, 314.

"I went down to our most advanced": Joseph Reed to Esther Reed, September 17, 1776, NYHS.

"I never felt such a sensation": Ibid.

"to recover that military ardor": George Washington to Patrick Henry, October 5, 1776, in *PGW,* VI, 479.

Washington ordered a counterattack: George Washington to John Hancock, September 18, 1776, in *PGW,* VI, 331.

"rushed down the hill": Joseph Hodgkins to Sarah Hodgkins, September 30, 1776, in *This Glorious Cause,* Herbert T. Wade and Robert A. Lively, eds. (Princeton, N.J.: Princeton University Press, 1958), 222.

Knowlton's encircling move: George Washington to John Hancock, September 18, 1776, in *PGW,* VI, 331.

"[We] drove the dogs": Henry Phelps Johnston, *The Battle of Harlem Heights, September 16, 1776* (New York: Macmillan, 1897), 155.

"The pursuit of a flying enemy": Joseph Reed to Esther Reed, September 1776, in *Life and Correspondence of Joseph Reed,* William B. Reed, ed. (Philadelphia: Lindsay & Blakiston, 1847), 238.

"They were seen to carry off": Joseph

Hodgkins to Sarah Hodgkins, September 30, 1776, in *This Glorious Cause,* Herbert T. Wade and Robert A. Lively, eds. (Princeton, N.J.: Princeton University Press, 1958), 222.

"greatest loss": Joseph Reed to Esther Reed, September 17, 1776, NYHS; George Washington to John Washington, September 22, 1776, in *PGW,* VI, 374.

"a pretty sharp skirmish": George Washington to Philip Schuyler, September 20, 1776, in *PGW,* VI, 357.

"They find that if they stick": Henry Knox to William Knox, September 23, 1776, NYHS.

"Our people beat the enemy": Nathanael Greene to William Ellery, October 4, 1776, in *PNG,* I, 307.

"impetuosity": Sir Henry Clinton, *The American Rebellion,* William B. Willcox, ed. (New Haven, Conn.: Yale University Press, 1954), 46.

"as if they were a thousand": Tench Tilghman, *Memoir of Lieutenant Colonel Tench Tilghman* (New York: Arno Press, 1971), 143.

"If we cannot fight them": Joseph Reed to Esther Reed, October 11, 1776, in *Life and Correspondence of Joseph Reed,* I, William B. Reed, ed. (Philadelphia:

Lindsay & Blakiston, 1847), 244.

"many fair houses": Ambrose Serle, September 19, 1776, in *The American Journal of Ambrose Serle, 1776–1778*, Edward H. Tatum, Jr., ed. (San Marino, Calif.: Huntington Library, 1940), 109.

"The shore of the Island": Frederick Mackenzie, *Diary of Frederick Mackenzie*, I (Cambridge, Mass.: Harvard University Press, 1930), 66.

"The infinite pains": Ambrose Serle, September 19, 1776, in *The American Journal of Ambrose Serle, 1776–1778*, Edward H. Tatum, Jr., ed. (San Marino, Calif.: Huntington Library, 1940), 109.

"judge for themselves": Troyer Steele Anderson, *The Command of the Howe Brothers During the American Revolution* (New York: Oxford University Press, 1936), 160.

"pyramid of fire": Frederick Mackenzie, *Diary of Frederick Mackenzie*, I (Cambridge, Mass.: Harvard University Press, 1930), 60.

"The sick, the aged": Ibid.

"thrown into the flames": Ibid., 59.

"There is no doubt": Ibid., 59–60.

"lurking": Henry Steele Commager and

665

Richard B. Morris, eds., *The Spirit of 'Seventy-Six*, I (Indianapolis: Bobbs-Merrill, 1958), 475.

"The Yankees [New York Loyalists]": James Grant to Richard Rigby, September 24, 1776, James Grant Papers, LOC.

called it an accident: George Washington to John Hancock, September 22, 1776, in *PGW,* VI, 369.

"Providence, or some good honest fellow": George Washington to Lund Washington, October 6, 1776, in *PGW,* VI, 495.

"New England man": *New York Gazette,* September 30, 1776.

"a person named Nathan Hales": Frederick Mackenzie, *Diary of Frederick Mackenzie* (Cambridge, Mass.: Harvard University Press, 1930), 61.

"too frank and open": Henry Phelps Johnston, *Nathan Hale, 1776* (New Haven, Conn.: Yale University Press, 1914), 106.

"reflect, and do nothing": Ibid., 107.

"I only regret that I have but one life": Henry Steele Commager and Richard B. Morris, eds., *The Spirit of 'Seventy-Six,* I (Indianapolis: Bobbs-Merrill, 1958), 476.

"We hung up a rebel": I. N. Phelps Stokes,

The Iconography of Manhattan Island, 1498–1909, I (New York: Arno Press, 1967), 1025.

"A spirit of desertion": Joseph Reed to Congress, in William B. Reed, ed., *Life and Correspondence of Joseph Reed,* I (Philadelphia: Lindsay & Blakiston, 1847), 240.

Reed had seen a soldier running: Joseph Reed to Esther Reed, in William B. Reed, ed., *Life and Correspondence of Joseph Reed,* I (Philadelphia: Lindsay & Blakiston, 1847), I, 238.

"I should have shot him": PGW, VI, 367, n. 3.

"presenting his firelock": George Washington, General Orders, September 22, 1776, in *PGW,* VI, 366.

"suffer death without mercy": George Washington, General Orders, September 23, 1776, in *PGW,* VI, 375.

"To attempt to introduce discipline": Joseph Reed to Esther Reed, October 11, 1776, in William B. Reed, ed., *Life and Correspondence of Joseph Reed,* I (Philadelphia: Lindsay & Blakiston, 1847), 243.

"Unless some speedy, and effectual measures": George Washington to John Hancock, September 23, 1776, in *PGW,* VI, 394.

"fly hastily and cheerfully": Ibid.

"To place any dependence": Ibid., 396.

"lust after plunder": Ibid., 399.

"atrocious offenses": Ibid., 398.

"Such is my situation": George Washington to Lund Washington, September 30, 1776, in *PGW,* VI, 441–442.

"That in the parlor": Ibid., 442.

"To our surprise and mortification": George Washington to John Hancock, October 8–9, 1776, in *PGW,* VI, 507.

"little more to fear": Nathanael Greene to Nicholas Cooke, October 11, 1776, in *PNG,* I, 315.

"Tweedledum business": Sir Henry Clinton, July 6, 1777, *The American Rebellion,* William B. Willcox, ed. (New Haven, Conn.: Yale University Press, 1954), 49, n. 23.

"their former scheme": George Washington to Nicholas Cooke, October 12–13, 1776, in *PGW,* VI, 546.

"absurd interference": John R. Alden, *General Charles Lee: Traitor or Patriot?* (Baton Rouge: Louisiana State University Press, 1951), 142.

"retained as long as possible": George Washington, Council of War, October 16, 1776, in *PGW,* VI, 576.

"obstruct effectually": William James Morgan, ed., *Naval Documents of the*

American Revolution, VI (Washington, D.C.: U.S. Department of the Navy, 1972) 1221.

"As the movements of the enemy": George Washington, General Orders, October 17, 1776, in *PGW,* VI, 582.

"one of the others gave it a shove": Joseph Plumb Martin, *A Narrative of a Revolutionary Soldier* (New York: Penguin, 2001), 46.

"Oh! The anxiety of mind": Henry Steele Commager and Richard B. Morris, eds., *The Spirit of 'Seventy-Six,* I (Indianapolis: Bobbs-Merrill, 1958), 487.

enemy dead: George Athan Billias, *General John Glover and His Marblehead Mariners* (New York: Holt, 1960), 121.

"The sun shone bright": William Heath, *Heath's Memoirs of the American War* (New York: A. Wessels Co., 1904), 88.

"Yonder is the ground": George F. Scheer and Hugh F. Rankin, *Rebels and Redcoats* (New York: Da Capo Press, 1957), 194.

"The air and hills smoked": Peter Force, *American Archives,* III (Washington, D.C.: M. St. Clair and Peter Force, 1837–1853), 474.

Washington ordered more men: PGW, VII, fn. 3, 52–53.

"Opinions here are various": Joseph Reed to Esther Reed, November 6, 1776, in William B. Reed, ed., *Life and Correspondence of Joseph Reed*, I (Philadelphia: Lindsay & Blakiston, 1847), 248.

"Others, and a great majority": Ibid.

"without attempting something more": George Washington to John Hancock, November 6, 1776, in *PGW*, VII, 97.

"If we cannot prevent": George Washington to Nathanael Greene, November 8, 1776, in *PGW*, VII, 115–116.

"His Excellency General Washington": Nathanael Greene to Henry Knox, November [17], 1776, in *PNG*, I, 351.

"The movements and designs": George Washington to John Hancock, November 14, 1776, in *PGW*, VII, 154.

"No wind for some days past": Frederick Mackenzie, *Diary of Frederick Mackenzie*, I (Cambridge, Mass.: Harvard University Press, 1930), 99.

"probably be against Fort Washington": Ibid.

"the first object": Ibid., 95.

William Diamond: Ibid.

"dreaming, sleepy-headed": Ambrose Serle, December 8, 1776, *The American Journal of Ambrose Serle, 1776–1778*, Edward H. Tatum, ed. (San Marino,

Calif.: Huntington Library, 1940), 156.

"It is easy to see": Ibid., November 10, 1776, 138–139.

"of much service to General Howe": Frederick Mackenzie, *Diary of Frederick Mackenzie,* I (Cambridge, Mass.: Harvard University Press, 1930), 97.

"from the general appearance": Ibid., 105.

"Sir, if I rightly understand": PGW, VII, n. 1,162.

"it being late at night": George Washington to John Hancock, November 16, 1776, in *PGW,* VII, 163.

"what was best to be done": Nathanael Greene to Henry Knox, November [17], 1776, in *PNG,* I, 352.

"There we all stood": Ibid.

"every obstacle was swept aside": "The Capture of Fort Washington, New York. Described by Cpt. Andreas Wiederhold," *Pennsylvania Magazine of History and Biography,* XXIII (1899), 96.

"At last, however": Henry P. Johnston, *The Battle of Harlem Heights, September 16, 1776* (New York: The Macmillan Company, 1897), 230.

"surmounted every difficulty": James Grant to Richard Rigby, November 22, 1776,

James Grant Papers, LOC.

"Before I was near the fort": John Adlum, *Memoirs of the Life of John Adlum in the Revolutionary War*, Howard H. Peckham, ed. (Chicago: Caxton Club, 1968), 69–70.

"indifferently clothed": Frederick Mackenzie, *Diary of Frederick Mackenzie*, I (Cambridge, Mass.: Harvard University Press, 1930), 111–112.

"They had been pretty well pelted": James Grant to Richard Rigby, November 22, 1776, James Grant Papers, LOC.

"The carnage would then have been dreadful": Frederick Mackenzie, *Diary of Frederick Mackenzie*, I (Cambridge, Mass.: Harvard University Press, 1930), 110.

"I am wearied almost to death": George Washington to John Washington, November 6–9, 1776, in *PGW,* VII, 105.

"I feel mad, vexed, sick": Nathanael Greene to Henry Knox, Nov. [17], 1776, in *PNG,* I, 352.

"I must entreat": George H. Moore, *The Treason of Charles Lee* (Port Washington, N.Y.: Kennikat Press, 1970), 42.

"Draw off the garrison": Ibid.

"Had I the powers": Ibid.

"why would you be over-persuaded": Charles

Lee to George Washington, November 19, 1776, in *PGW,* VII, 187.

7. DARKEST HOUR

"dead flat": George Washington to Charles Lee, November 21, 1776, in *PGW,* VII, 193.

"I saw him . . . at the head": Arthur S. Lefkowitz, *The Long Retreat: The Calamitous American Defense of New Jersey, 1776* (Metuchen, N.J.: Upland Press, 1998), 82.

"A deportment so firm": Ibid.

"broken and disspirited": George Washington to Charles Lee, in *PGW,* VII, 193.

dictated to Joseph Reed: Ibid., 195.

"most earnestly": George Washington to Joseph Reed, November 30, 1776, in *PGW,* VII, 238, n. 1.

"My neck does not feel": William S. Stryker, *Battles of Trenton and Princeton* (Trenton: Old Barracks Association, 2001), 5.

"critical state of our affairs": John Hancock to George Washington, November 24, 1776, in *PGW,* VII, 203.

"divided and lethargic": Thomas Mifflin to

George Washington, November 26, 1776, in *PGW,* VII, 219.

"The sufferings we endured": William M. Dwyer, *The Day Is Ours: November 1776–January 1977* (New York: Viking Press, 1983), 41.

"I can only say": Worthington Chauncey Ford, ed., *Correspondence and Journals of Samuel Blachley Webb, 1772–1775,* I (Lancaster, Pa.: Wickersham Press, 1893), 172.

"Common Sense and Col. Snarl": PNG, I, 330.

"passion of patriotism": David Freeman Hawke, *Paine* (New York: Harper & Row, 1974), 59.

"These are the times": Ibid.

"safe and secure route": George Washington to Charles Lee, November 24, 1776, in *PGW,* VII, 210.

"The fact is": Henry Steele Commager and Richard B. Morris, *The Spirit of 'Seventy-Six,* I (Indianapolis: Bobbs-Merrill, 1958), 497.

"This, in all probability": Sir Henry Clinton, *The American Rebellion: Sir Henry Clinton's Narrative of His Campaigns, 1775–1782,* William B. Willcox, ed. (New Haven, Conn.: Yale University Press, 1954), 55.

true eighteenth-century English artistocrat: Franklin Wickwire and Mary Wickwire, *Cornwallis: The American Adventure* (Boston: Houghton Mifflin, 1970), 8.

lost sight in one eye: Ibid., 7.

"I love that army": Ibid., 75.

"All the army marched": Archibald Robertson, *Archibald Robertson: His Diaries and Sketches in America, 1762–1780* (New York: New York Public Library, 1930), 114.

"The enemy gave us": George Washington to William Heath, November 29, 1776, in *PGW,* VII, 227–228.

"My former letters": George Washington to Charles Lee, November 27, 1776, in *PGW,* VII, 224.

"I received your most obliging": Charles Lee to Joseph Reed, November 24, 1776, in *PGW,* VII, 237, n. 1.

"the enclosed was put into my hands": George Washington to Joseph Reed, November 30, 1776, in *PGW,* VII, 237.

"I was hurt not because": George Washington to Joseph Reed, June 14, 1777, *The Writings of George Washington, From the Original Manuscript Sources 1745–1799,* VIII, John C. Fitzpatrick, ed. (Washington, D.C.: U.S. Govern-

ment Printing Office, 1933), 60.

"very good intelligence": *Pennsylvania Journal,* November 27, 1776.

"much alarm": Paul H. Smith, ed., *Letters of Delegates to Congress, 1774–1789,* V (Washington, D.C.: Library of Congress, 1979), 543.

"torpor": Ibid., 553.

"Oh how I feel for Washington": Ibid., 558.

"I will not however despair": George Washington to William Livingston, November 30, 1776, in *PGW,* VII, 236.

"Two brigades left us": PNG, I, 362.

"or your arrival may be too late": George Washington to Charles Lee, December 1, 1776, in *PGW,* VII, 249.

"The enemy are fast advancing": George Washington to John Hancock, December 1, 1776, in *PGW,* VII, 244.

"totally inadequate": Ibid.

"It being impossible": George Washington to John Hancock, December 1, 1776, in *PGW,* VII, 245.

"When we left Brunswick": PNG, I, 362.

"The inhabitants of Princeton": Paul H. Smith, ed., *Letters of Delegates to Congress, 1774–1789,* V (Washington, D.C.: Library of Congress, 1979), 581.

"I have not heard a word": George Washington to John Hancock, December 3,

1776, in *PGW,* VII, 256.

"reap the benefit": Peter Force, American Archives, 4th Series, V (Washington, D.C.: M. St. Clair and Peter Force, 1837–1853), 927–28.

"You can come down": William M. Dwyer, *The Day Is Ours: November 1776–January 1777, An Inside View of the Battles of Trenton and Princeton* (New York: Viking Press, 1983), 77.

"to act at his own discretion": Charles Stedman, *The History of the Origin, Progress, and Termination of the American War,* I (New York: Arno Press, 1969), 243.

"a cloud of dust": Captain Johann Ewald, *Diary of the American War: A Hessian Journal,* Joseph P. Tustin, ed. (New Haven, Conn.: Yale University Press, 1979), 18.

"We do not want to lose any men": Ibid.

"of ending the war amicably": Ibid., 25.

"It is said by some persons": I. N. Phelps Stokes, *The Iconography of Manhattan Island, 1498–1909,* I (New York: Arno Press, 1969), 1040.

"Scandalous behavior": Stephen Kemble, *Journals of Lieutenant-Colonel Stephen Kemble, 1773–1789, and British Army Orders: General Sir William Howe,*

1775–1778; *General Sir Henry Clinton, 1778; and General Daniel Jones, 1778* (Boston: Gregg Press, 1972), 98.

"[I] shudder for New Jersey": Ibid.

"All the plantations in the vicinity": Captain Johann Ewald, *Diary of the American War,* Joseph P. Tustin, ed. (New Haven, Conn.: Yale University Press, 1979), 18.

"On this march": Ibid., 22.

"The Hessians are more infamous": Ambrose Serle, *The American Journal of Ambrose Serle, Secretary to Lord Howe, 1776–1778,* Edward H. Tatum, Jr., ed. (San Marino, Calif.: Huntington Library, 1940), 246.

"The friend and the foe": Charles Stedman, *History of the Origin, Progress, and Termination of the American War,* I (New York: Arno Press, 1969), 242.

"They lead the relentless foreigners": PNG, I, 368.

"The enemy's ravages": Nathanael Greene to Nicholas Cooke, January 10, 1777, in *PNG,* II, 4.

"Their footsteps are marked with destruction": PNG, I, 365.

"But give me leave": Robert J. Taylor, ed., *Papers of John Adams,* V (Cambridge, Mass.: Belknap Press, 1983), 95.

"*The possession of Trenton*": Troyer Steele Anderson, *The Command of the Howe Brothers During the American Revolution* (New York: Oxford University Press, 1936), 206.

"*Our retreat should not be neglected*": *PNG*, I, 269.

"*a grand but dreadful*": Lillian Miller, ed., *The Selected Papers of Charles Willson Peale and His Family*, V (New Haven, Conn.: Yale University Press, 2000), 50.

"*With a handful of men*": Moncure Daniel Conway, *Writings of Thomas Paine*, I (New York: Putnam, 1894), 178.

"*a combination of unlucky circumstances*": Henry Knox to Lucy Knox, December 8, 1776, NYHS.

"*He was in an old dirty blanket*": Lillian B. Miller, ed., *Selected Papers of Charles Willson Peale and His Family* (New Haven, Conn.: Yale University Press, 2000), 50.

"*From several accounts*": George Washington to John Hancock, December 9, 1776, in *PGW*, VII, 283.

"*Philadelphia beyond all question*": George Washington to Charles Lee, December 11, 1776, in *PGW*, VII, 301.

"*in a very spirited manner*": George Washington to Jonathan Trumbull, Sr., December 12, 1776, in *PGW,* VII, 321.

"General Lee . . . is on his march": Ibid.

"Entre nous": Henry Steele Commager and Richard B. Morris, *The Spirit of 'Seventy-Six,* I (Indianapolis: Bobbs-Merrill, 1958), 500.

"I ordered my men to fire": Ibid., 502.

"unfortunate": General James Wilkinson, *Memoirs of My Own Times,* I (Philadelphia: Abraham Small, 1816), 106.

"We have captured General Lee": William M. Dwyer, *The Day Is Ours: November 1776–January 1777* (New York: Viking Press, 1983), 150.

"This coup de main*":* Henry Steele Commager and Richard B. Morris, eds., *The Spirit of 'Seventy-Six,* I (Indianapolis: Bobbs-Merrill, 1958), 503.

"combination of evils": PNG, I, 368.

"this unhappy accident": George Washington to James Bowdoin, December 18, 1776, in *PGW,* VII, 365.

"Unhappy man!": George Washington to Lund Washington, December 10–17, 1776, in *PGW,* VII, 290.

"the weather": William S. Stryker, *Battles of Trenton and Princeton* (Trenton: Old Barracks Association, 2001), 38.

"Sir William, he": John R. Alden, *A History*

of the *American Revolution* (New York: Knopf, 1969), 303.

"The Delaware now divides": George Washington to James Bowdoin, December 18, 1776, in *PGW,* VII, 365.

"Strain every nerve": George Washington to Israel Putnam, December 21, 1776, in *PGW,* VII, 405.

"Expense must not be spared": George Washington to Brigadier Generals James Ewing, Hugh Mercer, Adam Stephen, and Lord Stirling, December 14, 1776, in *PGW,* VII, 332.

"Use every possible means": George Washington to Lord Stirling, December 14, 1776, in *PGW,* VII, 339.

"General Howe is certainly": John Cadwalader to George Washington, December 15, 1776, in *PGW,* VII, 342.

"Our only dependence": George Washington to Lund Washington, December 10–17, 1776, in *PGW,* VII, 291.

"so destitute of shoes": William Heath, *Heath's Memoirs of the American War* (New York: A. Wessels Co., 1904), 107.

"We have been on the march": Joseph Hodgkins to Sarah Hodgkins, December 20, 1776, in *This Glorious Cause: The Adventures of Two Company Officers in Washington's Army,* Herbert

T. Wade and Robert A. Lively, eds. (Princeton, N.J.: Princeton University Press, 1958), 227.

"the enemy being near": Ibid., 228.

"Ice for a passage": George Washington to Robert Morris, December 22, 1776, in *PGW,* VII, 412.

"the full confidence of his Excellency": Nathanael Greene to Catharine Greene, January 20, 1777, in *PNG,* II, 7.

"His Excellency": Nathanael Greene to Christopher Greene, January 20, 1777, in *PNG,* II, 8.

"I cannot desert a man": William Tudor to Delia Jarvis, December 24, 1776, MHS.

"Will it not be possible": Joseph Reed to George Washington, December 22, 1776, in *PGW,* VII, 415.

"lucky blow": George Washington to Jonathan Trumbull, Sr., December 14, 1776, in *PGW,* VII, 340.

hoped this was true: Robert Morris to George Washington, December 21, 1776, in *PGW,* VII, 404.

"For Heaven's sake": George Washington to Joseph Reed, December 23, 1776, in *PGW,* VII, 423.

"profound silence": George Johnston to Leven Powell, December 29, 1776, in

PGW, VII, 437, editorial note.

"much depressed": George W. Corner, ed., *The Autobiography of Benjamin Rush* (Westport, Conn.: Greenwood Press, 1970), 124.

"affecting terms": Ibid.

"Victory or Death": Ibid., 125.

"I am determined": George Washington to John Cadwalader, December 25, 1776, in *PGW,* VII, 439.

"I agree with you": George Washington to Robert Morris, December 25, 1776, in *PGW,* VII, 439.

"extraordinary exertions": General James Wilkinson, *Memoirs of My Own Times,* I (Philadelphia: Abraham Small, 1816), 128.

"almost incredible": Henry Knox to Lucy Knox, December 28, 1776, NYHS.

"Over the river": John Greenwood, *The Revolutionary Services of John Greenwood,* Isaac J. Greenwood, ed. (New York: De Vinne Press, 1922), 38–39.

it was three o'clock: George Washington to John Hancock, December 27, 1776, in *PGW,* VII, 454.

"I well knew we could not": Ibid.

"and after two battalions": William B. Reed, ed., *Life and Correspondence of Joseph Reed,* I (Philadelphia: Lindsay &

Blakiston, 1847), 276.

"with the most profound silence": Henry Knox to Lucy Knox, December 28, 1776, NYHS.

"I recollect very well": John Greenwood, *The Revolutionary Services of John Greenwood*, Isaac J. Greenwood, ed. (New York: De Vinne Press, 1922), 39.

"in a deep and solemn voice": William S. Powell, "A Connecticut Soldier Writing Home: Elisha Bostwick's Memoirs of the First Years of the Revolution," *William and Mary Quarterly*, 3rd series, VI (1949), 102.

"Tell the general to use": William S. Stryker, *Battles of Trenton and Princeton* (Trenton: Old Barracks Association, 2001), 190.

"This was not unusual": John Greenwood, *The Revolutionary Services of John Greenwood*, Isaac J. Greenwood, ed. (New York: De Vinne Press, 1922), 40.

criticized Rall after his death: Rodney Atwood, *The Hessians: Mercenaries from Hessian-Kassel in the American Revolution* (Cambridge, Eng.: Cambridge University Press, 1980), 89.

"We have not slept one night": William S. Stryker, *Battles of Trenton and Princeton*

(Trenton: Old Barracks Association, 2001), 484.

"certain intelligence": James Grant to General Harvey, December 26–27, 1776, LOC.

"equal to the attempt": Ibid.

"The storm continued": Henry Knox to Lucy Knox, December 28, 1776, NYHS.

"seemed to vie": George Washington to John Hancock, December 27, 1776, in *PGW*, VII, 456.

"in the twinkling of an eye": Henry Knox to Lucy Knox, December 28, 1776, NYHS.

"The storm of nature": Nathanael Greene to Catharine Greene, December 30, 1776, in *PNG*, I, 377.

"After having marched off": Henry Knox to Lucy Knox, December 28, 1776, NYHS.

"The general, with the utmost sincerity": George Washington, General Orders, December 27, 1776, in *PGW*, VII, 448.

"I am willing to go upon": John Greenwood, *The Revolutionary Services of John Greenwood*, Isaac J. Greenwood, ed. (New York: De Vinne Press, 1922), 40.

"On my approach": General James Wilkin-

son, *Memoirs of My Own Times*, I (Philadelphia: Abraham Small, 1816), 131.

"The troops behaved": Henry Knox to Lucy Knox, December 28, 1776, NYHS.

"I looked at him": John Adlum, *Memoirs of the Life of John Adlum in the Revolutionary War*, Howard H. Peckham, ed. (Chicago: Caxton Club, 1968), 102.

"I did not wait": Ibid., 102–103.

"It appears to us": Executive Committee of the Continental Congress to George Washington, December 28, 1776, in *PGW*, VII, 465.

"But troops properly inspired": John Hancock to George Washington, January 1, 1777, in *PGW*, VII, 505.

" 'Tis an infamous business": James Grant to General Harvey, December 26, 1776, LOC.

"as safe as you are in London": Ibid.

his leave canceled: Franklin Wickwire and Mary Wickwire, *Cornwallis: The American Adventure* (Boston: Houghton Mifflin, 1970), 95.

"I feel the inconvenience": George Washington to John Hancock, January 1, 1777, in *PGW*, VII, 504.

"I thought it no time": George Washington to the Executive Committee of the Continental Congress, January 1,

1777, in *PGW*, VII, 500.

"in the most affectionate manner": Sergeant R——, "Battle of Princeton," *Pennsylvania Magazine of History and Biography*, XX (1896), 515–516.

"My brave fellows": Ibid.

"God Almighty": Nathanael Greene to Nicholas Cooke, January 10, 1777, in *PNG*, II, 4.

"use every endeavor": John Hancock to George Washington, December 27, 1776, in *PGW*, VII, 462, n. 1.

"Happy it is for this country": William S. Stryker, *Battles of Trenton and Princeton* (Trenton: Old Barracks Association, 2001), 244.

"Instead of thinking myself": George Washington to Executive Committee of the Continental Congress, January 1, 1777, in *PGW*, VII, 500.

"The year 1776 is over": Robert Morris to George Washington, January 1, 1777, in *PGW*, VII, 508.

"The enemy pushed our small party": Henry Knox to Lucy Knox, January 7, 1777, NYHS.

"The American army": George W. Corner, ed., *The Autobiography of Benjamin Rush* (Westport, Conn.: Greenwood Press, 1970), 128.

"If Washington is the general": William S. Stryker, *Battles of Trenton and Princeton* (Trenton: Old Barracks Association, 2001), 268.

"bag him": Franklin Wickwire and Mary Wickwire, *Cornwallis: The American Adventure* (Boston: Houghton Mifflin, 1970), 96.

"We . . . durst not attack them": Archibald Robertson, *Archibald Robertson,* Harry Miller Lydenberg, ed. (New York: New York Public Library, 1930), 119.

"They could not possibly suppose": Henry Knox to Lucy Knox, January 7, 1777, NYHS.

"I shall never forget": George F. Scheer and Hugh F. Rankin, *Rebels and Redcoats: The American Revolution Through the Eyes of Those Who Fought and Lived It* (New York: Da Capo Press, 1957), 219.

"Parade with us": Alfred Hoyt Bill, *The Campaign of Princeton: 1776–1777* (Princeton, N.J.: Princeton University Press, 1948), 108.

"A resolution was taken": David Hackett Fischer, *Washington's Crossing* (New York: Oxford University Press, 2004), 336.

"It's a fine fox chase": Alfred Hoyt Bill, *The*

Campaign of Princeton (Princeton, N.J.: Princeton University Press, 1948), 110.

"by aiming at too much": George Washington to John Hancock, January 5, 1777, in *PGW,* VII, 523.

"If there are spots": Douglass Southall Freeman, *George Washington: A Biography,* IV (New York: Scribner, 1951), 359.

"The two late actions": Nathanael Greene to Thomas Paine, January 9, 1777, in *PNG,* II, 3.

"the fashion in this army": Henry Steele Commager and Richard B. Morris, eds., *The Spirit of 'Seventy-Six,* I (Indianapolis: Bobbs-Merrill, 1958), 524.

"I am apt to think": L. H. Butterfield, *Adams Family Correspondence,* II (Cambridge, Mass.: Harvard University Press, 1963), 151.

"The energetic operation": Mercy Otis Warren, *History of the Rise, Progress, and Termination of the American Revolution,* I (Indianapolis: Liberty Fund, 1989), 195.

"Nothing could have afforded me": William Cobbett, *The Parliamentary History of England from the Earliest Period to the Year 1803,* XVIII (London: T. C.

Hansard, 1813), 1366–1368.

"disagreeable": *London General Evening Post,*
March 4, 1777.

Lord Germain saw at once: K. G. Davies,
ed., *Documents of the American Revolution, 1770–1783,* XIV (Dublin: Irish
University Press, 1976), 46–47.

"A people unused to restraint": George
Washington to Lord Stirling, January
19, 1977, in *PGW,* VIII, 110.

"He will be the deliverer": Nathanael Greene
to James Varnum, September 7, 1781,
in *PNG,* X, 36.

Bibliography

A NOTE ON SOURCES

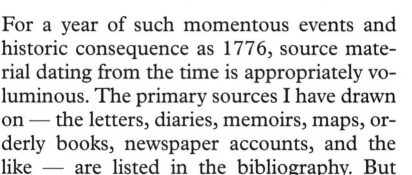

For a year of such momentous events and historic consequence as 1776, source material dating from the time is appropriately voluminous. The primary sources I have drawn on — the letters, diaries, memoirs, maps, orderly books, newspaper accounts, and the like — are listed in the bibliography. But those of the utmost importance have been the letters of George Washington, Nathanael Greene, Henry Knox, Joseph Reed, and Joseph Hodgkins. That these men found the time, and energy, to write all that they did, given the circumstances, is a wonder, and ought to be acknowledged as another of their great services to their country. Washington, in the time covered by this narrative, from July of 1775 to the first week of 1777, wrote no fewer than 947 letters!

On the British side, the letters of the irrepressibly opinionated James Grant were also a particularly rich and welcome source. Privately held at Ballindalloch

Castle in Scotland, the ancestral home of the Grants, the papers are now available on microfilm at the Library of Congress.

Of the more than seventy diaries I have consulted, much the most valuable have been those of Jabez Fitch, James Thacher, Philip V. Fithian, Ambrose Serle, Archibald Robertson, Frederick Mackenzie, and Johann Ewald. Of the memoirs, those of Alexander Graydon, Joseph Plumb Martin, and John Greenwood are outstanding.

I have drawn a great deal also from three of the earliest histories of the Revolutionary War, all published in the last decade of the eighteenth century, when memories were still relatively fresh and many of the principals were still alive. *The History of the American Revolution* by David Ramsay and *The History of the Rise, Progress, and Establishment of the Independence of the United States of America* by William Gordon are both the works of Americans. (Ramsay was a physician from South Carolina; Gordon, a Massachusetts clergyman.) The third is the first full account by an Englishman and by someone who actually fought in the war: *The History of the Origin, Progress, and Termination of the American War* by Charles Stedman.

In addition, I have relied on a number of

exceptional secondary works on the war overall: *Angel in the Whirlwind* by Benson Bobrick; *The War for America, 1775–1783* by Piers Mackesy; *The Glorious Cause* by Robert Middlekauff; *A Revolutionary People at War* by Charles Royster; and *A People Numerous and Armed* by John Shy.

Christopher Ward's two-volume *The War of the Revolution*, published more than fifty years ago, remains an excellent military study. Don Higginbotham's *The War of American Independence* is masterful, clear, and balanced. (Its bibliographical essay is especially valuable.) And the grand old multivolume classic, *The American Revolution* by Sir George Otto Trevelyan, first published in 1899, is a joy for the prose alone, but also filled with illuminating observations and details to be found almost nowhere else.

Of the books on the war in 1776, four are first-rate and essential: *Washington's Crossing* by David Hackett Fischer; *1776: Year of Illusions* by Thomas Fleming; *The Year That Tried Men's Souls* by Merritt Ierly; and *The Winter Soldiers* by Richard M. Ketchum. And four skillfully edited anthologies of the letters and reminiscences of many who played a part in the war, both American and British, have been mainstays: *The Spirit of 'Seventy-Six,* in two volumes, edited by Henry Steele Commager and Richard B. Morris; *The Revolution Remembered,* edited by John C. Dann; *Rebels and Redcoats,* edited by George F. Scheer and Hugh F. Rankin; and *Letters on the American Revolution, 1774–1776,* edited by Margaret Wheeler Willard.

One of the early surprises of my research was to find how very much material there is on the Siege of Boston. (I could readily have focused on that alone.) Yet for some strange reason, it is a subject that has been largely overlooked by historians for years. The one book of consequence, *The First Year of the American Revolution* by Allen French, was published in 1934. But it is an expert study, and in combination with Mr. French's extensive notes, on file at the Massachusetts Historical Society, it has been invaluable.

For the war in New York, the best accounts are *Under the Guns* and *Battle for Manhattan,* both by Bruce Bliven, Jr.; *The Battle of Long Island* by Eric I. Manders; *The Battle of Brooklyn, 1776* by John J. Gallagher; and *The Battle for New York* by Barnet Schecter. The earliest scholarly work, *The Campaign of 1776 Around New York and Brooklyn,* written by Henry P.

Johnston and published by the Long Island Historical Society in 1878, has been indispensable.

The best study of the Siege of Fort Washington is "Toward Disaster at Fort Washington," by William Paul Deary, an unpublished dissertation submitted to the Columbian School of Arts and Sciences, George Washington University, in 1996.

Of the books devoted to the campaign in New Jersey, I have drawn from the first serious work on the subject, William S. Stryker's *Battles of Trenton and Princeton*, published in 1898, as well as Arthur S. Lefkowitz's more concise *The Long Retreat*, published in 1998; *The Campaign of Princeton, 1776–1777* by Alfred Hoyt Bill; and *The Day Is Ours* by William M. Dwyer.

The biographies that have been of continuous value throughout my work include first and foremost Douglas Southall Freeman's *George Washington*, and especially volumes III and IV. Though a bit old-fashioned in manner, Freeman's *Washington* still stands second only to *The Papers of George Washington* in its comprehensive treatment of Washington's leading part in the war and in its plenitude of exceptional footnotes.

Other biographies repeatedly consulted

are *George III: A Personal History* by Christopher Hibbert; Theodore Thayer's *Nathanael Greene*; *The Life of Nathanael Greene* by George Washington Greene; North Callahan's *Henry Knox*; John Richard Alden's *General Charles Lee*; *General John Glover and His Marblehead Mariners* by George Athan Billias; William B. Willcox's insightful study of Sir Henry Clinton, *Portrait of a General*; *The Howe Brothers and the American Revolution* by Ira D. Gruber; *The Command of the Howe Brothers During the American Revolution* by Troyer Steele Anderson; and *Cornwallis: The American Adventure* by Franklin and Mary Wickwire.

The American Rebellion, another mainstay, is Sir Henry Clinton's own narrative of his campaigns, edited by William B. Willcox.

And, like all who write about the Revolutionary War, I am everlastingly indebted to *The Iconography of Manhattan Island, 1498–1909* by I. N. Phelps Stokes, *American Archives* by Peter Force, and the *Encyclopedia of the American Revolution* by Mark Mayo Boatner III.

I have, as well, referred repeatedly to portraits by John Trumbull, most of whose works are at the Yale University Art Gallery, and by Charles Willson Peale, particularly those at the National Independence Park in Philadelphia. In the works of these two great painters, both of whom served in the war, we see not only the faces of the protagonists on the American side but a delineation of character.

Finally, I must include five historic houses that figure in the story:

The old white-frame homestead at East Greenwich, Rhode Island, where Nathanael Greene was born and raised, still stands and still belongs to the Greene family. Its treasures include the cradle Nathanael Greene was rocked in, numbers of his books, and even the musket he bought from a British deserter before marching off to war. The handsome, four-square house Greene built shortly before he was married also still stands at Covington, Rhode Island, near the site of his iron foundry.

Mount Vernon, Washington's home in Virginia, is in many ways the autobiography that Washington never wrote, in all that it tells us about him. Then there are two that served as his headquarters during the course of 1776, the magnificent Longfellow House, as it has long been known, on Brattle Street in Cambridge, and the

Morris-Jumel Mansion on Jumel Terrace in New York City, off 160th Street. With the exception of the Greene homestead at East Greenwich, all of these great houses are open to the public, and in their way their old walls can truly talk.

MANUSCRIPT COLLECTIONS

American Antiquarian Society,
   Worcester, Mass.
      Newspaper, manuscript,
         and broadside collections
American Philosophical Society,
   Philadelphia
      Nathan Sellers Journal
Boston Public Library
Clements Library, Ann Arbor, Mich.
      Loftus Cliffe Papers
      Henry Clinton Papers
      James S. Schoff Revolutionary War
      Collection
Colonial Williamsburg Reference Library,
   Williamsburg, Va.
Harvard University Archives, Cambridge,
   Mass.
      John Winthrop Papers
Historical Society of Delaware, Wilmington

Historical Society of Pennsylvania, Philadelphia
    Edward Hand Papers
Library of Congress, Washington, D.C.
    Peter Force Archives
    Geography and Map Division
    James Grant Papers
    Consider Tiffany Papers
    George Washington Papers
Longfellow House National Historic Site, Cambridge, Mass.
    George Washington Papers and Park Service Archives
Massachusetts Historical Society, Boston
    John Adams Papers
    Reverend Samuel Cooper Diary
    Allen French Papers
    Richard Frothingham Papers
    Henry Knox Diary
    Timothy Pickering Papers
    Samuel Shaw Papers
    William Tudor Papers
    Lieutenant Richard Williams Papers
    Hannah Winthrop and Mercy Warren Correspondence
Mount Vernon Department of Collections, Mount Vernon, Va.
Museum of the City of New York Archives
National Archives, Washington, D.C.
    Revolutionary Pension Records

New-York Historical Society,
   New York City
      William Alexander, Lord Stirling,
         Correspondence
      Lachlan Campbell Journal
      William Duer Papers
      Nathan Eells Papers
      Henry Knox Papers
         (Gilder-Lehrman Collection)
      Alexander McDougall Papers
      Solomon Nash Journal
      Joseph Reed Papers
Pierpont Morgan Library, New York City
      John Trumbull Papers
Public Records Office, Kew Gardens,
   London
      Lord William Howe Papers
      Loyalist Claims Records
      Sir George Osborn Papers
Rhode Island Historical Society,
   Providence
      Thomas Foster Papers
      Nathanael Greene Papers
      Captain Stephen Olney Papers
Society of Cincinnati, Washington, D.C.
      Manuscript, Map, and Graphic
         Material Collections
Yale University Art Gallery, New Haven,
   Conn.

BOOKS

Abbott, W. W., ed. *The Papers of George Washington,* Colonial Series. Vol. I. Charlottesville: University Press of Virginia, 1983.

Adair, Douglass, and John A. Schutz, eds. *Peter Oliver's "Origin and Progress of the American Rebellion: A Tory View."* San Marino, Calif.: Huntington Library, 1961.

Adams, Charles Francis, ed. *The Works of John Adams.* Vols. III, IX. Boston: Little, Brown, 1856.

Adams, Hannah. *A Summary History of New-England: From the First Settlement at Plymouth to the Acceptance of the Federal Constitution, Comprehending a General Sketch of the American War.* Dedham, Mass.: H. Mann & J. H. Adams, 1799.

Adams, Randolph G. *Sir Henry Clinton Maps: British Headquarters Maps and Sketches.* Ann Arbor, Mich.: William L. Clements Library, 1928.

Alden, John R. *General Charles Lee: Traitor or Patriot?* Baton Rouge: Louisiana State University Press, 1951.

———. *A History of the American Revolution.* New York: Knopf, 1969.

The American Revolution in New York: Its Political, Social, and Economic Significance. (Prepared by the Division of Archives and History) Albany: University of the State of New York, 1926.

Anderson, Fred. *Crucible of War: The Seven Years' War and the Fate of Empire in British North America, 1754–1766.* New York: Knopf, 2000.

Anderson, Troyer Steele. *The Command of the Howe Brothers During the American Revolution.* New York and London: Oxford University Press, 1936.

Andrews, John. *History of the War with America, France, Spain, and Holland.* Vol. II. London: John Fielding, 1785–1786.

The Annual Register; or, A View of the History, Politics, and Literature for the Year 1775. London: Printed for J. Dodsley, 1776.

Arch, Nigel, and Joanna Marschner. *Splendour at Court: Dressing for Royal Occasions Since 1700.* London and Sydney: Unwin Hyman, 1987.

Atwood, Rodney. *The Hessians: Mercenaries from Hessen-Kassel in the American Revolution.* Cambridge, Eng.: Cambridge University Press, 1980.

Bailyn, Bernard. *Faces of Revolution: Personalities and Themes in the Struggle for American Independence. New York: Knopf, 1990.

Bakeless, John. Turncoats, Traitors, and Heroes. Philadelphia: J. B. Lippincott, 1959.

Balch, Thomas, ed. Papers Relating Chiefly to the Maryland Line During the Revolution. Philadelphia: Printed for the Seventy-Six Society, 1857.

Bancroft, George. History of the United States. Vol. IX. Boston: Little, Brown, 1866.

Barck, Oscar Theodore, Jr. New York City During the War for Independence. New York: Columbia University Press, 1931.

Barnum, H. L. The Spy Unmasked; or, Memoirs of Enoch Crosby. Harrison, N.Y.: Harbor Hill Books, 1975.

Beatson, Robert. Naval and Military Memoirs of Great Britain from 1727 to 1783. Vol. VI. Boston: Gregg Press, 1972.

Becker, John. The Sexagenary; or, Reminiscences of the American Revolution. Albany, N.Y.: J. Munsell, 1866.

Berger, Joseph, and Dorothy Berger, eds. Diary of America. New York: Simon & Schuster, 1957.

Bill, Alfred Hoyt. The Campaign of

Princeton: 1776–1777. Princeton, N.J.: Princeton University Press, 1948.

Billias, George Athan. *General John Glover and His Marblehead Mariners.* New York: Henry Holt, 1960.

———. *George Washington's Generals.* New York: Morrow, 1964.

Black, Jeremy. *Pitt the Elder: The Great Commoner.* Gloucestershire, Eng.: Sutton Publishing, 1999.

Blakeslee, Katherine Walton. *Mordecai Gist and His American Progenitors.* Baltimore: Daughters of the American Revolution, 1923.

Bliven, Bruce, Jr. *Battle for Manhattan.* New York: Holt, 1955.

———. *Under the Guns: New York, 1775–1776.* New York: Harper & Row, 1972.

Blumenthal, Walter Hart. *Women Camp Followers of the American Revolution.* Philadelphia: George S. MacManus Co., 1952.

Bobrick, Benson. *Angel in the Whirlwind: The Triumph of the American Revolution.* New York: Simon & Schuster, 1997.

Bolton, Charles Knowles, ed. *Letters of Hugh Earl Percy from Boston and New York: 1774–1776.* Boston: Gregg Press, 1972.

———. *The Private Soldier Under Washington.* Port Washington, N.Y.: Kennikat Press, 1964.

Bowman, Allen. *The Morale of the American Revolutionary Army.* Washington, D.C.: American Council on Public Affairs, 1943.

Bowne, William L. *Ye Cohorn Caravan: The Knox Expedition in the Winter of 1775–76.* Schuylerville, N.Y.: NaPaul Publishers, 1975.

Bridenbaugh, Carl. *Cities in Revolt: Urban Life in America, 1743–1776.* New York: Knopf, 1955.

Brooke, John. *King George III.* London: Constable, 1972.

Brookhiser, Richard. *Founding Father.* New York: Free Press, 1996.

Brooks, Noah. *Henry Knox: A Soldier of the Revolution: 1750–1806.* New York and London: Putnam, 1900.

Brooks, Victor: *The Boston Campaign: April 1775–March 1776.* Conshohocken, Pa.: Combined Publishing, 1999.

Buckley, Gail. *American Patriots: The Story of Blacks in the Military from the Revolution to Desert Storm.* New York: Random House, 2001.

Buel, Joy Day, and Richard Buel, Jr. *The Way of Duty: A Woman and Her Family in Revolutionary America.* New York: Norton, 1984.

Burgoyne, Bruce E., ed. *Enemy Views: The American Revolutionary War as Recorded by the Hessian Participants.* Bowie, Md.: Heritage Books, 1996.

———. *The Hesse-Cassel Mirbach Regiment in the American Revolution.* Bowie, Md.: Heritage Books, 1998.

Burke, Edmund. *The Correspondence.* Vol. III. *July 1774–June 1778.* Cambridge, Eng.: Cambridge University Press, 1961.

Burnaby, Rev. Andrew. *Travels Through the Middle Settlements in North America in the Years 1759 and 1760.* 3rd ed. London: For T. Payne, 1798.

Burrows, Edwin G., and Mike Wallace. *A History of New York City to 1898.* New York and Oxford: Oxford University Press, 1999.

Butterfield, L. H., ed. *Adams Family Correspondence.* Vols. I–II. Cambridge, Mass.: Harvard University Press, 1963.

———. *Letters of Benjamin Rush.* Vols. I–II. Princeton, N.J.: American Philosophical Society, 1951.

Callahan, North. *Henry Knox: General Washington's General.* South Brunswick, Maine: A. S. Barnes & Co., 1958.

Chase, Philander; W. W. Abbott; and Dorothy Twohig, eds. *The Papers of George Washington.* Vols. I–VIII. Charlottesville: University Press of Virginia, 1985–1998.

Chidsey, Donald Barr. *The Tide Turns: An Informal History of the Campaign of 1776 in the American Revolution.* New York: Crown Publishers, 1966.

Churchill, Sir Winston. *The Great Republic: A History of America.* New York: Modern Library, 2001.

Clark, William Bell, ed. *Naval Documents of the American Revolution.* Vols. III–VII. Washington, D.C.: U.S. Department of the Navy, 1968–1976.

Cobbett, William. *The Parliamentary History of England from the Earliest Period to the Year 1803.* Vol. XVIII. London: T. C. Hansard, 1813.

Coffin, Charles, ed. *The Lives and Services of Maj. Gen. John Thomas, Col. Thomas Knowlton, Col. Alexander Scammell, Maj. Gen. Henry Dearborn.* New York: Egbert, Hovey & King, 1845.

Colley, Linda. *Britons Forging the Nation, 1707–1837.* New Haven, Conn.: Yale University Press, 1992.

Collins, Varnum Lansing, ed. *A Brief Narrative of the Ravages of the British and Hessians at Princeton, 1776–1777.* Princeton, N.J.: University Library, 1999.

Commager, Henry Steele, and Richard B. Morris, eds. *The Spirit of 'Seventy-Six: The Story of the American Revolution as Told by Participants.* Vols. I–II. Indianapolis: Bobbs-Merrill, 1958.

Conway, Moncure Daniel. *Writings of Thomas Paine.* Vol. I. New York: Putnam, 1894.

Cook, Don. *The Long Fuse: How England Lost the American Colonies, 1760–1785.* New York: Atlantic Monthly Press, 1995.

Copley, John Singleton. *Letters and Papers of John Singleton Copley and Henry Pelham, 1739–1776.* Boston: Massachusetts Historical Society, 1914.

Corner, George W., ed. *The Autobiography of Benjamin Rush: His Travels Through Life, Together with His 'Commonplace Book' for 1789–1813.* Westport, Conn.: Greenwood Press, 1970.

Coupland, R. *The American Revolution and the British Empire.* New York: Russell & Russell, 1965.

Crary, Catherine S. *The Price of Loyalty:*

Tory Writings from the Revolutionary Era. New York: McGraw-Hill, 1973.

Cumming, W. P., and Hugh Rankin. *The Fate of a Nation: The American Revolution Through Contemporary Eyes.* London: Phaidon Press, 1975.

Cunliffe, Marcus. *George Washington: Man and Monument.* New York: New American Library, 1958.

Custis, George Washington Parke. *Recollections and Private Memoirs of Washington.* New York: Derby & Jackson, 1860.

Cutter, William. *The Life of Israel Putnam, Major General in the Army of the American Revolution.* Boston: Sanborn, Carter, Bazin & Co., 1846.

Dalzell, Robert F., Jr., and Lee Baldwin Dalzell. *George Washington's Mount Vernon.* New York: Oxford University Press, 1998.

Dann, John C., ed. *The Revolution Remembered: Eyewitness Accounts of the War for Independence.* Chicago: University of Chicago Press, 1980.

Davies, K. G., ed. *Documents of the American Revolution, 1770–1783.* Colonial Office Series. Vols. XI, XIV. Dublin: Irish University Press, 1976.

Dawson, Henry B., ed. *New York City*

During the American Revolution: Being a Collection of Original Papers from the Manuscripts of the Mercantile Library Association of New York City. New York: Privately printed for the Association, 1861.

Deary, William Paul. "Toward Disaster at Fort Washington, November 1776." Dissertation, George Washington University, 1996.

Decker, Malcolm. *Brink of Revolution: New York in Crisis, 1765–1776.* New York: Argosy Antiquarian, 1964.

Defoe, Daniel. *A Tour Thro' Great Britain, 1742.* Vol. II. New York & London: Garland Publishing, 1975.

Diamant, Lincoln. *Chaining the Hudson: The Fight for the River in the American Revolution.* Carol Publishing Group, 1994.

——. *Revolutionary Women in the War for American Independence.* A one-volume revised edition of Elizabeth Ellet's 1848 Landmark Series. Westport, Conn.: Praeger, 1998.

Drake, Francis S. *Life and Correspondence of Henry Knox.* Boston: Samuel G. Drake, 1873.

Drake, Samuel Adams. *General Israel Putnam: The Commander at Bunker*

Hill. Boston: Nichols & Hall, 1875.

———. *Old Landmarks and Historic Personages of Boston*. Boston: James R. Osgood & Co., 1873.

Draper, Theodore. *A Struggle for Power: The American Revolution*. New York: Times Books, 1996.

Drinkwater, John. *Charles James Fox*. New York: Cosmopolitan Book Corp., 1928.

Duer, William Alexander. *The Life of William Alexander, Earl of Stirling, with Selections from His Correspondence*. Published for the New Jersey Historical Society. New York: Wiley & Putnam, 1847.

Duncan, Louis C. *Medical Men in the American Revolution*. Jefferson, N.C., and London: McFarland & Co., 1998.

Dwyer, William M. *The Day Is Ours: November 1776–January 1777, An Inside View of the Battles of Trenton and Princeton*. New York: Viking Press, 1983.

Eliot, Ellsworth, Jr. *The Patriotism of Joseph Reed*. New Haven, Conn.: Yale University Library, 1943.

Ellet, Elizabeth F. *The Women of the American Revolution*. Vol. III. Philadelphia: George W. Jacobs & Co., 1900.

English, Frederick. *General Hugh Mercer: Forgotten Hero of the American Revolution.* Lawrenceville, N.J.: Princeton Academic Press, 1975.

Fenn, Elizabeth A. *Pox Americana: The Great Smallpox Epidemic of 1775–82.* New York: Hill & Wang, 2001.

Ferris, Robert G., and Richard E. Morris. *The Signers of the Declaration of Independence.* Flagstaff, Ariz.: Interpretive Publications, 1982.

Field, Thomas W. *Battle of Long Island.* Brooklyn: Long Island Historical Society, 1869.

Fields, Joseph E. *Worthy Partner: The Papers of Martha Washington.* Westport, Conn.: Greenwood Press, 1994.

Fischer, David Hackett. *Paul Revere's Ride.* New York: Oxford University Press, 1994.

———. *Washington's Crossing.* New York: Oxford University Press, 2004.

Fisher, Sydney George. *The True History of the American Revolution.* Philadelphia: J. B. Lippincott, 1902.

Fiske, John. *The American Revolution.* Vols. I–II. Boston: Houghton Mifflin, 1891.

Fitzpatrick, John C., ed. *George Washington Accounts of Expenses.* Boston: Houghton Mifflin, 1917.

——. *George Washington Himself.* Indianapolis: Bobbs-Merrill, 1933.

——. *The Writings of George Washington from the Original Manuscript Sources, 1745–1799.* Vols. I–VIII. Washington, D.C.: U.S. Government Printing Office, 1931–1933.

Fleming, Thomas. *Now We Are Enemies: The Story of Bunker Hill.* New York: St. Martin's Press, 1960.

——. *1776: Year of Illusions.* New York: Norton, 1975.

Flexner, James Thomas. *George Washington: The Forge of Experience, 1732–1775.* Vol. 1. Boston: Little, Brown, 1965.

——. *George Washington in the American Revolution, 1775–1783.* Vol. II. Boston: Little, Brown, 1967.

——. *The Young Hamilton: A Biography.* Boston and Toronto: Little, Brown, 1978.

Flood, Charles Bracelen. *Rise, and Fight Again: Perilous Times Along the Road to Independence.* New York: Dodd, Mead, 1976.

Foner, Philip S., ed. *The Complete Writings of Thomas Paine.* 2 vols. New York: Citadel Press, 1945.

Forbes, Esther. *Paul Revere and the World*

He Lived In. Boston: Houghton Mifflin, 1942.

Force, Peter. *American Archives: Consisting of a Collection of Authentick Records, State Papers, Debates, and Letters and Other Notices of Public Affairs.* 4th series. 9 vols. Washington, D.C.: M. St. Clair and Peter Force, 1837–1853.

Ford, Paul Leicester. *Washington and the Theatre.* New York: Dunlap Society, 1899.

Fortescue, Sir John, ed. *The Correspondence of King George the Third from 1760 to December 1783.* Vol. III. London: Macmillan, 1927–1928.

———. *The War of Independence: The British Army in North America, 1775–1783.* London: Greenhill Books, 2001.

Fowler, William, Jr. *The Baron of Beacon Hill: A Biography of John Hancock.* Boston: Houghton Mifflin, 1980.

———. *Rebels Under Sail: The American Navy During the Revolution.* New York: Scribner, 1976.

Freeman, Douglas Southall. *George Washington.* Vols. I–II. *Young Washington.* New York: Scribner, 1948–1949.

———. *George Washington.* Vol. III. *Planter and Patriot.* New York: Scribner, 1951.

———. *George Washington.* Vol. IV. *Leader of*

the Revolution. New York: Scribner, 1951.

French, Allen. *The First Year of the American Revolution.* Boston: Houghton Mifflin, 1934.

———. *The Siege of Boston.* New York: Macmillan, 1911.

Frey, Sylvia R. *The British Soldier in America: A Social History of Military Life in the Revolutionary Period.* Austin: University of Texas, 1981.

Frothingham, Thomas G. *History of the Siege of Boston, and of the Battles of Lexington, Concord, and Bunker Hill.* New York: Da Capo Press, 1970.

———. *Washington: Commander in Chief.* Boston: Houghton Mifflin, 1930.

Fruchtman, Jack, Jr. *Thomas Paine, Apostle of Freedom.* New York: Four Walls Eight Windows, 1994.

Gallagher, John J. *The Battle of Brooklyn, 1776.* New York: Sarpedon, 1995.

Garrett, Wendell. *George Washington's Mount Vernon.* New York: Monacelli Press, 1998.

Gerlach, Larry R., ed. *New Jersey in the American Revolution: 1763–1783.* Trenton, N.J.: New Jersey Historical Commission, 1975.

Gillett, Mary C. *The Army Medical Depart-*

ment, 1775–1818. Washington, D.C.: U.S. Government Printing Office, 1995.

Gordon, William. *The History of the Rise, Progress, and Establishment of the Independence of the United States of America.* Vols. I–II. London, 1788.

Greene, Albert. *Recollections of the Jersey Prison Ship.* Bedford, Mass.: Applewood Books, 1961.

Greene, George Washington. *The Life of Nathanael Greene.* Vol. I. Freeport, N.Y.: Books for Libraries Press, 1962.

———. *Nathanael Greene: An Examination of Some Statements Concerning Major General Greene in the Ninth Volume of Bancroft's "History of the United States."* Boston: Ticknor & Fields, 1866.

Griffiths, Thomas Morgan. *Major General Henry Knox and the Last Heirs to Montpelier.* Monmouth, Maine: Monmouth Press, 1965.

Gruber, Ira D. *The Howe Brothers and the American Revolution.* New York: Atheneum, 1972.

Hamilton, John C. *The Life of Alexander Hamilton.* Vol. I. New York: Halsted & Voorhies, 1834.

Hammond, Otis G., ed. *Letters and Papers of Major-General John Sullivan.* Vols.

I–III. Concord: New Hampshire Historical Society, 1930–1939.

Harcourt, Edward William, ed. *The Harcourt Papers.* Vol. XI. Oxford, Eng.: James Parke & Co., 1884.

Harrison, Peleg. *The Stars and Stripes and Other American Flags.* Boston: Little, Brown, 1914.

Hawke, David Freeman. *Paine.* New York: Harper & Row, 1974.

Heller, Charles E., and William A. Stofft, eds. *America's First Battles, 1776–1965.* Lawrence: University Press of Kansas, 1986.

Hibbert, Christopher. *George III: A Personal History.* New York: Viking Press, 1998.

———. *Redcoats and Rebels.* New York: Avon Books, 1990.

Higginbotham, Don. *George Washington and the American Military Tradition.* Athens: University of Georgia Press, 1985.

———, ed. *George Washington Reconsidered.* Charlottesville: University Press of Virginia, 2001.

———. *George Washington: Uniting a Nation.* Lanham, Md.: Rowman & Littlefield Publishers, 2002.

———. *The War of American Independence: Military Attitudes, Policies, and Practice,*

1763–1789. New York: Macmillan, 1971.

Hill, George Canning. *Gen. Israel Putnam: "Old Put," a Biography*. Boston: E. O. Libby & Co., 1858.

Hirschfield, Fritz. *George Washington and Slavery*. Columbia: University of Missouri Press, 1997.

Hofstra, Warren R., ed. *George Washington and the Virginia Backcountry*. Madison, Wis.: Madison House Publishers, 1998.

Holmes, Richard. *Redcoat: The British Soldier in the Age of Horse and Musket*. New York: Norton, 2001.

Houlding, J. A. *Fit for Service: The Training of the British Army, 1715–1795*. Oxford, Eng.: Clarendon Press, 1981.

Huddleston, F. J. *Gentleman Johnny Burgoyne*. Garden City, N.Y.: Garden City Publishing, 1927.

Humphreys, David. *An Essay on the Life of the Honourable Major-General Isaac Putnam*. Indianapolis: Liberty Fund, 2000.

——. *The Life, Anecdotes, and Heroic Exploits of Israel Putnam*. Cleveland: M. C. Younglove & Co., 1849.

——. *Life of General Washington*. Athens: University of Georgia Press, 1991.

Ierley, Merritt. *The Year That Tried Men's Souls: A Journalistic Reconstruction of the World of 1776.* South Brunswick, N.J.: A. S. Barnes & Co., 1976.

Jesse, J. Heneage. *Memoirs of the Life and Reign of King George the Third.* Vol. II. 2nd ed. London: Tinsley Bros., 1867.

Johnston, Elizabeth Bryant. *George Washington Day by Day.* New York: Baker & Taylor Co., 1895.

Johnston, Henry Phelps. *The Battle of Harlem Heights, September 16, 1776.* New York: Macmillan, 1897.

———. *The Campaign of 1776 Around New York and Brooklyn.* Brooklyn: Long Island Historical Society, 1878.

———. *Nathan Hale, 1776.* New Haven, Conn.: Yale University Press, 1914.

———. *Yale and Her Honor Roll in the American Revolution, 1775–1783.* New York: Privately printed, 1888.

Jones, E. Alfred. *The Loyalists of Massachusetts.* London: St. Catherine Press, 1930.

Jones, Michael Wynn. *Cartoon History of the American Revolution.* New York: Putnam, 1975.

Jones, Thomas. *History of New York During the Revolutionary War.* Vols. I–II. New York: New-York Historical Society, 1879.

Kammen, Michael. *Colonial New York: A History.* New York: Scribner, 1975.

——. *A Season of Youth: The American Revolution and the Historical Imagination.* New York: Knopf, 1978.

Ketchum, Richard M. *Decisive Day: The Battle for Bunker Hill.* New York: Doubleday, 1962.

——. *Divided Loyalties: How the American Revolution Came to New York.* New York: Holt, 2002.

——. *The Winter Soldiers.* Garden City, N.Y.: Doubleday, 1973.

——. *The World of George Washington.* New York: American Heritage, 1974.

Kidder, Frederic. *History of the First New Hampshire Regiment in the War of the Revolution.* Albany, N.Y.: Joel Munsell, 1968.

Lancaster, Bruce. *From Lexington to Liberty: The Story of the American Revolution.* Garden City, N.Y.: Doubleday, 1955.

Langford, Paul, ed. *The Writings and Speeches of Edmund Burke.* Oxford, Eng.: Clarendon Press, 1996.

Lawrence, Vera Brodsky. *Music for Patriots, Politicians, and Presidents.* New York: Macmillan, 1975.

Lefferts, Lt. Charles M. *Uniforms of the*

American, British, French, and German Armies in the War of the American Revolution. New York: New-York Historical Society, 1926.

Lefkowitz, Arthur S. *The Long Retreat: The Calamitous American Defense of New Jersey, 1776*. Metuchen, N.J.: Upland Press, 1998.

Lewis, W. S., and John Riely, eds. *Horace Walpole's Miscellaneous Correspondence*. Vol. II. New Haven, Conn.: Yale University Press, 1980.

Lewis, Wilmouth Sheldon. *Three Tours Through London in the Years 1748, 1776, 1797*. New Haven, Conn.: Yale University Press, 1941.

Longmore, Paul K. *The Invention of George Washington*. Berkeley: University of California Press, 1988.

Lundin, Leonard. *Cockpit of the Revolution: The War for Independence in New Jersey*. Princeton, N.J.: Princeton University Press, 1940.

Lushington, S. R. *The Life and Services of General Lord Harris*. 2nd ed. London: John W. Parker, 1845.

Lutnick, Solomon. *The American Revolution and the British Press, 1775–1783*. Columbia: University of Missouri Press, 1967.

Mackesy, Piers. *The War for America: 1775–1783*. London: Longmans, Green & Co., 1964.

Maier, Pauline. *American Scripture: Making the Declaration of Independence*. New York: Knopf, 1997.

Manders, Eric I. *The Battle of Long Island*. Monmouth Beach, N.J.: Philip Freneau Press, 1978.

Marshall, John. *The Life of George Washington, Commander-in-Chief of the American Forces*. Vol. II. Philadelphia: C. P. Wayne, 1804.

Martyn, Charles. *The Life of Artemas Ward, the First Commander-in-Chief of the American Revolution*. New York: Artemas Ward, 1921.

Mason, George C. *The Life and Works of Gilbert Stuart*. New York: Scribner, 1879.

McCullough, David. *John Adams*. New York: Simon & Schuster, 2001.

McKenzie, Matthew G. *Barefooted, Bare Leg'd, Bare Breech'd: The Revolutionary War Service of the Massachusetts Continental Line*. Boston: Massachusetts Society of the Cincinnati, 1995.

Middlekauff, Robert. *The Glorious Cause: The American Revolution, 1763–1789*. New York: Oxford University Press, 1982.

Middleton, Richard. *Colonial America: A History, 1585–1776.* 3rd ed. Oxford, Eng.: Blackwell Publishers, 2002.

Miller, Lillian B., ed. *Selected Papers of Charles Willson Peale and His Family.* Vols. I, V. New Haven, Conn.: Yale University Press, 1983, 2000.

Mitchell, L. G. *Charles J. Fox.* Oxford, Eng.: Oxford University Press, 1992.

Montross, Lynn. *The Reluctant Rebels: The Story of the Continental Congress, 1774–1789.* New York: Barnes & Noble, 1950.

——. *The Story of the Continental Army, 1775–1783.* New York: Barnes & Noble, 1967.

Moore, Frank. *Diary of the American Revolution.* Vols. I–II. New York: Charles Scribner, 1860.

Moore, George H. *The Treason of Charles Lee.* Port Washington, N.Y.: Kennikat Press, 1970.

Morgan, Edmund S. *The Genius of George Washington.* New York: Norton, 1977.

Morgan, Edwin V. *Slavery in New York.* Half Moon Series edition. Vol. II, No. 1. New York: Putnam, 1898.

Morgan, William James, ed. *Naval Documents of the American Revolution.* Vols. IV–VI. Washington, D.C.: U.S. Department of the Navy, 1969–1972.

Morrissey, Brendan. *Boston, 1775: The Shot Heard Around the World*. London: Osprey, 1995.

Murray, Rev. James. *An Impartial History of the War in America*. Vol. II. Newcastle, Eng.: Printed for T. Robson, 1780.

Norton, J. E., ed. *The Letters of Edward Gibbon*. Vol. II. *1774–1784*. New York: Macmillan, 1956.

Norton, Mary Beth. *Liberty's Daughters*. Boston: Little, Brown, 1980.

Olsen, Kirstin. *Daily Life in 18th-Century England*. Westport, Conn.: Greenwood Press, 1999.

Onderdonk, Henry, Jr. *Revolutionary Incidents of Suffolk and Kings Counties*. New York: Leavitt & Co., 1849.

Otten, Robert M. *Joseph Addison*. Boston: Twayne Publishers, 1982.

Pain, Nesta. *George III at Home*. London: Eyre Methuen, 1975.

Paine, Thomas. *The American Crisis*. London: T. W. Shaw, 1775.

———. *"Rights of Man" and "Common Sense."* New York: Knopf, 1994.

Palmer, Dave Richard. *The Way of the Fox: American Strategy in the War for America, 1775–1783*. Westport, Conn.: Greenwood Press, 1975.

Partridge, Bellamy. *Sir Billy Howe*. London: Longmans, Green & Co., 1932.

Pearson, Michael. *Those Damned Rebels*. New York: Da Capo Press, 1972.

Peckham, Howard H., ed. *The Toll of Independence*. Chicago: University of Chicago Press, 1974.

Peterson, Harold L. *The Book of the Continental Soldier*. Harrisburg, Pa.: Stackpole Co., 1968.

Phillips, Brig. Gen. Thomas R., ed. *Reveries on the Art of War: Marshal Maurice de Saxe*. Harrisburg, Pa.: Military Service Publishing Co., 1944.

Plumb, J. H. *The First Four Georges*. London: Fontana/Collins, 1956.

Preble, George Henry. *Origin and History of the American Flag*. Philadelphia: Nicholas L. Brown, 1917.

Putnam, Alfred P. *A Sketch of General Israel Putnam*. Salem, Mass.: Eben Putnam, 1893.

Quarles, Benjamin. *The Negro in the American Revolution*. Chapel Hill: University of North Carolina Press, 1961.

Ramsay, David. *The History of the American Revolution*. Vols. I–II. London: Printed for John Stockdale, 1793.

——. *Life of George Washington*. Ithaca, N.Y.: Mack, Andrus & Woodruff, 1840.

Raphael, Ray. *A People's History of the American Revolution: How Common People Shaped the Fight for Independence.* New York: New Press, 2001.

Rasmussen, William M. S., and Robert S. Tilton. *George Washington: The Man Behind the Myths.* Charlottesville: University Press of Virginia, 1999.

Rawson, Jonathan. *1776: A Day-by-Day Story.* New York: Frederick A. Stokes Co., 1927.

Reed, William B., ed. *Life and Correspondence of Joseph Reed.* Vol. I. Philadelphia: Lindsay & Blakiston, 1847.

Reich, Jerome R. *British Friends of the American Revolution.* Armonk, N.Y.: M. E. Sharpe, 1998.

Reid, Stuart. *Wolfe: The Career of General James Wolfe from Culloden to Quebec.* Staplehurst, Eng.: Spellmount, 2000.

Reilly, Robin. *Wolfe of Quebec.* London: Cassell & Co., 2001.

Rhodehamel, John, ed. *The American Revolution: Writings from the War of Independence.* New York: Library of America, 2001.

———. *George Washington: Writings.* New York: Library of America, 1997.

Rhoden, Nancy L., and Ian K. Steele, eds. *The Human Tradition in the American*

Revolution. Wilmington, Del.: Scholarly Resources, 2000.

Riding, Christine, and Jacqueline Riding. *The Houses of Parliament: History, Art, Architecture.* London: Merrell, 2000.

Ritcheson, Charles R. *British Politics and the American Revolution.* Westport, Conn.: Greenwood Press, 1981.

Roberts, Jane, ed. *George III and Queen Charlotte: Patronage, Collecting, and Court Taste.* London: Royal Collection Enterprises, 2004.

Robson, Eric, ed. *Letters from America, 1773–1780.* Manchester, Eng.: Manchester University Press, 1951.

Roche, John F. *Joseph Reed: A Moderate in the American Revolution.* New York: Columbia University Press, 1957.

Rossman, Kenneth R. *Thomas Mifflin and the Politics of the American Revolution.* Chapel Hill: University of North Carolina Press, 1952.

Royster, Charles. *A Revolutionary People at War: The Continental Army and American Character, 1775–1783.* Chapel Hill: University of North Carolina Press, 1979.

Sabine, Lorenzo. *Biographical Sketches of Loyalists of the American Revolution.* 2 vols. Port Washington, N.Y.: Kennikat Press, 1966.

Sabine, William H. W. *Murder, 1776 and Washington's Policy of Silence.* New York: Theo. Gaus' Sons, Inc., 1973.

Sayen, William Guthrie. "A Compleat Gentleman: The Making of George Washington, 1732–1775." Dissertation, University of Connecticut, 1998.

Schecter, Barnet. *The Battle for New York: The City at the Heart of the American Revolution.* New York: Walker & Co., 2002.

Scheer, George F., and Hugh F. Rankin. *Rebels and Redcoats: The American Revolution Through the Eyes of Those Who Fought and Lived It.* New York: Da Capo Press, 1957.

Schroeder, John Frederick, ed. *Maxims of George Washington.* Mount Vernon, Va.: Mount Vernon Ladies Association, 1989.

Schwarz, Philip J., ed. *Slavery at the Home of George Washington.* Mount Vernon, Va.: Mount Vernon Ladies Association, 2001.

Scott, John Anthony. *Trumpet of a Prophecy: Revolutionary America, 1763–1783.* New York: Knopf, 1969.

Sellers, Charles Coleman. *Charles Willson Peale.* Vol. I. *Early Life.* Philadelphia:

American Philosophical Society, 1947.

Seymour, William. *The Price of Folly: British Blunders in the War of American Independence*. London: Brassey's, 1995.

Sheppard, Edgar. *Memorials of St. James's Palace*. Vol. I. London: Longmans, Green & Co., 1894.

Showman, Richard K., ed. *The Papers of Nathanael Greene*. Vols. I, II, X. Chapel Hill: University of North Carolina Press, 1976, 1980, 1998.

Shy, John. *A People Numerous and Armed: Reflections on the Military Struggle for American Independence*. Ann Arbor: University of Michigan Press, 1990.

Simms, W. Gilmore, ed. *The Life of Nathanael Greene*. New York: George F. Cooledge and Bro., 1849.

Sizer, Theodore, ed. *The Autobiography of Colonel John Trumbull*. Library of American Art. New York: Da Capo Press, 1970.

Smith, Paul H., ed. *Letters of Delegates to Congress, 1774–1789*. Vols. I–V. Washington, D.C.: Library of Congress, 1976–1979.

Smollett, Tobias. *Adventures of Roderick Random*. London: Hutchinson & Co., 1904.

——. *The Expedition of Humphrey Clinker.* Oxford, Eng.: Oxford University Press, 1966.

Stark, James H. *The Loyalists of Massachusetts and the Other Side of the American Revolution.* Boston: W. B. Clarke Co., 1910.

Stedman, Charles. *The History of the Origin, Progress, and Termination of the American War.* Vol I. London: J. Murray, 1794; reprint, New York: Arno Press, 1969.

Stiles, Henry R. *History of the City of Brooklyn.* Vol. I. Albany, N.Y.: J. Munsell, 1869.

Still, Bayrd. *Mirror for Gotham New York as Seen by Contemporaries from Dutch Days to the Present.* New York: University Press, 1956.

Stokes, I. N. Phelps. *The Iconography of Manhattan Island, 1498–1909.* Vols. I, IV, V. New York: Arno Press, 1967.

Stryker, William S. *Battles of Trenton and Princeton.* Trenton, N.J.: Old Barracks Association, 2001.

Surtees, R. S. *Mr. Sponge's Sporting Tour.* London: Folio Society, 1950.

Taylor, Maureen Alice, and John Wood Sweet. *Runaways, Deserters, and Noto-*

rious Villains. Vol. II. Rockport, Maine: Picton Press, 2001.

Taylor, Robert J., ed. *Papers of John Adams.* Vols. III–V. Cambridge, Mass.: Belknap Press, 1979, 1983.

Thayer, Theodore. *Nathanael Greene: Strategist of the American Revolution.* New York: Twayne Publishers, 1960.

Thomas, Peter D. G. *Lord North.* New York: St. Martin's Press, 1976.

Thompson, Eben Francis. *A Brief Chronicle of Rufus Putnam and His Rutland Home.* Worcester, Mass.: Privately printed, 1930.

Trevelyan, Sir George Otto. *The American Revolution.* Vols. I–IV. New York: Longmans, Green & Co., 1899.

Tuchman, Barbara W. *The March of Folly: From Troy to Vietnam.* New York: Ballantine Books, 1984.

Turberville, A. S., ed. *Johnson's England: An Account of the Life and Manners of His Age.* Oxford, Eng.: Clarendon Press, 1933.

Tyler, Moses Coit. *The Literary History of the American Revolution.* Vols. I–II. New York: Frederick Ungar Publishing Co., 1957.

Valentine, Alan. *Lord Stirling: Colonial Gentleman and General in Washington's*

Army. New York: Oxford University Press, 1969.

Van Doren, Carl. *Secret History of the American Revolution*. Garden City, N.Y.: Garden City Publishing Co., 1941.

Van Tyne, Claude Halstead. *Loyalists in the American Revolution*. Gansevoort, N.Y.: Corner House Historical Publications, 1999.

Wade, Herbert T., and Robert A. Lively, eds. *This Glorious Cause: The Adventures of Two Company Officers in Washington's Army*. Princeton, N.J.: Princeton University Press, 1958.

Ward, Christopher. *The War of the Revolution*. Edited by John Richard Alden. Vols. I–II. New York: Macmillan, 1952.

Warden, G. B. *Boston: 1689–1776*. Boston: Little, Brown, 1970.

Warren, Mercy Otis. *History of the Rise, Progress, and Termination of the American Revolution*. Edited by Lester H. Cohen. Vols. I–IV. Indianapolis: Liberty Fund, 1989 (orig., 1805).

Warren-Adams Letters. Vol. I. *1743–1777*. New York: AMS Press, 1972.

Washington, George. *Rules of Civility and Decent Behavior in Company and Conversation*. Mt. Vernon, Va.: Mount

Vernon's Ladies Association, 1989.

Weigley, Russell F. *History of the United States Army.* New York: Macmillan, 1967.

Wheeler, Richard. *Voices of 1776: The Story of the American Revolution in the Words of Those Who Were There.* New York: Thomas Y. Crowell Co., 1972.

Whitehill, Walter Muir. *Boston: A Topographical History.* Cambridge, Mass.: Belknap Press, 1968.

Whiteley, William G. *The Revolutionary Soldiers of Delaware.* Wilmington, Del.: James & Webb Printers, 1875.

Wick, Wendy C. *George Washington, an American Icon: The Eighteenth-Century Graphic Portraits.* Washington, D.C.: Smithsonian Institution Traveling Exhibition Service and the National Portrait Gallery, 1982.

Wickwire, Franklin, and Mary Wickwire. *Cornwallis: The American Adventure.* Boston: Houghton Mifflin, 1970.

Willard, Margaret Wheeler, ed. *Letters on the American Revolution, 1774–1776.* Boston: Houghton Mifflin, 1925.

Willcox, William B. *Portrait of a General: Sir Henry Clinton in the War of Independence.* New York: Knopf, 1962.

Winsor, Justin, ed. *The Memorial History of*

Boston. Vol. III. Boston: James Osgood & Co., 1881.

Wood, Gordon S. *The Creation of the American Republic, 1776–1787.* Chapel Hill: University of North Carolina Press, 1969.

Wood, W. J. *Battles of the Revolutionary War: 1775–1781.* New York: Da Capo Press, 1995.

Wortley, The Honorable Mrs. E. Stuart, ed. *A Prime Minister and His Son: From the Correspondence of the Third Earl of Bute and of Lieutenant General the Honorable Sir Charles Stuart.* London: John Murray, 1925.

Wright, Esmond. *Fabric of Freedom: 1763–1800.* New York: Hill & Wang, 1961.

REFERENCE WORKS

Black, Jeremy, and Roy Porter, eds. *The Penguin Dictionary of Eighteenth-Century History.* London: Penguin Books, 1994.

Boatner, Mark M., III, ed. *Encyclopedia of the American Revolution.* New York: David McKay Co., 1966.

———. *Landmarks of the American Revolu-*

tion. Harrisburg, Pa.: Stackpole Books, 1973.

Cappon, Lester J., ed. *The Atlas of Early American History: The Revolutionary Era, 1760–1790.* Princeton, N.J.: Princeton University Press, 1976.

Carnes, Mark C., and John A. Garraty. *Mapping America's Past: A Historical Atlas.* New York: Holt, 1996.

Dexter, Franklin Bowditch. *Biographical Sketches of the Graduates of Yale College.* Vol. III. *1763–1778.* New York: Holt, 1903.

Foner, Eric, and John A. Garraty, eds. *Reader's Companion to American History.* Boston: Houghton Mifflin, 1991.

Grizzard, Frank E., Jr. *George Washington: A Biographical Companion.* Santa Barbara, Calif.: ABC-Clio, 2002.

Homberger, Eric. *Historical Atlas of New York City.* New York: Holt, 1944.

Johnson, Allen, ed. *Dictionary of American Biography.* 11 vols. New York: Scribner, 1936–1964.

Ketchum, Richard M., ed. *The American Heritage Book of the Revolution.* New York: American Heritage, 1958.

Kiple, Kenneth F. *Cambridge World History of Human Disease.* Cambridge, Eng.: Cambridge University Press, 1992.

Marshall, P. J., ed. *The Oxford History of the British Empire: The Eighteenth Century.* Vol. II. Oxford, Eng.: Oxford University Press, 1998.

Mollo, John, and Malcolm McGregor. *Uniforms of the American Revolution in Color.* New York: Macmillan, 1975.

Nebenzahl, Kenneth, ed. *Atlas of the American Revolution.* Chicago: Rand McNally, 1974.

Purcell, L. Edward, and David F. Burg, eds. *World Almanac of the American Revolution.* New York: World Almanac, 1992.

Sebastian, Anton. *Dictionary of the History of Medicine.* New York: Parthenon Publishers, 1999.

Shipton, Clifford K., ed. *Sibley's Harvard Graduates,* Vols. XIII, XVII. Boston: Massachusetts Historical Society, 1965, 1975.

Stember, Sol. *The Bicentennial Guide to the American Revolution.* Vol. II. New York: Saturday Review Press, 1974.

Stephen, Sir Leslie, and Sir Sidney Lee, eds. *Dictionary of National Biography.* Vols. I–LX. Oxford, Eng.: Oxford University Press, 2004.

Symonds, Craig L. *A Battlefield Atlas of the American Revolution.* Baltimore: Nautical & Aviation Publishing, 1986.

DIARIES, JOURNALS, AND MEMOIRS

Adlum, John. *Memoirs of the Life of John Adlum in the Revolutionary War.* Edited by Howard H. Peckham. Chicago: Caxton Club, 1968.

Amory, Thomas C. "Memoir of General Sullivan." *Pennsylvania Magazine of History and Biography.* Vol. II. Philadelphia: Published for the Society, 1878.

Anderson, Enoch. *Personal Recollections of Captain Enoch Anderson.* Vol XVI of the *Papers of the Historical Society of Delaware.* Wilmington: Historical Society of Delaware, 1896.

Baldwin, Jeduthan. *The Revolutionary Journal of Col. Jeduthan Baldwin, 1775–1778.* Edited by Thomas Williams Baldwin. Bangor, Maine: Printed for the DeBurians, 1906.

Bangs, Isaac. *Journal of Lieutenant Isaac Bangs: April 1, 1776–July 29, 1776.* Edited by Edward Bangs. Cambridge, Mass.: John Wilson & Son, 1890.

Barker, John. *The British in Boston: The Diary of Lieutenant John Barker.* Edited by Elizabeth Ellery Dana. New York: Arno Press, 1969.

Bixby, Samuel. "Diary of Samuel Bixby,

August 3–12, 1775." *Proceedings of the Massachusetts Historical Society.* Vol. XIV (1875–1876).

Black, Jeannette D., and William Greene Roelker, eds. *A Rhode Island Chaplain in the Revolution: Letters of Ebenezer David to Nicholas Brown, 1775–1778.* Clements Library, Ann Arbor, Mich.

Boyle, Joseph Lee, ed. *From Redcoat to Rebel: The Thomas Sullivan Journal.* Bowie, Md.: Heritage Books, 1997.

Bradford, S. Sidney, ed. "A British Officer's Revolutionary War Journal, 1776–1778." *Maryland History Magazine,* Vol. LVI (June 1961).

Bray, Robert, and Paul Bushnell, eds. *Diary of a Common Soldier in the American Revolution: 1775–1783.* DeKalb: Northern Illinois University Press, 1978.

Burgoyne, Bruce E. *An Anonymous Hessian Diary, Probably the Diary of Lieutenant Johann Heinrich von Bardeleben of the Hesse-Cassel von Donop Regiment.* Bowie, Md.: Heritage Books, 1998.

——, ed. *Defeat, Disaster, and Dedication: The Diaries of the Hessian Officers Jakob Piel and Andreas Wiederhold.* Translated from manuscripts in the New York Public Library. Bowie, Md.: Heritage Books, Inc., 1997.

Campbell, Lachlan. "British Journal from Aboard Ship in Boston Commencing January 1776 and Then Moving to New York." New-York Historical Society.

Carter, Lt. William. *A Genuine Detail of the Several Engagements, Positions, and Movements of Royal and American Armies During the Years 1775 and 1776.* London: Printed for the Author, 1784.

Chastellux, Marquis de. *Travels in North America in the Years 1780, 1781, and 1782.* Vols. I–II. Edited by Howard C. Rice. Chapel Hill: University of North Carolina Press, 1963.

Cheever, William. "William Cheever's Diary, 1775–1776." *Proceedings of the Massachusetts Historical Society.* Vol. LX (October 1926–June 1927).

Clinton, Sir Henry. *The American Rebellion: Sir Henry Clinton's Narrative of His Campaigns, 1775–1782.* Edited by William B. Willcox. New Haven, Conn.: Yale University Press, 1954.

Cresswell, Nicholas. *The Journal of Nicholas Cresswell, 1774–1777.* New York: Dial Press, 1924.

Curwen, Samuel. *The Journal of Samuel Curwen, Loyalist.* Vols. I–II. Edited by

Andrew Oliver. Cambridge, Mass.: Harvard University Press, 1972.

"Diary of Reverend Benjamin Boardman" (July 31, 1775–Nov. 12, 1775). *Proceedings of the Massachusetts Historical Society.* 2nd series. Vol. VII (1891–1892).

"Diary of Obadiah Brown." *Quarterly Bulletin of the Westchester County Historical Society.* Nos. 4–5 (1928–1929).

Diary of Reverend Samuel Cooper. Massachusetts Historical Society.

Diary of John Kettel. Massachusetts Historical Society.

Diary of Loyalist Thomas Moffatt. Peter Force Papers. Library of Congress.

"Diary of Nathan Sellers, 1776." American Philosophical Society.

"A Diary of Trifling Occurrences: Sarah Fisher Logan." *Pennsylvania Magazine of History and Biography.* Vol. LXXXII (1958).

"Diary of Ebenezer Wild." *Proceedings of the Massachusetts Historical Society.* 2nd series. Vol. VI (1891).

Duane, William, ed. *Diary of Christopher Marshall, 1774–1781.* Albany, N.Y.: Joel Munsell, 1877.

Emerson, William. *Diaries and Letters of William Emerson, 1743–1776.* Edited by

Amelia Forbes Emerson. Boston: Thomas Todd, 1972.

Ewald, Captain Johann. *Diary of the American War: A Hessian Journal.* Edited by Joseph P. Tustin. New Haven, Conn.: Yale University Press, 1979.

Fitch, Jabez. "Boston Siege Diary of Jabez Fitch." *Proceedings of the Massachusetts Historical Society.* 2nd series. Vol IX (1894–1895).

——. *The New York Diary of Lieutenant Jabez Fitch of the 17th (Connecticut) Regiment from August 2, 1776, to December 15, 1777.* Edited by W. H. W. Sabine. New York: Colburn & Tegg, 1954.

Fithian, Philip Vickers. *Philip Vickers Fithian: Journal, 1775–1776, Written on the Virginia-Pennsylvania Frontier and in the Army Around New York.* Edited by Robert Greenhalgh Albion and Leonidas Dodson. Princeton, N.J.: Princeton University Press, 1934.

Graydon, Alexander. *Memoirs of His Own Time: With Reminiscences of the Men and Events of the Revolution.* Edited by John Stockton Littell. Philadelphia: Lindsay & Blakiston, 1846.

Greenwood, John. *The Revolutionary Ser-*

vices of *John Greenwood of Boston and New York, 1775–1783*. Edited by Isaac J. Greenwood. New York: De Vinne Press, 1922.

Gruber, Ira D., ed. *John Peeble's American War: The Diary of a Scottish Grenadier, 1776–1782*. Mechanicsburg, Pa.: Stackpole Books, 1998.

Hanson, Robert Brand, ed. *The Diary of Dr. Nathaniel Ames of Dedham, Massachusetts, 1758–1822*. Camden, Maine: Picton Press, 1998.

Heath, Major General William. *Heath's Memoirs of the American War*. Edited by Rufus Rockwell Wilson. New York: A. Wessels Co., 1904.

Hutchinson, Thomas. *The Diary and Letters of His Excellency Thomas Hutchinson Esq*. Edited by Peter Orlando Hutchinson. Boston: Houghton Mifflin, 1884.

Inman, George. "George Inman's Narrative of the American Revolution." *Pennsylvania Magazine of History and Biography*. Vol. VII (1883).

"Journal of Samuel Correy, New Jersey Militia." Clements Library.

"A Journal Kept by John Leach, During His Confinement by the British, in Boston 'Gaol' in 1775." *New England*

Historic and Genealogical Register. Vol. XIX (1865).

"Journal of Ensign Nathaniel Morgan, April 21 to December 11, 1775." *Collections of the Connecticut Historical Society.* Vol. VII (1889).

"Journal of Nathaniel Ober." Massachusetts Historical Society.

"Journal of Lieutenant Williams." New-York Historical Society.

"Journal of Captain James Wood, Third British Battalion, Royal Artillery, 1775." New-York Historical Society.

"Journal of Sergeant William Young." *Pennsylvania Magazine of History and Biography.* Vol. VIII (1884).

Kemble, Stephen. *Journals of Lieutenant-Colonel Stephen Kemble, 1773–1789, and British Army Orders: General Sir William Howe, 1775–1778; General Sir Henry Clinton, 1778; and General Daniel Jones, 1778.* Boston: Gregg Press, 1972.

Kipping, Ernst, ed. *At General Howe's Side, 1776–1778: The Diary of General William Howe's Aide de Camp, Captain Friedrich von Muenchhausen.* Monmouth Beach, N.J.: Philip Freneau Press, 1974.

Knox, Henry. "Knox's Diary During His

Ticonderoga Expedition." *New England Historic and Genealogical Register.* Vol. XXX (1876).

Leggett, Abraham. *The Narrative of Major Abraham Leggett.* New York: Arno Press, 1971.

Lender, Mark E., and James Kirby Martin, eds. *Citizen Soldier: The Revolutionary War Journal of Joseph Bloomfield.* Newark: New Jersey Historical Society, 1982.

Lyman, Simeon. *Journal of Simeon Lyman of Sharon, August 10 to December 28, 1775. Collections of the Connecticut Historical Society.* Vol. VII (1899).

Lynn, Mary C., ed. *An Eyewitness Account of the American Revolution and New England Life: The Journal of J. F. Wasmus, German Company Surgeon, 1776–1783.* New York: Greenwood Press, 1990.

Martin, Joseph Plumb. *A Narrative of a Revolutionary Soldier: Some of the Adventures, Dangers, and Sufferings of Joseph Plumb Martin.* New York: Penguin Putnam, 2001.

McKenzie, Frederick. *Diary of Frederick Mackenzie.* Vol. I. Cambridge, Mass.: Harvard University Press, 1930.

Montresor, John. *"Journals of Captain John*

Montresor." Edited by G. D. Scull. Collections of the New-York Historical Society, 1881.

Morris, Margaret. *Private Journal Kept During the Revolutionary War.* New York: Arno Press, 1969.

Murray, James. *Letters from America, 1773 to 1780: Being the Letters of a Scots Officer, Sir James Murray.* Edited by Eric Robson. New York: Barnes & Noble, 1874.

Nash, Solomon. *Journal of Solomon Nash, a Soldier of the Revolution, 1776–1777.* Edited by Charles I. Bushnell. New York: Privately printed, 1861.

"The Papers of General Samuel Smith." *Historical Magazine.* 2nd series. Vol. VII (February 1870).

Rau, Louise, ed. "Sergeant John Smith's Diary of 1776." *Mississippi Valley Historical Review.* Vol. XX (1933–1934).

Rawdon, Reginald Lord. *Report on the Manuscripts of the Late Reginald Rawdon Hastings.* 4 vols. London: Her Majesty's Stationery Office, 1930–1947.

"Recollections of Incidents of the Revolution: General Jeremiah Johnson." *Journal of Long Island History.* Vol. XII, No. 2 (Spring 1976).

Robertson, Archibald. *Archibald Robertson: His Diaries and Sketches in America, 1762–1780.* Edited by Harry Miller Lydenberg. New York: New York Public Library, 1930.

Rowe, John. *Letters and Diary of John Rowe, Boston Merchant, 1759–1762, 1764–1779.* Edited by Anne Rowe Cunningham. Boston: W. B. Clarke Co., 1903.

Sargent, Winthrop, ed. "Letters of John Andrews, Esq. of Boston: 1772–1776." Cambridge, Eng.: Press of J. Wilson & Sons, 1866.

Scull, G. D., ed. *Memoir and Letters of Captain W. Glanville Evelyn, 1747–1776.* Oxford, Eng.: James Parker & Co., 1879.

Serle, Ambrose. *The American Journal of Ambrose Serle, Secretary to Lord Howe, 1776–1778.* Edited by Edward H. Tatum, Jr. San Marino, Calif.: Huntington Library, 1940.

Sleeper, Moses. *Diary of a Soldier, June 1775–September 1776.* Longfellow House National Historic Site, Cambridge, Mass.

Stabler, Lois K., ed. *Very Poor and of a Lo Make: The Journal of Abner Sanger.* Portsmouth, N.H.: Historical Society of Cheshire County, 1986.

Stark, John. *Memoir and Official Correspondence of General John Stark*. Edited by Caleb Stark. Boston: Gregg Press, 1972.

Stiles, Ezra. *The Literary Diary of Ezra Stiles: President of Yale College*. Edited by Franklin Bowditch Dexter. Vols. I–II. New York: Scribner, 1901.

Tallmadge, Benjamin. *Memoir of Colonel Benjamin Tallmadge*. New York: Arno Press, 1968.

Thacher, James, M.D. *Military Journal During the American Revolution, 1775–1783*. Boston: Richardson & Lord, 1823.

Trumbull, Benjamin. "Journal of the Campaign at New York, 1776–1777." *Collections of the Connecticut Historical Society*. Vol. VII (1899).

Tudor, John. *Deacon Tudor's Diary*. Boston: Press of W. Spooner, 1896.

Washington, George. *The Diaries of George Washington, 1780–1781*. Vol. III. Edited by Donald Jackson. Charlottesville: University Press of Virginia, 1978.

Webb, Samuel Blachley. *Correspondence and Journals of Samuel Blachley Webb: 1772–1777*. Vol. I. Edited by Worthington Chauncey Ford. Lancaster, Pa.: Wickersham Press, 1893.

——. *Family Letters of Samuel Blachley Webb, 1764–1807.* Edited by Worthington Chauncey Ford. New York: Cambridge University Press, 1912.

Wilkinson, General James. *Memoirs of My Own Times.* Vol. I. Philadelphia: Abraham Small, 1816.

Williams, Elisha. "Elisha Williams' Diary of 1776." *Pennsylvania Magazine of History and Biography.* Vol. XLVIII (1924).

ARTICLES

Anderson, Fred W. "The Hinge of the Revolution: George Washington Confronts a People's Army, July 3, 1775." *Massachusetts Historical Review.* Vol. I (1999).

Baker, William S. "Itinerary of General Washington from June 15, 1775, to December 23, 1783." *Pennsylvania Magazine of History and Biography.* Vol. XIV, No. 2 (1890).

"British Officer in Boston 1775." *Atlantic Monthly.* April 1877.

Brookhiser, Richard. "A Man on Horseback." *Atlantic Monthly.* January 1996.

Brown, Wallace. "An Englishman Views

the American Revolution: The Letters of Henry Hulton, 1769–1776." *Huntington Library Quarterly*. Vol. XXXVI (1972–1973).

"The Capture of Fort Washington, New York. Described by Cpt. Andreas Wiederhold." *Pennsylvania Magazine of History and Biography*. Vol. XXIII (1899).

"Contemporaneous Account of the Battle of Trenton, *Pennsylvania Evening Post*, December 28, 1776." *Pennsylvania Magazine of History and Biography*. Vol. IV (1880).

Conway, Stephen. "From Fellow-Nationals to Foreigners: British Perceptions of the Americans, circa 1739–1783." *William and Mary Quarterly*. 3rd series. Vol. LIX, No.1 (January 2002).

Davis, General W. W. H. "Washington on the West Bank of the Delaware 1776." *Pennsylvania Magazine of History and Biography*. Vol. IV, No. 2 (1980).

Delancy, E. F. "Mount Washington and Its Capture on the 16th of November, 1776." *Magazine of American History*. Vol. I (February 1877).

Gelb, Norman. "Winter of Discontent." *Smithsonian Magazine*. May 2003.

Gordon, Reverend William. Letters, *Pro-*

ceedings of the Massachusetts Historical Society. Vol. LX (October 1926–June 1927).

Greene, George Washington. "Major-General Nathanael Greene." *Pennsylvania Magazine of History and Biography.* Vol. II (1878).

Gruber, Ira. D. "Lord Howe and Lord George Germain: British Politics and the Winning of American Independence." *William and Mary Quarterly.* 3rd series. Vol. XXII, No. 2 (April 1965).

Heathcote, Charles William. "General Israel Putnam." *Picket Post* (Valley Forge Historical Society). February 1963.

"House of Lords and the House of Commons." *Mirror of Literature, Amusement, and Instruction.* No. 688 (November 1, 1834).

Ketchum, Richard M. "Men of the Revolution: Israel Putnam." *American Heritage.* Vol. XXIV (June 1973).

Koke, Richard J. "Forcing the Hudson River Passing." *New-York Historical Society Quarterly.* Vol. XXXVI (October 1952).

Kranish, Michael. "Washington Reconstructed." *Boston Globe,* February 17, 2002.

Kurtz, Henry I. "Victory on Dorchester

Heights." *American History Illustrated.* Vol. IV (December 1969).

"Late House of Commons and Antiquities of St. Stephen's Chapel." *Mirror of Literature, Amusement, and Instruction.* No. 690 (November 8, 1834).

"Letter of Reverend William Gordon to Samuel Wilcon, April 6, 1776." *Proceedings of the Massachusetts Historical Society.* Vol. LX (1926–1927).

"Letters from a Hessian Mercenary." *Pennsylvania Magazine of History and Biography.* Vol. LXII, No. 4 (October 1938).

"Letters Written During the Revolutionary War by Colonel William Douglas to His Wife Covering the Period July 19, 1775, to December 5, 1775." *New-York Historical Society Bulletin.* Vols. XII–XIII (January 1929–January 1930).

Luther, F. S. "General Israel Putnam." *Proceedings of the Worcester Society of Antiquity for the Year 1904.* Vol. XX, No. 4 (1905).

"Major General John Thomas." *Proceedings of the Massachusetts Historical Society.* 2nd series. Vol. XVIII (1903–1904).

"Occupation of New York City by the British." *Pennsylvania Magazine of His-*

tory and Biography. Vol. IV (1980).

Paltsits, Victor Hugo. "The Jeopardy of Washington, September 15, 1776." *New-York Historical Society Quarterly.* Vol. XXXII (October 1948).

Pogue, Dennis J. "General Washington: One of the Wealthiest Men in American History?" Mount Vernon Library (2002).

Powell, William S. "A Connecticut Soldier Writing Home: Elisha Bostwick's Memoirs of the First Years of the Revolution." *William and Mary Quarterly.* 3rd series. Vol. VI (1949).

R———, Sergeant. "Battle of Princeton." *Pennsylvania Magazine of History and Biography.* Vol. XX (1896).

"Sermon of Rev. John Rodgers, Jan. 14, 1776." *New York Times,* March 16, 2003.

Shelton, William Henry. "Nathan Hale Execution." *New York Times,* September 22, 1929.

Vernon-Jackson, H. O. H. "A Loyalist's Wife: Letters of Mrs. Philip Van Cortlandt, 1776–1777." *History Today.* Vol. XIV (August 1964).

Wakin, Daniel J. "Pastor's Call to Arms in 1776 Has Echoes in 2003." New York Report in *New York Times,* March 16, 2003.

Warren, ——. "Uniform of the Revolutionary Army." *Proceedings of the Massachusetts Historical Society.* Vol. IV (1858–1860).

"Washington's Headquarters in New York." *National Historical Magazine.* July 1944.

Wertenbaker, Thomas Jefferson. "The Battle of Princeton." In *The Princeton Battle Monument.* Princeton, N.J.: Princeton University Press, 1922.

Whitehorne, Joseph. "Shepardstown and the Morgan-Stevenson Companies." *Magazine of the Jefferson County Historical Society.* Vol. LVIII (December 1992).

NEWSPAPERS AND JOURNALS

Boston Gazette
Boston Newsletter
Boston Transcript
Connecticut Gazette and Universal Intelligencer (New London)
Connecticut Journal (New Haven)
Essex Gazette (Salem, Mass.)
Essex Journal (Newburyport, Mass.)
Freeman's Journal (Philadelphia)
Gentleman's Magazine (London)

Hartford (Connecticut) Courant and
  Weekly Intelligencer
Lloyd's Evening Post and British Chronicle
  (London)
London Chronicle
London Gazette
London Gazette and New Daily Advertiser
London General Evening Post
London Public Advertiser
Massachusetts Gazette and Boston Weekly
  Newsletter
Massachusetts Spy (Boston)
Mirror of Literature, Amusement,
  and Instruction (London)
Morning Chronicle and London
  Advertiser
New England Chronicle and Essex Gazette
  (Cambridge, Mass.)
New Haven Journal
Newport (Rhode Island) Mercury
New York Constitutional Gazette
New York Gazette
New-York Packet
New York Sun
Pennsylvania Evening Post (Philadelphia)
Pennsylvania Gazette (Philadelphia)
Pennsylvania Journal and Weekly
  Advertiser (Philadelphia)
Pennsylvania Packet (Philadelphia)
Providence Gazette

St. James's Chronicle (London)
Universal Magazine (London)
Virginia Gazette (Williamsburg)